Crisis and Hope

Crisis and Hope
The Educational Hopscotch of Latin America

Edited by
Stephen J. Ball, Gustavo E. Fischman,
and **Silvina Gvirtz**

Routledge
Taylor & Francis Group

LONDON AND NEW YORK

First published 2003 by RoutledgeFalmer

Published 2017 by Routledge
2 Park Square, Milton Park, Abingdon, Oxfordshire OX14 4RN
711 Third Avenue, New York, NY 10017, USA

First issued in paperback 2017

Routledge is an imprint of the Taylor & Francis Group, an informa business

Library of Congress Cataloging-in-Publication Data

Crisis and hope : the educational hopscotch of Latin America /
edited by
Gustavo E. Fischman, Stephen Ball and Silvina Gvirtz.
    p. cm. — (Reference books in international education)
Includes bibliographical references and index.

   ISBN 0-415-93535-0 (Hardcover : alk. paper)
   1. Education—Latin America. 2. Educational change—Latin America.
I. Fischman, Gustavo. II. Ball, Stephen J. III. Gvirtz,
Silvina. IV. Series.
   LA541 .C76 2003
   370'.98—dc21

                                        2002152243

ISBN 13: 978-1-138-96696-3 (pbk)
ISBN 13: 978-0-415-93535-7 (hbk)

POLITICS OF EDUCATIONAL
INNOVATIONS IN DEVELOPING
COUNTRIES
*An Analysis of Knowledge and
Power*
edited by Nelly P. Stromquist and
Michael L. Basile

EDUCATIONAL RESTRUCTURING IN
THE CONTEXT OF GLOBALIZATION
AND NATIONAL POLICY
edited by Holger Daun

TEACHING IN JAPAN
A Cultural Perspective
by Nobuo K. Shimahara

CIVIC EDUCATION IN THE ASIA-
PACIFIC REGION
Case Studies across Six Societies
edited by John J. Cogan, Paul
Morris, and Murray Print

HEGEMONIES COMPARED
*State Formation and Chinese School
Politics in Postwar Singapore and
Hong Kong*
by Ting-Hong Wong

PROFESSIONAL DEVELOPMENT OF
SCIENCE TEACHERS
*Local Insights with Lessons for the
Global Community*
edited by Pamela Fraser-Abder

CONSTRUCTING EDUCATION FOR
DEVELOPMENT
*International Organizations and
Education for All*
by Colette Chabbott

SCHOOL LEADERSHIP AND
ADMINISTRATION
Adopting a Cultural Perspective
edited by Allan Walker and Clive
Dimmock

DEVELOPMENT EDUCATION IN JAPAN
*A Comparative Analysis of the
Contexts for its Emergence, and Its
Introduction into the Japanese
School System*
by Yuri Ishii

DAUGHTERS OF THE THARU
*Gender, Ethnicity, Religion, and the
Education of Nepali Girls*
by Mary Ann Maslak

EDUCATION, CRISIS AND HOPE
Crisis and Change in Latin America
edited by Stephen J. Ball, Gustavo
E. Fischman and Silvina Gvirtz

Contents

Series Preface

This series of scholarly works in comparative and international education has grown well beyond the initial conception of a collection of reference books. Although retaining its original purpose of providing a resource to scholars, students, and a variety of other professionals who need to understand the role played by education in various societies or world regions, it also strives to provide accurate, relevant, and up-to-date information on a wide variety of selected educational issues, problems, and experiments within an international context.

Contributors to this series are well-known scholars who have devoted their professional lives to the study of their specializations. Without exception these men and women possess an intimate understanding of the subject of their research and writing. Without exception they have studied their subject not only in dusty archives, but have lived and traveled widely in their quest for knowledge. In short, they are "experts" in the best sense of that often overused word.

In our increasingly interdependent world, it is now widely understood that it is a matter of military, economic, and environmental survival that we understand better not only what makes other societies tick, but also how others, be they Japanese, Hungarian, South African, or Chilean, attempt to solve the same kinds of educational problems that we face in North America. As the late George Z. F. Bereday wrote more than three decades ago: "[E]ducation is a mirror held against the face of a people. Nations may put on blustering shows of strength to conceal public weakness, erect grand façades to conceal shabby backyards, and profess peace while secretly arming for conquest, but how they take care of their children tells unerringly who they are" (*Comparative Methods in Education*, New York: Holt, Rinehart and Winston, 1964, 5).

Perhaps equally important, however, is the valuable perspective that studying another education system (or its problems) provides us in understanding our own system (or its problems). When we step beyond our own limited experience and our commonly held assumptions about schools and learning in order to look back at our system in contrast to another, we see it in a very different light. To learn, for example, how China or Belgium handles the education of a multilingual society, how the French provide for the funding of public education, or how the Japanese control access to their universities enables us to better understand that there are reasonable alternatives to our own familiar way of doing things. Not that we can borrow directly from other societies. Indeed, educational arrangements are inevitably a reflection of deeply embedded political, economic, and cultural factors that are unique to a particular society. But a conscious recognition that there are other ways of doing things can serve to open our minds and provoke our imaginations in ways that can result in new experiments or approaches that we may not have otherwise considered.

Since this series is intended to be a useful research tool, the editor and contributors welcome suggestions for future volumes, as well as ways in which this series can be improved.

Edward R. Beauchamp
University of Hawaii

Introduction
Toward a Neoliberal Education?
Tension and Change in Latin America

GUSTAVO E. FISCHMAN
STEPHEN J. BALL
SILVINA GVIRTZ

In surveying the impact of neoliberalism in Latin America as we inch anxiously into the twenty-first century, it is not difficult to find educational and social programs and practices to be critical about. Skepticism and disdain are easy. The challenge of finding a coherent political, theoretical, or ethical base from which to develop purposive critiques and alternative plans of action is not so easy. For those committed to the ideals of fairness and equality of social and civil rights as the bases of a substantive democracy, critique and innovation are even more difficult. Neoliberalism stands, as we suggest in this introduction, as an ideology without ideology, beyond politics. Part of its success is that it evades and eschews the conflicts and disputes that arise around struggles for social justice. Rather it promises "a better life" by releasing individuals to do what they do best. It offers betterment, in a sense, without effort, as a side effect. Against this the plans, interventions, and bureaucracy of social democracy look out-moded. It is increasingly difficult to find "another place" from which to be heard. Thus, like many others, we start with critique—but in this volume as a whole, we also offer evaluation and some possibilities for hope.

The policy orthodoxies of national economic development are now well established, and there is no shortage of policy. Levin goes so far as to call it a global "policy epidemic." Similar policies are pursued in very different political and economic locations. Certainly during the 1990s countries throughout Latin America experienced an accelerated process of change and witnessed the implementation of new social and economic models of development (Reimers 2000; Torres and Puiggrós 1997; UNESCO-OREALC 2000) associated with the implementation of neoliberal programs.

Basically, these models were either directly related to the "conditionality" requirements of IMF and World Bank loans or their regional agents, or were taken up by local politicians committed to the normativities of northern development directions. In either case pacing was typically sacrificed for speed, often with dire consequences. At the level of global policy the changes in the welfare regimes in many developed and developing countries—and the attendant transformation of public sector organizations and the further opening up of these economies to global capitalist institutions—are part of a process of alignment with the "inviolate orthodoxy" (Stiglitz 2002, 43) espoused by organizations like the OECD, World Trade Organization (WTO), and the World Bank. The World Bank and International Monetary Fund (IMF) in particular are firmly committed to what is sometimes called the Americanization of the world economy. Joseph Stiglitz, reflecting on his time as chief economist at the World Bank, describes major decisions taken by the IMF as "made on the basis of what seemed a curious blend of ideology and bad economics, dogma that sometimes seemed to be thinly veiling special interests" (xiii).

However, while the use of the term neoliberalism is very common in Latin America, a definite assessment of its impact is made somewhat difficult by the looseness and ambiguity with which the term is used. Lynne Phillips (1998) among others points out: "Neo-liberalism is the process of growing reliance on the market for organizing social and economic activities. Why this process has taken place in Latin America is still a matter of debate" (xvi). Lidia Henales and Beatrice Edwards describe this situation by pointing out that:

> Generally, critics of neo-liberalism describe it as economic and social strategies that together constitute the renovation of the old liberal mercantilist ideal. However, those who currently design and implement these policies reject the term neo-liberal and instead use such terms as privatization, decentralization, deregulation, and tax reform to convey the same meaning. In this way they successfully disown the long ideological continuum from which they have evolved, while simultaneously promoting neo-mercantilism as new and diverse. (2000, 1)

Most of the programs aimed at bringing about privatization, decentralization, deregulation, and tax reform were justified as the only possible solution to the economic and social problems faced by the Latin American countries because only these policies were attuned to the worldwide process of globalization.[1] In this case globalization was equated with modernization and implied the acceptance of the expansion of transnational capital, the supranational character of productive decision making, increasing trends pressuring in the direction of the homogenization of information and cultural consumption, and the connection of geographically and culturally distant places in such a way that local events are shaped, as well as influenced, by events occurring in remote places.[2]

Neoliberal economic policy discourse has become hegemonic in the public sphere and all but overwhelmed the articulation of alternative social conceptions that emphasize the need for greater democracy and the improvement of the quality of life—measured not only in economic terms but also in preventing environmental collapse and creating equal access to job opportunities, education, culture, health, and welfare. There is a hegemonic inevitability about neoliberal reforms, but it is an inevitability that is carefully "policed" by inter-national agencies. In practice and in political discourse, neoliberal reforms are presented as simply rational-technical solutions to the problems of underde-velopment, and separated from their ideological and philosophical origins.[3] Terry Eagleton's reflections are helpful here:

> Many a ruling class has sought to erase from historical memory the blood and squalor in which it was born. As Blaise Pascal admonishes with arresting candor in his Pensées, "The truth about the [original] usurpation must not be made apparent; it came about originally with-out reason and has become reasonable. We must see that it is regarded as authentic and eternal, and its origins must be hidden if we do not want it soon to end" (Eagleton 2002, 119).

Eagleton's point underlines the importance of trying to understand and de-construct the neoliberal perspective and the arguments of its supporters that propose its "nonexistence" and work against the possibility of "thinking other-wise." In the simplest sense educators and researchers need to address the rele-vance of policies based on economic and business practices to the ethical/ intellectual processes of education. More specifically, it is important to under-stand how the hegemonic position of neoliberalism in Latin American coun-tries works on the fears, concerns, perspectives, and strategies of social subjects that are reinterpolated within a discourse of responsibility and a "vocabulary and ethics of enterprise" producing in turn a new "style of conduct" (Weber 1915/1948). The market, competitiveness, and choice involve not simply a new and more efficient mechanism for the delivery of public sector services but also the basis for a new moral economy. It brings with it a new set of values and a new ethical framework within which relationships and practices in public sector organizations are reworked.

Defining the neoliberal perspective in education

Steve Klees (1999) has noted that economic theory and policies, from the early writings of Adam Smith to the current discussion of neoliberalism and the IMF and World Bank sponsored structural adjustment programs, have always been anchored in the debates about the role and balances between the force and presence of the market and the state. While the defining characteristics of neoliberalism follow the central elements of classic economic liberalism with regard to the role of the state, there are key differences here, which are funda-mental to understanding the current politics of education in the Latin Amer-ica. Mark Olssen's clear statement of the differences between neoliberalism and classic economic liberalism is worth quoting in its entirety:

> Whereas classical liberalism represents a negative conception of state power in that the individual was to be taken as an object to be freed from

the interventions of the state, neo-liberalism has come to represent a positive conception of the state's role in creating the appropriate market by providing the conditions, laws and institutions necessary for its operation; although for many developing societies these conditions for the market are dictated by international lenders and multi-lateral agencies. In classical liberalism, the individual is characterized as having an autonomous human nature and can practice freedom. In neo-liberalism the state seeks to create an individual who is an enterprising and competitive entrepreneur. In the classical model the theoretical aim of the state was to limit and minimize its role based on postulates which included universal egoism (the self-interested individual); invisible hand theory which dictated that the interests of the individual were also the interests of the society as a whole; and the political maxim of laissez-faire. In the shift from classical liberalism to neo-liberalism, then, there is an important element added, for such a shift involves a change in subject position from "homo economicus," who naturally behaves out of self-interest and is relatively detached from the state, to "manipulatable man" who is created by the state and who is continually encouraged to be "perpetually responsive." It is not that the conception of the self-interested subject is replaced or done away with by the new ideals of "neo-liberalism" but that in an age of universal welfare, the perceived possibilities of slothful dependence create necessities for new forms of vigilance, surveillance, performance appraisal and of forms of control generally. In this model the state has taken it upon itself to keep us all up to the mark. The state will see to it that each one makes a "continual enterprise of ourselves" . . . in what seems to be a process of "governing without governing." (Olssen 1996, 340)

This process of governing without governing involves not a deregulation and withdrawal of the state, but a re-regulation and a new kind of role. According to Olssen's description one of the main goals of the neoliberal state is the development of "an individual who is an enterprising and competitive entrepreneur" (Olssen 1996, 34). Similarly, Kless (1999, 1) notes that this emerging model of the state is "an integral part of neo-liberalism's attempt to delegitimate government and disengage government and society from any collective responsibility for social welfare." This shift from collective responsibility to entrepreneurial individualism has profound implications for the educational sector.

A central feature of the neo-liberal argument as applied to education systems is that schools must bring their policies and practices in line with the importance of knowledge as a form of production (Davies and Guppy 1997). Neoliberal educationalists largely blame public schools, state-monopolies, and "producer capture" for economic decline, and they argue that educational reform must therefore be responsive to the postindustrial labor market and the needs of a restructured global economy. Davies and Guppy explain that the renewal of school must follow: "Curricula concentrated on consumer relations, problem solving, entrepreneurialism, and cross-cultural 'multiskilling' are central to this economic transformation. Employers will recruit people with broad education and complement this with intensive on-the-job training" (1997, 439).

Neoliberal discourses both theoretically and ideologically rest on a belief in the self-correcting qualities of the corporatist logic of the free market as part of a self-proclaimed ideologically neutral discourse of efficiency and accountability. Within this discourse the market and the corporation are sanitized and romanticized. Market failings are erased and the "perfections" of competition are set over and against the "conservatism" of state bureaucracies. The role of the state in regulating markets—most recently highlighted by the hurried passing of the Sarbanes-Oxley Act in the U.S.—is glossed over in the enthusiasm of neoliberal politics. In this sense, the region is facing what Pierre Bourdieu refers to as the "gospel" of neoliberalism. This gospel is one that serves as a clarion call to combat "by every means, including the destruction of the environment and human sacrifice, against any obstacle to the maximization of profit" (1998, 126). It is worth quoting Pierre Bourdieu's description of neoliberalism at length:

A powerful economic theory whose strictly symbolic strength, combined with the effect of theory, redoubles the force of the economic realities it is supposed to express. It ratifies the spontaneous philosophy of the people who run large multinationals and of the agents of high finance—in particular pension-fund managers. Relayed throughout the world by national and international politicians, civil servants, and most of all the universe of senior journalists—all more or less equally ignorant of the underlying mathematical theology—it is becoming a sort of universal belief, a new ecumenical gospel. This gospel, or rather the soft vulgate which is put forward everywhere under the name of liberalism, is concocted out of a collection of ill-defined words—"globalization," "flexibility," "deregulation" and so on—which, through their liberal or even libertarian connotations, may help to give the appearance of a message of freedom and liberation to a conservative ideology which thinks itself opposed to all ideology. (1998, 126)

This ideology without ideology is set over and against the "failures" of social democracy, and the inability of welfare systems to meet the needs of all citizens. As Brenkman notes: "While liberal democracy offers an important discourse around issues of rights, freedoms, participation, self-rule, and citizenship, it has been mediated historically through the damaged and burdened tradition of racial and gender exclusions, economic injustice, and a formalistic, ritualized democracy, which substituted the swindle for the promise of democratic participation" (Brenkman 2000, 123 and in Giroux, forthcoming). At the same time, liberal and republican traditions of Western democratic thought have made possible the development of limited forms of social and political argumentation that at a minimum contained a "referent" for addressing the gap between the promise of a radical democracy and the existing forms of democratic governance.[4] Neoliberalism then gathers discursive strength and political influence from both its promises of a new kind of nonideological freedom and a telling critique of democratic failures. It represents, in its own terms, a move beyond politics back to a state of nature, back to the "natural" impulses of individualism and competition.

Neoliberalism and educational policies in Latin America

Neoliberal discourse can be subjected to thorough examination and critique, but this book's major task is to examine the material effects of neoliberal policies both at the level of whole economies and in the lives of those of the margins of global society—those to whom the "promises" of neoliberalism matter most. Arguably, over the last decade as a whole the macroeconomic indicators have improved from previous decades, and economic growth has somewhat resumed in most countries of the region. According to data of the Inter-American Development Bank (1999), between 1990 and 1997 Chile's GDP increased at a yearly rate of 6.9 percent—4 percent in Argentina, 2 percent in Bolivia, 2.7 percent in Peru, 3.6 percent in Uruguay, and below 2 percent in ten other countries. However, in the last two years growth has stalled and several Latin American economies—Bolivia, Argentina, and Uruguay in particular—now find themselves in free-fall and looking for further international loans. Even while it lasted, however, economic growth did not improve the basic picture of extreme inequality. Since 1990, unemployment rates have increased, and poverty and worsening living conditions are the everyday reality for a growing number of people. As a clearly conservative outlet such as *The Economist* pointed out: "The fundamental economic outlook is favorable but the poor cannot eat 'fundamentals.' What they see is that the region's traditionally wide gap between the incomes is widening further" (1996, 21).

As a region, Latin America still has one of the highest levels of income inequality in the world. On average, a quarter of national incomes is appropriated by the wealthiest 5 percent, and only 7.5 percent is distributed among the poorest 30 percent of the population. Between 1980 and 1997 the number of people living below country-specific poverty lines increased from 136 to 204 million, with 90 million living in conditions of extreme poverty. Many of the poor live in rural and indigenous areas, and the process of pauperization has also disproportionately affected women.[5]

In contrast, the wealthiest sectors of the population have enjoyed the bene-fits of the application of policies of "liberalization and modernization," which have increased their opportunities to access the latest world-market technol-ogy and consume fashionable goods. The simultaneous increase of wealth for a few and the expansion of poverty for many is the expression of the striking economic segmentation and its parallel process of social polarization of the region. Important transformations existed not only in the economy but also in the education sector.

And how does all of this relate to education? The short answer is: In a num-ber of complex ways. As we have suggested already, the overall relationship between education and the economy—both in terms of inputs and out-comes—is being reworked. Education itself is drawn ever more directly into the sphere of profit. There is the insertion of the habitus of private production and its commercial sensibilities and a concomitant "utilitarian morality" into educational practices. Education is commodified. In many ways we have as yet no well-developed language with which to describe and analyze the "marketi-sation" of education. Concrete developments have outrun the scope of our usual conceptual tools. Furthermore, increasing evidence suggests that the ef-fects of market structures in education may directly parallel the segmenting and polarizing effects of the neoliberal economy. The "new modernization" discourse developed a strong educational tone, stressing the importance of higher levels of educational efficiency and quality through school decen-tralization, autonomy, increased rigor, discipline, efficiency, efficacy, account-ability, and higher levels of private sector participation in the delivery of educational services.

The educational debate in Latin America at the beginning of the twenty-first century appears to be dominated by polemics about standards, testing, school autonomy, decentralization, accountability of the public sector, privati-zation, and vouchers, indicating that the center of the debate is how to best ac-commodate educational institutions to the demands of the market. As Hursh (2001) notes:

> The neo-liberal states, through the use of standards, assessments, and accountability, aims to restrict educators to particular kinds of thinking, thinking that conceptualizes education in terms of producing individu-als who are economically productive. Education is no longer valued for its role in developing political, ethical, and aesthetic citizens. Instead, the goal has become promoting knowledge that contributes to economic productivity and producing students who are compliant and produc-tive. Blackmore explains that: "educational policy has shifted emphasis from input and process to outcomes, from the liberal to the vocational, from education's intrinsic to its instrumental value, and from qualitative to quantitative measures of success." (2001, 34)

The processes noted by Hursh for the U.S. and the UK have their parallels in Latin America. The educational debate prior to the rise of neoliberalism centered on providing equality of opportunity and the imagined nexus between education and democracy. Within the neoliberal hegemony, the educational focus and agendas have shifted to financially driven and assessed programs of school reform. These agendas are centered on increasing the accountability and efficiency of the public systems of education through processes of "educational restructuring." This restructuring is mainly understood as a process of producing financial savings, while at the same time thoroughly transforming goals, epistemological bases, and methods and procedures of school systems. In some ways this is again a simple and powerful transposition of logic from the market into the public sector. Education is held to account; its efficiency is measured. But this is not simply a process of measurement and comparison; it also effects and changes what it measures, driven by the reductionist idea that everything is a matter of accounting (Readings, 1998) and the only things that are worthwhile are those that can be counted or measured. As Du Gay (1996, 190) puts it: "the generalization of an enterprise form to all forms of conduct may of itself serve to incapacitate an organization's ability to pursue its preferred projects by redefining its identity and hence what the nature of its project actually is."

Programs for increasing the efficiency and accountability of educational systems have become the primary strategy for dealing with public education. Many educational reform programs are now almost exclusively framed by the quality-efficiency equation, and the complex connections between education and democracy often have been displaced by these more "pressing" priorities—although some of the chapters in this collection highlight the conflicts and struggles that are inherent in the making and enactment of policies. There are several example of hybrid policies with mixed priorities.[6]

During the 1990s most Latin American countries were subject to multiple attempts at significantly restructuring their educational systems. Many of these attempts emphasized the rhetoric of choice, accountability, quality, and decentralization, though, as suggested already, they have frequently had the paradoxical effect of reducing school autonomy and enabling central governments to acquire even greater control over the daily life of educational institutions. Barry, Osborne, and Rose (1996) aptly describe the changing role and tactics of governmental and quasi-governmental organizations:

> Paradoxically, neo-liberalism, alongside its critique of the deadening consequences of the "intrusion" of the state into the life of the individual, has nonetheless provoked the invention and/or deployment of a whole array of organizational forms and technical methods in order to extend the field in which a certain kind of economic freedom might be

practiced in the form of personal autonomy, enterprise, and choice. (Barry et al., 10)

Currently, ministries of education in the region (both at the national or provincial level) not only have more power to determine school policies, curriculum changes, and evaluation processes, but also have tighter control over the performance of individual schools. These performances are linked to the goals of financial programs of economic adjustment, devised and supervised by international financial institutions such as the World Bank and the IMF. This type of control is not driven by educational principles or needs.

These processes of extending the presence of the state were implemented while the state simultaneously was withdrawing from intervention from its traditional sphere as guarantor of equal educational opportunities and provisions. Fernando Reimers makes the following comments:

> It should be acknowledged that the stark inequalities among primary schools serving different children occur in contexts of relatively low spending and quality for all children enrolled in public schools in Latin America. In spite of the fact that international organizations and governments have been more prone to emphasize reforms to improve resource utilization (which assumes that there is unutilized or poorly utilized capacity in the system) the public education systems in Latin America spend significantly less than the United States or the Caribbean. Expenditures per pupil in primary education, as a percentage of GNP per capita, exceed 2.5 percent only in Costa Rica and Cuba. In most other countries they are significantly below this level (Reimers 2000, 446)

As already noted, the Latin American reforms of the 1990s were formulated to advance two simultaneous goals: increasing the accountability of the educational systems and promoting school-level reform. In general terms, the changes proposed to achieve those goals were structured according to the following main strategies:[7]

- *Establishing new general laws for the educational sector (in those countries that did not already have them).* In Venezuela the "Ley Orgánica de Educación" (Organic Law of Education) was passed on July 26, 1980, and was established in 1986; in Chile the "Ley Orgánica Constitucional de la Enseñanza" (Organic Constitutional Law of Teaching) was passed in 1990; in Argentina the "Ley Federal de Educación" (Federal Law of Education) was passed in 1993; in Colombia the "Ley General de Educación" (General Law of Education) was passed in 1994; and in

Brazil the "Ley de Directrices y Bases de la Educación" (Law of Orientation and Foundations of Education) was passed in 1997.

- *Establishing processes of system decentralization.* In Chile the process of decentralization began in 1980 and ended in 1986. In Argentina, the greatest political effort was made in 1978 and concluded with passing the "Ley Federal de Educación" (Federal Law of Education) in 1994. In Venezuela, the "VIII Plan de la Nación" (VIII Plan of the Nation) was proposed to decentralize the administration of education. In Colombia, except for certain administrative aspects, the new law of education promoted processes of decentralization (Martínez Boom, 1993), as in Venezuela (Braslavsky and Gvirtz 2001)

- *Attempts to promote a managerial ethos in individual schools through "Proyectos Educativos Institucionales" (Institutional Education Projects).*[8] These programs have been carried out in Latin America since the 1990s (Argentina, Colombia, Venezuela, and later Brazil). The institutional projects intended to give each school the power to elaborate its own project, which had to include the objectives of the institution, the profile of graduates, and a master plan describing in detail the prioritized contents to be taught. All stakeholders in the institution were to participate in its elaboration and form work groups, as well as provide support in the decision-making process. This was to be done bearing in mind the priorities and problems of the school itself, while respecting the general guidelines presented by either the national state or the provincial states. The institutional projects' rationale should have allowed and promoted each school to create its own working method. Thus, the curricular sequence and organization, the teaching methods, and their pacing were to vary from one school to another according to their institutional differences. Perhaps the most innovative and ideologically different program promoting institutional autonomy is the Escola Cidadã Program (Citizen's School Project) developed by the Municipality of Porto Alegre (Rio Grande do Sul, Brazil) since 1989 (Fischman and McLaren, 2000). In this program, educators, students, parents, community organizations, and individuals have had the opportunity to express their opinions about the role that schools should play in the larger society, and reflect upon the type of social, political, and educational practices they would like to see in operation in the municipality's schools.[9]

- *The state's withdrawal from strict curricular regulation and development of national standards or "minimum curricular contents" were elaborated in Argentina, Brazil, Chile, Colombia, the Dominican Republic, and Mexico, replacing former national curricula that dictated in great detail the contents to be taught.*

- *Implementing national systems of school and student assessment.* Undoubtedly, systematic evaluation is not new in modern pedagogy; it was and is widely used in educational systems throughout the world. What makes its current implementation different in this case is that it was designed with the rationale of constituting the core of these reforms. It is gradually being applied in a significant number of countries of the region. So much importance is placed on this new mechanism that lawmakers are contemplating the creation of instruments for evaluating the systems, and the majority of Latin American countries have already created and implemented them. Chile pioneered the implementation of experiments in the evaluation of system quality in Latin America. Currently it has the "Sistema de Medición de la Calidad Educativa" (SIMCE) (System of Measuring Educational Quality). The national ministries of education have been carrying out this task of measuring quality since 1988. In Mexico, the Sistema Nacional de Evaluación (SNEE) (National Evaluation System) was created. Brazil has its so-called Sistema Nacional de Evaluación de la Educación Básica (SAEB) (National System for the Evaluation of Basic Education), Paraguay has the Sistema Nacional de Evaluación del Proceso Educativo (SNEPE) (National System for the Evaluation of the Educational Process). Costa Rica, Venezuela, Argentina, Colombia, and Uruguay have also used this type of evaluation. Evaluation in these countries has two primary goals: one is the technical goal of improving the quality of the system through the analysis of outcomes; the other is an explicit political goal in which some of the results are used to legitimize certain political discourses regarding the objectives of the reforms.[10]

If in the traditional organization of Latin American educational systems results were guaranteed by means of highly centralized curricula, and attempts to enforce uniform teaching methods by means of daily control were carried out by administrators and supervisors, the reforms of the 1990s hoped to guarantee educational performance through the evaluation of what students have learned or, perhaps more accurately, their performance on tests or examinations. Supervision is no longer intended to be a daily phenomenon; rather its application is to be systematic over time. Nonetheless, whatever our location, educators now operate within a baffling array of figures, performance indicators, comparisons, within the educational system and competitions—in such a way that the contentments of stability are increasingly elusive, purposes are contradictory, motivations blurred, and self worth slippery. For teachers, constant doubts about which judgements may be in play at any point mean that any and all comparisons to "supposedly good teaching performances" have to be attended to. What is produced is a state of conscious and permanent visibility at the intersection of government, organization, and self-formation.

The vast literature that addresses the contemporary changes in educational systems associated with the processes of globalization and capitalistic reorganization demonstrates above all that formal systems of schooling are positioned as one of the most important social policies of the state (Ozga 2000; Fischman and Stromquist 1999, Rizvi and Lingard 2000). In the new scenario of public education in Latin America, it appears that the authorities seek to employ forms of expertise in order to govern schools at a safe distance. As noted before, neoliberalism involves less a retreat from governmental "intervention" and more a transformation based on the reinscription of the techniques and forms of expertise required for the exercise of government. (Barry et al., 14) As Rose writes, the "formal political institutions" govern from a distance and "conceive of these actors as subjects of responsibility, autonomy, and choice, and seek to act upon them through shaping and utilizing their freedom" (Rose 1995, 53–4).

Nonetheless, the social "purposes" of education in the Latin American context and elsewhere are also firmly subordinated to the financial and economic policies and principles of neo-liberalism. In Latin America the neoliberal logic is made explicit by the policy recommendations presented in different documents formulated in international conferences (Jomtien, Thailand 1990; Santiago de Chile, 1998; Dakar, Senegal, 2000) and by regional and international entities such as the World Bank and CEPAL-OREALC.

Using the goals defined in these documents as an evaluative parameter it is possible to conclude that the reforms of the 1990s have had a very limited positive impact in terms of improving education in the region. Among the most relevant indicators of the limitations of these reforms are:

- Although educational systems expanded, incorporating more students, this was done within highly fragmented systems in which the disparities among groups and regions have increased. (Post 2001)
- The newly implemented systems of educational assessment give empirical proof that the educational systems have achieved very low levels of learning. (Post, in press)
- The teaching workforce has not reached appropriate levels of compensation or professionalization. (Fischman 2000)
- The infrastructure needed to support the notion of education as lifelong learning has not reached adequate levels to attend to the needs of the adult population, reducing the services exclusively to basic education.

To conclude, the educational reforms in the 1990s developed a new organizational model of public schooling. This is a hybrid model (Braslavsky and Gvirtz 2001) and has advanced forms of decentralization and empowerment, which encouraged limited systems of local control and community participation while strengthening central authority and increased privatization. These changes are producing tensions in the character and orientation of the state and are reworking the relationships and patterns of influence between the state, the economy, and education. While the educational policies of the 1990s expanded the number of buildings, teachers, and students, their relevance for poor children and their families seems, thus far, limited, and they may well have resulted in new educational divisions and greater social polarization.

About the content of this book

The contributors to this volume are a mix of scholars from North America and Latin America, and their chapters display the richness and variety of approaches that is necessary if we are to begin to understand the complexities of educational policy and its multiple connections with the changing state, the changing economy, and the changing needs of diverse populations. As in any selection for an edited book, they cannot account for all of the historical, social, political, economical, and cultural patterns of national development and the organizational particularities of every system of education in the region. Nevertheless, seeing them as a whole, these chapters address some of the most important changes and continuities taking place in the educational sector in Latin America, and situate them within the context of the shifting dynamic forces of globalization. The writers do not take up a single, unified stance toward neoliberalism nor toward educational policy and its purposes. They also write with different points-of-view—gender, higher education, adult education, marginalized youth, rural schooling, educational elites, "local" policy making, comparisons between policies and between countries, and policy changes over time. Read individually they are fascinating; read together they constitute a powerful document of contemporary change in Latin America and its possibilities and problems.

Roberto Rodrìguez-Gómez and Armando Alcántara explore the role of several multilateral organizations in the configuration of a unified agenda to reform higher education in Latin America. Their main interest is to document the principal similarities and divergences in the policies and strategies that these agencies advocate in order to transform Latin America's higher education systems.

Daniel Schugurensky analyzes the changes in the field of adult education policy and practice during the 1990s, indicating that the application of neoliberal economic and social policies in the region had several implications for adult education policy and practice. First, increasing inequality of income places a greater burden on adult education as a "compensatory measure for the poor." Education in general, and adult education in particular, is increasingly turned to as the remedy for solving social problems such as poverty or unemployment. Secondly, the rapid and unfinished transition to democracy in Latin America requires broad, popular preparation for participation in democratic society and in the development of democratic values, particularly in times when formal democratic institutions are not living up to expectations, and novel means of democratic participation need to be designed. This entails, at a minimum, universal adult literacy that allows for a more informed public, and widespread education in citizenship, particularly the knowledge, skills, and attitudes that prepare individuals for active political participation. In his conclusions, Schugurensky emphasizes that adult education alone cannot solve all the social problems, and certainly not of the problems faced by the one hundred and fifty million Latin American youth and adults who have never had access to school or have been forced out of it. However, in connection with other actors and initiatives, it can offer a significant contribution to a more sustainable, just, democratic, and equitable development. It can also make a modest contribution to the collective development of alternatives to the hegemonic neoliberal perspective.

Pia L. Wong and Ramon Balestino arrive at a similar conclusion in their discussion of educational reforms in Brazil. This chapter examines three critical questions related to the education of marginalized young people in Brazil: (1) to what extent does current government policy prioritize the education of marginalized young people; (2) what alternative models exist for addressing their educational needs and interests; and (3) what kind of policies are needed next to maximize educational opportunities for this population? Wong and Ballestino discuss three approaches used in the education of marginalized young people and show how the Brazilian policy makers have made "nods of the head," acknowledging the existence of marginalized young people but continuing to use conventional practices to address their concerns. Wong and Balestino conclude their article by making recommendations for new collaborative forms of policy making in which grassroots groups and state entities work in partnership to prioritize the educational rights of marginalized young people. This type of partnership may offer compelling alternatives for a mediated, mitigated neoliberalism.

Patrick J. McEwan's and Luis Benveniste's chapter addresses the history and politics of rural education reform in Colombia, with particular attention to the Escuela Nueva program. These two scholars conceptualize educational change not as a result of a unified or enduring policy package but as a dynamic process that is continuously shaped and reshaped as political actors and institutions compete for influence and scarce resources in a variable social arena. In particular, they assess the motivations of the Colombian state in promoting a comprehensive reform of its rural schools. They argue that Colombia's unique political context was, in large part, responsible for its novel approach to school reform. As the political context shifted, however, so to did the state's posture to rural schooling. The authors track the Escuela Nueva program through three phases (grassroots, formalized, and decoupled) to demonstrate how social actors, their interests at a specific point in time, and the distribution of power among them are crucial elements for understanding the motivation and outcomes of social policy making.

Jorge M. Gorostiaga Derqui offers an analysis of the characteristics of decentralization policies and their relationship with neoliberalism in Argentina, Brazil, Chile, and Mexico. The objective of this chapter is not to arrive at a "correct" interpretation of the relationships between the two phenomena (neoliberalism and decentralization), but rather to explore different views and the complexity of the topic. Gorostiaga Derqui argues that school decentralization—or "school autonomy," the transferring of functions and responsibilities from the state to schools—appears as a new and extended reform that was accompanied by more traditional forms of decentralization during the 1990s such as provincialization or municipalization. These decentralization policies were coupled with processes of centralization of planning and evaluation at the national level. This new form of centralization/decentralization is seen as linked to the neoliberal restructuring of the state, to pressures from globalization processes and forces, and to various internal demands for improving quality and efficiency in the delivery of education.

Mariano Narodowski's and Milagros Nores's work intends to provide evidence of the complexity of the relationships between economic and educational reform, and they argue that the concept of neoliberalism contributes little to the understanding of education reforms, especially in the cases of Argentina and Chile. They contrast the inequalities of Chile's market system with those of Argentina's state system and ask difficult questions about which system is worse.

Luís Armando Gandin and Michael W. Apple situate the processes of educational policy and reform within the larger Brazilian sociopolitical context. They discuss the ways in which a set of "local" policies has had what seem to be extensive and long-lasting effects on educational participation. These authors describe and analyze the policies of the "Popular Administration" in Porto Alegre, Brazil. The focus of this chapter is on the "Citizen School" and on proposals that are explicitly designed to radically change both the municipal schools and the relationship between communities, the state, and education.

Susan Street's chapter addresses the new centrality of schools—and teacher actions within them. Street addresses school reform programs as they have evolved in Mexico from the perspective of subaltern actors—the teachers' dissident movement—and the efforts of this movement to disengage its struggle for democracy from the traditional leftist posture of taking over state power (democratizing the teachers' union). The alternative is the development of a pedagogical movement deemed necessary to revolutionize teaching and schooling at the community level, as the struggle for popular or radical democracy continues and deepens.

In her chapter, Nelly P. Stromquist examines some of the manifestations of neoliberalism in education from the perspective of gender using political economy frameworks. Specifically, this chapter seeks to show the myriad ways, the variety of actors, and the consequences through which neoliberalism is impacting womens' education and use of education as a liberating tool. The political economy perspective highlights the material, as opposed to discursive properties, of neoliberal dynamics and, in so doing, exposes the tensions among institutional actors as new equilibrium are sought, prevented, and negotiated.

Patricia Vanegas focuses on the international influence exerted on educational reform in Colombia. Specifically, she addresses how global trends of thought, in this case neoliberalism, pervade the contexts of policy making. Vanegas defines and describes this influence as a relationship of power between the international context and the Colombian educational policy-making elite. Vanegas uses the concept of Northern Influence to explore the specificities of this relationship of power. She argues that the Northern Influence does not simply happen as a result of imposition from the north to the south, but rather through a complex of relationships, influences, interests, and dependencies that impact upon the capability of individuals to "think otherwise" about policy.

Notes

1. The position of Jeffrey Puryear and José Brunner, two of the most renowned social scientists in Latin America, illustrates this tendency: "The current development model has placed new demands, on both citizens and the state. Globally-integrated, open economies require an internationally competitive work force, strong in science and technology. With the return to democracy after military dictatorships, people have made new demands on public services at the same time that government needs its citizens to be more informed and responsible. The decentralization of public administration puts more emphasis on participation, autonomy and civic responsibility at the local level" (Jeffrey M. Puryear and José J. Brunner, "Una agenda para la reforma educacional en América Latina y El Caribe.")
2. Granted, globalization is one of the hottest and most argued concepts in terms of its meaning and outcomes among social scientists (Rhoten 2000). Stephen Ball, in a paper about global citizenship and educational policy (1998), points out that very often globalization is defined from the top but there are also "down perspectives." The "top perspective" conceptualizes globalization as a process of cooperation between the most developed and industrialized nations, multinational corporations, and local elites, in which there is widespread attempt to sustain free market rules through the acceptance of a "consumerist ethos." (Ball 1998, 121). From the "down perspective," or for the vast majority of poor and impoverished middle classes within Third World countries, globalization has been received with less optimism. The "global market" has not delivered all the benefits its public defenders have promised. In fact, the globalized economy is largely controlled by the operations of multinational corporations and the similar interests of the G-7 countries, international financial institutions, and supranational organizations. Since the mid-1970s the MNCs have grown more rapidly than the world economy. In 1976, the fifty largest industrial corporations worldwide had sales of $540 million and received $25 billion in profits. In 1990, sales figures for the top fifty had climbed to $2.1 trillion and their profits had reached $70 billion. In real terms, whereas the U.S. economy was growing at an annual rate of 2.8 percent (the OECD average was 2.9 percent), the MNCs' annual sales growth was about 3.5 percent during the 1975–1990 period (Brown and Lauder 1997, 173).
3. Rosa Nidia Buenfil (1998) provides a good example of how the implementation of neoliberal–inspired policies are often masked by the state: "The Mexican government assumes 'social liberalism' (a euphemism for neoliberalism) as the philosophical axis of this reform, thus subordinating education to economic views: (e.g. education as investment), economic needs (e.g. schooling as unemployed depot) and pace (e.g. education as training), thus inscribing on education a managerial administration."

4. For these reasons it would be a mistake not to examine the complex and contradictory histories of personal and collective struggles that have contributed to and benefited from the welfare state. To dismiss the fact that, accompanied by severe contradictions, the condition of public schools as a component of the welfare state did vastly improve—in relative ways—the social conditions of economically and socially oppressed groups is not only politically disingenuous, but also an inadequate exercise in historical reasoning.

5. Several studies (CEPAL 1995; IRELA 1995; Stromquist 1997) have asserted that structural adjustment programs have been particularly pernicious to women. For a thorough discussion of the critical shortcomings for women in structural adjustment models of development, see Kabeer 1995.

6. We are not suggesting that the current neoliberal discourse in Latin America has replaced a previous discourse of democracy and social justice (or at least compensatory education). What the debates are showing is that neoliberal policies are promoted alongside a discourse of equity and poverty reduction.

7. We cannot fail to mention that there have been some limited "choice-based" experiments, as in the case of Chile, where the national government, through a decree issued on June 2, 1989, authorized the use of "vouchers" to subsidize the demand for education. In most other countries in the region, the chief reform strategies currently applied tend to subsidize and improve the supply of education.

8. This is the denomination given to the forms of implementation of autonomy in Colombia and Argentina.

9. This process of educational reform expresses the articulation of democratic ideals, community experiences, the legacy of the popular education movement, and a firm commitment to create a new model of schooling even amid a dramatic financial and economic crisis, and provides one of the most radical experiences of popular participation in school management, including a process of competitive and accountable system of budget allocation.

10. Regarding the political use of assessment instruments, David Post notes, "In the 1990s, separate attempts were made by UNESCO and by the International Association for the Evaluation of Achievement (IEA) to assess language and mathematics achievement in Latin America. Even when ministries were convinced to participate, the results of these assessments have been kept secret in several countries (including Peru and Mexico). National pride, and a concern to save face, will always politicize the measurement of quality." (Post 2001, 6)

References

Ball, S. (1998). "Cidadania Global. Consumo e Politica Educacional." *A Escola Cidada no Contexto da Globalizacao*. L. Heron Da Silva. Petropolis, Editora Vozes.

Barry, A., T. Osborne, and N. Rose. (1996). *Foucault and Political Reason: Liberalism, Neoliberalism, and Rationalities of Government*. Chicago: University of Chicago Press.

Bourdieu, P. (1998). *Acts of Resistance: Against the Tyranny of the Market*. New York: The New Press.

Bourdieu, P. (1999). *The Weight of the World: Social Suffering in Contemporary Society*. Stanford: Stanford University Press.

Braslavsky, C., and S. Gvirtz. (2001). *"Nuevos desafíos y dispositivos en la política educacional Latinoamericana de fin de siglo."* Madrid, Organización de los Estados Iberoamericanos.

Brenkman, John. 2000. "Extreme Criticism." In *What's Left of Theory*, edited by J. Butler, J. Guillary, and K. Thomas. New York: Routledge.

Brown, P., and H. Lauder. (1997). "Observations on Global/Local Articulations of the Regendering and Restructuring of Educational Work." *International Review of Education* 43, no. 5–6: 439–461.

Brunner, Joaquin, and Jeff Puryear. (1995). *Educación, Equidad y Competitividad Económica en las Américas: An Interamerican Dialogue: Vol 1, Key Issues*. Washington, D.C.: Organization of American States.

Buenfil, Rosa Nidia. (1998). Globalization, Education and Discourse Political-Analysis Ambiguity and Accountability in Research *Qualitative Studies in Education*

CEPAL (1995). *"Panorama Social de América Latina."* Santiago, Chile, CEPAL.

Davies, Scott, and Neil Guppy. (1997). "Globalization and Educational Reforms in Anglo-American Democracies." *Comparative Education Review* 41(4):435–459.

Du Gay, P. (1996). *Consumption and Identity at Work*. London: Sage.

Eagleton, Terry. (2002). "Capitalism and Form." *New Left Review* 14: 119.

Economist, The. November 30th, (1996). "Latin America's Blacklash." *The Economist* 341 (7994):19–23.

Fischman, G. and N. Stromquist. (1999). "Globalization and Higher Education in Developing Countries." *Higher Education: Handbook of Theory and Research* 15: 501–22.

Fischman, G. E. (2000). *Imagining Teachers: Rethinking Gender Dynamics in Teacher Education*. Lanham, Md.: Rowman and Littlefield.

Fischman, G. and P. McLaren. (2000). "Schooling for Democracy: Toward a Critical Utopianism." *Contemporary Sociology* 29, no. 1: 168–80.

Giroux, Henry. (2003). "Thinking Politics and Resistance as a form of Public Pedagogy." In *Critical Theories, Radical Pedagogies and Global Conflicts,* edited by G. Fischman, P. McLaren, and H. Sunker. Lanham: Rowman and Littlefield Publishers, 1–12.

Henales, Lidia and Beatrice Edwards. (2000). "Neo-liberalism and Education Reform in Latin America." *Current Issues in Comparative Education* 2, no. 2: 1.

Hursh, David. (2000). "Neoliberalism and the Control of Teachers, Students, and Learning: The Rise of Standards, Standardization, and Accountability." *Cultural Logic* 4 (1):1–6.

Inter-American Development Bank. (1999). *Facing Up Inequality in Latin America*. Washington, D.C.: Inter-American Development Bank.

IRELA. (1995). *Poverty in Latin America: Causes and Consequences*. London; IRELA.

Kabeer, N. (1994). *Reversed Realities: Gender Hierarchies in Development Thought*. London, New York: Verso.

Klees, Steven J. (1999). "Privatization and Neoliberalism: Ideology and Evidence in Rhetorical Reforms." *Current Issues in Comparative Education* 1, no. 2, 1.

Krawczyc, N. and M. C. Maria, et al., eds. (2000). *O cenário educacional Latino-americano no liminar do seculo XXI*. Reformas en debate. Campinas, Editora Autores Associados.

Levin, B. (1998). "An Epidemic of Education Policy: What Can We Learn for Each Other?" *Comparative Education* 34, no. 2, 131–42.

Martínez Boom, A. (1993). "*Ley General de Educación. Alcances y Perspectivas*." Bogotá: Fundación Tercer Milenio.

Olssen, M. (1996). "In Defense of the Welfare State and Publicly Provided Education." *Journal of Education Policy* 11: 337–62.

Ozga, J. (2000). *Policy Research in Educational Settings: Contested Terrain*. Buckingham: Open University Press.

Phillips, Lynne. (1998). "Introduction: Neoliberalism in Latin America." In *The Third Wave of Modernization in Latin America: Cultural Perspectives on Neoliberalism,* edited by L. Phillips. Wilmington, DE: Jaguar Books, xi–xxiv.

Post, D. (2001). *Children's Work, Schooling, and Welfare in Latin America: Chile, Peru, and Mexico Compared*. Boulder, Colo.: Westview Press.

Readings, Bill. (1996). *The University in Ruins*. Camgridge, MA: Harvard University Press.

Reimers, F., Ed. (2000). *Unequal Schools, Unequal Chances: The Challenges to Equal Opportunity in the Americas*. Cambridge, Mass.: DRCS-Harvard University.

Rhoten, D. (2000). "Education Decentralization in Argentina: A 'Global-Local Conditions of Possibility' Approach to State, Market, and Society Change." *Journal of Education Policy* 15, no. 6: 593–619.

Rizvi, F., and B. Lingard. (2000). "Globalization and Education: Complexities and Contingencies." *Educational Theory* 50, no. 4: 419–426.

Stiglitz, J. (2002). *Globalization and Its Discontents*. London: Penguin Books

Stromquist, N. (1997). *Literacy for Citizenship: Gender and Grassroots Dynamics in Brazil*. Albany, SUNY Press.

Torres, Carlos A., and Adriana Puiggrós. (1995). "The State and Public Education in Latin America." *Comparative Education Review* 39 (1):1–27.

UNESCO-OREALC. (2000). *Regional Report of the Americas: An Assessment of the "Education for All" Program in the Year 2000*. Santiago, Chile: UNESCO-OREALC.

Weber, Max. (1964). *Basic Concepts in Sociology*. Edited and translated by H. P. Secher. New York: Citadel Press.

1
Toward a Unified Agenda for Change in Latin American Higher Education
The Role of Multilateral Agencies

ROBERTO RODRÍGUEZ-GÓMEZ
ARMANDO ALCÁNTARA

Introduction

This chapter explores the role of several multilateral organizations in the configuration of a unified agenda to reform higher education in Latin America. Our main interest is to document the principal policies and strategies that these agencies advocate in order to transform Latin America's higher education systems. A central purpose of the chapter is to identify both similarities and divergences in the approaches to policy design and implementation that are being used by the multilateral agencies participating in the ongoing debates.

During the last two decades the higher education systems of Latin America have experienced a number of structural changes including a dramatic increase in enrollments, systemic territorial expansion of institutions, diversification of the system through the founding of new institutional types, and opening to private investment in third level education. In addition, legal reforms have been adopted at a national level that have weakened institutional autonomy. It could be said that the most significant changes are those that are intended to increase institutional accountability to the state and which have resulted in a variety of policy instruments aimed at improving the system's productivity, efficiency, and quality. Accordingly, there are now policies mandating performance-based pay for faculty; funding for programs that are contingent on compliance with predetermined quality assurance indicators, and incentives to encourage faculty to earn the doctorate in order to achieve their professionalization.

Despite the uniqueness of each nation's system of higher learning, there is remarkable agreement and similarity in the ways in which their governments are pursuing their modernization. Thus, our first hypothesis is that in the realm of higher education policies in Latin America, there is a tendency towards the creation of a unified agenda for reform, which would follow—albeit with some years of delay and under less favorable circumstances—the same path to transformation as has been followed in the more economically developed countries (Goedegebuure, Leo et al., 1994, Morsy and Altbach, 1998).

A second hypothesis proposed in this chapter is that multilateral agencies, through recommendations, their own policies and their programs, have assumed a leading role in shaping the higher education reform agenda in Latin America. We have to acknowledge, however, that the production of and socialization to a "unified agenda" is a rather complex process. On the one hand, the perspective of multilateral organizations is not homogeneous although a convergence exists in a number of crucial aspects. On the other hand, it is worth distinguishing between the development of criteria for reform, which is the province of the government and their implementation, which is under the province of the academic community. It is within the academic community that we witness strong resistance to reforms which are perceived as eroding institutional autonomy and academic freedom. As a consequence, in the current debates the compromises and negotiations that ensue have had the effect of placing the multilateral agencies on one side of the table, and the institutions of higher education (or their representing organizations), on the other.

In this chapter we examine only one aspect of the problem: that which corresponds to the different perspectives on higher education reform in Latin America being held by some of the principal multilateral organizations. We wish to note that a more comprehensive view of the issue under consideration would have to take into account the specific political processes of each country and their effect on the implementation of the transformation agenda that has been outlined by the multilateral agencies.

Our main interest in this chapter is to compare the perspectives of organizations representing the multilateral banking system and the organizations whose principal objective is the search of political consensus for social and economic development. The first case under scrutiny is that of the World Bank and the Inter American Development Bank; the second case is represented by the United Nations Education, Science and Culture Organization (UNESCO) along with the Economic Commission for Latin America (ECLA). A number of questions guide our analysis: What is the position of these agencies with respect to higher education in Latin America? What are the reform initiatives they support? What are the similarities and differences in the reform initiatives being proposed by these agencies? Answer to these questions will allow us, to outline some of the basic elements that constitute the current "unified agenda" and to raise issues that are of critical importance for the near future.

International agencies and higher education

The notion of international agencies covers a complex institutional constellation with purposes that go from economic exchange to the formation of political consensus. These agencies cover a variety of subjects that have cooperation and the regulation of competition in common. Some of them represent regional blocks, others have worldwide coverage and yet others form conglomerates on matters of shared interest (Jallade, Lee and Samoff, 1994).

In the Latin American educational field and particularly in the university, the participation of multilateral agencies has a continuous trajectory. Some of them, like the Union of Latin American Universities (UDUAL) or the Higher Education Regional Commission of UNESCO for Latin American and the Caribbean (CRESALC) have worked for decades to stimulate regional university cooperation. However, in recent years, the presence of multilateral development banks has been a factor in the definition of higher education policies in the countries of the region and has opened up a debate, which is still going on, about the pertinence of its recommendations. Other intergovernmental agencies, that propose the search for consensus with respect to development problems, have also made pronouncements on higher education and constitute a point of reference in the processes of change in Latin American universities (Tünnermann, 1995; Kent, 1995; Coraggio, 1998; Alcántara; 2000; Rodríguez-Gómez, 2000).

For these reasons, it is important to compare the perspective of these two types of organizations on higher education reform. Beyond the obvious differences arising from the very nature of the organizations, what is the position of the international agencies with respect to higher education at present and in the future? The following text is an attempt to answer this question. To do so, we divided the presentation into two groups, the first represents the broadest level of discussion, exemplified by the cases of UNESCO and the World Bank, both agencies with a worldwide coverage including all the countries of Latin America. The second group is comprised of regional level organizations and is illustrated with the cases of ECLA and IADB.

UNESCO

UNESCO is a specialized agency of the United Nations Organization (UN), founded in 1948 with the purpose of "promoting education for everyone, cultural development, protection of nature, cultural heritage, as well as scientific cooperation, freedom of the press and communication". In its Declaration of Principles, the associate countries made the commitment to offer "complete and egalitarian educational opportunities" and procure an "unrestricted search for objective truth and the free exchange of ideas and knowledge". Although more than 180 countries belong to the agency, some have opted to cease being members; such is the case of the United States in 1984 and the United Kingdom and Singapore in 1985 (UNESCO, 1999).

From its creation, UNESCO has been a central instance in the international educational debate. As well as the General Conference that meets every two years in ordinary sessions, thematic world conferences are held periodically: in 1998 the World Conference on Higher Education (Paris) took place and in 1999 the World Conference on Science (Budapest); agreements and resolutions were made in both that are pertinent to our analysis.

In Latin America, UNESCO is present through a decentralized unit (the Regional Education Office for Latin America and the Caribbean, OREALC) which is responsible for supporting the countries of the region in educational improvement (UNESCO, 1998c). The work of OREALC is complemented by the activities of the recently constituted International Institute of UNESCO for Higher Education in Latin America and the Caribbean (IIESALC) to substitute CRESALC. The Institute is responsible for promoting the debate on university problems, disseminating studies on higher education and providing technical assistance for planning and implementing programs.

World Bank

Like UNESCO, the origins of the World Bank go back to the nineteen forties. It was founded in 1944 with the initial purpose of supporting the material reconstruction of the allied European block, but with time it has become the main multilateral instrument for financing development projects and also a highly effective means to promote the economic policy positions of the advanced capitalist countries.

The World Bank currently groups together 180 countries and mobilizes a volume of credits for US$30,000,000,000 a year that are distributed under three principal modalities: project loans, sectoral loans and structural adjustment loans. Each country has a number of votes in terms of their shareholding which, in turn, is determined by the size of their economies in relation to the world economy; thus the Group of 7 (Canada, France, Germany, Italy, Japan, United Kingdom and United States) represent 45% of the capital of the World Bank and the United States another 17%. The World Bank member countries participate simultaneously in the International Monetary Fund (IMF) and, in accordance with the normativity in force, only developing countries are subject to the Bank's credit.

In different stages, the World Bank has assumed different missions. Once the reconstruction phase was ensured, the Bank turned to financing modernization projects through loans for infrastructure and equipment. In the eighties, it fostered economic liberalization processes and approved credits for the payment of foreign debt and structural adjustment. From the beginning of 1990, the Bank concentrated on a strategy "to combat poverty" that included the objective of "investing in people, particularly through the promotion of basic health and education; environmental protection; the fostering of private sector development; the strengthening of governments' capacity to provide quality services in a sufficient, transparent way; the promotion of reforms to create a stable macroeconomic environment, and to direct investment and long term planning strategies". (World Bank, 1999a). These objectives represent a second generation of structural adjustment programs and coincide with the purpose of sustaining the viability of the macroeconomic reform and alleviating its social and political impacts. In this way, the part of the loans that the World Bank channels to financial and public sector management tended to decrease: in the eighties, approximately one half of the loans were directly linked to the macroeconomic adjustment program, while in the nineties, this proportion decreased to one third (World Bank, 2000).

The World Bank began operating in the educational field in 1963. In the sixties and seventies, loans were focused on training and technical formation; and in this period the proportion of resources for education was marginal given the total number of loans approved. In the eighties, the situation began to change: from 1980 to 1995 the volume of loans to the educational sector tripled and its share in total World Bank credits doubled. In the nineties, the overall average for education was 8.2%, with a peak of 10.9% in 1995. In the Latin American region the average for the decade was 8.6%, with a maximum of 12.3% in 1995, which in absolute terms represents more than US$600,000,000 a year.

The World Bank focus on educational priorities has also varied. In 1990, a preference for basic education was established as the central part of resource distribution; during the decade projects associated with primary and secondary education consumed more than half the credits of the sector. In 1995, a priority was established in education for girls and an interest in the educational needs of ethnic minorities and indigenous groups, while infrastructure loans began to decrease and loans for other educational inputs to increase (World Bank, 1995). In spite of this approach, the Bank continued approving credits for post-basic educational programs. In Latin America several projects to reform higher education were approved, as is the case of Argentina (1996), Mexico (1998) and Chile (1999) with credits for US$165,000,000, US$180,200,000 and US$165,000,000 respectively (World Bank, 1999b).

In its most recent document on sectoral policy, the World Bank proposes four global priority areas: basic education, with special attention to girls and the poorest sector of the population; early interventions, with programs aimed at early childhood and school hygiene; innovative delivery, including distance education, open learning and new technologies; and systemic reform considering actions such as: determination of standards, curricular reform, achievement assessment, governance and decentralization (World Bank, 1999c).

The Bank recognizes that these priorities are not necessarily the same for all regions and countries given the diversity of conditions and results the different educational systems and structures present. For Latin America, it suggests the following order of priorities: "to improve the learning-teaching process; to include those who are excluded; to meet the needs of young people; to reform institutional management; to use technology to improve education and reform higher education" (World Bank, 1999c) and with respect to higher education reform it recommends; "diversifying tertiary education in order to raise quality and efficiency, improving university access for the lowest two-fifths in terms of income and strengthening the role of the private sector in financing and providing higher studies". (World Bank, 1999d).

ECLA

The Economic Commission for Latin America was founded in 1948 by a resolution of the Economic and Social Council of the UN, with the following objectives: to carry out studies and research; to promote economic and social development through cooperation and integration; to collect, organize, interpret and disseminate information and data relative to the economic and social development of the region; to provide advisory services to governments; implement technical cooperation and assistance programs for development; organize meetings of intergovernmental groups and groups of experts; to sponsor training courses, symposia and seminars; and contribute to the regional perspective of world problems being taken into account.

Throughout its history, ECLA has played an important role in defining development options for Latin America (Bielschowsky, 1998). In the fifties, the Commission recommended import substitution as the basis of an industrialization strategy suitable for Latin American reality, while it also insisted on stimulating exports and intraregional exchange. It also underlined the virtues of planning and recommended investment in human capital as a premise for technological advance. In the sixties, ECLA's thinking was sustained on two fundamental theoretical bodies: dependency theory and the thesis of structural heterogeneity. Through this reflection, that incorporated new analytical dimensions to the subject of appropriate development, it underlined the need for a more equitable social distribution of the product in order to respond to the demands unleashed by the modernizing process.

The discussion in the seventies centered around "development styles", a concept suggesting a broader definition of development, not only economic but also social, political and cultural. In the face of the world economic crisis of 1973–1974, the Commission recommended a better combination of the use of the internal market and an export drive. In the context of Latin American militarism and during the crisis of the eighties, ECLA lost its role as protagonist as an instance promoting development strategies in the region—a role that was assumed by the IMF with its structural adjustment programs. Nevertheless, it continued with its work on theoretical reflection and the formulation of recommendations. Thus, in relation to adjustment policies, the Commission proposed that the recessive adjustment of the balance of payments be substituted by an expansive adjustment. At the end of the eighties, ECLA opened up a discussion on the long-term growth process, centered on the thesis of productive transformation with equity. In the nineties, the development model recommended by the Commission, in tune with the new conditions of global exchange, emphasized competitive trade liberalization based on the addition of intellectual value to exports.

In ECLA's trajectories, the theme of education is a constant. It insists on its key role in national and regional development with different shades of meaning. ECLA's influence on Latin American educational thought is also relevant and it parts from long term research projects (suffice it to remember the Development and Education in Latin America project of the eighties) and a vast editorial production on the subject.

IADB

The Interamerican Development Bank (IADB) was established in 1959—in the context of the Cold War and at the request of the American government—with the purpose of "accelerating the economic and social progress of Latin American and the Caribbean". Today, this bank is the main source of multilateral financing for Latin America and the Caribbean: since it was founded it has channeled direct loans for almost US$100,000,000,000. IADB belongs to 46 countries; 28 are "regional members" (the American continent) and the remaining countries are "extraregional" (from Europe, Asia and the Middle East). As in the case of the World Bank, the voting power of each country is derived from its shareholding; at present, 51% of the votes correspond to the conglomerate of Latin American and Caribbean countries, 32% to the US, 4% to Canada and the remaining 13% to non-regional members.

During the 1960's and 1970's, IADB was a pioneer in the multilateral financing of social projects in the areas of health and education; moreover, in the same period, it contributed to the creation of some hundred higher education institutions. In spite of this, the loans for basic infrastructure (roads, hydraulic works and energy, transport and housing) consumed most of the resources. In the eighties, the debt crisis put pressure on the Bank to operate principally as an instance of financial assistance. Indeed, the projects approved operated as resource transfer vehicles and not as IADB intended—to make investments that would foster productivity and economic reform. In this context, a debate arose within the agency between two positions, one that insisted on its role providing financial and technical assistance and the other that adjudicated it with a central role in promoting the economic policy recommended by the "Washington Consensus"; that is, in favor of structural adjustment. In 1994, some conciliation was achieved and put into writing in the "IADB-8 Agreement". This agreement authorized the eighth increase in the financial fund of IADB since its creation, increasing authorized resources from US$60,000,000,000 to US$100,000,000,000. The agreement also indicated the "appropriate combination" with which the Bank may distribute loans for economic policy reforms and for social investments.

Recently, IADB reformulated its priorities on the basis of a broader definition of development, understood as "equitable, which supposes the integration of the poor, women and minorities in the benefits and obligations proper to development; balanced, in the sense that it demands the participation of the public sector to an equal extent as the private sector and civil society, and sustainable, bearing in mind its impact on the environment and the need to have more vigorous institutions" (IADB, 1999a). At the end of the decade, IADB did a five year planning exercise that included, among other goals, "to make US$40,000,000,000 available to the region in the next five years; devote half this sum to the social sectors and duplicate the amount of loans dedicated to education so that they will reach a minimum of US$5,000,000,000 in the five year period" (IADB, 1999b).

In the educational field, IABD's loans have supported different areas and programs in accordance with the criteria in force in each state. At present, priority is given to reform and extension of secondary education projects, the strengthening of higher technical, non-university education and the consolidation of the national science and technology systems; in the 1990's, Mexico and Brazil contracted credits under this last concept. In 1993, the Mexican project "Science and Technology Program" was approved with a total cost of US$300,000,000 of which IADB contributed US$180,000,000 and the national government a further US$120,000,000. This project includes a sub-program for Support to the Technological Modernization of Industry that the National Council for Science and Technology (CONACyT) is in charge of, and is aimed at distributed direct financing to micro and small, private enterprises so that they can carry out research and development projects, and a sub-program on the Formation of Human Resources that consists in an educational project at the National Autonomous University of Mexico (UNAM) for scientific and technological development (IADB, 1997b). In the Brazilian case, in September 1995, a similar credit was approved for the "Science and Technology Program" project with a total cost of US$320,000,000 to which IADB contributed 50%. As in the previous case, the project consists of a sub-program for the technological modernization of local enterprises through which reimbursable resources are distributed to those involved, and an academic sub-program that transfers non-reimbursable resources and funds for research to public universities and public or private research centers (IADB, 1998). In both loans, amortization terms are over 20 years.

From the characterization provided so far, we should add that both the World Bank and the Interamerican Development Bank are included in the definition of lending banks, that is, the investor countries are exclusive credit subjects. In practice, the developing countries are the borrowers, but they have minimum power of decision in the definition of the banks' policies, since their contributions to the fund limit their voting capacities. The influence of multi-lateral banking on the economic and social policy trends of developing countries is derived from this condition of basic inequality and operates under the logic of "crossed conditioning" (Manchón, 1995), based on the shared views of the actors with greatest weight in the international financial community. The political benefit obtained by the investor countries is nothing to be despised; in part because it ensures a continuous renovation of alignment in the world balance of power today in the framework of competition between regional economic blocks and, also in part, as a distension factor to avoid pressures arising from the erosion in living conditions in the poorest countries (Vilas, 1995).

The complexity of the system of international relations is not reduced, of course, to interactions between multilateral banks and countries; the role of intergovernmental adjustment agencies, like UNESCO and ECLA, already described, must be added. These last agencies lack tax instruments or ways of conditioning similar to those of the multilateral banks. Their recommendations are indicative and their power of conviction is based, almost exclusively, on their capacity to articulate and transfer rationality to the emerging social development models. Historically, there have been convergences, differences and frank opposition between the postures of multilateral banking and the consensus agencies, which is indicative of the contingent character in which the definition of said models occurs, a situation in which we can locate the debate on educational policy. For these reasons, it is necessary to go into the specific traits, into nuances and even into the details of the different educational policy proposals of the multilateral agencies considered here, an aspect that we shall look at below.

Perspective of the international agencies with respect to higher education

In this section, we examine the proposals for higher education reform that the agencies included in our study have developed. It should be pointed out that we have reviewed documents with different dates (although all from the nineties) and issued in different contexts. Nevertheless, it seems to us that they reflect the principal policy approaches suggested and that, as a whole, they allow us to appreciate the essential and superficial differences that interest us.

The World Bank and the lessons of experience

In 1994, the World Bank published "Higher Education: Lessons of Experience" (World Bank, 1994) in which it presents a general diagnosis of what, from the perspective of the agency, constitutes the critical matters in higher education in developing countries. Although the empirical analysis concentrates principally on the African region, the inferences, conclusions and recommendations devolve upon the set of developing countries.

Among the problems diagnosed in the document (Kent, 1995) the following should be mentioned: 1) The bad quality of higher education as a result of a rhythm of expansion imposed on the national higher education systems in a context of limited economic resources. In the eighties, while net growth of the gross domestic product was minimal and in some cases regressive, university expansion continued, giving rise to "do more with less" strategies that, in the end, would be counterproductive for academic quality. 2) Problems with efficiency in the institutional use of government resources and subsidies. For various, although convergent, reasons, (statutes of autonomy, absence of an accountability culture, university governability based on relations of clientage, lack of efficient methods and systems of administration, corruption, etc.), both the handling of resources and productivity are diagnosed as inefficient. As the rates of terminal efficiency in the developing countries are also low, costs per graduate tend to be higher than those prevailing in the developed countries. 3) Problems in equity since, according to the World Bank, the priority granted to higher education in the developing countries caused a severe distributive imbalance giving rise to the university institutions consuming resources that could have been destined to basic or secondary education or the technological segment. Since, as a group, university students come from the middle and upper classes, university subsidies imply a biased subsidy in favor of these social groups, and in detriment to the education support needs of lower class sectors. This bias is translated into an inequitable distribution of opportunities and income among the population.

Based on this line of analysis, the recommendations contained in the document cover three public policy areas suggested in the following objectives: a) to increase institutional differentiation, b) to strengthen the institutions' financial base, and c) to improve the quality of teaching and research. As a corollary to the recommendations, the need to redefine the role of government in relation to national higher education systems is emphasized. Since the document is also offered as "a guide to support the developing nations in the formulation of effective reform strategies", the chapter on proposals is illustrated with examples of cases that have successfully implemented solutions and projects attending the objectives mentioned above.

"To increase institutional differentiation" is a proposal for redistributing the demand for higher education, avoiding excessive concentration of preferences in saturated areas and professional positions. Instead of a curricular structure concentrated on the traditional liberal professions, according to the World Bank, there should be a trend towards a system that, as well as the conventional degree, can offer short cycle technological modalities, higher technological studies, above all those focused on new technologies, postgraduate studies for research, teaching and specialized professional practice, among others. Together with the above, it is proposed to demolish bureaucratic barriers that until today have prevented adequate mobility of students among cycles, modalities and degree courses.

"To strengthen the financial base of the institutions" is a proposal that suggests such actions as: combining government subsidies with registration fees and supporting this combination with educational credit systems independent of the government; diversifying the sources of institutional financing through projects with technological applications and through the sale of services; differentiating government subsidy through competition for programs for which funding is offered and by means of institutional productivity assessment instruments. Furthermore, recommendations are made in the sense of improving university administration and pressing for transparent accountability, as well as favoring competition between private individuals in the supply of higher education.

"Improve the quality of teaching and research" is also a general postulate that translates into a set of concrete proposals. The need is emphasized to have external evaluation instances that will give rise to positive competition between institutions and will favor the standardization of the quality of the results. The importance of constructing links between universities and the productive sectors is underlined since in this way it is possible to construct a higher education system more pertinent and sensitive to market needs and productive transformation.

As several specialists have noted, an uncompromising economic supposition underlies the World Bank's approach: higher education is significant in terms of value added, that is, to the extent that the individual returns the investment and to the extent that the national economy is favored through competitiveness. The subject of educational expenditure as investment has been the subject of interest of the World Bank for a long time and refers to the calculation of the "rates of return" of schooling. Until the beginning of the nineties, the Bank's economists had sustained that, in developing countries, basic and secondary education generate the greatest rates of return at both individual and aggregate level, which justifies government investment in these levels. In contrast, the higher education subsidy is regressive for national economies and should therefore be transferred to students and their families (Psacharopoulos, 1994). This orthodox thesis has been debated and modified in the thematic groups of the Bank (Betts, 1999) and, although the debate has not been closed, a broader view on the subject can be seen that is translated, for example, into proposals of a shared subsidy for higher education (Colclough, 1996).

Of course, the problematic of higher education is not exhausted in a discussion on financing, diversification and reform of contents and methods. Questions on the meaning, mission and functions of the universities appear together with these subjects, subjects that UNESCO has tried to recover through a broad discussion of the social, political and humanistic objectives of higher education.

Agenda 21 of UNESCO

In October 1998, the World Conference on Higher Education sponsored by UNESCO was held, an act in which work commenced three years earlier with the publication of the organization's policy document "Change and Development in Higher Education" (UNESCO, 1995) was culminated. Between 1996 and 1998, several Regional Conferences were held in different parts of the world with the purpose of collecting the points of view of the communities of academics, directors, civil society groups, government bodies and other social actors on four key subjects: relevance, quality, financing and administration, and international cooperation. With this thematic agenda the following Conferences took place: Havana (November 1996), Dakar (April 1997), Tokyo (July 1997), Palermo (September 1997) and Beirut (March 1998). Another two meetings of experts at regional level were also organized: one with the Council of Europe (Strasbourg, July 1998) and another with the countries of North America in Toronto (April, 1998) in which Canada and the United States participated as well as representatives from Mexico and Puerto Rico.

The result of this program was an enormous amount of documents arising from declarations, conclusions, minutes and other texts that, taken as a whole, offer a complete view of higher education problems in the world, while providing a range of solutions with which to face the educational challenges of the twenty-first century. Similarly, the base documents were prepared for the thematic debates, that were held in parallel to the sessions of the World Conference, dealing with such aspects as education and culture, the new information technologies, the students' view, the role of the woman, sustainable human development, education for peace, the problematic of employment and the role of educational research, among others.

As expected, the documents approached the subjects contained in the 1995 text. Nevertheless, each document reaches a level of development and depth of analysis that is really remarkable. Similarly, these texts are outstanding for their explicit formulation of political and value commitments that, in each case, provide the fundaments for the orientation and postures presented. Of course, to review the content of all these documents exceeds the limits of this article, even more so if it is considered that they are syntheses. Nevertheless, we shall refer to one of them in particular given that it illustrates the general sense of the discussion and its main themes.

The text, "Towards an agenda 21 for higher education" (UNESCO, 1998b) synthesizes the challenges and tasks for the coming century seen in the light of the results of the Regional Conferences. It begins with a list of the missions that the contemporary university and higher education systems fulfil and should tackle more deeply in the immediate future. Thus, it indicates, in first place, that "the eminent mission of higher education is to serve mankind and society", that "through its research function, its courses of study and training, its cooperative activities and its alliances with several social sectors, higher education is called to make a key contribution to opening up and illuminating new paths towards a better future for society and the individual and to give direction and orientation to that future". Based on such principles, higher education has two important missions before it: "to actively participate in solving the main global, regional and local problems (such as poverty, malnutrition, illiteracy, social exclusion, exacerbation of inequalities between nations and individuals, widening of the gap in science and technology between industrialized and developing countries, and environmental protection), and to work intensely on the generation of proposals and recommendations that promote sustainable human development, the extension of knowledge, universal respect for human rights, equality of opportunities between men and women, justice and the application of democratic principles within their own institutions and in society, understanding between nations and ethnic groups, religions, cultures and other groups, in favor of a culture of peace and non-violence and in the construction of intellectual and moral solidarity".

It is similarly considered that the traditional mission of maintaining, increasing and disseminating knowledge through research and intellectual creation is fundamental, as is the teaching and dissemination of said knowledge. This mission must include the task of "developing endogenous capacities to acquire and apply existing knowledge and to create new knowledge". Similarly, it is the task of higher education "to educate responsible, informed and active citizens as well as highly qualified specialists". It should be added with respect to this vision that one of the most important missions of higher education is concerned with ethic and cultural aspects: "to preserve and affirm cultural identity, promote the propagation and creation of cultural values, to protect and foster cultural diversity and to participate actively in the development of intercultural understanding". Finally, it is mentioned that higher education must "contribute to the implementation of lifelong learning for everyone". In this sense, higher education is considered to "have a great responsibility with respect to the educational system as a whole and the educational activities of society".

Another part of the document stresses the importance of higher education systems establishing and harmonizing relations with the different instances comprising society and the State. Emphasis is given to the strategic role of partnerships between higher education institutions and the different social actors in order to promote the development of said institutions in the perspective of reaching higher levels of pertinence and to promote the notion of co-responsibility in the educational enterprise. The subject of innovation is then approached. Innovation must be promoted so that higher education can successfully face the challenges of a labor market that demands greater competences and knowledge, as well as the need for most of the population to have them. One challenge that is outlined on the horizon is how to take higher education to the groups and sectors that need to be updated in order to confront their new employment conditions. In this discussion, the notion of lifelong learning is the key and diversification and flexibility actions appear as feasible responses in the reform that is required.

The subject of access to higher education is central throughout the document. It is one point on which the documents produced by the Regional Conferences found convergence, from different points of view, when they indicate that: "All persons must have the possibility, at some stage in their lives, of access to education and to have an opportunity to go back to university life (Havana); it is important to extend and diversify opportunities so that each citizen can be a beneficiary of higher education, as well as competence and knowledge (Tokyo); diversification of demand implies institutional diversification, as well as new policies and flexibility to guarantee access (Palermo); special measures are required to facilitate access to those who have begun their working life or have had to give up their studies prematurely (Beirut); there is a need for policies aimed at specific goals to increase the number and rate of participation of women in higher education, in teaching and in positions of responsibility as well as in science and technology careers (Dakar)".

"Agenda 21" also considers the subject of university students and professors, recognizing that they are "the main protagonists in higher education". It is noted that, even recognizing the potential of distance teaching technologies, the professor-student interaction and the relations among students, with respect to human contacts, are formative and educational to such an extent that they are determinants of the quality and the results of the teaching-learning process. With respect to the students, the importance of their "playing an active role in higher education institutions" is stressed as is the importance of this role being recognized by the institutions and translated into the opening up of possibilities for them and their organizations to participate in decision making and in the design of courses of action. It is mentioned that "everything that concerns the students is of interest to the professors and vice versa", in such a way that "the formation and updating of the teaching body is a key aspect to being able to raise the levels of educational quality." Furthermore, it is recognized that "the participation of professors in research, as well as the link between research and teaching is essential in ensuring quality and effectiveness in higher education in order to contribute to the progress of knowledge and develop endogenous research and research and development capacities." This chapter of the document closes with a pronouncement on the need to increase mobility of professors and students on national, regional and international planes and the need to develop institutional networks to facilitate the exchange and mutual certification of knowledge.

The following point considers the topics of autonomy and accountability, academic freedom, objectivity and intellectual rigor. It indicates that "academic freedom in higher education and its wide autonomy are essential for the institutions to perform their mission" and it mentions that autonomy presupposes responsibilities in the face of society. The document ends with a section on research and anticipation functions. To begin, it indicates that research is a fundamental mission and a principal function of higher education, that the task of advancing in knowledge and focusing it on solving fundamental social problems is the responsibility of the institutions, but also of the academics in particular. Moreover, it notes that higher education institutions must have sufficient resources to do research and that the State is mainly responsible for the task of financing research, although other social agents must also commit themselves to this task. Finally, it indicates that anticipation is an important task of higher education. In this sense, universities must assume the function of anticipating the future needs and requirements of the societies that contain them in order to offer alternatives to the challenges they are facing.

As indicated above, the vision of UNESCO, product of a wide consensus that collects the points of view of a large variety and diversity of actors in education, attempts to create a balance between the requirements of the contemporary world and the traditional, permanent mission of the university. Similarly, it takes into account not only the function of higher education in economic development, but its cultural role, its importance for individual and social development, as well as its weight in the construction of a democratic space. But are these two visions, that is, that of the World Bank concentrated on the profitability of higher education and its contribution to development, and the broad view of UNESCO, totally incompatible? Or are there perhaps possibilities for a synthesis that would recover the economic and social imperatives of the contemporary university? One tentative reply to these dilemmas can be found in the joint work of the World Bank and UNESCO that we review below.

World Bank + UNESCO = Peril and promise

In March of the year 2000 a document was put into circulation entitled "Higher Education in Developing Countries: Peril and Promise" that was drawn up by a task force jointly sponsored by the World Bank and UNESCO, as follow-up to the agreements of the World Conference in Paris 1998 (World Bank and UNESCO, 2000). The document in question consists of six sections.

The first deals with longstanding problems and new realities. This chapter constitutes the context of the whole analysis and examines the expansion of demand, tendencies to diversification in higher education systems and potential implications of the knowledge revolution. Chapter two, "Higher education and the public interest" emphasizes the contribution of higher education to the economic, social, political and cultural development of nations and therefore its public interest. This argument is set against the traditional approach of measuring benefits according to the "economic rates of return" derived from public or private investments in higher education. The third chapter considers the higher education systems, discusses the theme of functional diversification of the university systems and indicates that the conception of free market, according to which systems tend to adjust themselves through competition, is mistaken in the case of higher education. This idea is opposed to the need for a non-centralized coordination of systems that seeks to protect university autonomy, foster competition between similar institutions and give coherence and rationality to the system as a whole. At the end of the section, it concludes that "governmental guidance is an essential part of any solution."

Governability constitutes the principal theme of the fourth chapter, indicating in first place the general principles of good institutional government: academic freedom, cooperative government, clear rights and responsibilities, selection for academic merit, financial stability and accountability. It also develops a set of 'instruments' with which to achieve the objectives of good government: effective, capable collegiate bodies, organs of government with broad vision, practices of responsible, flexible, transparent financial programming and administrative control, access to data for decision making, solid leadership, selection and promotion of academic and management personnel based on academic merit, security of employment, adequate remuneration and internal and external evaluation and accreditation systems. The fifth chapter is devoted to examining science and technology and it notes the backwardness of the developing countries in this terrain, as well as the need to promote science and technology systems through government resources and the construction of links and alliances with both enterprises and international cooperation. It also stresses the responsibility of governments to promote science and technology activities given the incipient character of university and industry cooperation.

In chapter six the document pleads for the establishment of liberal education in some higher education institutions of the developing countries, since this approach is pertinent for the formation of flexible professionals with the capacity to adapt themselves to a rapidly changing environment. Unlike the traditional approach that underlines the need to offer specialized technical formation, an argument is presented in favor of liberal studies, providing measures are taken to offer a solid, updated, flexible formation. Finally, in the conclusion section recommendations are postulated around two groups of objectives. The first has to do with the need to increase resources and the second with improving efficiency in handling them. It is necessary to extend the financial base to 1) improve educational infrastructure, particularly computers, networks, science laboratories and equipment, although they are also needed to reinforce conventional infrastructure: classrooms, libraries, dormitories, recreational spaces and cultural installations, 2) design, test and implement new programs and curricular designs, as well as expanding or introducing liberal education, 3) recruit, retain and motivate a permanent academic staff, 4) increase access to socially unfavored populations, 5) foster teaching and research in basic and applied science areas. In order to improve efficiency in university management, institutional measures are proposed such as a) reinforcing internal government, b) improving the quality of academic programs, c) developing and motivating academic personnel. It is also suggested that government instances develop the architecture of a more rational higher education system that will, at the same time, promote mass education and excellence, as well as attending the character of public interest in higher education. Similarly, it stresses the importance of implementation for, as it is said, "the field of international development is plagued with good ideas that have never been seen to bear fruit". For this reason, the document concludes, "we must above all be practical if we wish to achieve a successful reform".

The perspective of the UNESCO-World Bank task force on higher education reform allows us to suppose that the position of multilateral banks in the future will assume a profile of greater flexibility, more sensitive to the political and social dimensions of change. The outline of a new profile can begin to be glimpsed in the credit preferences of the World Bank, with greater aperture towards post-basic teaching and higher education proposals and also through the pronouncements of some of the most influential intellectuals in the design of the World Bank policies on education. Thus, an attitude more favorable to the strengthening of the higher education, science and technology systems of developing countries would be expected providing projects which are congruent with the "hard" lines of the proposal: pragmatism, reinforcement of private participation, insistence on quality and efficacy, formulas of social compensation, use of distance education options, lifelong education approach, among the principal aspects. Below we shall see the Latin American view of the subject.

ECLA: Education as the nucleus of productive transformation with equity

The proposal "productive transformation with equity" reflects the conceptual tendency behind ECLA's proposal with respect to Latin American development at the end of the "decade lost to development", as the Commission itself characterized the nineteen eighties. This proposal sustains a central thesis: deliberate, systematic incorporation and diffusion of technical progress constitutes the pivot of productive transformation while making it compatible with political democratization and a growing social equity. The set of actions recommended by the Commission to reach sustainable development, appropriate to Latin American reality, is articulated around this idea (ECLA, 1990).

The proposal distinguishes two types of economic growth: one that makes it possible to raise the standard of living of the population by means of an increase in productivity and one based on the depredation of natural resources and the reduction in real remuneration. In the first case, technical progress acts as the variable that articulates the objectives in tension: competitiveness and social sustainability. According to ECLA, to activate technical progress it is necessary to strengthen the entrepreneurial base, have a technological infrastructure, participate in the international economy and propitiate the formation of human resources with capacity to handle new knowledge. However, the Commission indicates that backwardness in education and in the field of the generation of knowledge are obstacles that prevent advances in this direction.

On this conceptual basis, the Commission elaborated a general and a specific proposal for education. The first, entitled "Equity and Productive Transformation, an Integrated Approach", prepared for the twenty-fourth period of sessions of the Commission at the beginning of 1992, discusses the means to reach a situation of convergence between growth and social equity. The second, published that same year, entitled "Education and Knowledge, Nucleus of Productive Transformation with Equity" (ECLA, 1992) establishes the purpose of "contributing to the creation, in the coming decade, of certain educational conditions, training and the incorporation of scientific-technological progress that permit the transformation of the productive structures of the region into a framework for progressive social equity".

Below we present a summary of ECLA's document, specifying the arguments and proposals most closely related to educational reform and the scientific and technological research systems.

From ECLA's perspective, education is strategic for development. This condition comes from its role in the formation of subjects with the values and behavior of modern citizenship and their functions in the construction of the capacities and skills that generate productivity. The strengthening of the knowledge production and diffusion system which, of course, includes education at all its levels, is understood as a decisive instrument for facing both the internal challenge of citizenship and the external challenge of competitiveness. This perspective is recognized in the developed countries and in those with late industrialization and has been translated into important policies to foster education, science and technology. In contrast, in the developing countries, even when valuing the relation between education and technical progress, there is a persistent backwardness and the effort to improve has been insufficient, generally ineffective and with unsatisfactory results. In effect, although the Commission admits that the educational, training and science and technology systems of the region have experienced an important quantitative expansion, it indicates that insufficiencies in the quality of the results persists in most countries and there is little pertinence with respect to the requirements of the environment and evident problems in equity in the social distribution of access opportunities. Furthermore, the institutionality of the system is characterized for its rigidity, bureaucratization and lack of linkage with the productive and social milieu.

Based on the ideas and the diagnosis presented, ECLA establishes the need for a strategy to stimulate the transformation of education and training and to increase the scientific-technological potential of the region with a view to forming modern citizenship, linked to both democracy and equity and international competitiveness. The proposal defines competitiveness as the central objective, performance as policy guideline and decentralization as a component of the institutional scheme. The Commission states that the proposal recognizes tensions between citizenship and competitiveness, equity and performance, and integration and decentralization, but concentrates on the sphere of complementariness that exists on each of these planes.

The strategy for change is oriented towards the following directions: i) from a political point of view, attempt to assume knowledge production and diffusion activities as strategic, long term tasks that require the broadest consensus possible between the different social actors and a stable financial commitment to their development; ii) from a contents point of view, to focalize action on the results of education, training and science and technology and on their articulation with performance demands from people, enterprises and institutions in the different spheres of society; iii) from an institutional point of view, break the isolation of the educational establishment and the generation and the transmission of knowledge and introduce action modalities in which the actors have more room for autonomy in decisions and greater responsibility for results.

In order to reach these objectives, the proposal defines actions in seven policy fields. The first refers to the need to overcome the isolation of the educational, training and acquisition of scientific and technological knowledge systems, opening them up to social requirements. The following two fields refer to the results sought with this aperture: to ensure universal access to codes of modernity, and promote creativity in access, diffusion and innovation in scientific-technological matters. The following four are of an instrumental character: responsible institutional management; professionalization and protagonism of the educators; financial commitment of society to education, training and the scientific-technological effort, and regional and international cooperation. In these different spheres of policy, guidelines are established that influence the different components of formal education (pre-school, primary, secondary and higher), training and the scientific-technological effort and, very specially, the links between them and the productive sector. The preparation and specification of policies, as well as their application in various national circumstances, is a task that falls to each country.

ECLA's document stresses the role of regional and international cooperation to reach the objectives indicated. On this subject, it proposes the formation of human resources in the countries of Latin America and the Caribbean with a view to a more efficient use of installed capacity in universities and academic centers of the region. In specific terms, the following lines of cooperation are stressed: improvement in quality; innovations at middle education level; accreditation of institutions, programs and units of higher education, formation of academics and researchers; institutional reform and local administration; technical training; educational research; student exchange and strategic cooperation.

In spite of the fact that ECLA's document omits particular recommendations on higher education reform in Latin America, it is clear that the principal challenges evolve around notions of pertinence, integration and linkage. Pertinence, in the sense of a better relation between university supply and the demands of society. Integration, understood as the effort to harmonize the set of subsystems that comprise the educational structure in each country. Linkage, in the sense of relating the needs of the productive structure with the capacities generating knowledge in the higher education institutions through specific projects. (Cf. Labastida, et al., 1993).

The document does not ignore the need for greater financial backing from multilateral banks for projects involving education in general and the knowledge producing sector in particular. In this respect, it notes that during the eighties, these organizations decreased their reply in these areas in terms of resources and the profile of their activities. However, ECLA concludes that in the nineties there are new economic and political conditions that permit greater collaboration between governments, consensus agencies and development banks through which support is given to the performance of tasks directly linked to education and the production of knowledge as the nucleus of productive transformation with equity. On this last aspect, it is of interest to know the proposal of the Interamerican Development Bank, a subject we will consider below in order to close the section on an analysis of the documents on strategies for university reform issued by the multilateral agencies.

IADB's proposal for reforming higher education in Latin America

The document entitled "Higher Education in Latin America and the Caribbean: Strategy Paper", published in 1997, presents the position of IADB on higher education in the region, as well as a strategy to improve it (IADB, 1997a). It also attempts to appraise its position and its implications in policy matters. It similarly attempts to take into account what lies beyond the universities and the social task they are associated with. One of the central arguments of the document is that higher education performance in Latin America and the Caribbean varies substantially in the different countries and sectors as well as between institutions and internal units of the institutions themselves. It attributes such heterogeneity to different functions the university establishments fulfil.

As well as stressing the social importance of higher education, beginning with what it means for the life of the people and with its demographic and economic aspects, the document emphasizes that the need for persons formed through advanced education has never been as great as it is now. In this sense, it affirms that the modernization and integration of Latin America within an increasingly globalized economy and society depend to a very large extent on higher education. Based on this, IABD rejects the view that higher education is marginal to national development or that the State is removed from higher education. But it also opposes the perspective that higher education can only perform its role well if it is expanded and strengthened with greater public funds. The document insists that the development of higher education requires a reorientation and redistribution of rules and resources, a process that IABD is willing to promote through work with reformers in each country.

After enumerating the achievements and limitations of higher education in the region to date, the document focuses on an analysis of what it considers to be its main functions: academic leadership; professional tasks and work; formation and technical development; and liberal education. These four functions are considered fundamental for the diagnosis, reform and strategy of IADB. It recognizes that the typology has a strong economic emphasis and stresses the teaching and learning process. It also proves to be complicated and difficult to apply in institutional contexts in which a juxtaposition of functions can frequently be observed.

Further on, three crucial aspects of sector policy are reviewed: equity and public subsidies; incentives, financing and government; and improvement in quality and control. Each of these aspects is focused on the four functions mentioned above. Finally, it points out that IADB will support applications whose goal is to favor broad reforms that reasonably seek to improve quality and efficiency. Another objective is to support programs whose results exceed the benefits that students can obtain individually. They will also favor applications that promote equality, as for example, scholarships for students with economic needs and aid for institutions in impoverished countries and regions. As a consequence, it is considered that a typical project would contain a budget item for organizational reform that would be administered by the educational authorities, and a competitive fund to support the initiatives of individual institutions or programs within institutions.

IADB's proposals are similar to those of the World Bank in several aspects, such as promoting efficiency and quality through reforms in the academic and administrative structure of the institutions, stimulating general evaluation and accreditation mechanisms, establishing mechanisms for mixed financing, facilitating the articulation of the higher education system with the social and productive environment, and propitiating transparent, systematic accountability. In spite of these coincidences, that show that there is a shared approach by both agencies to higher education and the possibilities of reforming it, there are also important differences, above all at the level of priority assigned to higher education projects (in practice, IADB has conceded greater importance to initiatives of this type) and also on the operative plane that range from the financial conditions under which loans are agreed on to modes of supervision and evaluation of the respective projects, subjects that merit a detailed study.

Final comments

In this article we have attempted to offer the reader an overview of the debate under way on higher education in Latin America from the perspective of the multilateral agencies. It should be stressed that this is an open, well-developed discussion, in which the interlocutors influence one another and tend to agree, in principle, on postures. For example, it is essential to support higher education and scientific research in order to advance towards a society of knowledge; it is necessary to expand and differentiate higher education systems and add quality to the teaching-learning processes; care must be taken to guarantee equity in supply and equality of opportunities based on academic merit; new, more solid links must be forged between higher education and the social system in order to obtain better levels of pertinence and effectiveness; it is important to attend administrative and government aspects so that institutions can become more efficient and can concentrate on innovation; a greater effort is needed to consolidate academic staff and thus improve the formation of professionals up to the task of facing present challenges.

Important differences can be found, however, with respect to the means proposed to carry out transformations like the ones indicated and also with respect to the actors who are considered capable of being the driving force behind them. For example: What should the role of the State be in higher education and science and technology policy? In what way should the private sector participate in order to stimulate the formation of professionals and scientific and technological research? Who should pay for higher education and through which mechanisms? What types of assessment translate into quality and innovation? How can an improvement in the academic level of professors be promoted? What means can be used to advance towards the objectives of equity and pertinence? What is the optimum distribution of the educational modalities comprising the higher education system? What priority should be given to the development of open and distance education options? What type of social contract should be established in order to reach an appropriate balance between the demands of society and the possibilities of response from universities? How can labor market conditions and a formation in higher education be harmonized? What are considered to be desirable scenarios in the middle and long term and how can progress be made towards constructing them?

It is precisely around these questions that a definition of policy guidelines for higher education opens up new avenues. In this context the role of multilateral agencies becomes critical and goes along two complementary ways, each having a different kind of impact:

a) The first way is created through research, diagnoses, and consultation that, after being systematized is transformed into recommendations and proposals for reform or in positions in favor of specific courses of action. We also find that these agencies promote their views by sponsoring a variety of activities such as debates, courses, workshops and seminars. The technical assistance that these agencies provide in response to the request of national governments also provide an opportunity to communicate their agenda. Finally, the numerous publications (printed and electronic) produced by these agencies play an important role in the diffusion of information that reinforces their perspectives.

b) In the case of the multilateral banking system, the equivalent strategy consists of offering educational credits for programs aimed at implementing specific reforms. In the case of Latin America, the main programs being promoted through this mechanism are those linked to evaluation and accreditation of programs, the strengthening of professorial bodies, the linking of research units to private firms, and scholarship programs that strengthen the private sector of higher education.

Although it has not been the purpose of this paper to provide a detailed analysis of the dynamics between the market and the state with respect to higher education, we agree with Torres and Schugurensky (forthcoming), that the current changes in Latin American higher education cannot be examined in isolation from larger political and economic changes in the region. These changes, in turn, are related to the dynamics of globalization. Furthermore, it should also be noticed that global trends are promoted, resisted, and negotiated differently in each national context and in each individual institution. Finally, the very dynamics of the debate we pointed out in this article advises against any attempt to characterize the postures of the different types of multilateral agencies through an excluding polarity. Instead, the need can be seen to delve deeply into subjects on which it is possible to reflect. If this contribution encourages the reader to look into the debates it describes, it will have faithfully fulfilled its objectives.

Bibliography

Alcántara, Armando (2000). "Tendencias mundiales en la educación superior: El papel de los organismos multilaterales", in Cazes, Daniel, Eduardo Ibarra and Luis Porter (editors). *Encuentro de Especialistas en Educación Superior*, Mexico, CEIICH-UNAM, pp. 81–102.

Betts, Julian R. (1999). "Returns to Quality in Education", *The World Bank Economics of Education Series*, 1, June.

Bielschowsky, Ricardo (1998). "Evolución de las ideas de la CEPAL", *Revista de la CEPAL*, núm. extraordinario.

Colclough, Christopher (1996). "Education and the Market: Which Parts of the Neoliberal Solution are Correct?", *World Development* 24 (4): 589–610.

CEPAL (1990). *Transformación productiva con equidad. La tarea prioritaria del desarrollo de América Latina y el Caribe en los años noventa*, Santiago de Chile, CEPAL (LC/G.1601-P).

CEPAL (1992). *Educación y conocimiento. Eje de la transformación productiva con equidad*, Santiago de Chile, CEPAL (LC/G.1702/Rev.2-P).

Coraggio, José Luis. (1998). "Investigación educativa y decisión política. El caso del Banco Mundial en América Latina". *Perfiles Educativos*, 79–80, pp.43–57.

Goedegebuure, Leo, Frans Kaiser, Peter Maassen, Lynn Meek, Frans van Vught, and Egbert de Weert (1994). "International perspectives on trends and issues in higher education policy", in Goedegebuure, Leo, Frans Kaiser, Peter Maassen, Lynn Meek, Frans van Vught, and Egbert de Weert (eds.), *Higher Education Policy. An International Comparative Perspective*, Oxford, Pergamon Press, pp. 315–348.

IADB (1997a). *Higher Education in Latin America and the Caribbean. Strategy Paper*, Washington DC, IADB.

IADB (1997b). *Proyecto: México, Programa de Ciencia y Tecnología* (804/OC-ME; 001/SPQ-ME), Washington DC, IADB.

IADB (1998). *Project: Brazil, Science and Technology Program* (880/OC-BR), Washington DC, IADB.

IADB (1999a). "La Renovación del Compromiso frente al Desarrollo", Washington DC, IADB.

IADB (199b). "Información Básica 1999", http://www.iadb.org/

Jallade, Lucila, Eddy Lee and Joel Samoff (1994). "International Cooperation", in: Samoff, Joel (ed.). *Coping with Crisis: Austerity, Adjustment and Human Resources*, Paris, Cassell-UNESCO.

Kent, R. (1996). "The World Bank and UNESCO on Higher Education", International Higher Education, 4, pp. 3–5.

Labastida, Julio, Giovanna Valenti and Lorenza Villa Lever, eds. (1993). *Educación, ciencia y tecnología. Los nuevos desafíos para América Latina*, Mexico, UNAM.

Malo, Salvador and Samuel Morley (1996). *La Educación Superior en América Latina y el Caribe. Memoria de un Seminario de Rectores.* Washington DC BID-UDUAL.

Manchón, Federico (1995). "Globalización, regionalización y comportamiento financiero", in: J.L. Calva, *Globalización y bloques económicos. Mitos y realidades*", Mexico, Juan Pablos, pp. 40–57.

Morsy, Zaghouol and Philip G. Altbach (eds.) (1998). *Higher Education in an International Perspective: Critical Issues*, New York, Garland.

Psacharopoulos, George (1994). "Returns to Investment in Education: A Global Update", *World Development*, 22(9), September, pp.1325–43.

Rodríguez, Roberto (2000). "La reforma de la educación superior. Señas del debate internacional de fin de siglo", *Revista Electrónica de Investigación Educativa*, 2 (1), http://redie.ens.uabc. mx/vol2no1/

Schugurensky, Daniel (1998). "La reestructuración de la educación superior en la era de la globalización. ¿Hacia un modelo heterónomo?", in Alcántara, Armando, Ricardo Pozas and Carlos A. Torres (coords.), *Educación, Democracia y Desarrollo en el Fin de Siglo*, Mexico, Siglo XXI, pp.118–49.

Schwartzman, Simón (1999). "Prospects for Higher Education in Latin America", *International Higher Education*, 17, fall, pp.9–10.

The Task Force on Higher Education and Society (2000). *Higher Education in Developing Countries. Peril and Promise*, Washington DC, The World Bank.and UNESCO

Torres, Carlos Alberto (1996). *Las Secretas Aventuras del Orden. Estado y Educación*, Buenos Aires, Miño y Dávila Editores.

Torres, Carlos Alberto and Daniel Schugurensky (forthcoming). "The Political Economy of Higher Education in the Era of Neoliberal Globalization: Latin America in Comparative Perspective". *Higher Education.*

Tünnermann, Carlos (1995). *Una Nueva Visión de la Educación Superior*, San José de Costa Rica, CSUCA.

UNESCO (1995). *Documento de Política para el Cambio y el Desarrollo de la Educación Superior*, Paris, UNESCO.

UNESCO (1998a). *La Educación Superior en el Siglo XXI. Visión y Acción (Documento de Trabajo)*, Paris, UNESCO.

UNESCO (1998b). *Towards an Agenda for Higher Education: Challenges and Task for the Twenty-First Century Viewed in the Light of the Regional Conference*, Paris, UNESCO.

UNESCO (1998c). *La UNESCO y la Educación en América Latina y el Caribe 1987–1997*, Santiago de Chile, UNESCO-OREALC.

UNESCO (1999). "What is UNESCO?", http://www.unesco.org/general/eng/about/
Vilas, Carlos M. (1995). "Estados nacionales y mercados transnacionales en la búsqueda de un desarrollo alternativo", in: J.L. Calva, *Globalización y bloques económicos. Mitos y realidades*, Mexico, Juan Pablos, pp.310–333.
World Bank (1994). *Higher Education, The Lessons from Experience*, Washington DC, The World Bank.
World Bank (1995). *Priorities and Strategies for Education. A World Bank Review*, Washington DC The World Bank.
World Bank (1999a). "The World Bank Mission", http://www.worldbank.org
World Bank (199b). "Latin America & The Caribbean Bank Assistance", http://www.worldbank.org/html/extpb/annrep/lac1.htm
World Bank (1999c). *Education Sector Strategy*, Washington DC, The World Bank.
World Bank (1999d). *Education Change in Latin America and the Caribbean: A World Bank Strategy Document*, Washington DC, The World Bank.
World Bank (2000). *Informe Anual 1999*, Washington DC, The World Bank.

2

Two Decades of Neoliberalism in Latin America

Implications for Adult Education

DANIEL SCHUGURENSKY

Any discussion of adult education in Latin America cannot be isolated from a context of poverty and increasing income polarization. Neither of these issues can be isolated from larger economic and political changes in the region, which in turn cannot be examined without reference to global dynamics. As we move full swing into the twenty-first century, Latin America continues to be the most unequal region of the planet. Current trends in many Latin American countries suggest that this situation is not improving, and in some countries it is actually getting worse. With a few exceptions (such as Costa Rica, Uruguay, and Cuba), more than 30 percent of Latin America's total income is concentrated in just 10 percent of the households, and in many countries the figure is over 35 percent. In contrast, the portion of total income corresponding to the poorest 40 percent of households falls between 9 and 15 percent (CEPAL 2002a). For large sectors of the region's population, such inequality is expressed in high levels of unemployment, underemployment, malnutrition, and overall poverty. Presently, about 220 million Latin Americans (about 45 percent of the total population) are living in poverty. Among them, about 90 million are below extreme poverty, living in indigence. This is the context in which Latin American educators face the reality of 42 million illiterate people and 110 million adults who have not completed primary school.

Poverty and inequality are indeed serious problems endured by the region, but not the only ones. With more or less emphasis, depending on the situation of each particular country, most Latin American societies are facing a combination of serious social, political, and economic challenges. An exhaustive analysis of these problems is beyond the scope of this chapter. The following list, not organized in any particular order, calls our attention to ten of the most pressing problems affecting Latin America today (see Stevens 1999, Zarco 2000, Schugurensky and Myers 2001):

1) Increasing levels of poverty, along with deepening social, gender, and racial inequalities;

2) Fragile and dependent economies with high levels of bankruptcy, unemployment, underemployment, and speculative capital;

3) Weak parliamentary democracies and little autonomy of the judiciary system;

4) High rates of delinquency, organized crime, and daily violence, and regular—sometimes massive—human rights violations;

5) High rates of child poverty and malnutrition, child labor, and school dropout and repetition;

6) High levels of tax evasion and corruption, particularly among the political and business elite, and significant decreases of public confidence in political institutions and the political class;

7) Increasing difficulty in incorporating issues related to sustainable development and social justice in trade agreements such as North American Free Trade Agreement (NAFTA) and the Free Trade Agreement of the Americas (FTAA), which both put an emphasis on economic integration under a hegemonic "hub-and-spokes" configuration;

8) Rapid environmental degradation;

9) Fragility of reconciliation processes with justice (after civil wars or state terrorism), and even a return to violent armed conflicts;

10) An ever-growing external debt that swallows up growing portions of national revenues and increases dependency on foreign financial institutions, coupled with capital flight and difficulties exporting due to tariffs and subsidies in countries of the North.

These dynamics have taken place in a context of increasing urbanization, intensified subordination to the global economy, and adoption of market principles in the public realm. Given current trends, it is plausible that several of these challenges will remain during the rest of this decade. On the political front, Latin American countries are likely to continue experiencing the difficult transition from predominantly authoritarian regimes to formally democratic ones. This transition has been affected by widespread political corruption (present in all three branches of representative institutions), high levels of violence, and a low trust in elected governments to solve the region's most pressing social problems. Aware of the tenuous nature of democracy in the region, fifteen presidents from the nineteen-nation Rio Group signed the Cartagena Declaration in June 2000, in which they declared a commitment "to consolidating and strengthening representative democracy" in Latin America, and described democracy as the only legitimate political system and a requirement for peace and development. This statement may be interpreted in light of increasing threats to democracy in the region—particularly in the Andean countries, which have been the most politically unstable during the last decade, but also in the context of a relatively low popular confidence in democratic institutions.[1] At the same time, the most recent elections in Brazil and Ecuador suggest the beginning of a new wave of post-neoliberal regimes in the region, and a new twist in political processes to improve the standard of living of the majority population.

Economically, Latin American's position of structural dependency in the world system (not only in terms of commercial trade and finances, but also in terms of research and development) does not show signs of reversing; on the contrary, it seems to be deepening every year. In the social arena, redistributive policies that were part and parcel of the different Latin American weak expressions of the welfare state were gradually eliminated during the 1980s and the 1990s, and continue to be replaced by a set of neoliberal policies promoting deregulation, competition, and privatization of public enterprises and agencies. Neoliberal policies, through a variety of mechanisms of market liberalization, also replaced the previous development strategy of import substitution industrialization and protectionism (based on high tariffs restricting access to domestic markets by foreign imports in favor of domestic production) that characterized the region's development strategy during the previous decades. These processes, coupled with the implementation of structural adjustment policies and budget cuts, provided a combination that has amounted to the partial "dismantling and remantling" of the welfare state and the emergence of the neoliberal state (Graff 1995, Pannu 1996). The costs of implementing neoliberal policies and the continuous drain of resources via the repayment of the external debt are becoming increasingly evident in the failure to reduce poverty and income inequality in the region.

In Latin America today, the promise of full employment and social inclusion that was characteristic of the golden years of the welfare state has vanished. As unemployment becomes a structural feature of neoliberal capitalism, the working class is now considered privileged for having the opportunity to be exploited. They are indeed privileged with respect to the unemployed, who desperately seek the possibility of being exploited. And the unemployed, who are potentially in conditions of being exploited, are in turn a privileged group in relation to the unemployable, who by virtue of factors such as old age or unmarketable skills cannot even aspire to be exploited (Gentili and Alencar 2001, Schugurensky 1997).

It is in this difficult political, social, and economic landscape that adult education policies and practices are located today. Such a context poses a variety of challenges for adult education that range from developing effective adult literacy, family literacy, and adult basic education programs to implementing innovative training programs for the formal and informal economy, promoting community development programs linked to the creation of productive and social alternatives, and creating a variety of interventions in peace education, environmental education, gender education, and citizenship education, to name only a few. Paradoxically, and sadly, the challenges for adult education are expanding at the same time as its budgets are contracting.

This chapter discusses neoliberal policies in Latin America, with a focus on adult education. After outlining the macro-level educational policies that have impacted Latin America during the nineties, I provide an overview of the main issues facing adult education in Latin America and explore some of the reasons for the continuing peripheral status of adult education in policy circles. In the final section, I discuss some of the efforts currently carried out by the Latin American adult education community to develop an alternative agenda for the field.

Two decades of neoliberal medicine: Promises and realities

After twenty years or more of experimenting with neoliberal recipes, Latin American societies (and particularly, but not exclusively, the poor and marginalized) are still waiting for the realization of the original economic and political promises. Two decades ago, many expected that market-oriented policies would bring more democracy and prosperity to the region, and that everybody would benefit from such prosperity. Metaphors such as "rising tides that lift all boats," causal relationships between trade and democracy, recurrent allusions to spillovers that would distribute wealth to all members of society, and continuous references to the inherent inefficiency and corruption of state bureaucracies vis-à-vis the efficiency and transparency of the markets succeeded in capturing the imagination and the hopes of many who thought that the new policies would bring about positive change to the region. In some countries, the promise was framed by elected representatives as the only possibility for their societies to enter into "the first world."

Two decades later, in a context of increasing poverty, recession, violent conflicts, income polarization, and political corruption, those promises, and the premises behind them, are put into question. Neoliberal reforms, undertaken by many governments in the region since the seventies and eighties with support and assistance from international agencies such as the World Bank, the International Monetary Fund (IMF), and the Inter-American Development Bank, were premised on two main assumptions: a) that the market operates on a set of natural laws in opposition to the artificial (human-made) political laws embodied in the state, and b) that a market free from government regulations benefits all classes and social groups through trickle-down effects.

Regarding the first assumption, neoliberal theory claims that a fair and efficient global marketplace can effectively operate under a model of "general competitive equilibrium," in which supply and demand are basically regulated by the invisible hand of the market. The problem with this argument is that concrete dynamics of "competitive equilibrium" are difficult to find in the real world. In other words, "overall competitive equilibrium" is more a theoretical abstraction than a descriptive model of reality. On this topic, William Rees, a professor at the University of British Columbia, points out that, despite the evidence that refutes it, all major national governments and mainstream international agencies continue to perpetuate the myth that global development and poverty alleviation rest on unlimited economic expansion fueled by open markets and more liberalized trade. Likewise, economist James K. Galbraith, who teaches at the University of Texas, claims that the available empirical evidence "flatly contradicts" the major premises of neoliberal economic analysis. In the same vein, Joseph Stiglitz, a Nobel Laureate and former chief economist of the World Bank who is now disenchanted with neoliberal theory, argues that market-based development is not neutral, as the theory contends, and in reality can do real harm to entire peoples and the ecosystem (Galbraith 1999, Rees 2002, Stiglitz 2002).

On the second assumption, it is becoming increasingly clear that the "trickle-down" effect, which was expected to spill wealth over the whole society, has become in reality a "sucking-up" effect, as wealth is more concentrated today than two decades ago. The promise of globalization, which would allegedly integrate all economies into a global village from which everyone would benefit, has kept protectionism intact in the North and relaxed labor and environmental standards in the South, increasing international asymmetries. The increasing concentration of wealth in fewer individuals and economic corporations suggests that leaving the market to the self-regulation of the "invisible hand" of supply and demand often leads to monopolies and oligopolies, with resulting income polarization. In the 1960s, three dollars flowed North for every dollar flowing South; by the late 1990s, the ratio had grown to seven to one. In the last twenty-five years, the ratio between the income of the top 20 percent and the bottom 20 percent doubled, from 32:1 in 1975 to 78:1 in 1995; and today, for every $100 of economic growth, $86 go to the richest one-fifth, while only $1.10 goes to the poorest one-fifth. Today, the assets of the top three billionaires of the world are larger than the combined gross national product (GNP) of all least developed countries and their 600 million people. The assumption of the "spillover effect" is not only questioned by critics of neoliberalism. Even the World Bank has admitted in its 1999 World Development Report that, in spite of its previous forecasts, growth does not necessarily trickle down. The "new" lesson learned by the bank, then, was that development must address human needs directly. For many Latin America governments, this warning may be a wake-up call about the limits of the market to solve issues of poverty and inequality.

Some empirical studies have challenged both spillover and competitive equilibrium—the two main neoliberal assumptions. For instance, in research on Mexico, Veltmeyer et al. (1997, 139–62) showed that privatization intensified the concentration of wealth without increasing economic efficiency through competition. To make matters worse, unemployment increased (300,000 to 1 million jobs were lost), the real value of wages drastically decreased (from 35 percent to 50 percent), and poverty generally spread. Moreover, neoliberalism encouraged the proliferation of *maquiladora* industries, which are directed to exports and exploit workers, especially women, for low-cost labor.

Admittedly, in many countries of the region neoliberal policies have managed to stabilize the economies, reduce inflation, and occasionally spur economic growth. At the same time, however, those policies were largely responsible for increasing unemployment, poverty, income inequality, and the informal economy. According to some studies (Oomen 1997, Rosenzvaig 1997, Morley 1994 and 2001, Berry 1998, Ocampo 1998, Veltmeyer et al. 1997, Loser and Guerguil 2000), neoliberal policies produce worsening income distribution and exact a disproportionately high social cost to the popular classes.

In short, today, after two decades of structural adjustment medicine, poverty levels and income distribution in Latin America are still worse than before the crisis of the 1980s. Latin America's poor are as poor or even poorer than they were two decades ago, and in many countries they are joined by large contingents of "new poor," former members of the middle class experiencing a rapid process of downward social mobility. At the same time, the promise of prosperity for all did not materialize, and Latin America continues to be the most unequal region of the world in terms of wealth distribution. For this reason, some analysts such as James Petras (2002) argue that neoliberalism is not so much a neutral economic theory but an imperial strategy for capturing control over markets, national enterprises, and natural resources.

The fruits of structural adjustment: Toward the end of *pensamiento único?*

The discontent with the gap between neoliberal promises and their results has been growing in Latin America, which is witnessing increasing demonstrations of discontent by a wide range of social actors, including factory workers, the unemployed and underemployed, public employees, and those sectors of the middle class experiencing a process of proletarianization. More recently, the frustration has been evident even among high public officials. Those politicians who usually vent these types of concerns in private are becoming more vocal in explicitly expressing their disillusion with the neoliberal model. This feeling could be observed in the recent Conference on Funding Development held in Monterrey, México, in March 2002. Speaker after speaker (and not only from Latin America, but also from other regions of the developing world) made the point that after two decades of experimenting with neoliberal recipes, the situation of their countries has not improved or has worsened.

For instance, one Latin American president spoke of the dangers of the international trading and monetary systems and argued that a new model of development should put the equitable distribution of wealth at its core. Caribbean and Central American representatives claimed that, despite the substantial reforms undertaken and the painful social sacrifices made under structural adjustment over the past twenty years, expectations have not been realized. Challenging one of the main premises of neoliberal economics, the

Brazilian representative argued that it is self-deluding to believe that the invisible hand of the market will address the exclusionary tendencies of the current socioeconomic systems. The remarks made by elected officials in this and other meetings, coupled with other events such as the recent electoral results in Brazil, Ecuador, and Bolivia and the social uprising in Argentina, show that many Latin Americans are losing patience after two decades of neoliberal policies have accomplished very little and prolonged the suffering of their people. Many Latin Americans are calling for a new social contract that puts people before profit.

Advocates of neoliberal globalization could claim that Latin Americans need to be patient because short-term suffering and recession is a necessary step toward economic prosperity; in the long run, the argument goes, the fruits of market reform will produce the expected benefits. However, as John M. Keynes pointed out decades ago in his widely quoted words, "in the long run we are all dead." Keynes also uttered another famous phrase particularly relevant for Latin America's current situation, after two decades of waiting for the potential prosperity to be brought about by neoliberal policies: "The difficulty lies not so much in developing new ideas as in escaping from old ones." These words encapsulate the difficulties Keynes faced in challenging the orthodoxy of the laissez-faire economic theory prevailing at his time, but also help to explain the roadblocks in breaking from the neoliberal framework, which has become so dominant and entrenched in economic and social policy circles that it is known in Latin America as *pensamiento único* ("the only possible thought"), and by the English acronym TINA ("there is no alternative").

Those roadblocks were particularly hardy during the nineties, when in many Latin American countries, challenging the epistemological premises and the hopeful promises of neoliberal economics equated to something close to heresy. But that was then, and now is now. As the data on the impact of market-oriented policies becomes known, the neoliberal model is losing support from a variety of constituencies, including vast sectors of the middle class. The emerging statistics from the social realities of the nineties strongly suggest that the neoliberal policies implemented during the last two decades did little to improve the standard of living of the Latin American people. In those twenty years, the number of poor in the region increased more than 50 percent (from approximately 136 million to the current 220 million), and the process does not seem to be stopping. From 1997–2002 alone, the number of poor in Latin America increased by 20 million. In Peru, the government statistics agency Instituto Nacional de Estadisticae Informatica (INEI) reported that the poverty rate at the beginning of 2002 had reached 54.8 percent of the population, up from 48.4 percent in 2000. In parts of Argentina, poverty levels have almost doubled during the same period.

The process of pauperization affected both urban and rural populations, but it had a harder impact on women and indigenous populations, which are still enduring a disproportionate burden of the Latin American economic crisis. In many indigenous communities of Chiapas, for instance, most families suffer the death of two or more children under five years of age. In those communities, infant malnutrition is close to 80 percent, child labor is central to family survival, and 72 percent of the children do not complete even the first year of elementary school (Gentili and Alencar 2001). Unfortunately, the tragic situation of Chiapas' indigenous communities is not an exception in Latin America, a continent where, according to the International Labor Organization, 17.4 million children between the ages of 5 and 17 have to work in order to contribute to their family's economic survival. In El Salvador, 17 percent of all children have to work, a figure that rises to 21 percent in Honduras and an astonishing 33 percent in Guatemala. In the past, Argentina used to feed the world and attain high levels of educational achievement, but is now experiencing unprecedented levels of child malnutrition and school dropout. Even in Costa Rica, a country that historically has a social welfare tradition, 147,000 Costa Rican children (15 percent) work in agriculture, fishing, street vending, and child prostitution. Ten years ago, this figure was only 8 percent, and the tendency is on the rise (International Labor Organization 2002). Many of these Latin American children will likely be adult illiterates by 2015, the target year set by governments in the Dakar Declaration to reduce adult illiteracy by half.

As the social reality of Latin America is not showing strong signs of improvement, more and more people (including disenchanted economists and traditional politicians) think it is time to revisit the main premises of the neoliberal model. Slowly but steadily, political and intellectual circles once infatuated with the model are now beginning to challenge some of its key assumptions and the evidence used to support them. A departure from the corset of market fundamentalism that prevails in neoliberal thinking does not equate to a radical paradigm shift in economic and social policy but, as Keynes suggested, provides a first step in developing new ideas. Developing a new framework that breaks with neoliberal economics, avoids the shortcomings of the main competing models of the twentieth century (such as the welfare state and socialism), and achieves validity in today's globalized context will not be an easy task. It is a task that requires a delicate balance between imagination and pragmatism, and in turn requires a vigorous and broad societal debate that goes beyond ideological cliches and overgeneralizations. A few groups and institutions in Latin America are starting to imagine alternative economic and social models and develop alternative social and educational policies. Some adult education movements in the region are part of these initiatives.

Neoliberal policies and practices in Latin America

In current debates about the implementation of neoliberal policies in Latin America, it is possible to observe at least five common myths or misperceptions. The first misperception is that the neoliberal reforms implemented in

Latin America during the last decades followed an orthodox, monolithic, and universal application throughout the region. In reality, while it is possible to say that there was a general pattern, it is also true that the policies varied from country to country (and from political regime to political regime within a given country) depending on a variety of other factors, such as the specific issue at stake, the correlation of forces at the national level, or the intellectual and organizational capacity of the actors involved in the negotiations (Puiggrós 1999, Coraggio and Torres 1999).

The second misperception is that the policies were easily imposed from outside due to the weak position of power of the internal actors who opposed them, but had no alternative than to accept them. This tends to portray a dichotomous picture of bad and powerful external actors on the one hand, and good but powerless internal actors on the other. The reality is not so simple. The implementation of neoliberal policies in each country was the result of a complex set of alliances and struggles among internal and external actors. While many large sectors of the Latin American population opposed those policies, it is also true that most reforms would not have occurred without the strategic support provided by a critical mass of powerful and influential sectors of local political, intellectual, and business groups, including those who own the most important media conglomerates.

The third misperception is that those neoliberal policies provided great benefits to the creditor countries and great poverty to all in the debtor countries. Again, this is a simplistic portrayal of reality that ignores the existence of "pockets of beneficiaries" in the debtor countries. It should not be forgotten that many neoliberal policies and the variety of arrangements related to them (particularly during the process of privatizing public companies) provided important benefits (financial and otherwise) to select segments of local political and business elites, including national presidents. Recent corruption scandals related to irregularities in natural resources and the process of privatizing public enterprises (such as bribes and overprized and underprized assets) suggest that an informal system of rewards was in place in several countries.

The fourth misperception is that neoliberalism requires a minimal and weak state, and ideally the disappearance of the state so the market forces of supply and demand can operate freely, without political interference and bureaucratic regulation. In reality, beyond its anti-state rhetoric, capitalism (even its laissez-faire variety) needs the state, and not necessarily a weak one. It needs a strong and business-friendly state capable of reducing social expenditures, eroding redistributive policies, and relaxing labor legislation while controlling the ensuing social discontent. That is, neoliberalism requires a state that has the capability to suppress or co-opt those sectors that can potentially contest and challenge the "rights" of capital to operate in uncontrolled markets. In this sense, even if the welfare state retrenches, the need for the state still continues under neoliberal regimes. Indeed, the double role of the state continues to be, as much as in Gramsci's time, ensuring the social order and building hege-mony through a combination of coercion and persuasion. The state is needed today as much as before to provide the conditions for capital accumulation and promote the legitimation of the status quo. In the post-welfare era, the state has been redirecting its energies to accumulation, which is leading to a crisis of legitimation with the consequent ascendance of social conflict. In sum, neoliberalism can operate through democratically elected governments or (when legitimation fails) through ruthless military dictatorships, but it al-ways needs the assistance of the state. And not necessarily a minimalist state, as the myth suggests, but a different type of state. Neoliberalism does not de-mand the dismantling of the state but rather its restructuring.

The fifth recurring misperception is that the infusion of capital provided by the International Monetary Fund and the World Bank was essential to the sur-vival of Latin American economies, social programs, and educational systems, and therefore Latin American countries had no other choice than to desper-ately seek those loans. The reality, however, is that the IMF and World Bank's contribution to the national economies was negligible. According to the World Bank itself, its financial loans represent only less than 1 percent of the educa-tional expenditures of developing countries (World Bank 1995). Likewise, in Argentina, since 1998 the loans of the IMF represented just 1.7 percent of all the aggregated expenditures of the public sector (federal, provincial, and mu-nicipal). It is interesting to note that seldom in the private sector does a minor partner have so much decision power on policy matters (Hourest and Lozano 2002).

Neoliberalism, social development, and educational achievement: Two suggestive examples

For different reasons, today Argentina and Cuba are two suggestive case stud-ies attracting the attention of those interested in examining the impact of neoliberal policies on the standard of living of the people. Cuba probably is the only country in the region that has not been following the neoliberal recipes advanced by multilateral agencies and international financial institutions. In-deed, Cuba is the only developing country besides North Korea that did not re-ceive any assistance, either in advice or in aid, from the World Bank in the last forty years. Argentina is studied because it has applied the neoliberal medicine for several decades under the leadership of economist Domingo Cavallo and it has been showcased during the nineties as a successful model of development. During those years, Argentina was the IMF's preferred model and most obedi-ent student."[2]

In spite of not receiving financial aid or advice from the IMF and the World Bank (or perhaps precisely because of it) Cuba stands out among Latin Amer-ican countries for its achievements in social welfare, particularly in the fields of health and education. For instance, whereas the infant mortality rate is 30 per 1,000 live births in Latin America and the Caribbean, the figure for Cuba is close to 6 per 1,000 live births. Likewise, while the mortality rate for children under age five in the region is 38 per 1,000, in Cuba it is from 8 to 13 per 1,000. Moreover, life expectancy in Cuba is the highest in the region.

In education, the accomplishments of the island are also impressive. In spite of the economic crisis, Cuba has been able to keep social development as a priority, with public spending on education amounting to 6.7 percent of the GNP, twice the proportion of many Latin American countries. Likewise, net primary enrollments are the highest in the region, and the teacher-student ratio (twelve students per teacher) is half of the Latin American average. It could be claimed, however, that these statistics do not necessarily reflect the real measure of success of an educational system, which is the quality of learning. In this regard, the Cuban case suggests a strong correlation between investment in education and student achievement. For instance, the youth illiteracy rate in Cuba is close to zero, a figure unmatched by any other Latin American country, where the average is 7 percent. This is confirmed by the results of a comparative evaluation of learning undertook by UNESCO-OREALC in thirteen Latin American countries. The data for the study emerged from mathematics and language tests with students in grade 3 and 4. Overall, Cuban students showed the highest level of achievement (UNESCO-OREALC 1998, 2000; World Bank 1999).

According to the latest figures in the World Development Indicators published by the World Bank in April 2001, Cuba continues to surpass virtually all other Latin American countries in its health and education statistics. It is interesting to note that these accomplishments in social welfare were attained in the context of a relatively poor economy and a long-term, continuous blockade on trade imposed by the United States, which makes the accomplishment more impressive.

Faced with this evidence, in a surprising statement made in April 2001, the president of the World Bank, James Wolfensohn, publicly admitted that the Cuban government was doing good work in providing for the social welfare of its people. Addressing a news conference after the release of the World Development Indicators, Wolfensohn pointed out that "Cuba has done a great job on education and health and, if you judge the country by education and health, they've done a terrific job." Then he added: "It was not with our advice but it was not without our advice either. We just have nothing to do with them." This is ironic because Cuba's economic and social policies are generally the opposite of the World Bank's recommendations for the countries of the region. Or perhaps it is not so ironic, as Cuba's success in education and health could be explained precisely by its resolve to avoid taking loans from international financial institutions. As is well known, these loans usually come with conditions, which generally demand the privatization of state services and cutting provisions to the poor. The combined result of these conditions and the drain of financial resources through high interest rates is ever-growing and unpayable debts, which in turn lead to more recession, poverty, unemployment, and hunger.

The recent collapse of Argentina's economy illustrates this situation with particular drama. Although there is no doubt that high levels of corruption were part and parcel of the current Argentinean agonies, it is also clear that the so-called eternal debt played an important role in the problem—and for some, even the primary role. According to a recent study carried out by the Center for Economic and Policy Research (a Washington-based think tank), the financial crisis of Argentina was due more to insurmountable debt than to profligate government spending. The study, conducted by economists Mark Weisbrot and Dean Baker, claims that from 1993 to 2000, Argentina's primary government spending (funding for salaries, government programs, and operations) was essentially flat, whereas interest payments on the government debt rose threefold (Bussey 2002). Unemployment, homelessness, and poverty in Argentina are now reaching unprecedented levels, and the impact on education is becoming increasingly evident. A recent study conducted by Save the Children and United Nations Children's Fund (UNICEF) in the province of Buenos Aires (one of the wealthiest in the country) revealed that half of the students who start secondary school do not complete it. The data also reveals the existence of great inequalities, as most of these students are poor. Whereas among the wealthiest 20 percent of the population the great majority (92 percent) finish secondary school, among the poorest 40 percent of the population only 15 percent of those who start it complete it (Dandan 2002).

If Argentina represents a good example of the application of neoliberal policies, and Cuba represents a good counter-example, there is no evidence to suggest that the health of the economy and the social fabric are necessarily correlated positively with the implementation of those policies. This does not mean that Cuba's model of a centralized state economy and its one-party system is a perfect one, or that the Argentinean model of privatization, structural adjustment, pegged currency, and debt escalation of the nineties was all wrong. Both models have negative and positive aspects (Argentina, for instance, managed to control hyperinflation and stabilize the economy). However, the overall impact of the implemented policies on the welfare of the population (and particularly the poor sectors), wealth distribution, and educational achievement suggest that, at least in Latin America, neoliberal theory needs further examination before receiving further uncritical endorsement by domestic policy makers.

Neoliberalism and education in Latin America

In terms of education, one of the main features of the neoliberal model has been the replacement of a pedagogical relationship with an economic logic imported from business practices and market dynamics. The new buzzwords, in Latin America as well as in most parts of the world, are "standards," "testing," "decentralization," "economic competitiveness," "accountability," "privatization," and "vouchers" (Fischman and Gvirtz 2001; Wong and Balestino 2001).

Several developments have resulted from this shift from the previous discourse centered on public provision and equality of opportunity. First, efficiency and productivity criteria used by private companies have been extended to schools, sometimes inappropriately. Second, the emphasis in policy priorities, discourse, and practice has shifted from learner-centered curriculum to job-related outcomes and vocational training. Third, education is increasingly conceived of as another marketable commodity and less as a public good or inalienable human right. Fourth, teachers' autonomy and control over their work is reduced by workplace bureaucracy and standardized procedures. Fifth, institutional efficiency was pursued through decentralization strategies, but given that the decentralization process was seldom complemented with enough financial and technical support, in many cases it increased inequalities among regions and schools. In this transition, foreign aid agencies, through direct and indirect means, and particularly through the power of the purse, have become increasingly influential in educational policy, to the extent that in many countries the agenda-setting process is shaped by the priorities of the funding agencies of the day, which also have a large influence on research priorities, the nature of the findings, and the way the results are used (Samoff 1994, Stromquist and Monkman 2000, Coraggio and Torres 1999).

In this regard, Fischman and Gvirtz (2001) argue that the new controls on educational performance devised and supervised by international financial institutions were not driven by educational principles or need but by adjusting the systems to the budgetary restrictions of structural adjustment programs. Paradoxically, they suggest, the state increased its presence in education through a variety of control mechanisms, and at the same time it withdrew from its traditional role as guarantor of equality of both educational opportunity and provision. A similar pattern is taking place in higher education, with a push toward entrepreneuralism, applied research, competition among institutions, and privatization. With increasing market imperatives and state controls, the pendulum is shifting from autonomy to heteronomy—in the sense that its institutional mission, agenda, and operational principles are more contingent upon an external logic than self-determined by its internal actors (Schugurensky 1999, Rodríguez-Gomez and Alcantara 2001).

As a hypothesis, it is possible to suggest that the relative success of the neoliberal forces in advancing their educational project in Latin America was based on at least two dynamics: on one hand, a deliberate strategy engineered by international agencies to influence local centers of political decision-making through different means, from conditional loans to specific recommendations to reduce potential conflict derived from reform implementation; on the other hand, a syncretic discourse that managed to garner the support of different constituencies by reconciling traditionally contradictory values. For instance, the neoliberal discourse on education appealed simultaneously to quality and equity, to accountability and autonomy, and to competition and integration. This broad appeal, at least at the rhetorical level, to these three conceptual pairs that are usually seen as antithetic probably played an important role in the hegemony-building strategies of the neoliberal agenda (for an elaboration of this argument, see Schugurensky 2000).

As noted earlier, the discourse of neoliberalism also included a strong emphasis on decentralization policies. In practice, what could be observed in Latin America was a double and concurrent dynamic of decentralization and centralization. In the educational systems of the region, this means that the central state apparatus downloaded functions and responsibilities (including financial) to lower levels of governments and schools at the same time that they centralized planning and evaluation. This amounts to relaxing process control but strengthening product control—that is, delegating the control over institutional processes to local agents while tightening the control of the general direction and expected outcomes of educational policies (Braslavsky and Gvirtz 2001, Gorostiaga 2001).

What was the overall impact of neoliberal policies on education? After a thorough examination of the main five arguments for and against neoliberal education policies in Latin America, Robert Arnove (1997) concludes that those policies have not improved the education of the majority of Latin American children and adults. Furthermore, Arnove claims that these policies, within a context of increasing impoverishment and a growing gap between the rich and the poor, lead to larger inequities in educational access and outcomes. Based on the impact of past neoliberal policies in the region, Arnove predicts that they will be unlikely to meet the challenges of providing universal primary education and eliminating large-scale illiteracy, and contends not only that the promises of neoliberal policies to substantially alter the educational landscape are deceptive, but that, on the contrary, they have serious limitations and deleterious consequences. In sum, the available evidence suggests that the theoretical model of rational choice theory applied to education (based on consumers' selection of educational institutions that compete among themselves) has not proven useful to solve the problems of inequality of opportunity. As Samoff (1994) pointed out in a pioneering work on this topic, what we have seen instead is a fixation on finances that relegated concerns for the quality of learning processes to the backburner. As a result, foreign advisers, national and provincial policy makers, and even educators are losing sight not only of the broader (and often difficult to measure) goals of education, such as self-reliance, citizenship, self-confidence, equity, or solidarity, but also of the importance of improving teaching-learning processes. Rather, they focus almost exclusively on spending less and on measuring standardized outcomes, promoting cost-recovery, privatization, and national examinations, with the risk of transforming education into a mere delivery system.

Implications for adult education

For adult education programs in Latin America, the situation during the last two decades was not so much of close alignment with the market, but of oblivion. A field traditionally marginalized in terms of education funding and policy, adult education during this period was further marginalized by international agencies and national governments. What is particularly ironic about this process is that the near abandonment of the field of adult education in Latin America (and for that matter, worldwide) occurred at the same time that there was a clear mandate to revitalize it. The mandate was articulated in the Education for All conference held in 1990 in Jomtien, Thailand, and subsequently ignored during most of the decade both by national governments and by international agencies that influence Latin American education policy.

For the field of adult education, the post-Jomtien decade constitutes a sad example of overcommitment and underachievement, which reflects the gap between expansive rhetoric and contracting agenda. Indeed, most educational policies for "including the excluded" implemented during the last decade have themselves excluded adult education from the repertoire of potential interventions, and have excluded adults from their policy radar.[3] Although the recommendations emanating from Jomtien in 1990 supposedly included "all," in practice, as Rosa Maria Torres (2000) points out, the agenda "shrunk" to exclude almost everything beyond basic education for children. For Almazan-Khan (2000) this situation has continued in the 2000 Dakar conference (whose policy strategy was supposed to rectify the mistakes of the last ten years), to the extent that she asks whether "EFA" stands for "Education for All," or "Except for Adults." In other words, the impact of the educational policies implemented during the nineties on the field of adult education was not so much in terms of drastic restructuring (as it was in other levels of the system) but in terms of cutbacks and outright neglect.

In the postwar history of Latin American adult education, seldom had this sector received so little support at both the national and international level as it did in the nineties. Although a myriad of local programs remained in place, the large-scale initiatives and the legitimacy of the field characteristic of the previous four decades practically vanished. Despite their occasional rhetoric of lifelong education, the emphasis of the overall education strategy of bilateral and multilateral organizations, national governments, and donor agencies lay almost exclusively on schools rather than on nonformal education, and on children rather than on youth and adults. Moreover, whereas in the past Latin

American adult education (and particularly the popular education movement) was a permanent source of innovation and creativity that inspired programs all over the world, it has been argued that during the nineties the most interesting innovations in the region came from the school system (Stromquist 1997, UNESCO-OREALC 2000, La Belle 2000, Torres 2000).

Many things are expected from adult education, from fostering ecologically sustainable development to promoting democratization, social justice, gender equity, economic growth, peace building, and the empowerment of marginalized groups (CONFINTEA 1997). While the potential for that contribution exists, and in some contexts adult education made significant contributions in one or more of those areas, in general terms the role of adult education in capitalist societies does not contradict prevailing structures of class, gender, and race inequalities (Puiggrós 1999, Youngman 2000).

At the same time, however, adult education has great potential for counterhegemonic projects. Today the region is witnessing revitalization of the tradition of popular education, which brought to the center of its agenda some themes that were at its margins in previous decades (such as ecopedagogy, gender equity, indigenous education, or active citizen participation in local governments) while keeping its traditional Freirian focus on conscientization, popular organization, and participatory action research. Indeed, the economic, political, and social crisis is propelling many groups in the Latin American adult education community to recover the social change paradigm that was so prominent in the seventies.

At a broader level, the Latin American adult education movement is experiencing a momentary identity crisis due to the difficulties in clarifying the boundaries of the field. The dynamics of the discussions tend to pull adult educators into the opposite directions of expansion and contraction. Some adult educators argue that, in order to gain relevance and overcome its current crisis, adult education should expand beyond its traditional activities and programs, and make clear connections with the main issues that affect the lives of youth and adults in the region. In other words, adult education should actively engage with issues related to human rights, poverty, the environment, gender, ethnicity, democracy, citizenship, employment, rural development, unions, migration, violence, local governance, health, consumers' rights, indigenous autonomy, peace, and the like. Other adult educators counterargue that this type of agenda puts excessive demands on the field and inevitably leads to dispersion and frustration. In their view, the solution to the crisis lies in concentrating its scarce resources on the few areas in which there is a history of accumulated expertise, such as literacy, adult basic education, and vocational training, and doing these things with efficiency and quality. Only this, they argue, will build confidence in the field among internal and external constituencies (Schugurensky and Myers 2001). This is a Catch-22 situation. In order to be more effective and attract more people, literacy and adult basic education programs have to become more relevant to the lives of the learners and their communities. At the same time, the achievement of higher relevance usually implies a diversification of programs, contents, and methods, which in turn creates dispersion and could reduce effectiveness and quality if adequate coordination mechanisms are not in place.

The only way out of this dilemma is to avoid an exclusive choice between breadth and depth, which constitutes a mental straightjacket. The practical choice is not between broad expansion and rigorous contraction, but between a superficial expansion that spreads the field too thin and ends inevitably in self-exhaustion, dispersion, and paralysis, and a well thought-out, creative, and collaborative intersectoral expansion that articulates quality and relevant efforts carried out by adult educators in governmental and nongovernmental institutions as well as other areas. More importantly, this collaborative strategy must actively involve the adults and youth themselves in the definition of goals and strategies. The task is no longer to promote an adult education for the people, but to develop with them an inclusive educational movement. The transition from a "for" to a "with" mentality is an important step for a field traditionally characterized by top-down approaches, compensatory logic, and deficit theories. The incipient experiments of local democracy in several Latin American cities provide a fertile ground for experimenting with these types of democratic models. The work of the Movimento de Alfabetização (MOVA) and the Serviço de Educação de Jovens e Adultos (SEJA) in Porto Alegre are interesting examples in this regard.

Summary and conclusions

During the last two decades, the bulk of economic and social policy in Latin America has been guided by the doctrine of neoliberalism. Since the early eighties, most Latin American countries began to depart from their already weak versions of the welfare state model and embarked on a variety of initiatives to develop a more market-friendly state. One by one, sooner or later, most Latin American countries implemented the central recipes of structural adjustment, privatization, and deregulation. Due to the real and perceived problems related to state bureaucracies (such as inefficiency, corruption, etc.), it was expected that this model would lead to economic prosperity, efficiency in the provision of services, and an overall increase in the standard of living (either through the direct impact of the policies or through the so-called spillover effect).

In exchange for loans, Latin American countries agreed to implement a structural adjustment package promoted by international lenders. Although this package varied from country to country, in general terms it led to privatizing many industries and public services, instituting or raising user fees, eliminating subsidies of all kinds, cutting public services, raising interest rates, downsizing the public sector, and opening the nation's economy to world competition. The expected results were job gains in export industries (which would offset temporary losses in the domestic labor market), a healthier and more competitive economy, and a more efficient state. In most parts of Latin America, those expectations were far from realized. Indeed, today it is increasingly clear that after twenty years of experimenting with more or less orthodox varieties of the neoliberal model, its outcomes are not living up to its original promises.

The economic and social circumstances described in this chapter have several implications for adult education policy and practice. First, increasing income inequalities place a greater burden on adult education as a "compensatory measure for the poor." Education in general, and adult education in particular, is increasingly turned to as the remedy for solving social problems such as poverty or unemployment. Second, the rapid and unfinished transition to democracy in Latin America requires broad popular preparation for participation in democratic society and in the development of democratic values—particularly in times when formal democratic institutions are not living up to expectations and novel means of democratic participation need to be designed. This entails, at a minimum, universal adult literacy that allows for a more informed public and widespread education in citizenship, particularly the knowledge, skills, and attitudes that prepare individuals for active political participation. Lastly, neoliberal policies and market values are reflected in the privileging of vocational training in adult education, which creates an adult educational system subservient to the economy and divorced from individual educational needs, social development, or democratic participation.

Notwithstanding a few exceptions, and even considering that a certain degree of autonomy exists in every system, it may be naive to expect that institutionalized adult education in Latin America will promote an emancipatory pedagogical model that challenges the hegemonic model. While the transformative potential of state-controlled adult education should not be overestimated, it is possible to suggest that alternative values, political agendas, and pedagogical practices are more likely to be found in the active field of popular education and in the educational activities of social movements and community organizations (Jarvis 2002).

This does not mean that popular education should not engage with the state and with mainstream adult education. On the contrary, as Gadotti suggests, popular education should have one foot on the state apparatus and the other in social movements: tactically inside, strategically outside. (Gadotti 1992: 71).

In sum, adult education alone cannot solve all social problems, and not even all of the problems faced by the 150 million Latin American youth and adults who have never accessed or have been pushed out from school. However, in connection with other actors and initiatives, it can offer a significant contribution to a more sustainable, just, democratic, and equitable development. It can also make a modest contribution to the collective development of alternatives to the *pensamiento único*. Perhaps a post-neoliberal era is indeed possible, and adult education can play an important role in moving us in that direction.

Notes

1. For example, a poll conducted by the newspaper *Folha de São Paulo* found that only 47 percent of Brazilians believe that "democracy is best," while 18 percent support the idea that "at times dictatorship is the best option," and almost one-third of the respondents (29 percent) thought that it did not matter whether the country was run by a democracy or a dictatorship (The Globe and Mail, July 17, 2000, A13). A recent poll in Argentina found that immediately after unemployment and recession (48 percent and 37 percent respectively), 35 percent of people identify the political class as one of the main national problems. While unemployment and recession have been identified as problems for over a decade, now the political class is clearly perceived as a problem. This is expressed in other symptoms like voters' absenteeism, spoiled ballots, and the main slogan of the *cacerolazos* (pot-banging demonstrations), "que se vayan todos, que no quede ni uno solo," meaning that all members of the political class should leave office. Other recent events hostile to the deepening of democracy in the region include accusations of electoral fraud in Peru (followed by a corruption scandal that led the president to flee the country), and coup attempts in Venezuela, an unprecedented crisis of governability in Argentina, and an intensification of armed conflict and external intervention in Colombia. The most recent elections in Brazil and Ecuador, however, bring renewed hope in elected representatives to address the most pressing social issues.

2. Alberto Acosta "¡Llora por mi Argentina! (f) FMI," from *Hoy*, Quito, January 30, 2002, p. 2, in *Globalización. Portal latinoamericano en globalización*, http://www.globalizacion.org/argentina/ArgentinaAcostaFMI.htm.

3. An example of this situation can be found in a recent policy document in which the World Bank outlines its educational strategy and lending policies for Latin America and the Caribbean. In the section on priorities, the WB claims that the overarching goal for Latin America and the Caribbean "is to raise the Region's human capital, especially that of the poor" (World Bank 2000, 11). Such a statement can raise the hopes of Latin American adult educators for a few seconds, but such optimism would probably evaporate after reading the following paragraphs, in which the bank describes its six strategic priorities to achieve this goal. Throughout them, there is an absence of references to adult education and nonformal education. Even the discussion of the first priority, which calls for "including the excluded by, whenever possible, targeting interventions to the poor," makes no allusions to the potential role of adult education programs. There are references to a variety of interventions such as early childhood programs, school feeding, school health programs, improvement of quality of learning and school attendance through financial incentives to poor families, or the expansion of opportunities for secondary and tertiary education through income-contingent scholarships. The other five priorities deal with the quality of teaching and school revitalization, secondary education, decentralization of education ministries, tertiary education reform, and educational innovations, especially in the use of education technology.

References

Acosta, Alberto. (2002). "!Llora por mi Argentina! (f) FMI." Published in *Hoy*, Quito, January 30, 2002, p. 2, and reproduced in *Globalización. Portal latinoamericano en globalización*, http://www.globalizacion.org/argentina/ArgentinaAcostaFMI.htm (last accessed November 15, 2002).

Almazan-Khan, M. L. (2000). "Does EFA Stand for 'Except for Adults'?" *ICAE News* (spring), p. 3.

Arnove, Robert. (1997). "Neoliberal Education Policies in Latin America: Arguments in Favor and Against." In Carlos A. Torres and Adriana Puiggrós, eds. *Latin American Education: Comparative Perspectives.* Boulder, Colo.: Westview Press, 79–102.

Arnove, R., S. Franz, M. Mollis, and C. A. Torres. (1999). "Education in Latin America at the End of the 1990s." In R. Arnove and C. A. Torres, eds. *Comparative Education: The Dialectic of the Global and the Local*. Lanham, Md.: Rowman and Littlefield, 305–28.

Berry, A. (1998). "The Income Distribution Threat in Latin America." In A. Berry, ed. *Economic Reforms, Poverty, and Income Distribution in Latin America*. Boulder, Colo.: Lynne Rienner.

Braslavsky, Cecilia, and Silvina Gvirtz. (2001). "Nuevos desafíos y dispositivos en la política educacional latinoamericana de find de siglo." Madrid: Organización de los Estados Americanos.

Buenfil, Rosa Nidia. (2000). "Globalization and Educational Policies in Mexico 1988–1994: A Meeting of the Universal and the Particular." In Nelly Stromquist and Karen Monkman, eds. *Globalization and Education: Integration and Contestation across Cultures*. Maryland, Md.: Rowman and Littlefield.

Bussey, Jane. (2002). "The Debt Did It: Argentina's Economic Crisis Is a Result of Huge Interest Payments, Not Runaway Spending, a Study Says." *The Miami Herald*, March 24, 2002.

Carnoy, Martin. (2000). "Globalization and Educational Reform." In Nelly Stromquist and Karen Monkman, eds. *Globalization and Education: Integration and Contestation across Cultures*. Maryland, Md.: Rowman and Littlefield.

CEPAL. (2002a). Panorama social de América Latina 2001–2002. Santiago de Chile: CEPAL.

CEPAL. (2002b). Current Conditions and Outlook. Economic Survey of Latin America and the Caribbean, 2001–2002. Santiago de Chile: CEPAL.

CONFINTEA. (1997). Adult Education: The Hamburg Declaration and the Agenda for the Future. Fifth International Conference on Adult Education 14–18 July, 1997. Hamburg: UNESCO.

Coraggio, Jose Luis, and Rosa Maria Torres. (1999). "La educación segun el Banco Mundial." Madrid: Pedro Miño.

Dandan, Alejandra. (2002). "Pobres en vías de extinción en la secundaria. La desercion escolar en el segundo nivel se disparó." *Pagina* 12 (marzo 14).

Fischman, Gustavo, and Silvina Gvirtz. (2001). "An Overview of Educational Policies in the Countries of Latin America during the 1990s." *Journal of Education Policy* 16, no. 6: 499–506.

Gadotti, Moacir (1992). Estado e educa? popular: Bases para uma educa? p??ca popular, in M. Gadotti and C. A. Torres (eds.), Estado e educa? popular na Am?ca Latina. Sao Paulo: Instituto Paulo Freire.

Galbraith, J. (1999). The Crisis of Globalization. *Dissent* 46 no. 3, 12–16.

Gentilli, Pablo, and Chico Alencar. (2001). "Educar na esperança em tempos de desencanto." Rio de Janeiro: Vozes.

Gorostiaga, Jorge. (2001). "Educational Decentralization Policies in Argentina and Brazil: Exploring the New Trends." *Journal of Education Policy* 16, no. 6: 561–84.

Graff, W. (1995). The State in the Third World, *Socialist Register*.

Hourest, Martin, and Claudio Lozano (2002). La democracia y el FMI: Entre la mentira y el crimen. Revista Realidad Económica. Buenos Aires (Argentina) núm. 187-1, abril al 15 mayo de 2002, 36–55.

International Labor Organization. (2002). A Future without Child Labour: Global Report under the Follow-up to the ILO Declaration on Fundamental Principles and Rights at Work. International Labour Conference, 90th Session. Report I (B). Geneva: ILO Bureau of Publications.

Jarvis, Peter. (2002). "Globalisation, Citizenship and the Education of Adults in Contemporary European Society." *Compare* 32, no. 1:5–20.

La Belle, T. (2000). "The Changing Nature of Non-formal Education in Latin America." *Comparative Education* 36, no. 1:21–36.

Loser, C., and Guerguil, M. (2000). "The Long Road to Financial Stability." *Finance and Development* 37, no. 1:7–12.

Morley, S. A. (1994). Poverty and Inequality in Latin America: Past Evidence, Future Prospects. Policy Essay no. 13. Washington D.C.: Overseas Development Council (ODC).

Morley, S. A. (2001). The Income Distribution Problem in Latin America and the Caribbean. ECLAC/CEPAL: Santiago de Chile.

Ocampo, J. (1998). Income Distribution, Poverty, and Social Expenditure in Latin America. *CEPAL Review*.

Oomen, T. K. (1997). "Social Movements in the Third World." In Staffan Lindberg and Arni Sverrison, eds. *Social Movements in Development: The Challenge of Globalization and Democratization*. Basingstoke, UK: Macmillan, 46–66.

Pannu, R. S. (1996). Neoliberal Project of Globalization: Prospects for Democratisation of Education. In *Alberta Journal of Educational Research* 42, no. 2:87–101.

Petras, James. (2002). U.S. Offensive in Latin America: Coups, Retreats, and Radicalization. *Monthly Review* 54, no. 1.

Puiggrós, Adriana. (1999). *Neoliberalism and Education in the Americas.* Boulder, Colo.: Westview Press.

Rees, William E. (2002). "Squeezing the Poor." *Toronto Star*, April 22, A16.

Rivero, J. (1999). *Educación y exclusión en America Latina: Reformas en tiempo de globalización.* Lima: Tarea.

Rodríguez-Gomez, Roberto, and Armando Alcantara. (2001). "Multilateral Agencies and Higher Education Reform in Latin America." *Journal of Education Policy* 16, no. 6: 507–25.

Rosenzvaig, E. (1997). Neoliberalism: Economic Philosophy of Postmodern Demolition, *Latin American Comparative Perspectives.* Boulder, Colo.: Westview Press.

Samoff, J. (1994). "Responses to Crisis: (Re)setting the Education and Training Policy Agenda." In Joel Samoff, ed. *Coping with Crisis: Austerity, Adjustment, and Human Resources.* London: Cassell-Unesco.

Schmelkes, S. (1994). "Research Trends in Adult Education in Latin America." Paper presented at the International Seminar on Research Trends in Adult Education. Paris: UNESCO.

Schugurensky, Daniel. (1997). "Forward to the Past? Globalization, Neoliberalism, and Adult Education." In *Questions de formation/Issues in Adult Education* 8, no. 15. Reprinted in *ABET Journal—A South African Journal of Adult Basic Education and Training,* 2.

Schugurensky, Daniel. (1999). "Higher Education Restructuring in the Ear of Globalization: Toward a heteronomous model." In Robert Arnove and Carlos A. Torres, eds. *Comparative Education: The Dialectic of the Global and the Local.* Lanham, Md.: Rowman and Littlefield, 283–304.

Schugurensky, Daniel. (2000). "Syncretic Discourses, Hegemony Building, and Educational Reform." *Education and Society* 18, no. 2: 75–94.

Schugurensky, Daniel, and John P. Myers. (2001). "Cinderella and the Search for the Missing Shoe: Latin American Adult Education Policy and Practice during the 1990s." *Journal of Education Policy* 16, no. 6: 527–46.

Stevens, Willy J. (1999). *Desafios para America Latina.* Ed. Taurus: Mexico.

Stiglitz, Joseph. (2002). "Lo que aprendi de la crisis economica mundial." *Revista Veintitres.* Buenos Aires, February 85–88.

Stromquist, Nelly. (1997). *Literacy for Citizenship: Gender and Grassroots Dynamics in Brazil.* Albany, N.Y.: SUNY Press.

Stromquist, Nelly, and Karen Monkman. (2000). "Defining Globalization and Assessing Its Implications on Knowledge and Education." In Nelly Stromquist and Karen Monkman, eds. *Globalization and Education: Integration and Contestation across Cultures.* Maryland, Md.: Rowman and Littlefield.

Torres, R. M. (2000). *One Decade of Education for All: The Challenge Ahead.* Buenos Aires: International Institute for Educational Planning.

UNESCO-OREALC. (1998). First International Comparative Study of Language, Mathematics, and Associated Factors in Third and Fourth Grades. First Report. Santiago de Chile: UNESCO.

UNESCO-OREALC. (2000). First International Comparative Study of Language, Mathematics, and Associated Factors in Third and Fourth Grades. Second Report. Santiago de Chile: UNESCO.

Veltmeyer, H., J. Petras, and S. Vieux. (1997). "Neoliberalism and Capitalism in Mexico 1983–1995: Model of Structural Adjustment?" In Veltmeyer, Petras, and Vieux, eds. *Neoliberalism and Class Conflict in Latin America: A Comparative Perspective on the Political Economy of Structural Adjustment.* New York: St. Martin's Press.

World Bank. (1995). "Priorities and Strategies for Education: A World Bank Sector Review." Washington D.C.: World Bank.

World Bank. (1999). "Entering the Twenty-first Century. World Development Report 1999/2000." Washington D.C.: World Bank.

Youngman, Frank. (2000). *The Political Economy of Adult Education.* Leicester: Zed Books.

Zarco, Carlos. (2000). "Educacion, ciudadania, derechos humanos, y participacion de las personas jovenes y adultas," in Unesco et al., eds. *La educacion de personas jovenes y adultas en America Latina y el Caribe.* Prioridades de Accion en el Siglo XXI. Unesco: Santiago de Chile.

3

Prioritizing the Education
of Marginalized Youth in Brazil
A Collaborative Approach

PIA L. WONG
RAMON BALESTINO

This chapter examines three critical questions related to the education of marginalized youth in Brazil: 1) To what extent did government policy from 1995–1999 prioritize the education of marginalized youth? 2) What alternative models exist for addressing their educational needs and interests? 3) What parameters can be further developed to maximize educational opportunities for this population? The research draws from a broad range of archival materials including federal/state publications, legislation, publications from nongovernmental organizations and multilateral institutions, and a set of in-depth interviews conducted over a four-year period. Youth in Brazil—a group that is unique in its characteristics, needs, and dynamics—are continuously isolated from policy discourse. In making this argument, we present three models or responses that specifically target the education of marginalized youth. Each model encompasses distinct dynamics and power relations between grassroots groups, state agencies, and the youth themselves. This analysis emerges at a time when Brazilian policymakers must negotiate a risky crossroads—they must determine the extent to which future legislation, policy and programs will faithfully adhere to neoliberal policies, which are damaging to the population targeted in this study or deviate from them. Recommendations posed herein for new collaborative forms of policy making where grassroots groups and state entities work in partnership to prioritize the educational rights of marginalized youth may offer compelling alternatives for a mediated, mitigated neoliberalism.

Providing quality public education accessible to all children has been an historic challenge in Brazil. A brief analysis of federal education policies prior to 1995 reveals vast inequities on several dimensions: 1) the development of a sophisticated postgraduate system took priority over expanding access to and enhancing the quality of elementary and secondary education; 2) resources and materials distributed unevenly funded large cities and the Southeastern

67

regions at the expense of other areas of the country; and 3) poorly defined distribution of educational resources and responsibilities among the three levels of government (municipal, state, and federal) created detrimental inefficiencies and redundancy (Barros and Lam 1996; Birdsall, Bruns, and Sabot 1996; Plank, Sobrinho, and Xavier 1996). The result of these trends and others (such as poor teacher preparation, low teacher salaries, decaying infrastructure, etc.) is an educational system that has consistently privileged an economic and political elite and marginalized low-income, working class, and even middle-class families (O'Cadiz, Wong, and Torres 1998).

Diminishing access to educational resources and the poor quality of the limited existing resources have curtailed educational opportunities in general, and have most severely affected low-income and working-class youth in particular. Lacking access to a quality public education severely limits the professional and life opportunities available to low-income youth in a country with notorious and growing income disparities (Wolfensohn 1999). Limited educational opportunities further isolate these youth who are already marginalized by their social class and, often, ethnic identity.

Within this group of marginalized youth are so-called *meninos/as da rua* or street children.[1] This group is typically characterized by youth who spend the majority of their time on the streets—outside their families, communities, and schools, the three core settings that ensure a child's healthy growth and development. Children choose to be outside of these three settings for a variety of unique reasons and circumstances, including poverty, unhealthy family environments, low quality neighborhood public schools, and violent or unproductive community surroundings. The relationship between being on the streets and poverty and unhealthy family and community environments is well documented (Swift 1991, Rizzini 1994, Scheper-Hughes and Hoffman 1994). Although so-called street kids can come from the farthest reaches of rural areas, the majority are born to rural migrant families who reside in urban squatter villages. Accordingly, many end up on the streets of Brazil's larger cities: Rio, São Paulo, Belo Horizonte, Brasilia, Recife, and Salvador. Extreme violence, exploitation, and poor health (including addiction to solvents, high risk to HIV and sexually transmitted diseases, and malnutrition) are some of the daily dangers the youth confront while on the streets.[2]

A further dilemma Brazilian youth face, and the thrust of our research, is the opportunity and desire to continue their education in a formal school setting, despite formidable odds. Many have, at one time or another, been enrolled in school; however, several factors contribute to a lack of student engagement. Personal and familial problems often contribute to sporadic attendance, dropout, or failure to enroll in school at all. For low-income families in general, the opportunity costs of attending school are high; for children attempting to survive on their own, these opportunity costs can be prohibitive. In addition, inflexible curriculum, overcrowded classrooms, and teachers who do not have the resources or time to adequately address the needs and realities of these youth combine to "push" students out of school (Rizzini 1994, Fine 1991).

To better understand the roots of these issues we briefly highlight major initiatives concerning the education of marginalized sectors in Brazilian society. Then, we analyze the significant pieces of federal education legislation enacted between 1995 and 1999 and related policy documents published by the Ministry of Education and the National Education Council. We situate our discussion within a broader and critical analysis of the neoliberal context within which the policy making has occurred. We then describe three possible models for policy and program development processes that target the educational needs and interests of marginalized youth. These models encompass distinct dynamics and power relations among the various actors involved (such as grassroots groups, state agencies, and the children themselves).

One model involves educational work outside the system through a grassroots social movement that adapts its pedagogical method to the "street," enabling a flexible form of learning that can be shaped to the diverse needs and challenging environments of the youth. An example of this model comes from the Movimento Nacional de Meninos/Meninas da Rua (MNMMR or the National Movement of Street Children). A second model arises from the work of an activist state, which deliberately builds a progressive education program around the interests and needs of marginalized communities. The educational initiatives and programs implemented by the Partido dos Trabalhadores (PT, or Workers' Party) administrations in such cities as São Paulo (1989–1993) and Porto Alegre (1992–present) provide compelling examples of this model. A third model involves an active and negotiated partnership between an interested state and a mobilized grassroots group. We describe examples from the collaborative efforts of Projeto Axê and the municipal government of Salvador, Bahia, under the leadership of the Partido da Frente Liberal (PFL, or Liberal Front Party) to illuminate the principle parameters of this third model. We conclude with recommendations for new collaborative forms of policy making, program development, and implementation where grassroots groups and state entities work as partners to fulfill the educational rights of marginalized youth.

Data and methods

The findings and discussions in this chapter draw from archival research and a set of interviews conducted over a four-year period. Archival documents include publications of the Ministerio de Educação e Cultura (MEC, or Ministry of Education and Culture), legislation passed by the Brazilian Congress, MNMMR documents, bulletins, training manuals, and educational materials, and publications of nongovernmental organizations (NGOs) (such as Instituto Paulo Freire [Paulo Freire Institute], Brazil Network, Americas Watch, and Amnesty International) and multilateral institutions (such as United Nations Children's Fund [UNICEF], Inter-American Development Bank [IDB], The World Bank, and the United Nations Development Program [UNDP]). Content analysis was conducted on national legislation and MEC publications. Documents were thoroughly reviewed and analyzed; references to items of interest (such as poverty, the working class, marginalized youth, social class, race, ethnicity, etc.) were identified with a computer-aided word/phrase search as well as through manual review.[3] Program documents and policy materials from MNMMR, Projeto Axê, and the Municipal Secretariats of São Paulo and Porto Alegre were reviewed for basic information about programs and policies. Interviews were conducted with primary informants, particularly Benedito Rodrigues dos Santos, a founder of MNMMR and movement coordinator from 1988–1992; Cesare De Florio La Rocca, Senior Director of Projecto Axê; Paulo Freire, past Municipal Secretary of Education in São Paulo (MSE-SP); Ana Maria Saul, past Director of Technical Orientation, MSE-SP; José Clovis de Azevedo, Municipal Secretary of Education, Porto Alegre (MSE-PA); Antonio Fernando Gouvêa da Silva, technical assistant to MSE-SP (1989–1993) and Secretariats of Education in Angra dos Reis and Porto Alegre; Ana Lucia Amaral, past Sub-Secretary of Education, Minas Gerais; Ramiro Wahrhaftig, Secretary of Science, Technology and Higher Education, Paraná. Interviews were used to supplement and clarify document analysis.

A history of neglect

Brazil's public education system was developed as a project of a liberal state seeking to enhance its own legitimacy, bolster modernization policies, and consolidate a sense of national identity and cohesion (Torres and Puiggrós 1995, Boli and Ramirez 1992). Policy makers framed public education as a tool for human capital development (Schultz 1961), forecasting the pay-off of a productive labor base and increasing social mobility. These idealized objectives for the public education system have fallen far short in reality. Despite significant educational expansion in the 1960s and 1970s, indicators of educational quality and quantity have declined since the 1980s. And, after more than a decade of neoliberal policies, statistics from the mid-1990s paint a grim picture (MEC 1999). Illiteracy stood at 16 percent. Only 50 percent of the children who began elementary school finished all eight grades, and those who finished took an average of twelve years to do so. Teachers as a group were under-prepared to deliver high quality education; on average (and this varies dramatically between regions), teachers had about eight years of schooling themselves resulting in a tenuous grasp of relevant subject matter.[4] Teachers' salaries were famously low. During the 1990s the basic salary was as low as 60 percent of the national minimum wage in some areas (Hanuschek et al. 1996); even when it approximated the national minimum wage, teachers earned so little that they were often forced to work several shifts (most Brazilian schools in urban areas run between two and four shifts per day) (Wong 1995). Minimal investments in basic facilities and instructional materials further contributed to the deterioration of educational quality (Barros and Lam 1996). Federal subsidies of private schools and their graduates' education in federal and state universities further distort educational indicators.[5] The state of education in Brazil prior to 1995 underscored a history of privilege for children from elite groups and a history of neglect for children from working-class and poor families.

A history of struggle

Marginalized groups in Brazil have mobilized against the inequities of this system, protesting from within the injustices of educational policy and working from outside the system to create alternative educational opportunities. Two historical examples illustrate the nature of the popular struggle for basic educational rights. Following World War I, a burgeoning middle and working class, concentrated in rapidly expanding urban centers, mobilized to form the *Escola Nova* movement of the 1920s and 1930s. The *escola novistas* demanded the democratization of access to high-quality education and pedagogical and curricular reforms to link school practices with the economic and social realities of their surrounding communities. These activists scored a major victory in the 1934 constitution that addressed the government's role in setting educational policy and guaranteed universal schooling and government financing (10 percent of revenues for federal government and municipalities, no less than 20 percent for states and the federal district) (Aragão 1985; Helenir 1987).

With the onset of the political regime of the *Estado Novo* (1937–1945) under populist leader Getulio Vargas, any advances made by the *escola novistas* were lost. The constitution of 1937 thwarted the move toward mass education by declaring the freedom of private initiative in education to be a primary goal. Reversing gains made in the 1934 and 1937 constitutions, the Vargas regime legitimated the elite's belief in their exclusive entitlement to high-quality schooling and solidified a system that restricted access to public primary education, reserving entry to the "free" prestigious public universities for those with means to attend private secondary schooling (Helenir 1987).

The *escola novistas* applied pressure to the system. Others chose to initiate efforts outside the system, though the system (that is, the structure of capitalism and associated institutions) was viewed as an eventual target of transformation. Key in these nonformal efforts was the work of Paulo Freire and others involved in the Movimento de Cultura Popular (MCP, or Movement for Popular Culture) of the late 1950s and early 1960s. The *MCP* had roots in the counterhegemonic struggles occurring against the Catholic Church through base ecclesial communities and the grassroots practices of liberation theology. It sought to awaken the critical consciousness of the Brazilian masses through a transformative educational praxis. Popular education á la Freire arose from a political and social analysis of the living conditions of the poor and their outstanding problems (such as unemployment, malnourishment, and poor health), and attempted to engage the poor in individual and collective awareness of those conditions (Freire 1973).

There are key features in this theoretical and practical educational model. The pedagogical practices drew from collective and individual previous experiences (understood as previous knowledge) and stressed work in groups rather than individually. The education provided by these projects is based on the concrete skills or abilities that they try to instill in the poor (such as literacy or numeracy) with experiences designed to arouse pride, a sense of dignity, personal confidence, and self-reliance among the participants. Most importantly, these projects use the development of skills (e.g. literacy) and attitudes (e.g. self-confidence and class awareness) to deepen the students' ability to critically understand and analyze their realities and situations so as to have better prospects of intervening and changing those circumstances (O'Cadiz et al. 1998, Freire 1973). The 1964 military coup d'etat clamped down on the popular education movement and halted important policy changes that were poised to emerge from this movement.

Following the *abertura* (early 1980s), mobilization around issues of educational quality and access have gradually come to occupy a more important position both among grassroots groups and in the state, though their respective foci are decidedly different. Localized grassroots movements (such as in large metropolitan areas like São Paulo) have had active educational initiatives in several instances, particularly related to adult education and literacy.[6] Organizations mobilizing policy makers, such as Conselhos de Secretários de Educação (Councils of State Secretaries of Education, or CONSED), provide a forum for discussion and debate of policies and programs, a sharing of ideas and results, and a force for lobbying federal policy makers and legislators (Plank 1996). Liberal political parties have initiated efforts to democratize access, transform curricula, and enhance the school/community relationship (such as Brizola's Centros Integrados do Educação Pública, CIEP in Rio de Janeiro State). Progressive and radical parties such as the PT have implemented transformative educational projects (discussed below). In the decade following the transition from military rule, such efforts were sporadic and based on local—municipal or state—factors rather than launched in response to leadership demonstrated at the federal level. In the section below, we consider current federal educational policy and discuss the extent to which it charts a new educational course for marginalized youth.

Current federal "policy talk": "Openings" or mandates?

The election of Fernando Henrique Cardoso as President of Brazil in 1995 gave many hope for new federal policies that would vigorously promote equity and social justice, despite the significant political compromises made on the campaign trail. While his administration has not addressed many of the deep structural issues that persistently thwart educational equity (such as public subsidy of private schooling, top-heavy K-16 systems, and lack of articulation among municipal, state, and federal providers, etc.), it has developed a series of policies that promise to substantially affect traditional modes of education in Brazil.

In this section, we analyze "policy talk" (Tyack and Cuban 1995) at the federal level by reviewing several of the major pieces of legislation passed between 1995 and 1999 (with this period representing the legislative cycle of Cardoso's first term). We critique these pieces of legislation not as exemplars of practice but as indicators to local actors of the national priorities and thus the areas earmarked for resources, support, and attention. Thus, despite our careful analysis, we understand that policy talk may differ markedly from institutional practices.

We identify several relevant actors in the policy arena, though our analysis is not exhaustive and does not include all stakeholders in the policy-making process. Primarily, we draw from federal educational legislation passed during the 1995–1999 legislative session and from resolutions and opinion pieces issued by the Ministry of Education and National Education Council, created by national law in 1995 and operating in conjunction with the Ministry of Education. First, we analyze the Lei de Diretrizes e Bases da Educação Nacional (LDB, or National Law of Directives and Bases for Education) and all relevant resolutions. Next, we review the Parametros Curriculares Nacionais (PCN, or National Curriculum Parameters) and accompanying legislation related to teacher education. Finally, we describe other educationally related initiatives such as the school lunch program and a national assessment system. We use two evaluative categories to analyze each piece of legislation, attempting to determine whether elements in the legislation either *mandate* programs or practices to address the educational needs of marginalized youth or *provide an opening* for programming by states, municipalities, or other entities (such as grassroots groups) that could target this population.

It is important to note that this current round of policy making exemplifies an interesting twist on standard issue educational policies articulated by such neoliberal champions as the International Monetary Fund (IMF) and the World Bank (the latter being a major international donor for Brazilian education projects). Carnoy (1999) argues that neoliberal reforms are primarily driven by concerns that are manifested into three policy orientations (1) increased competitiveness, (2) increased efficiency and decreased governmental financing of public goods (e.g., education), and (3) increased equality of opportunity.

Competitiveness-driven and finance-driven reforms both aspire to a similar goal: improve the productivity of labor. The means for doing so differs and competitiveness-driven reforms are more likely to tolerate increased educational spending, whereas finance-driven reforms have as an explicit objective sharp reductions in educational spending, regardless of the effects on educational quality (which will likely be negative but, under this model, predicted as only temporary). In competitiveness-driven reforms, the aim is to improve the quality of labor most typically by increasing educational attainment. Under competitiveness-driven reforms, several key policies are common: decentralization, accountability systems that include standards and routine testing, improved management of educational resources, and enhanced teacher training and recruitment. Finance-driven reforms use a different set of policies: prioritizing funding of lower levels of education over higher levels, privatization of secondary and higher education, and the reduction of costs at all levels of the system.

The third model put forth by Carnoy emphasizes equity and is characterized by such policies as: provision of high-quality basic education to the lowest-income populations including youth and adults without basic skills, and special programming that targets such subsectors of the population as women, rural residents, and students with special needs. Equity-driven reforms are typically the least favored by those following a neoliberal agenda.

In Brazil, the policy elites appear to favor the competitiveness-driven reforms though the process of drafting the legislation discussed below signals important concessions made to those with a more equity-oriented focus. Because of Brazil's strong ties with the World Bank, in particular, the tendency toward competitiveness-driven and finance-driven reforms is strong and evidenced in a series of efforts that mirror those outlined above: decentralization, national standards, national testing, transfer of federal resources to states and municipalities to shore up basic education, and reductions in spending per pupil across the board.

Nevertheless, in drafting the 1996 legislation, involvement of civil actors with a public equity agenda occurred at a high level. Development of the curriculum guidelines (Parâmentros Curriculares Nacionais, or PCN) in particular involved a range of actors known for their activism around equity issues including: Instituto Plural, the Geledés Institute of Black Women, the Institute of Anthropology and the Environment, and the Interministerial Working Group to develop policies valuing the black population (Brooks 2001). Moreover, these guidelines were supervised by the Ministerio de Educação e Cultura (MEC, or Ministry of Education and Culture) and the Conselho Nacional de Educação (CNE, or National Education Council) *in conjunction* with the United Nations Education, Science, and Cultural Organization (UNESCO) and Brazil's National Human Rights Plan (Brooks 2001). It is apparent in the analysis below that the pieces of legislation that emerged during this period were subject to intense negotiation among the various actors as they attempted to find a workable coexistence for their divergent orientations.

Lei de Diretrizes e Bases da Educação Nacional

In 1996, the Brazilian Congress passed Lei 9394, the Lei de Diretrizes e Bases da Educação Nacional (LDB, or National Law of Directives and Bases for Education), outlining curricular, pedagogical, governance, and financial policies for education to be implemented in a decentralized form at the state and municipal levels. Though there had been comprehensive federal education legislation in the past, the scope and specificity of the 1996 LDB was unique (MEC 1999). For those advocating educational change, the passage of the LDB (which had been proposed in prior legislative sessions) was a significant victory. Subsequent legislation in the late 1990s related to curriculum, and teacher preparation added further specificity to the provisions in the LDB. The Cardoso administration developed additional measures to support the reform efforts directed toward schools and universities.

The LDB contains nine titular provisions. The first clarifies the term "education," and defines the basic parameters related to how it occurs, who can provide it, and what its purposes are. Of note in Title I is the explicit identification of social movements as locations in which educational processes occur. Title II of the LDB outlines eleven principles and objectives for the national educational system. They range from guaranteeing equality of conditions related to access and continued enrollment in school and assuring the plurality of ideas and pedagogical concepts to promoting democratic governance of schools and encouraging linkages between education in schools, work, and social practices. *Title II of the LDB offers no mandates* for targeting marginalized youth; but its emphasis on democratic school governance and the linkages between education in schools, work, and *social practices* could provide openings, particularly if, through decentralized implementation in local contexts, grassroots groups are included in democratic governance structures and their educational efforts integrated in some manner into schoolwide projects and initiatives.

In Title III, the LDB spells out the rights of students and the responsibilities of educational institutions. Included in the rights of students are such principles as the provision of free and compulsory education through grade 8 and gradually extending it into the tenth grade, services for students with special needs, free and universal preschool programs, and the availability of educational programs for young adults and working students. Complementing the educational rights of students is a series of articles related to the administrative duties of different levels of the educational system (municipal, state, federal) in guaranteeing maximum access to free public education and to the responsibilities of parents in advocating for students' rights.

Title IV outlines the organization of the educational system delineating responsibility and areas of oversight for municipal, state, and federal educational agencies in the determination of educational standards and assessment processes. *Neither mandates nor openings specifically for marginalized youth appear in Title III or Title IV of the LDB.* Though working youth are identified in Title IV, the government has not traditionally conceptualized this group as part of marginalized youth.

Title V is the most detailed of the provisions in the LDB as it outlines procedures and expectations for content and pedagogy. It is divided into five chapters. The first delineates the two levels of education—pre-kindergarten through the completion of high school and higher education. The second chapter outlines the basic policy for preschool and elementary education, covering such diverse topics as organization of student groups (graded, non-graded, multi-age, etc.), academic calendars, general procedures for judging student competence at various grade levels, student-teacher ratios, strategies for increasing efficiency and reducing grade repetition, curriculum content, and special considerations for rural schools. Chapter 3 guarantees professional education and professional development, either within formal school structures or in the workplace. Chapter 4 focuses on higher education, which is charged with stimulating cultural production and developing students' scientific spirit and reflective thinking. Processes for regular evaluation and accreditation of institutions of higher education are outlined and guidelines for academic calendars, institutional governance, students' rights, faculty rights, and budgeting are presented. Chapter 5 of Title V attends to the provision of special education, with major emphasis on providing for special education students within regular schools and regular education programs. Despite the specificity of Title V of the LDB, marginalized youth do not emerge as a category for special attention. It is curious that in instances where the particular challenges of educating marginalized youth are addressed, as in Chapter 2's discussion of enrollment and repetition, the provisions are quite conventional and speak more to improving efficiency and enrollment processes than to initiating alternative measures such as outreach through community groups or transformation of pedagogy and curricula.

Title VI establishes federal policy for educators and emphasizes two fundamental principles: the links between theory and practice and a professional development trajectory that builds on prior experiences and activities (such as schooling, coursework, professional experience, etc.). Title VII addresses issues related to salaries, budgets, and other expenditures on education. It outlines the funding bases for the educational system and provides a funding formula for federal contributions to various educational programs and to states and municipalities. Title VIII deals with two major items: education for indigenous people and distance education. Titles VI, VII, and VIII of the LDB offer neither mandates nor openings directed towards the educational needs and interests of marginalized youth.

Finally, Title IX is dedicated to the Decade of Education/Education for All proclaimed by the United Nations and details Brazil's response to this mandate. Four major policy statements combine to charge all levels of the system with: enrolling all school age children, providing special courses or distance education to undereducated youth and adults, creating professional development courses and programs for educators, and integrating all of the sites of a jurisdiction within the national system of educational evaluation and production. (Other provisions in Title IX deal with the timeframe for various entities to implement the LDB.) An opening emerges in Title IX of the *LDB* through the references to full enrolment and special courses for undereducated youth, both of which could motivate increased attention to the educational needs and special circumstances of marginalized youth. It is still unclear, however, whether the federal government envisions incremental changes to their existing systems to make them "work better" or whether it will be acknowledged that improvements to a system that has never included marginalized youth are unlikely to create future successes with this population. As the examples from MNMMR below illustrate, marginalized youth, a transient and somewhat resistant group, will likely not respond eagerly to official campaigns touting the benefits of school. Similarly "special courses" must go beyond merely holding school after the work day is completed, particularly if that work day is envisioned in terms of conventional business hours.

Parametros Curriculares Nacionais (National Curriculum Parameters) and related resolutions

In addition to the LDB, subsequent resolutions (specifically Resolution CEB #2, 4/19/99, Resolution CEB #3, 6/26/98, and Resolution CEB #2, 4/7/98) issued by the CNE present detailed directives for national curriculum at the basic and middle levels of the system (prekindergaren through tenth grade). These directives together with the PCN (created by legislative decree and elaborated by the Ministry of Education and CNE) define education as the means for providing the nation's students with preparation for democratic citizenship and the workplace. Core content areas include: Portuguese literature and language, science, mathematics, history, geography, physical education, art, and foreign language. Furthermore, the curriculum is expected to facilitate students' development of creativity, curiosity, innovation, imagination, and appreciation of quality, subtlety, leisure, and sexuality. Several crossdisciplinary themes are identified: ethics, the environment, cultural pluralism, health, sex education, work, and consumption. The PCN delineates the core areas of curriculum content and identifies key student learning outcomes; surprisingly issues of social class, poverty, and marginalized youth do not factor as special categories for consideration.

Finally, the PCN directs educators to develop curriculum according to the twin organizing concepts of interdisciplinarity and contextualization. Interdisciplinarity refers to the creation of curriculum that does not isolate content areas from each other but facilitates the use of multiple disciplines in pursuing knowledge about fundamental issues. Contextualization provides guidance for what those fundamental issues might be—issues that emerge out of the students' reality, the school community, the larger neighborhood. The PCN's twin organizing concepts of *interdisciplinarity* and *contextualization* comprise the first significant mandate in federal policy for both the educational work done by grassroots groups and for the inclusion of marginalized youth and their realities in the day-to-day workings of public classrooms. There are multiple interpretations of these two concepts, however. Because the legislation is rather brief in its explication of them, those with a more critical perspective would appear to have latitude in their interpretation and implementation of these ideas in curriculum development.

From a critical perspective (one that is held by the grassroots groups and the activist states discussed in this text), curriculum that builds on interdisciplinarity and contextualization does several important things vis à vis marginalized youth. Contextualization requires that the educator, via pedagogical strategies and curricular choices, recognize and build on the experiences and knowledge brought to the classroom by marginalized youth; in building on this intellectual and cultural capital, the classroom can be a place where these experiences and this knowledge can be better understood, critiqued, deepened, and consequently elevated in status (Pernambuco 1993, Habermas 1987, Freire 1997). Contextualization also opens up possibilities for the development of curriculum that is oriented toward issues, concepts, and problems present in students' realities rather than focusing on a catalogue of facts and ideas that are distant from and possibly even contradictory to the real interests and needs of this population.

Interdisciplinarity is a logical partner for contextualization. Interdisciplinarity, in its most ample definition, is not merely the de-emphasis of the rigid boundaries artificially separating the disciplines but rather implies an entirely different conceptualization of epistemology and the process of knowledge construction. By its very nature, an interdisciplinary curriculum is one that integrates the analytic tools and knowledge base of various disciplines for the purposes of finding rich solutions and responses to compelling issues and challenges. Thus, interdisciplinarity requires a connection between the social world (relationships, history, culture) and the production of knowledge, and rejects the notion of knowledge as static, a commodity to be deposited into the heads of learners (Faundez 1990, Freire 1990a, Delizoicov 1982, Fazenda 1979, Japiassú 1976).

The federal mandate for educators to develop curriculum that is guided by interdisciplinarity and contextualization legitimates the educational work of grassroots groups and poses a significant challenge to educators in the public school system to transform their educational practice in ways that better meet the educational interests and needs of marginalized youth.

Teacher preparation and professional development
In addition to the basic curricular and organizational parameters established by federal legislation, we include an analysis of federal guidelines for teacher preparation and professional development. There have been significant

changes in this area, and many consider these changes positive (Amaral 1996, Wahrhaftig 2000). The primary thrust of the government's initiatives related to teachers focuses on establishing norms of professionalism through increased certification requirements (all teachers must have a B.A. equivalent and a credential by 2007), increased autonomy to schools and responsibility to teachers to develop site-based education plans, and parameters for monitoring educational quality and maintaining accountability for outcomes.

To accomplish this, the National Education Council's Resolution CEB #2, 4/19/99 related to the LDB identifies a number of policies for teacher preparation and on-going professional development. Article 1 of this resolution reaffirms the necessity of appropriate teacher preparation and content development for prospective teachers; it emphasizes special skills in providing education to indigenous peoples and to students with special needs. In Section 2 of Article 1 states general orienting principles for the educational programs to be developed at educational institutions. Article 2 mandates teacher preparation programs to educate teachers who will be able to develop and evaluate educational programs of high quality; identify and address issues and challenges that emerge in the school setting; use educational practices and strategies that prepare students for their future roles in the social and political world, taking into context their learning styles, socioeconomic reality, cultural diversity, ethnicity, religion, and gender; evaluate program and policy outcomes; and utilize technology.

Article 3 deals with the core curricular areas that future teachers must dominate and urges teacher preparation programs to develop competency-based evaluation systems for their graduates. It sets out minimum requirements for teacher preparation programs. In addition to teaching the curricular areas outlined in the PCN, Section 3, Article 3 of Resolution #2 mandates teacher preparation programs to ground future teachers' studies in the disciplines of philosophy, sociology, history, educational psychology, anthropology, communication, information technology , arts, culture, and linguistics.

Article 4 indicates that there should be coherence among the requirements of practicing teachers (such as participation in school governance, the development of school plans, etc.) and the coursework and field-based experiences of preservice teachers. Article 5 underscores the importance of teacher preparation and establishes the knowledge base found in higher education as the benchmark for teacher professional knowledge.

In Article 6, mandates for school administration are outlined and include: supporting educational practices that foster student independence, and responsibility and ability to be proactive in their social world and consider cultural, socioeconomic, gender and ethnic realities. In developing school-based education plans, educators are urged to consider the school as a social institution with internal dynamics and relationships that extend beyond the school to support human rights, the common good, and democratic order. They are also reminded that students undergo different phases of development that should be taken into consideration when developing school-based plans. Articles 7, 8, 9, and 10 address issues of minimum program requirements, program evaluation, and relationships with other teacher preparation institutions at different levels of the system.

This directive on teacher preparation includes important mandates that have the potential to translate into educational benefits for marginalized youth. Article 2 provides the most forceful language in identifying students' socioeconomic realities as an important variable to be considered in the educational process. Article 2 further directs teacher preparation programs to employ strategies that will make students' socioeconomic reality a part of the learning process. Finally, Article 6 charges school leadership with creating educational programs that foster student independence and ability to be *proactive* in their social world and aware of cultural, socioeconomic, gender, and ethnic realities. The combination of the mandate for interdisciplinarity and contextualization found in the PCN and Articles 2 and 6 in Resolution CEB #2 sends a compelling message about the possibilities for the education of marginalized youth.

Related educational legislation and initiatives

In addition to these major pieces of legislation, the Cardoso administration has pursued supplementary educational initiatives, including the School (Subsidized) Lunch Program and the National Miminum Wage Guarantee program. Investments in the School Lunch Program have been doubled under Cardoso's administration, and resources have been decentralized to the municipal level where local factors can be taken into consideration with regard to schedule and menu (MEC 1999). The National Minimum Wage Program provides families with incomes below the minimum wage with extra subsidies upon monthly proof of matriculation and regular attendance in school of their school-age children. The MEC states that this program has benefited over 500,000 families and has contributed to more stabilized patterns of school attendance, decreased tendencies toward urban flight, and reduced indices of child labor (MEC 1999).

Finally, the Cardoso government, in concert with state governments (e.g., Minas Gerais) and with guidance and resources from international aid agencies like the World Bank, has supported innovative programs at the state level such as the Programa de Aceleração de Aprendizagem (the Accelerated Learning Program) where students who are repeating or at risk of repeating a grade engage in an intensive program of study with teachers who have effective track records and have received specialized training in new methods and strategies (MEC 1999, Amaral 1996). Assessment and evaluation have emerged as a cornerstone of the federal educational initiatives. The Instituto Nacional de Estudos e Pesquisas (INEP, or National Institute for Educational Studies and

Research) has been reoriented to function as an independent entity responsible for the entire system of obtaining, evaluating, and storing information concerning the country's education overall (Souza 2000). One of its core activities is the on-going implementation of the Sistema da Avaliação do Ensino Basico (SAEB, or Evaluation System for Basic Education), which examines pupil performance at elementary and secondary levels. Already, data generated by the SAEB has led the government to declare that it is not access to schooling that must be addressed but the quality of schooling and the experiences of the students once they are actually in school (MEC 1999).

Federal legislation and the MEC supporting documents cover considerable ground and address controversial issues. Unlike analyses of prior national policy making (Plank 1996), our review shows concerted attention in the 1996 LDB to issues related to promoting and enhancing the public good and genuine leadership/accountability for implementation of said policies. There are significant opportunities to increase internal efficiency, articulation, and cohesion. Issues such as special education, education for indigenous peoples, cultural pluralism, and sexual orientation figure prominently in MEC documents and federal legislation. Thoughtful educational programs and accompanying curriculum that respond to the federal mandate will certainly contribute to the robustness of Brazil's emerging democratic institutions and civil society.

Meager beginnings for marginalized youth

In analyzing federal legislation and related policy documents through the lens of the educational needs and interests of marginalized youth, however, it is evident that, despite strong directives in the PCN and Resolution CEB #2, current national policy mostly offers "openings" that might be used by grassroots groups and progressive educators to serve the target population. We interpret these openings as figurative "nods of the head" that indicate that policy makers acknowledge the existence of marginalized youth but continue to use conventional practices to address their concerns. That is, marginalized youth are still conceived of as having dropped out of school or failed to enroll in school rather than being viewed as having been pushed out of a system that is not designed to recognize their unique characteristics and is not flexible enough to bend to serve them adequately (Fine 1991). These openings are new and may signal an important shift both in the potential responsiveness of the system to marginalized youth and in the opportunities available to this group. The future of both push and pull factors must be deliberately addressed if the educational opportunities for marginalized youth are to improve concretely.

Our analysis of educational policy making during this period also highlights apparent tensions within the neoliberal paradigm followed by the Cardoso administration. It is apparent that the elite and powerful in Brazil and beyond (such as multilateral organizations and donor countries) favor the competitiveness- and finance-driven reforms as the most effective path for Brazil's future. However, if this future is to include any measure of hope for the significant numbers of marginalized youth in Brazil, the educational course set by policy makers in Brazil must be steered in part by those who favor equity-driven reforms. One can only surmise that the inclusion of such groups as the Instituto Plural and the use of reference points provided by UNESCO and the Brazil Human Rights Plan forced attention in the policy development phases to issues of educational equity (Brooks 2001). It is our opinion that such equity objectives will only become a part of the educational vision if the government continues to include in its policy-making processes those representatives of civil society that have the most to lose under finance- and competitiveness-driven reforms and the most to gain from increased consolidation of democratic processes and equity-driven reforms. Though Margaret Thatcher, queen mother of neoliberalism, was inclined to declare "there is no alternative" (George 1999), we submit that there are alternatives to neoliberalism that must enter the policy discourse if we are to have a hope of breaking the hegemony of neoliberalism.

In the following section, we offer three models or "responses" that specifically target the education of marginalized children. As the analysis of the LDB, PCN, and related legislation reveals, there are limited mandates and openings in which issues of social class, poverty, and the educational needs of marginalized youth can be inserted into official dialogue and consideration. These models present possibilities for capitalizing on the still narrow policy space devoted to these issues, while simultaneously pressuring official policy makers to expand this space. At the same time, these models represent new ways of envisioning equity-driven policies and programs amidst neoliberal pressures.

Model I

A grassroots answer to educating marginalized youth

During the 1980s, in response to the growing phenomenon of youth seeking the streets in Brazil, the National Movement of Street Children (MNMMR) was formed to encourage so-called street children to acquire the desire to learn and in the process become organized and empowered.[7] MNMMR set out to accomplish this through embracing two pedagogical principles: (1) educational work with street children—as protagonists of the movement—should be developed within the parameters of their realities; and (2) children have legitimate rights and therefore must transform their educational reflection into action and participate as citizens in decisions that affect their lives.[8] Composed of a nationwide coalition of marginalized youth, educators, and advocates, MNMMR has taken the leading position in developing a pedagogy of popular education through which both child and educator learn to exercise citizenship.

Street educators are the social actors that promote this pedagogical process of popular education. The educators have the seemingly impossible task of going to the streets, marketplaces, plazas, and peripheral communities to engage and organize the youngsters. They are trained to adapt teaching methods to these children in the street, rather than expecting the children to conform to a pedagogy developed for those youth in more privileged situations.

Education aimed at marginalized youth cannot be strictly academic. Rather, instruction must gel with the young person's reality and encourage reflection in a manner that informs of guaranteed rights, strengthens ability to combat violence, and enhances competence to organize and mobilize. Street education, however, is not an elementary procedure. A successful pedagogy cannot be secured by simply mastering some methodological rules or following a standard routine. Instead, the educators must be extremely flexible, markedly creative, and engage in a constant process of evaluation, reflection, and refinement. Shadowing Paulo Freire's consciousness raising pedagogy (Freire 1973), the educators develop educational processes together with the youth. Swift (1997, 56) outlines seven Freirean principles that serve as touchstones in the practice of MNMMR's street educators:

1. The educator is not the owner and dispenser of knowledge, but the sharer, facilitator, and companion in the production of knowledge.
2. The educator cultivates respect, acceptance, and solidarity.
3. Children are active participants in their own learning, not passive recipients of ideas and values.
4. Children must be given the opportunity to experience themselves as members and contributors to their communities.
5. In constructing this experience, both the educator and child are learners and undergo transformation. The educator enters into the world of the marginalized youth where there is a simultaneous exploration of an oppressed reality in which they both seek a way out.
6. The educators' authority derives from the fact that they have a wider frame of reference and better access to information. Information should be used in ways the children perceive as valuable.
7. Both the participation and the organization of children are essential components to the process.

The *Nucleo de Base*, or Grassroots Nucleus is what MNMMR calls the organized spaces that street educators and youngsters construct. Benedito Rodrigues dos Santos, founder and national coordinator (1988–1992) of MNMMR, explains the *Nucleo*'s pedagogical purposes:

1. *Education for Citizenship.* The children learn to become part of a decision-making process;
2. *Mutual Support.* The children develop collective forms of solidarity through the exercise of mutual assistance; and,

3. *Referral for Services.* MNMMR does not provide basic services for children (food, shelter, clothing); therefore, the *Nucleo* serves as a safe, legitimate space where children can exchange information regarding service providers throughout their communities (dos Santos 1998).

Within the *Nucleos*, any one of four popular education projects is carried out. The projects are constructed to encourage the active participation of the youth. They afford children the opportunity to become a subject in the process of changing their own realities through identifying contradictions in their experiences. These methods are not just used for the children, but also by the children (MNMMR 1995):

1. *Pedagogical Workshops.* Workshops encourage a critical awareness among the youth, particularly relating to their lack of access and opportunity. The pedagogy is strongly oriented toward the experiences and perceptions of the group. The *Nucleos* understand the importance of including the families and communities within their pedagogy for change. Popular themes include children's rights as set forth in the Estatuto de Criança e Adolescente (ECA, or Child and Adolescent Statute),[9] prevention against the use and abuse of drugs, sex education, and the prevention of STDs.

2. *Cultural Activities.* A wide array of cultural activities are developed, including plastic art, painting, sculpture, *capoeira* (an Afro-Brazilian martial art/dance form), and popular theater that explores different dramatization techniques such as the Theater of the Oppressed.[10] The objectives of these activities are three-fold. First, artistic expression enhances the children's understanding of a topic or theme while at the same time building a strong bond within the group. Second, the activities are undertaken to celebrate and preserve the artistic aspects of Brazilian popular culture. Finally, the fun-filled, creative activities allow the youth to reclaim elements of their childhood, lost to their struggle to survive.

3. *Recreation, Sports, and Leisure.* The use of creative games, *brincadeiras* (improvised get-togethers), circus skills, and various sports provide an informal, participatory means of communication that enables the children to become more familiar with one another and more comfortable interacting in a group. Through participatory games, the children understand other members' realities, express their feelings, construct their identities, and develop dreams and aspirations. This project also cultivates democratic principles: cooperation, respect for others, and articulation of opinions and concerns.

4. *Defense of Children's Rights.* This pedagogical project seeks to educate and empower the youth to recognize and claim their rights as set

forth in the ECA. This is accomplished principally by disseminating information on the statute through debates, seminars, group dialogue, instructional manuals, and books. The objective of these activities is to inform, educate, and promote compliance with the mandates of *ECA*. Similar to the other three, this project respects the reality of the youth. As well, and in an effort to involve the community, activities are usually realized in community centers and schools.

The MNMMR provides a model for effective and progressive educational work with marginalized youth that occurs almost entirely outside of the formal system. This model is not viable on a large-scale or long-term basis or as a permanent solution to the challenges of educating marginalized youth. However, MNMMR offers several important lessons, particularly for those in the formal education system. MNMMR demonstrates that marginalized youth *can* be engaged in a structured and deliberate process of education to reach such goals outlined in the LDB and PCN as the creation of citizens for a democracy and youth with a sense of curiosity, creativity, and innovation. The MNMMR experience also highlights that this group has unique characteristics, needs, and dynamics that must be understood to ensure the success of any educational endeavor.

Finally, the MNMMR success underscores the importance of two important political dimensions of becoming educated. On one hand, the MNMMR models a creative, flexible form of education that simultaneously celebrates childhood and promotes a critical awareness (Balestino 1998). On the other, a formal space is created for youth to become more literate and/or numerate. Within this model, the orientation of MNMMR's critical pedagogy and its political emphasis necessitates formal learning in a manner that diversifies and amplifies the youngsters' abilities and skills set. True to its popular education roots, MNMMR constructs a political-pedagogical program that enables both teacher and student the opportunity to become citizens, and as such, better able to participate in decision-making processes that affect their lives.

Model II

The activist state

The creation of state initiatives targeted toward marginalized youth has been most evident in the municipal administrations of the Partido dos Trabalhadores (PT, or Workers' Party). Formed in 1980, the Workers' Party is anchored by the country's militant and radical trade unions but is also supported by organizations from poor communities and the middle-class intellectual elite (primarily university faculty). In 1989, the PT scored its first major political victory with the election of its candidate, Luiza Erundina, as mayor of the city of São Paulo. She in turn appointed internationally renowned educator, Paulo Freire, as secretary of education and his administration created a series of initiatives and reforms for the city's public schools. These reforms pursued five major objectives: (1) increased access to schooling, (2) democratization of school administration, (3) improved quality of instruction, (4) education for working youths and adults, and, (5) the formation of critical and responsible citizens (Secretaria 1990). To create a viable base for achieving these objectives, Freire's administration pursued several concrete financial initiatives, including securing the 25 percent of the municipal budget constitutionally mandated for educational expenditures but either not requested or not allocated during prior administrations (Freire 1990b). Significant allocations from this budget targeted teachers' salaries (which increased an incredible 112 percent in real terms during the first year of his administration and another 30 percent during the third year); modernizing school facilities (building repairs, new chairs and desks, etc.); providing instructional materials; and purchasing and installing computers and other forms of technology (O'Cadiz et al. 1998). These investments in the teaching and learning environment and the increased status that they provided teachers were necessary preconditions for the ambitious curriculum reform initiated by Freire's administration (detailed below).

The *Projecto da Interdisciplinaridade* (the Interdisciplinary Project, the "Inter Project") was the major vehicle for creating a popular public school, the major objective orienting all reform efforts in the elementary schools. This project used intensive teacher professional development (through the *Grupos de Formação*—Formation Groups—that met ten hours weekly) and an elaborated three-step process (study of the reality, organization of knowledge, and application of knowledge) to reorient the school curriculum, and with it pedagogical and organizational practices at the sites toward the educational needs and interests of low-income and working-class students. Though working within a formal and elementary education system, the Inter Project genuinely expressed the most compelling and transformative elements of its educational ancestor, popular education. (For further discussion, see O'Cadiz et al. 1998).

The São Paulo experience was relatively brief (1989–1993). However, its major innovations (the public popular school, interdisciplinary curriculum via generative themes, teacher formation groups, democratization of governance, etc.) have had continuity in the educational initiatives implemented by subsequent PT administrations in other cities. The PT administration in Porto Alegre (1992–present), for example, has greatly expanded some of the components piloted in São Paulo (Azevedo 1998). School governance and district-wide policy making have been further democratized in both their micro and macro dimensions. School site councils are mandated to have broad representation from school faculty and staff as well as from students and the community. School site councils now have wide authority over the school budget, which has been expanded through the decentralization of funds from the central administration. School directors (principals) are elected by the community at large and the hiring of other school faculty and staff is done through the site council. Porto Alegre added another innovation: a sophisticated system of periodic regional forums and municipal congresses that operate as a participatory system for developing policy objectives and formulating plans. Representatives from school sites attend these gatherings and use data and experiences to create and refine policy around such questions as: What are the features of the schools we currently have? To what extent do they serve the interests of popular classes? What are the features of the schools we would like to have? What initiatives will we need to transform our existing schools and how will we know we have accomplished this transformation? (Azevedo 1998) Further, practices piloted in the educational sector have influenced policy making in other arenas, including the development of municipal budget priorities that is now a regular participatory process.

In this model, an activist and progressive state creates a change agenda in which policy making and program development deliberately take on the challenges and contradictions facing the working class and the poor. Attempts are made to dismantle the historic structures that concentrate power and resources in the hands of the elite, devolving power to the base while simultaneously working to build their capacity for genuine participation. In this model, teachers and associated educators (e.g., administrators) are viewed as the focal actors in school and social change. Efforts are made to develop their skills and enhance their authority in intervening in the key teaching and learning dimensions of schooling. The concerns of the working class and the poor are deliberate targets for this intervention and more democratic and participatory means of decision making are developed as safeguards against co-optation or paternalism.

Model III

Partnership in pedagogy—grassroots and state

In our final model we find a culmination of the previous two: grassroots pedagogy and state mandates. This ongoing partnership unites the municipal government of Salvador, Bahia—through the Secretary of Education (under the municipal administration of the Partido da Fronte Liberal, PFL)—and *Projeto Axê* (Project Axê).[11] As a nongovernmental actor, *Projeto Axê* is bridging the space between innovative grassroots actors and the public sector. Contrary to focusing efforts exclusively on providing services, *Axê* strives to form partnerships with the public sector and incorporate into policy innovative pedagogical practices that target marginalized youth. Such coalitions seek to engage the public sector in policy dialogue and demonstrate "where there is a *will* to educate these youth, there is a *way*" (La Rocca 1999).

Following in the pedagogical footsteps of MNMMR, *Projeto Axê*'s initial activities (in the early 1990s) were aimed at Salvador's high concentration of children in the streets. *Axê*'s trained educators went to the streets to begin an educational process with the youth. Similar to MNMMR, *Axê*'s educators stimulate youth to develop an interest in learning through nonformal methods of education—always aimed at awakening critical curiosity in the youth regarding the conditions they face (Swift 1997, Balestino 1998).

Today, street education is still very much a part of the project. However, *Axê* has expanded its pedagogical reach to public schooling and established what is called the "School Monitoring Program"—a program carried out in partnership with the Salvador Municipal Secretariat of Education. The School Monitoring Program is an alliance between *Projeto Axê* and over sixty public schools in the city of Salvador. Within the program, *Axê* assumes three interdependent roles, operating as (1) a catalyst to increase the enrollment of marginalized children and adolescents into the public school system, (2) a bridge to strengthen relationships among the child, family, and school, and, (3) a trainer to empower teachers to learn alternative pedagogical techniques and utilize them in the formal school setting.

Once the marginalized children become involved in *Axê*, via the street educators' outreach efforts, *Axê* staff use a series of activities and strategies—what the project calls the Pedagogy of Desire—to awaken the youth's desire to enroll in public school.[12] Once enrolled in a partnering school, the children spend mornings in classes of formal instruction, while afternoons are devoted to complementary education in the arts: Afro-Brazilian culture, dance, music, theater, and fashion. This mixture of formal and nonformal education enriches the students' learning and increases the likelihood they will stay in school. Moreover, *Axê*'s presence within schools provides students with an advocate that reinforces the notion that these children have rights, desires, and life experiences that must be creatively addressed within educational practices (La Rocca 1999). Throughout this initial process, *Axê* remains involved with the students and ensures that there is a continued space for the children to learn and contribute within school.

Axê also acts to facilitate the participation of *family with child* and *community with school*, specifically through the School Monitoring Program. In order for children to become legally enrolled in public school, the state requires that a legal guardian sponsor them. Working together, *Axê* and the public schools use this requirement as a vehicle to reconnect the family with the marginalized child and encourage family participation within school. Because of *Axê*'s connection to the community, its educators are able to make sponsorship a reality. By encouraging dialogue between family and child, adults are made aware of the child's desire to enroll in school and the absolute necessity of their participation. This process has the potential of yielding three interconnected outcomes: first, the family member enrolls the child in school, resulting in increased interest on the part of families in the education of their children; next, *Axê*, the school, and parents develop a partnership whereby family members are encouraged to actively participate within the school; and third, a healthy space is constructed for potential reintegration of the child into his or her family.

Axê's final role demonstrates its intent to move beyond merely generating school enrollment and monitoring students' progress. Accordingly, public school teachers receive training on alternative methods of education for children who seek the streets. This occurs by inviting teachers to observe numerous forms of educational and evaluative methodologies carried out in *Axê*'s outreach centers. As well, *Axê* educators are invited into the schools to hold training on such various topics as children's rights, conflict resolution, or mediation strategies. As teacher trainers, *Axê* is seeking to incorporate its pedagogical success in educating marginalized youth into the formal school system. It is a political project that aims to change practice by training the school community to better educate and evaluate these children.

Axê's goal is to build a new model of education—together with the Municipality of Salvador—that affords marginalized children the chance to enroll and remain in formal educational settings. This is accomplished by using the strengths and experiences of both partners resulting in education that blends formal instruction with nonformal pedagogical methods. Due to its success in Salvador, *Projeto Axê* has received numerous requests to replicate its programs nationally and regionally (La Rocca 1999). Notwithstanding, the guiding principle is that replicating projects will not solve the so-called street kids dilemma. Instead, the solution must come from cooperative efforts between civil society and the public sector that translate into relevant, sustainable public policy.

The partnership between *Axê* and the municipality of Salvador represents our third model of ensuring basic educational rights for marginalized youth. In this model, the liberatory education processes common to progressive nonformal educational efforts have occupied a space in the formal system, potentially providing marginalized youth and other students with opportunities to benefit from the strengths of the two paradigms. Though this model shares elements with the second model, particularly as it has been enacted in São Paulo and Porto Alegre, a unique dynamic is the feature of grassroots groups operating in the public schools, in an integrated rather than additive manner and with continued control over the content and method of instruction of their particular component.[13] Further, in this third model, the partnership occurs not with an activist state, as may be ideal, but with a state that is relatively centrist in its leanings and thus, more representative of the political dynamics in the majority of regions in the nation.

Forging new partnerships

Each of the models above offers a distinct response to the educational needs of marginalized youth. The MNMMR is a case of liberatory education that unfolds outside of the formal system. In São Paulo and Porto Alegre an activist state deliberately reorients policy making and program development toward the interests of marginalized youth. The Project Axê–City of Salvador partnership joins a grassroots popular education effort with a centrist state to transform teaching and learning in classrooms.

Further, these models can act as exemplars for ways in which social movements, NGOs and other community organizations can further goals of educational equity despite persistent pressures for competitive- and finance-focused neoliberal policies.In each model, increased educational equity for marginalized youth is achieved in part because the process of policy and program development includes advocates (such as social movements and nongovernmental organizations, NGOs) for this population who articulate an alternative vision of the teaching and learning process and its outcomes. With the inclusion of a broad range of actors in the development of the LDB and the PCN, there is now a precedent at the federal level for a policy process that attempts to be democratic; the models we have presented also demonstrate the feasibility of this approach at local levels. It is imperative that advocates for marginalized children maintain pressure relentlessly on policy makers to be included in all phases of policy development and implementation and that they bring to this process their practical examples of educational work with marginalized children.

An ultimate objective would therefore be to create a much larger space in which a state-level commitment to the education of marginalized youth interacts cooperatively with the transfer of local knowledge and methodologies of the grassroots groups. We propose a collaborative process for policy making that integrates (but does not co-opt) grassroots expertise into formal policy and program development and implementation. Such a process is fraught with difficulties and possible contradictions, as grassroots groups often pursue outcomes that run contrary to state objectives and work under conditions that allow for more flexibility than formal bureaucracies (for in-depth analyses of state-grassroots partnerships, particularly those pursued by the PT in São Paulo, see O'Cadiz et al. 1998, Stromquist 1996, O'Cadiz 1994). We believe there are structured ways for grassroots groups and activist states to work in conjunction toward improved educational opportunities for marginalized youth. Several parameters are worth noting.

First, let us highlight the relative strengths of each entity. Grassroots groups tend to adapt their interventions to the needs of local communities. Their strength lies in tapping into the knowledge base at the local level and forming programs and initiatives that address concrete needs and issues. Also, grassroots groups are often more democratic in the processes that they use for knowledge transmission and construction and for organizational governance. As a result, they have more extensive and meaningful connections and working relationships with the population they serve and other important actors and groups in the local context. For example, important guidelines in the development of educational projects for the MNMMR include: (1) program goals formulated in conjunction with the youth that prioritize the empowerment and conscientization processes, (2) program curriculum that accounts for students' personal histories and particular realities and considers their level of emotional, social, and educational development, (3) the creation of a space that allows children to fully experience their reality and their stage of development, (4) the development of skills that empower youth to improve their conditions through formal political channels and informal actions, and (5) continual evaluation of program activities, particularly as they relate to the long- and short-term impact on the youth involved.

By contrast, governments have more comprehensive power; only states have the capacity to generate improvements in education on the scale required. It is the primary responsibility of the national government to create a policy framework in which marginalized children have quality access to public classrooms. The state has considerable resources, structures, and programs with which to shape educational efforts. Grassroots activists and others with a focus on educational equity for marginalized children must continue to demand a role in the decision-making process that allocates these resources and programs.

What are the potential benefits of a collaborative partnership between the state and grassroots groups? Grassroots groups have much to offer in the way of ideas for improving the relevance of curricula and teaching materials, the standard of teaching, and the motivation and engagement of marginalized children. The state can offer models and structures that allow grassroots groups to improve their programming, scale up their offerings, and enter into the policy dialogue. Both entities will need to work together to monitor a space for collaborative dialogue and co-constructed policies and programs in order to create new educational possibilities for marginalized youth.

Notes

This chapter was a collaborative effort and represents equal levels of commitment and work, despite the order of names in the title. We would like to recognize the courageous work of marginalized youth and their allies and hope that this text furthers, in some way, their struggle.

1. The term "street children" embraces girls and boys whose ages range from preschooler to late adolescent. Their situation can vary from those who are truly living on the streets, to those who work on the streets to support their families, to those who engage in illegal activities at the command of adults or for their own survival. Within this analysis we will largely use marginalized youth to incorporate the broad spectrum of children from popular classes who are dislocated from social, political, and economic opportunities, and thus denied their rights as children.

2. With this in mind, it is important to note that the image of street kids promoted by the media and the political system typically characterizes them in a dichotomous fashion: either as victims of their surroundings (the *problems of* street kids) or as threats to society (street kids *as the problem*). Rarely are the youth portrayed, as the bearer of a unique personal identity, complete with particular needs, special talents, and distinguished abilities.

3. Because of the substantial overlap between people of color, particularly those of Afro-Brazilian descent, and people in lower-income social classes (Puryear 1996), we also included race and ethnicity as key words in our analysis. They are used in this context as a proxy for social class.

4. A study on teacher knowledge revealed less than stellar results on a fourth grade criterion-referenced test, with scores in the Portuguese section in the 75 percent range and scores in the math section in the 87 percent range (Hanuschek, Gomez-Neto, and Harbison 1996).
5. Though federal universities do not charge tuition, admission is intensely competitive and generally unattainable for students who have not had access to high-quality private schooling or expensive preparatory courses for the *vestibular*, the national entrance exam (Plank 1996, Saúl 1992).
6. The most notable efforts include the work of the Movimento de Educação de Base (MEB), which is linked to the National Conference of Bishops of Brazil, *Centros de Movimentos Populares* (Center for Popular Movements), and São Paulo's Movimento de Alfabetização de Jovens e Adultos (MOVA, Movement for Youth and Adult Literacy) (see O'Cadiz 1994 and Stromquist 1997 for further description and analysis).
7. Empowerment in this context will be taken to signify the power to participate, the mastery of a skill, and the acquisition of political competence—which includes the ability to mobilize others.
8. The word "citizen" has a specific cultural dimension in Brazil, expressing the nation's aspiration for economic and social justice. Therefore, children as citizens implies that children should be able to participate in decision-making processes that affect their lives. In order to guarantee this, they must be granted full citizenship: the right to speak and act for themselves.
9. The ECA overturned long-standing Brazilian traditions in juvenile justice and child protection. ECA is broken down into three parts—all relating to the rights of children: (1) *Basic Social Policies* designed to protect the civil liberties of all children without regard to economic status, (2) *Social Assistance Policies* ensure that economically depressed children and their families receive a minimum level of well-being that preserves their dignity, and (3) *Special Protection Policies* directed toward children at personal and social risk such as drug addicts, homeless, orphans, children in institutions, victims of discrimination, negligence, and abuse. For more, see Irene Rizzini et al., "Brazil: A New Concept of Childhood," in Cristina Szanton Blanc, *Urban Children in Distress: Global Predicaments and Innovative Strategies* (Florence: UNICEF, 1994); Antonio Carlos Gomes Da Costa and Barbara Schmidt-Rahmer, "Brazil: Children Spearhead A Movement for Change," in *The Convention: Child Rights and UNICEF Experience at the Country Level* (Florence: UNICEF, 1991).
10. The creator of popular theater is Augusto Boal. For a complete understanding of his theatrical method see Augusto Boal, *Theater of the Oppressed* (New York, N.Y.: Theater Communications Group, Inc., 1979).
11. It is worth noting that the PFL, though it has a liberal political agenda, does not advocate radical systemic transformation, as does the PT. Thus, it is significant that this party engages in a transformative partnership with a grassroots organization.
12. *Axé*'s Pedagogy of Desire is a series of creative pedagogical steps designed ultimately to empower the youth to desire to learn. This takes place through three levels: (1) *Pedagogy of Stimulation*: a series of creative steps which builds confidence between the child and *Axé*; (2) *Pedagogy of Love*: encompasses such activities as securing or creating a birth certificate, receiving medical attention, and becoming aware of rights; and (3) *Pedagogy of Comfort*: targets specific skills training, reintegration into formal schools, and if feasable, reintegration into families.
13. Indeed, the PT administrations in both São Paulo and Porto Alegre have done groundbreaking work with state/grassroots partnerships, particularly in the area of adult education through MOVA. We have chosen to use the *Axé*-City of Salvador model instead because of its explicit focus on marginalized youth (in this case, typically street children) and because it has entered into a partnership not with an activist state but a state that is centrist to liberal in its ideology.

References

Amaral, Ana Lucia. (1996). Former sub-secretary of education, Minas Gerais. Personal Interview. September 19.

Aragão, R. (1985). "A instrução pública no Brasil." Rio de Janeiro: Editora de Fundação Getulio Vargas.

Arnove, R., P. Altbach, and G. Kelly, eds. (1992). *Emergent Issues in Education. Comparative Perspectives*. New York: SUNY Press.

Azevedo, J. C. (1998). Secretary of education, Porto Alegre. Personal interview. April 12, San Diego, CA.

Balestino, R. (1998). *Children, Conscientization, and Citizenship: A Case Study of Brazil's National Movement of Street Children.* Master's thesis. Sacramento: California State University.

Barros, R. and D. Lam. (1996). "Income and Educational Inequality and Children's Schooling Attainment." In Birdsall and Sabot, ed. *Opportunity Foregone: Education in Brazil.* Washington, D.C.: Inter-American Development Bank.

Birdsall, N., B. Bruns, and R. Sabot. (1996). "Education in Brazil: Playing a Bad Hand Badly." In Birdsall and Sabot, eds. *Opportunity Foregone: Education in Brazil.* Washington, D.C.: Inter-American Development Bank.

Boli, J. and Ramirez, F. (1992). "Compulsory Schooling in the Western Cultural Context." In Robert Arnove, Philip Altbach, and Gail Kelly, eds. *Emergent Issues in Education: Comparative Perspectives.* New York: SUNY Press.

Brooks, A. (2001). "Brazil's Politics of Educational Reform and New Discourse on Race and Rights: The National Curriculum Guidelines of 1997." Master's thesis. Stanford, Calif.: Stanford University.

Carnoy, M. (1999). *Globalization and Educational Reform: What Planners Need to Know.* Paris: UNESCO.

Delizoicov, D. (1982). *Concepção Problematizadora para o Ensino de Ciências na Educação Formal.* Master's thesis. São Paulo: Universidade de São Paulo.

de Freitas, L. (1988). "A questão da interdisciplinaridade: Notas para a reformulação dos cursos de pedagogia." (Mimeograph). Campinas: Universidade Federal.

dos Santos, B., Movement coordinator and founder, MNMMR. Personal interview. Berkeley, CA, May 27, 1998.

Faundez, A. "Dialogo e Multidisciplinaridade." (Mimeograph).

Fazenda, I. (1979). "*Integração e interdisciplinaridade no ensino brasileiro.*" São Paulo: Loyola.

Fine, M. (1991). *Framing Dropouts. Notes on the Politics of an Urban High School.* New York: SUNY Press.

Fischman, R., ed. (1987). *Escola Brasileira: Temas e Estudos.* São Paulo: Atlas.

Freire, P. (1973). *Education for Critical Consciousness.* New York: The Seabury Press.

Freire, P. (1990a). *Pedagogy of the Oppressed.* New York: Continuum.

Freire, P. (1990b). Personal interview. São Paulo, October 3.

Freire, P. (1997). Politics and Education. Trans. Pia Wong. Los Angeles: UCLA Latin American Center Publications.

George, S. (1999). "A Short History of Neoliberalism." Conference on Economic Sovereignty in a Globalizing World. March 24–26. www.globalpolicy.org/globaliz/econ/histneol.htm.

Gomes da Costa, Antonio. (1997). *Niños y niñas de la calle: Vida, pasion y muerte.* Argentina: UNICEF.

Gouvêa da Silva, Antonio Fernando. (1991 and 1992). Technical advisor. Secretaries of education. São Paulo, Porto Alegre. Personal interviews. September 15 and October 10.

Habermas, J. (1987). *The Theory of Communicative Action.* Vol. 2. *Lifeworld and System: A Critique of Functionalist Reason.* Trans. Thomas McCarthy. Boston: Beacon Press.

Hanuschek, E., J. Gomez-Neto, and R. Harbison. (1996). "Efficiency-Enhancing Investments in School Quality." In Birdsall and Sabot, ed. *Opportunity Foregone: Education in Brazil.* Washington, D.C.: Inter-American Development Bank.

Helenir, S. (1987). "A Educação nas Constituições Brasileiras." In Fischman, ed. *Escola Brasileira: Temas e Estudos.* São Paulo: Atlas.

Japiassú, H. (1976). *Interdisciplinaridade e patologia do saber.* Rio de Janeiro: Imago.

La Rocca, C. (1999). Senior director, Project Axé. Personal interview. August 9.

MEC. Ministerio de Educação e Cultura. (1999). *Educação Brasileira: Políticas e Resultados.* Brasilia: author.

MNMMR. Movimento Nacional de Meninos/Meninas da Rua. (1995). "Dez Anos de Movimento Nacional de Meninos/Meninas da Rua-1985/1995" Brasilia: author.

O'Cadiz, M. (1994). "Literacy, Social Movements, and Class Consciousness: Paths from Freire and the São Paulo Experience." *Anthropology & Education Quarterly* 25, no. 3; September.

O'Cadiz, M., P. Wong, and C. Torres. (1998). *Education and Democracy: Paulo Freire, Social Movements, and Educational Reform in São Paulo.* Boulder, Colo.: Westview Press.

Pernambuco, M. (1993). "Significações e Realidade: Conhecimento (a construção coletiva do programa)." In Nidia Nacib Pontuschka, ed. *Osadia no Diálogo: Interdisciplinaridade na escola pública.* São Paulo: Loyola.

Plank, D., J. Sobrinho, and A. Xavier. (1996). "Why Brazil Lags Behind in Educational Development." In Birdsall and Sabot, eds. *Opportunity Foregone: Education in Brazil.* Washington, D.C.: Inter-American Development Bank.

Puryear, J. (1996). *Implementing the Summit of the Americas: Reforming Educational Systems.* Miami: University of Miami, North-South Center.

Rizzini, I., et al. (1994). "Brazil: A New Concept of Childhood." In Cristina Szanton Blanc. *Urban Children in Distress: Global Predicaments and Innovative Strategies.* Florence: UNICEF.

Saúl, Ana Maria. (1992). Former director of technical orientation, municipal secretariat of education, São Paulo. Personal interviews. São Paulo. August–October.

Scheper-Hughs, N., D. Hoffmanm. (1994). "Kids Out of Place." In *NACLA* (May/June).

Schultz, T. (1961). "Investment in Human Capital." *American Economic Review* 51 (March): 1–17

Secretaria Municipal de Educação. (1990). *Cadernos de Formação: Um primeiro olhar sobre o projeto.* São Paulo: author.

Souza, P. (2000). "Education As a Key Tool for Development in the 21st Century." In *Education in Brazil: Reforms, Advances, and Perspectives.* Washington D.C.: IDB Brazil Seminar (April 11).

Stromquist, N. (1997). *Literacy for Citizenship: Gender and Grassroots Dynamics in Brazil.* New York: SUNY Press.

Swift, A. (1991). *Brazil: The Fight for Childhood in the City.* Florence: UNICEF.

Swift, A. (1997). *Children for Social Change.* Nottingham: Educational Heretics Press.

Torres, C. and Puiggrós. (1995). "The State and Public Education in Latin America." Introduction to the special issue on Latin America of the *Comparative Education Review* 39, no. 1, (February): 1–27.

Tyack, D. and L. Cuban. (1995). *Tinkering Towards Utopia.* Cambridge, Mass.: Harvard University Press.

Wahrhaftig, Ramiro. (2000). Secretary of science, technology, and higher education, Paraná. Personal interview. June 4.

Wolfensohn, J. (1999). President, The World Bank Group. "Remarks at the Council of the Americas." Washington, D.C., May 3.

Wong, P. (1995). "Constructing a Public Popular Education: Implementation of the Interdisciplinary Project in São Paulo Public Schools." *Comparative Education Review* 39, 1 (February).

4

A Local Reform Goes Global

The Politics of Escuela Nueva

PATRICK J. McEWAN
LUIS BENVENISTE

This chapter explores the history and politics of rural school reform in Colombia, focusing on the *Escuela Nueva* program. In particular, it assesses the motivations of the Colombian State in promoting a comprehensive reform of its rural schools. We argue that Colombia's unique political context was, in large part, responsible for its novel approach to school reform. As the political context shifted, however, so to did the state's posture to rural schooling. We track the *Escuela Nueva* program through three phases (grassroots, formalized, and decoupled) to demonstrate how social actors, their interests at specific points in time, and the distribution of power among them, are crucial elements for understanding the motivation and outcomes of social policy making. In other words, this research portrays education reform as a dynamic process that is continuously shaped and reshaped as political actors and institutions compete for influence and scarce resources in a variable social arena.

What motivates the state to pursue education reform? There are multiple theoretical answers to this question that often yield conflicting answers. Many adopt the functionalist view, implicitly or explicitly, that education reform is a technical means for states to promote economic and social development (see, for example, Cook 1991, for a critique of this position). In contrast, world institutionalists view reform as the result of attempts by governments to "appear" modern by adopting the signals of modernity (Meyer et al. 1997). Marxist analyses have a less benign view of state attempts to reform education (Bowles 1980, Bowles and Gintis 1976, Gintis and Bowles 1988). They interpret reform as the state's attempt to foster a hidden curriculum that promotes correspondence between the needs of capitalist production and the characteristics and attitudes of workers. Still other theorists interpret reform as a state response to a growing crisis of legitimation. For example, Jansen (1990) and Weiler (1993) explore why governments undertake programs of decentralization and curricular reform, finding the answer in the state's attempts to "retrieve its eroding legitimacy" (Jansen 1990, 30).

This chapter is not theoretical, but it attempts to shed light on these perspectives by closely examining the genesis and development of a particular education reform: the *Escuela Nueva* program in Colombia. As in many countries of Latin America, rural areas in Colombia are educationally and economically disadvantaged relative to cities. In contrast to other countries, the Colombian state has energetically pursued rural school reform in the guise of the *Escuela Nueva* program. The reform endowed rural, multigrade schools with special training and instructional materials. Its stated objectives were to encourage links between the school and community, and to promote new instructional strategies among rural teachers, including classroom discussions, work in small groups, and independent student research.

Independent evaluations find that *Escuela Nueva* has improved the academic achievement of participating students, compared with students in traditional rural schools (McEwan 1998a,b, Psacharopoulos, Rojas, and Vélez 1993). This occurred even though the program was, on occasion, not fully implemented (Benveniste and McEwan 2000). As a pedagogical model, *Escuela Nueva* is frequently cited as an example of "best practice" for other developing countries (Carnoy and de Moura Castro 1996, Lockheed and Verspoor 1991, 158–161, World Bank 1995, 61–62), and it has been replicated in several countries of Latin America and around the world.

This chapter assumes a broader perspective than prior work by exploring the historical and political context of multigrade schooling in Colombia. In doing so, it assesses the motivations of the Colombian state in promoting a comprehensive reform of its rural schools. The particular political context of Colombia largely shaped its innovative approach to school reform and rural development. But as the political environment changed, so to did the state's position toward rural schooling. This inevitably transformed the nature and extent of the *Escuela Nueva* program. At various points in time, different theories provide an attractive framework for "explaining" why the Colombian state did or did not promote rural schooling. Ultimately, however, the analysis emphasizes the importance of the historical and political context in comprehending the underlying logic that fuels educational change. Both elements are essential ingredients for understanding rural school reform. Education reform is a dynamic and malleable process, continuously adapting and adjusting, as political actors and institutions vie over the control of resources and influence in a shifting social environment.

To develop the arguments, the second part describes the political context in which the *Escuela Nueva* program was conceived. The third part focuses specifically on the evolution of multigrade school reform, identifying several "stages of development" between 1960 and the mid 1990s. The fourth part discusses the evolving motives of the Colombian state for promoting rural education reform in greater detail, as well as the relative influence of international organizations in Colombia and elsewhere. The final part summarizes and concludes.

The Colombian political context

Colombian educational development is inextricably linked to its political development, particularly the waves of political violence that have engulfed rural areas of the country since the beginning of the century. Thus, we begin with some political context, relying heavily on the accounts of Bushnell (1993) and Hanson (1986).

Colombia has traditionally been a country of great inequality, particularly between urban and rural areas. The latter were, and still are in most cases, economically and geographically isolated from urban areas. Education, too, has been relatively disadvantaged in rural areas. In 1903 the Organic Law of Public Education established the groundwork for the modern system of education (Hanson 1986). Though not compulsory until 1927, education was declared free and given to the control of state governments. The law further legislated that urban primary schools were to provide six years of education, while rural schools were to provide only three. One author, cited in Hanson (1986), asserts that

> In reality that law reveals [a] disinterest in rural education, a disinterest based on an ideology intended to justify and legitimate a social structure, and especially an agrarian structure, inherited from the colonial period. The perpetuation of rural illiteracy is one of the elements that permits the conservation of a traditional rural society. It slows horizontal movement (rural to urban), and vertical movement (aspirations for land redistribution).[1]

Enrollments in primary education began to grow sharply after 1945, though growth was less pronounced in rural areas.[2] In fact, the relative neglect of rural education was to continue for some years. Hanson (1986, 34) observes that a 1950 decree established three types of primary education: (1) rural schools with a two-year duration, in which boys attended one day and girls the next; (2) single-sex rural schools with a four-year duration; and (3) urban schools with a five-year duration. Thus, students in rural areas attended less school—when schools were available to enroll in—and they also had specialized curricula that provided a "practical rather than an intellectual preparation" (Hanson 1986, 34).

Only in the 1960s did the attitude toward rural education, and the role of rural areas in general, begin to change among politicians and the technocrats increasingly charged with mapping the course of Colombia's development. As a prelude to a deeper understanding of the reasons for this fundamental shift, it is necessary to delve deeper into Colombia's political history.

Colombia has, rather uniquely among developing countries, a strong tradition of bipartite politics and democratically elected governments. The liberals and the conservatives have traditionally vied for Colombia's presidency, with the liberal party in favor of reduced powers of the central government, and fewer influences of the Catholic church. The conservatives have stood for opposite positions. Liberals have generally supported progressive social reforms more than conservatives, although such distinctions are increasingly clouded in contemporary Colombian politics.

On April 9, 1948, the face of Colombian politics and society was fundamentally altered. Jorge Eliécer Gaitán, a populist liberal, was assassinated in the Colombian capital of Bogotá. Rioting and political violence, now referred to as the *Bogotazo*, erupted in the capital. For the next eighteen years, however, the brunt of violence was experienced in rural areas among adherents of the two political parties (Bushnell 1993). The period, simply referred to as *La Violencia*, led to the deaths of between one and two hundred thousand people.

In 1953, Colombia was subjected to one of its few authoritarian regimes when General Gustavo Rojas Pinilla assumed power in a coup d'etat. However, his inability to put an end to the violence still wracking the countryside, among other factors discussed by Bushnell (1993, 217–222), led to his exile in 1957. What followed is a novel power-sharing arrangement referred to as the "National Front." Its provisions called for the liberal and conservative parties to alternate the presidency every four years for the next sixteen years. Furthermore, at least 10 percent of the national budget was to be reserved for educational expenditures. These and other provisions were approved in a national plebiscite in 1957.

Successive regimes of the National Front made primary education one of their investment priorities. Between 1930 and 1958, around one to 1.4 percent of GNP was devoted to education. After the National Front assumed power, the figure rose to 3.5 percent (Hanson 1995). Educational investments came to symbolize the possibility for social mobility and modernization for the general citizenry in the context of a tightly controlled social and economic environment by the liberal-conservative political elite. Rural education was still relatively neglected, though rural areas leapt onto the development agenda in other ways. The distribution of agricultural lands, as in much of Latin America, was unequal. An attempt at land reform was made in the 1930s during a progressive regime, but did not advance very far. The first National Front regime of the liberal Alberto Lleras Camargo in the early 1960s placed land reform high on its list of priorities (Bushnell 1993). A 1961 law, despite heavy opposition from large land-owning interests, was enacted, which set up a reform agency: the *Instituto Colombiano de Reforma Agraria* (INCORA). Though expropriation was allowed, the law emphasized redistribution of existing public lands.

The law was implemented on a piecemeal basis until the third National Front regime of Carlos Lleras Restrepo in the late 1960s, also a liberal. Lleras Restrepo catalyzed reform through his sponsorship of the *Asociación Nacional de Usuarios Campesinos* (ANUC). The organization was designed to provide peasant farmers with access to services of the government, including extension and land redistribution. ANUC branch offices rapidly spread throughout the country, and by 1970 had become a strong political force.

While these reforms were being enacted, the political stage was being set for a tumultuous election in 1970. Shortly after his overthrow, General Rojas Pinilla had returned from exile. He began organizing a populist third party called the *Alianza Nacional Popular* (ANAPO). Much of his support was garnered from urban areas, especially the poorer classes and the unemployed. Among rural denizens, however, the traditional affiliations to liberal and conservative parties still ran deep. ANAPO did quite well in the Congressional elections of 1966, and prepared itself for a presidential challenge in 1970. Since the election was reserved for the conservatives by the National Front agreement, Rojas Pinilla ran as a conservative. The official candidate, Pastrana, narrowly edged Rojas Pinilla, amid some allegations of fraud. It is generally thought that the organization of the peasant vote by ANUC was a key factor in the conservative victory (Bushnell 1993).

Though the first waves of internecine political violence were subsiding by the mid-1960s, new forms of violence were emerging. Two Communist guerrilla insurgencies, the *Fuerzas Armadas Revolucionarias de Colombia* (FARC) and the *Ejército de Liberación Nacional* (ELN) were consolidated in different parts of Colombia. The FARC drew particular support from rural peasants, while the ELN was mainly composed of youth from the urban middle class. After the 1970 election, a third revolutionary force was created, the *Movimiento 19 de Abril* (M-19). Also urban in nature, it was mainly composed of disillusioned followers of Rojas Pinilla and ANAPO. Since their creation, the guerrilla groups, mainly the first two, have shown their ability to control wide swathes of territory in Colombia. Bushnell (1993, 247) observes that "the revolutionary left did succeed in establishing a series of mostly isolated, though fairly large, rural zones where different guerrilla organizations exercised control or at least prevented the state from establishing full authority. Often, of course, these were zones where state authority had been little more than nominal in the first place."

The conservative administration of Pastrana from 1970 to 1974 was lukewarm toward land reform, instead promoting a development program that emphasized urban construction and light industrialization. Even so, the political strength of ANUC continued to propel the reforms. The next administration of López Michelson, a liberal, made rural development the centerpiece of the administration, entitling the four-year development plan *Para Cerrar la Brecha* (To Close the Gap), referring largely to the urban-rural gap.[3] Though facing opposition on a number of counts from urban interests, it did spearhead the implementation of new programs for rural development in order to contain increasing rural-urban migratory currents triggered by recent urbanization initiatives. The program of *Desarrollo Rural Integrado* (DRI) has existed since the mid-1970s, its main goal to address the social and economic needs of small farmers (World Bank 1994). Much later, in 1982, the *Plan Nacional de Rehabilitación* (PNR) was instituted. Since then, various administrations have used it as a means of targeting economic and social assistance to municipalities that have particularly high indices of poverty and violence. By 1992, projects of the PNR affected nearly 25 percent of the Colombian population, mostly peasants in rural areas (World Bank 1994).

A brief history of multigrade schools

In many developing countries, rural teachers contend with students of multiple ages and abilities, crowded into classrooms with little instructional material of any sort (McEwan 1999). In this context, some countries have provided in-service training and teaching materials that are designed to maximize student learning in the multigrade context. The following paragraphs describe the evolution of the multigrade school in Colombia, culminating in the official establishment of the *Escuela Nueva* program.

From unitary schools to large-scale reform

Multigrade schools in Colombia have their roots in the "unitary complete schools methodology" promoted by UNESCO in the 1960s.[4] The methodology consisted of individualized instruction, active learning, the use of special self-instructional texts and "learning cards" and automatic promotion. The unitary schools movement acquired particular momentum after it was endorsed at a meeting of Ministers of Education held in Geneva in 1961 (Schiefelbein 1992). The first officially designated multigrade school was established, with the support of UNESCO, by the *Instituto Superior de Educación Rural* in the Colombian state of Norte de Santander. In 1967, the administration of Lleras Restrepo—also notable for its sponsorship of the rural organization ANUC—issued a decree that promoted the use of the unitary schools methodology in all one-teacher schools.

After the decree, various institutions experimented with the methodology throughout the country, each interpreting the model differently. There was still no nationwide program of multigrade schools, even though as many as 4,500 teachers were trained in the basic unitary schools methodology (Schiefelbein 1992). At this stage, teachers prepared learning cards, which were essentially teacher-designed lesson plans designed to work effectively in a multigrade setting. At this time, the educational system of Colombia was highly decentralized. While centrally financed, the central government possessed little direct control over basic aspects of the educational system such as the hiring of teachers. Hanson (1995) delineates the series of problems that this caused, such as the illegal hiring of personnel and the growth of bloated and underqualified staffs that then had to be paid by the central government. Lleras Restrepo, shortly after the unitary schools decree, initiated a program of administrative centralization that sought to subject state educational systems to some measure of accountability and control.[5]

The unitary schools movement had begun to lose some momentum "due to the amount of additional work required to prepare the learning cards . . . [and] lack of support from colleagues or supervisors" (Schiefelbein 1992, 57). Unitary schools movements in Argentina, Chile, and Uruguay ran into similar problems, and their pilot projects fell into disrepair. In Colombia, however, a steering group was created, composed of teachers, supervisors, and university professors in Norte de Santander (the site of the original pilot project) as well as a group from the national Ministry of Education. They worked toward the improvement of learning materials by selecting the best teacher-designed learning cards and compiling them into a self-instructional textbook. In addition to these ongoing efforts to reduce the burden on unitary school teachers, the steering committee worked to galvanize support for their approach by evangelizing the unitary methodology within the ministry. Still, of course, they were constrained by the lack of an official administrative structure to assist and supervise teachers, and the sustainability of the program was threatened (Colclough and Lewin 1993).

In 1975, the *Escuela Nueva* program was officially born. USAID had been searching for a new approach to funding education in Colombia, and found it in the unitary schools movement (McGinn 1996). The expansion of the program to roughly five hundred schools in three departments of Colombia, including the department where the original pilot project was undertaken, was financed between 1975 and 1978. Schiefelbein (1992, 60) observes that, in this period, "materials for students and teachers were revised; account was taken of the administrative and financial organization of the regions; schedules and materials for training and follow-up were up-dated; [and] the systems of production and distribution of materials were stream-lined."

Between 1979 and 1986, the program received ongoing financing from the Inter-American Development Bank, the Coffee Growers' Federation, and the Foundation for Higher Education. Over this period, program materials were systematized, and the program was codified in manuals distributed to teachers and used in training (Schiefelbein 1992). Overall, the program was expanded to over eight thousand rural schools.

During this time, and in later phases of *Escuela Nueva*, the organizational structure of the program was constantly evolving. Given its origins as a pilot program, first implemented in the decentralized system of the late 1960s, this is not surprising. Aristizabal (1991) reports that evaluations of *Escuela Nueva* in the 1990s show that the program is incorporated into the educational administrative structures of departments in numerous and not always coherent ways. For instance, in one department, it may be controlled by the Secretariat of Education; in another, it may still depend on the national ministry. Administratively, at least, it has rarely made sense to speak of *Escuela Nueva* as a homogeneous program.

In 1986, the program received its largest push in the form of financial assistance from the World Bank (McGinn 1996). The loan was intended to support the "scaling up" of the *Escuela Nueva* methodology to ten thousand additional rural schools. In the previous year the program had been designated as the official strategy to universalize rural primary schooling (Colbert, Chiappe, and Arboleda 1993). The key elements—or, at least, what were perceived to be key elements—were frozen in an official "kit" (Colbert et al. 1993, McGinn 1996, Schiefelbein 1992). Its transformation from an amorphous, evolving policy to a concrete, well defined one was complete.

Escuela Nueva: *The ideal and the actual*

Then, as now, the ideally implemented *Escuela Nueva* was supposed to contain certain characteristics, briefly described in the following paragraphs. These are described at greater length in McEwan (1998b) and Benveniste and McEwan (2000). Multigrade students advance through flexible, but not automatic, promotion. Individual student work, emphasized in traditional schools, is combined with work in small groups. Student work is oriented by self-instructional learning guides in mathematics, Spanish, science, and social studies. Units in the book include the learning objectives, guided activities to be completed, and free activities that require application of the knowledge gained. Some involve creative exploration and application of regional-specific knowledge. In general, the pedagogy of the *Escuela Nueva* can be characterized as "active," relying upon students, guided by the teacher, to acquire and construct knowledge for themselves.

Teacher in-service training is divided into three one-week courses conducted throughout the first school year, designed to provide teachers with pedagogical skills to implement in the multigrade classroom. Courses use a detailed manual organized similarly to student learning guides. Community involvement is a key element of *Escuela Nueva*. Substantial latitude is left to the teacher to design interventions, but several are suggested or required. For example, students and their family members collaborate in making a map of the surrounding community. Sometimes parents collaborate in the actual construction and maintenance of the school and furniture that facilitates implementation of the reforms (such as desks that facilitate group work, shelves for the learning corners, etc.).

Of course, we would be surprised if schools exactly resembled the vision painted above. More likely than not, the extent to which multigrade schools use the "ideal" methodology has varied over time and by region. Unfortunately, little information is available about the congruence between the ideal and the actual in the early stages of the development of multigrade schools. After the World Bank loan in 1986, data collection on the *Escuela Nueva* program increased, which allows us to make finer inferences.

In a 1992 sample of rural schools, evidence shows that only two-thirds of schools belonging to the *Escuela Nueva* program possessed the prescribed library.[6] Just 33 percent of third graders in Spanish and 29 percent in mathematics were using the official self-instructional textbooks; in fifth grade the figures were 46 and 40 percent. Slightly more recent data in 1993 indicate that, in a sample of fifth-grade mathematics instructors identifying themselves as *Escuela Nueva* teachers, only 64 percent had completed all of the three required in-service training courses, supposedly essential for program implementation. Ten percent completed two courses, 14 percent completed one, and 12 percent had not participated in any in-service training. Troubling issues have been raised regarding the quality of teacher training. The original hands-on nature of the teacher training was diluted in many instances to a less-effective lecture format (Aristizabal 1991).

Less evidence is available on the extent to which core educational practices have been appreciably altered in the manner prescribed by the official program materials. McEwan (1998b) cites data on instructional methods used by teachers in *Escuela Nueva* and traditional rural schools. The former, as expected, utilize techniques such as group work, library research, and exploration outside the classroom with greater frequency. Nonetheless, there is considerable variability in application of techniques that could be categorized under the rubric of active pedagogy. Many traditional school teachers use these techniques, while a substantial number of *Escuela Nueva* teachers use them less than would be expected under a full adoption of the program. Another study using a different sample of schools and teachers found no significant differences in teacher practices between the two school types (Loera and McGinn 1992, McGinn 1996). Aristizabal (1991) cites a number of qualitative studies of rural schooling in Colombia that suggest a great heterogeneity in the application of recommended pedagogies.

The "stages of development" of multigrade schools

The preceding discussion assists in identifying three clearly defined phases in the development and implementation of the multigrade rural education reform in Colombia: grassroots, formalized, and decoupled.

Grassroots reform (1961–1974) In this initial phase, the idea of unitary schools promoted by UNESCO sparked interest in some areas and institutions of Colombia; in others it quickly died out. It is fair to say that the unitary schools would have been completely unsustainable during this period without the grassroots support of many teachers. Both in their willingness to prepare learning cards and in their desire to implement key aspects of the unitary schools methodology in the classroom, they sustained the momentum of the program. A rural-based steering group also succeeded in providing an informal organizational structure to support and continue developing the ideas of the unitary school. Nonetheless, little formal administrative support existed in the way of financing or supervision of teachers, except perhaps for the fact that it enjoyed high-level political support in the form of a presidential decree.

Formalized reform (1975–1985)   In the next phase, the motivation and commitment of teachers to the program was complemented by financial support and new administrative structures (albeit heterogeneous from one department to another). In some sense, this was the "golden era" of *Escuela Nueva*. A sense of innovation still existed among teachers, who were still a relatively small and carefully selected group. Most, if not all, had received the appropriate training and classroom materials. They were probably more faithful to the classroom prescriptions of the program, though little concrete evidence exists in this regard. Toward the end of this phase, the gradual incorporation of more and more teachers into the program and problems in moving "to scale" foreshadowed problems to come.

Decoupled reform (1986–mid 1990s)   The provision of World Bank financing and the official "scaling up" of the program were the ironic precursors to *Escuela Nueva*'s gradual decline. The program was frozen into a "kit" form, easily transferred from one region to another. The requirements of implementing the program on a large scale and mass printing of textbooks meant that the program curriculum, already less flexible than in the 1960s, was even less adaptive. Toward the end of this period, evidence from schools and teachers indicates that being called an *Escuela Nueva* is less indicative of what actually occurs in the classroom.[7] In the language of sociologists, the program gradually became decoupled: administrative forms that impart directions and regulations exist and evolve, while actual practices in rural classrooms are less affected (Meyer and Rowan 1978).

It ought to be noted that there may be important exceptions to this pattern. It is commonly argued that the pedagogical model is more faithfully implemented in wealthier coffee-growing departments, such as Caldas and Santander, where the program has received strong and ongoing support from the private Coffee Growers' Federation. There is little direct empirical evidence on this point. However, anecdotal data suggests that study tours of the *Escuela Nueva*—partly intended to "showcase" the program—are often directed to schools in these regions.

More recently, the program has been imperiled at the administrative level. Interviews by the authors suggest that *Escuela Nueva* has lost some political support within the Ministry of Education and among the educational bureaucracy in Colombia. Key members of the original steering committee are no longer in the Ministry of Education. Vicky Colbert, for example, a former vice-minister of education and one of the program's most vigorous supporters, currently heads a nongovernmental organization—the "Back to the People" Foundation—devoted to reinvigorating the program from the private sector.

Discussion

Changing motives of the Colombian state

Rural areas in Colombia were extraordinarily disadvantaged in the first half of this century, and the state did little to change this. Indeed, the government made explicit attempts, reflected in rural school legislation, to limit the amount and quality of rural schooling. During the 1960s, however, the state's policy toward rural development experienced a sea change. Successive governments of the National Front expanded the coverage of rural education and implemented a series of land reforms. The earliest development of multigrade schools occurred largely due to the impulse of teachers and a few devoted staffers in the Ministry of Education. In 1967, however, a presidential decree of Carlos Lleras Restrepo officially supported the burgeoning use of the unitary schools methodology.

What motivated this dramatic shift in policy? In part, it is due to the violent context of Colombian politics. Initially, successive administrations of the National Front viewed rural education as a means of "civilizing" and "pacifying" the rural citizenry and thereby controlling the bloody political violence wracking the country. Toward the end of the 1960s, however, a broader set of motives drove the state to support rural education. Lleras Restrepo was under increasing pressure from the urban populist ANAPO movement of the former dictator Rojas Pinilla. He responded by strengthening land reform efforts and organizing peasants through ANUC, and throwing his support behind rural schooling as a means of incorporating rural peasants into the political process, and perhaps slowing rates of rural-urban migration (Bushnell 1993). The latter was already proceeding at a healthy clip and was adding the urban unemployed, a core constituency of ANAPO.

The narrow victory of the conservative National Front candidate over Rojas Pinilla in 1970 only reinforced the political necessity of garnering political support in rural areas. Unfortunately, ANUC and peasant land movements were becoming increasingly radicalized and outside the purview of high government officials. In any case, the conservative Pastrana was not an avid supporter of land reform. Thus, education became an even more important mechanism for acquiring political support among rural peasants. Indeed, the pace of enrollment in rural primary schools increased markedly. The liberal López Michelsen was elected in 1974, with his pro-rural agenda. Shortly thereafter, *Escuela Nueva* was born as an official program with USAID financing, and the importance of rural education in government policy was consolidated.

Toward the 1980s, violence was still prevalent in rural areas, but it had ceased to be a generalized phenomenon among the peasantry, pitting liberals against conservatives. Instead, violence was driven by guerrillas, drug traffickers, and right-wing paramilitary groups. Thus, the state was far less concerned, as in the 1960s, with "pacifying" the peasantry who were now mainly victims. Moreover, the ANAPO movement of Rojas Pinilla had fragmented into the M-19 urban guerrilla movement and no longer presented a political threat, at least in formal elections. Thus, the importance of "incorporating" rural denizens into the political process gradually lost importance.

As some motives waned in importance, others took their place. Confronted by escalating violence from guerrillas and drug traffickers, the state's credibility was increasingly threatened by its lack of presence or authority in rural areas. Rural schools were still the only tangible evidence of the state in some municipalities, and their consolidation represented an important means of shoring up eroding legitimacy. As the state's motives began to shift, however, so to did the functioning of multigrade schools, which became increasingly decoupled. That is, the form and structures of multigrade schools continued to exist, but the core educational practices of multigrade teachers began to resemble less and less the prescribed pedagogies of the ideal *Escuela Nueva*.

This is not coincidental. At least part of this decoupling was due to the state's reduced emphasis on "pacification" and "rural incorporation." As priorities shifted to reasserting state legitimacy, changing classroom practices came second to demonstrating a rural presence. In the context of a growing crisis of legitimation (Jansen 1990, Weiler 1993), the state emphasized the construction of schools, rather than the altering of core educational practices within them. Further, *Escuela Nueva* was identified as an expensive pedagogical intervention. The state's shifting priorities are perhaps best illustrated by its declining commitment to allocating necessary financial resources to the program and providing teachers with the training and materials required to fully implement the *Escuela Nueva* methodology.

This is not to say that the state was the only contributing factor to the decoupling of multigrade schools. Expanding the program at a rapid pace meant that more and more teachers needed to be trained and deployed. Newly incorporated teachers were becoming farther removed from the grassroots origins of the program, and may have lacked the motivation and commitment of earlier participants.[8] Whereas a good percentage of teachers in the original unitary school incarnation might have participated in designing learning cards or otherwise modifying the program, those who became *Escuela Nueva* teachers in the late 1970s and beyond were confronted with a "kit" that dictated in a fairly rigid fashion the form and functioning of their classroom. To be sure, the programmatic version of *Escuela Nueva* does emphasize teacher innovation, but the nature of innovation is qualitatively different that of earlier stages, when the "program" was still defined by its participants.

Escuela Nueva also lost some of its steam as the professional team that spearheaded its initial development and implementation left the Ministry of Education. The departure from government of its champions eroded the sense of ownership and identification needed to lead and invigorate this education reform program as it broadened its reach.

Indigenous versus international influences

The *Escuela Nueva* reform grew and reached its peak as much of Latin America was embarking on "neoliberal" education reform initiatives, oftentimes associated with structural adjustment plans sponsored by international organizations. Neoliberal reforms are usually characterized by a strong market orientation, the reduction of public sector intervention, a restraint in public expenditures, and a preference for locally administered (as opposed to centrally administered) programs. In many respects, *Escuela Nueva* appears to be linked to these neoliberal reforms. A largely community-driven education program, it came about at the recommendation of UNESCO and later expanded through support from USAID and the World Bank. However, these similarities are somewhat deceiving. We argue instead that *Escuela Nueva* was primarily an indigenous movement that enjoyed the local support from educators and the political establishment, especially in its earlier stages. This section explores two related issues, already touched upon previously: how *Escuela Nueva* came to be an "indigenous" reform and whether *Escuela Nueva* may be rightly positioned within a neoliberal education reform paradigm.

Three factors were decisive in creating local conditions for the growth and acceptance of *Escuela Nueva* in the initial stages of development. First, teachers from Norte de Santander developed their curricular materials for all basic subjects and grade levels to overcome some of the difficulties in the implementation of UNESCO's "Unitary Schools" approach. These schools were labeled "*Escuelas Nuevas*," although the notion of what this entailed was necessarily fluid. This fluidity, often perceived as an obstacle to education reform, created the conditions for teachers and other stakeholders to leave their mark on the program and adjust it to local conditions. Ultimately, it also created a sense of local "ownership" among teachers (McGinn 1996).

Second, the Coffee Producers' Committee played a key role in spreading *Escuela Nueva* in Caldas. As Fizbein and Lowden (1999, 22) observe:

> Combining the roles of cofounder, broker, and community leader, the committee was uniquely placed to use its well-established credentials both in the local community and the technical enclaves of the Ministry of Education to gradually undermine the endemic clientelism in the education system that had previously impeded the spread of the *Escuela Nueva* model.

In the 1980s, the committee bore 80 percent of the costs of teacher training and program management (Fiszbein and Lowden 1999). This financial and political support, largely at the local level, was crucial in developing and maintaining the program. By some accounts, it has ensured that *Escuela Nueva* has preserved a strong indigenous streak, even as international organizations have sought to give the program their imprimatur.

Third, a key element in *Escuela Nueva* becoming anchored as an indigenous movement was the creation of rural microcenters (funded mainly by UNICEF) that brought teachers and parents together in monthly meetings to discuss reform implementation. These provided social and educational forums for local participants to exchange ideas and contribute to program development. In the scaling-up process, the participation of these stakeholders was watered down, and the program's destiny began to slip from the grasp of its local champions. There are, of course, exceptions to this rule. In Caldas, the *Escuela Nueva* model is only offered under the express request of the community, assuring that the school is able to commit to the core objectives and expectations of *Escuela Nueva*. As Fizbein and Lowden (1999) observe, "this focus on the community reveals a shift from an assistential, centralized development approach to one of complementary contributions based on shared responsibility and goals." Not coincidentally, Caldas is one of the few regions in which program "decoupling" is arguably less pronounced.

International organizations have vigorously promoted *Escuela Nueva*, in Colombia and elsewhere, often side-by-side with market-oriented education reforms. Is there a link, then, between this approach to multigrade education and neoliberal reform initiatives? Although aggressively promoted by international organizations, *Escuela Nueva* provides a curious counterpoint to the wave of neoliberal education reforms in Latin America imported from the "North." First, the curriculum and methodology of *Escuela Nueva* were explicitly designed to foster creative self-expression and independent thought. If anything, the program is more closely aligned to a Freirian conceptualization of education as a critical dialogue, deeply involving the most disadvantaged beneficiaries of educational systems in how schooling functions and the construction of knowledge (Freire 1970). This is quite different from many governance and finance reforms, such as vouchers and decentralization, that ignore discussion of pedagogy and curriculum.

Second, *Escuela Nueva* is more costly than traditional rural schools. There is very little evidence on this point, but Psacharopoulos et al. (1993) suggest a figure on the order of 10 percent. This may well be compensated by gains in achievement, as evidenced by Psacharopoulos et al. (1993) and McEwan (1998b), suggesting some gains in cost-effectiveness of resource use relative to other possible interventions. Nonetheless, the increased costs place *Escuela Nueva* at odds with other elements of neoliberal reforms that emphasize cost control.

Third, the strategies of *Escuela Nueva* are not explicitly designed to promote market-based solutions. The program does rely on increased community involvement as a means to improve achievement. But this unique approach is largely theorized as a pedagogical innovation—allowing parents to confer with teachers on curriculum, instruction, and school organization—rather than as an accountability measure that prods schools and teachers to work more cost-efficiently.

A local reform goes global

The role of international organizations in the development of Colombian multigrade schools is significant in a financial sense, but probably less so if one is exclusively concerned with identifying the genesis of this form of educational change in Colombia. The funds of international development institutions certainly made it possible, and even gave additional incentive, for the state to pursue *Escuela Nueva*. But the idea, and many of the motivations of the Colombian state, existed prior to financing by USAID, the Inter-American Development Bank, the World Bank, and others. International organizations seized upon the program as a means of providing support to rural educational development (while simultaneously fulfilling their own institutional mandates) through their participation in a highly-visible and credible initiative proven to be pedagogically effective.

The role played by international organizations in the development and implementation of multigrade schooling policies is probably more significant in other countries of Latin America and around the world, where the *Escuela Nueva* methodology was promoted and applied with support from international agencies. In 1989, the World Bank singled out the *Escuela Nueva* movement as one of the three primary school experiments in the world that had succeeded in making educational innovations, and recommended that "the lessons of this experience be widely disseminated among policy makers in developing countries" (as cited in López, 1999, 15).

During the 1990s, there have been several experiments that replicated the experiences of Colombian multigrade classrooms. Perhaps the most successful replication has taken place in Guatemala. Under the auspices of USAID's Basic Education Strengthening Project, the Ministry of Education developed the *Nueva Escuela Unitaria* (NEU) program. Like its Colombian counterpart, the NEU program relied on student self-instructional workbooks and teacher guides, an integrated active pedagogy, the creation of teachers' circles (akin to *Escuela Nueva*'s microcenters) for in-service training and development of pedagogical materials, and extensive community involvement. The NEU model was soon adopted by a wide variety of private nonprofit and religious organizations, such as the Social Investment Fund, the Catholic Salesian Order of Don Bosco, *Plan Internacional*, and the Guatemalan Coffee Growers association. By 1998, privately-funded NEU schools outnumbered government-sponsored schools by 4 to 1 (Kline 2000).

In Vietnam, the Ministry of Education and Training, in collaboration with UNICEF, has launched a multigrade education initiative to reach ethnic minority communities in the northern part of the country (Aikman and Pridmore 2001). In contrast to other nations where multigrade classrooms in remote areas are led by teachers with little training or expertise, in Vietnam only the "best" teachers are selected for multigrade teaching. The project has established a number of "demonstration schools" staffed by master teachers to demonstrate the "ideal" multigrade classroom and train new teachers. Training modules have been developed on a variety of subjects, including classroom organization, independent learning, bilingual teaching, school-community linkages, and local low-cost materials production. When it started in 1991, this project served 20 schools in four provinces with 506 students. By 1999, over

2500 primary schools and 7000 teachers participate in this program (Hargreaves et al. 2001).

Many other countries have also followed suit. Peru is currently implementing a pilot program scheduled to go up to scale with World Bank support (Hargreaves et al. 2001). Similarly, Nicaragua, Philippines, and Uganda have launched multigrade demonstration schools that emulate the Colombian *Escuela Nueva* (López 2001, Odyek-Ocen 2000). Argentina and Chile have also experimented with multigrade methodologies, albeit with limited success (López 1999).

The *Escuela Nueva* experience has come to represent a practical option to provide educational services to children in remote locations. International agencies have played an instrumental role in supplying the technical and financial resources necessary to disseminate this educational approach worldwide. The appeal of *Escuela Nueva*, however, is not solely founded on its emphasis to reach the most marginal children. Perhaps most importantly, *Escuela Nueva* represents a high-quality pedagogical approach founded on teaching strategies that promote child-centered learning and forge a tight linkage between classrooms and the communities in which they are embedded.

Conclusions

The history of multigrade school reform in Colombia suggests that state motives were complex and evolving. Prior to the 1960s, rural areas were largely ignored by the state, and the quantity and quality of schooling were limited. Traditional Marxist analyses of education have a ready explanation for this, in that the government sought to reinforce the social relations of capitalist production (Bowles 1980, Bowles and Gintis 1976, Gintis and Bowles 1988). The creation of an educated and politically active citizenry in rural areas clearly did not contribute to this goal.

Why, then, did the state begin to shift its policies in the 1960s? We suggested two explanations. First, the state wished to "pacify" rural denizens on the heels of many years of political violence. Second, and somewhat later, the state wished to incorporate more rural individuals into the political process. Both suggest a pluralist explanation in which social demands on the political system are key in determining the shape and extent of state actions (Benveniste 1989, Pressman and Wildavsky 1986, Wirt and Kirst 1982). Throughout this period, the state was quite concerned with effecting change at the classroom level by altering core teaching practices, precisely because it was concerned with altering the attitudes and behavior of peasants.

Eventually, the state's motives shifted yet again. The state was increasingly faced by a crisis of legitimation in rural areas where its presence and authority were minimal (Jansen 1990, Weiler 1993). In these cases, its primary concern was to construct schools and make a public demonstration of its commitment to reform, rather than focus on actual changes in classroom practices. Not surprisingly, the *Escuela Nueva* program sometimes functioned in name only.

A careful analysis of the various incarnations of the *Escuela Nueva* program over time highlights the importance of embracing a dynamic conception of educational reform. Further, this type of historical institutional account draws attention to how social actors, their interests at a specific point in time, and the distribution of power among them are crucial elements for understanding the motivation and outcomes of political behavior (Thelen and Steinmo 1992). This approach moves away from a static conceptualization of educational change by focusing on how shifts in the cultural, political or economic environment ripple through reform design and implementation. In other words, education reform is a contested process continuously shaped and reshaped as political actors and institutions compete for influence and scarce resources in a variable social arena. The *Escuela Nueva* case study warns us against treating education change initiatives as a unified or enduring policy package. More precisely, it underscores the fluid political purposes that fuel apparently disinterested educational reform efforts.

Notes

An earlier version of this paper was published in the *Journal of Education* Policy, 2001, vol. 16, no. 6: 547–559. The authors wish to thank Adriana Jaramillo, Karen Mundy, Alberto Rodriguez, Tatiana Romero Rey and an anonymous referee for their comments and suggestions. Discussions with Vicky Colbert have contributed enormously to our understanding the program. These individuals are not responsible for any errors or interpretations. The findings, analyses, and conclusions expressed in this paper are entirely those of the authors.

1. Lebot (1972), cited in Hanson (1986, 30).
2. See Table 3.2 in Hanson (1986).
3. Hanson (1986, 44) cites the plan's main statement:
    The development plan which is now being presented to Congress is directed toward closing the gaps which the classic form of development has created. It is hoped that the gaps between the country and the city, between rich and poor urban neighborhoods, and between those who have access to educational and health services and the illiterate and undernourished will be closed. The program which we propose to the country is to change the ends of development policy, to attempt to protect the traditional sectors of the rural and urban economy, and to transfer public investment, primarily to small and medium-sized cities and rural areas where our poorest areas are found.
4. Unless otherwise noted, the following description relies heavily upon the work of Schiefelbein (1992) and Colbert, Chiappe, and Arboleda (1993).
5. In recent years, of course, Colombia has sought to reverse this process of centralization. Though interesting, consideration of the changing policies toward educational decentralization is beyond the scope of this paper. Hanson (1995) provides an illuminating discussion.
6. See McEwan (1998b) and Benveniste and McEwan (2000) for further details on program implementation.
7. Even so, recent evaluations of student achievement suggest that a partially implemented *Escuela Nueva* still worked better than traditional rural schools (McEwan 1998b, Psacharopoulos, Rojas, and Vélez 1993).
8. Benveniste and McEwan (2000) discuss several factors that may contribute to low levels of motivation and commitment among teachers, such as the lack of adequate incentives to serve in isolated rural areas.

References

Aikman, S. and P. Pridmore. (2001). "Multigrade Schooling in "Remote" Areas of Vietnam." *International Journal of Educational Development* 21: 521–536.

Aristizabal, A. (1991). "Análisis de las evaluaciones realizadas sobre el Programa Escuela Nueva." UNICEF, unpublished manuscript.

Benveniste, G. (1989). *Mastering the Politics of Planning.* San Francisco: Jossey-Bass.

Benveniste, L. A. and P. J. McEwan. (2000). "Constraints to Implementing Educational Innovations: The Case of Multigrade Schools. *International Review of Education* 46 (1/2): 31–48.

Bowles, S. and H. Gintis. (1976). *Schooling in Capitalist America.* London: Routledge and Kegan Paul.

Bowles, S. (1980). "Education, Class Conflict and Uneven Development." In J. Simmons, ed. *The Education Dilemma: Policy Issues for Developing Countries in the 1980s.* Oxford: Pergamon Press.

Bushnell, D. (1993). *The Making of Modern Colombia: A Nation in Spite of Itself.* Berkeley: University of California Press.

Carnoy, M. and C. de Moura Castro. (1996). *Improving Education in Latin America: Where to Now?* Washington: Inter-American Development Bank.

Colbert, V., C. Chiappe, and J. Arboleda. (1993). "The New School Program: More and Better Primary Education for Children in Rural Areas in Colombia." In H. M. Levin and M. E. Lockheed, eds. *Effective Schools in Developing Countries.* London: The Falmer Press.

Colclough, C. and K. Lewin. (1993). *Educating All the Children.* Oxford: Oxford University Press.

Cook, T. (1991). "Postpositivist Criticisms, Reform Associations, and Uncertainties About Social Research." In Anderson and Biddle, eds. *Knowledge for Policy: Improving Education Through Research.* London: Falmer Press.

Fiszbein, A. and P. Lowden. (1999). *Working Together for a Change: Government, Business, and Civic Partnerships for Poverty Reduction in Latin America and the Caribbean.* Washington, D.C.: World Bank).

Freire, P. (1970. *Pedagogy of the Oppressed.* New York: Seabury Press.

Gintis, H. and S. Bowles. (1988). "Contraindiction and Reproduction in Educational Theory." In M. Cole, ed. *Bowles and Gintis Revisited: Correspondence and Contraindiction in Educational Theory.* Philadelphia: The Falmers Press.

Hanson, E. M. (1986). *Educational Reform and Administrative Development: The Cases of Colombia and Venezuela.* Stanford: Hoover Institution Press.

Hanson, E. M. (1995). "Democratization and Decentralization in Colombian education." *Comparative Education Review* 39, no. 1: 101–119.

Hargreaves, E., C. Montero, N. Chau, M. Sibli, and T. Thanh. (2001). "Multigrade Teaching in Peru, Sri Lanka, and Vietnam: An overview." *International Journal of Educational Development* 21: 499–520.

Jansen, J. D. (1990). "Curriculum Policy as Compensatory Legitimation? A View From the Periphery." *Oxford Review of Education* 16, no. 1: 29–38.

Kline, R. (2000). "A Model for Improving Rural Schools: *Escuela Nueva* in Colombia and Guatemala." *Current Issues in Comparative Education.* 2, no. 2: http://www.tc.columbia.edu/cice/articles/ak122.htm.

Lebot, I. (1972). *Elements para la Historia de la Educación en Colombia en el Siglo XX.* Bogotá: Departamento Administrativo Nacional de Estadística.

Lockheed, M. and A. M. Verspoor. (1991). *Improving Primary Education in Developing Countries.* Oxford: Oxford University Press.

Loera, A. and N. F. McGinn. (1992). "La repitencia de grado en la escuela primaria colombiana." Education Development Discussion Papers, Harvard Institute for International Development.

López, A. (1999). "Colombia Exports its "New School" Blueprint." *UNESCO Courier* 6 (June): 14–16.

McEwan, P. J. (1998a). "La efectividad de la Escuela Nueva en Colombia." *Ensayos sobre Economía Cafetera* 13: 35–56.

McEwan, P. J. (1998b). "The effectiveness of multigrade schools in Columbia." *International Journal of Educational Development* 18, no. 6: 435–452.

McEwan, P. J. (1999). "Recruitment of Rural Teachers in Developing Countries: An Economic Analysis." *Teaching and Teacher Education* 15: 849–859.

McGinn, N. (1996). "Resistance to Good Ideas: *Escuela Nueva* in Colombia." Paper presented at 1996 Conference of the Nordic Association for the Study of Education in Developing Countries.

Meyer, J. and B. Rowan. (1978). "The Structure of Educational Organizations." In Meyer et al., eds. *Environments and Organizations*. San Francisco: Jossey-Bass.

Meyer, J., J. Boli, G. Thomas, and F. Ramirez. (1997). "World Society and the Nation-state." *American Journal of Sociology* 103, no. 1: 144–181.

Odyek-Ocen, M. (2000). "Ugandan Experience with Multigrade Teaching." Paper presented at Commonwealth Secretariat Regional Workshop on Multigrade Teaching Modules, Gaberone, Botswana.

Pressman, J. and A. Wildavsky. (1986). *Implementation*. Berkeley: University of California Press.

Psacharopoulos, G., C. Rojas, and E. Vélez. (1993). "Achievement Evaluation of Colombia's *Escuela Nueva: Is Multigrade the Answer?*" Comparative Education Review 37, no. 3: 263–276.

Schiefelbein, E. (1992). *Redefining Basic Education for Latin America: Lessons to Be Learned from the Colombian Escuela Nueva*. Paris: UNESCO, International Institute for Educational Planning.

Thelen, K. and S. Steinmo. (1992). "Historical institutionalism in comparative politics." In Steinmo, Thelen, and Longstreth, eds. *Structuring Politics: Historical Institutionalism in Comparative Analysis*. New York: Cambridge University Press.

Weiler, H. N. (1993). "Control versus Legitimation: The Politics of Ambivalence." In J. Hannaway and M. Carnoy, eds. *Decentralization and School Improvements: Can We Fulfill the Promise?* San Francisco: Jossey-Bass.

Wirt, F. and M. Kirst. (1982). *Schools in Conflict*. Berkeley: McCuthcan.

World Bank. (1994). *Poverty in Colombia*. Washington, D.C.: World Bank.

World Bank. (1995). *Priorities and Strategies for Education: A World Bank Review*. Washington, D.C.: World Bank.

5

Neoliberalism and Educational Decentralization Policies

The Experience of the 1990s

JORGE M. GOROSTIAGA DERQUI

This chapter offers an analysis of educational decentralization in Latin America during the 1990s, focusing on the cases of Argentina, Brazil, Chile, and Mexico. I explore the characteristics of decentralization policies and their relationship with neoliberalism in the four countries. The objective of this chapter is not to arrive at a "correct" interpretation of the relationships between the two phenomena (neoliberalism and decentralization), but rather to explore different views and the complexity of the topic.

The chapter argues that school decentralization (or "school autonomy"), the movement toward transferring functions and responsibilities to schools, appears as a new and extended reform accompanied by more traditional forms of decentralization—like provincialization or municipalization—during the 1990s. These decentralization policies were coupled with processes of centralization of planning and evaluation at the national level. This new form of centralization/decentralization is seen as linked to the neoliberal restructuring of the state, to pressures from globalization processes and forces, and to various internal demands for improving quality and efficiency in the delivery of education.

After a general discussion about the relationships between neoliberalism and educational decentralization in the Latin American context, I offer a brief historical account of centralization and decentralization processes in the region. The following two sections provide a description of the decentralization policies designed in Argentina, Brazil, Chile, and Mexico, and a discussion of their significance and their links to broader political, economic, and social changes.

Neoliberalism and decentralization

The 1990s in Latin America was a decade characterized by the democratization of political systems (at least in their formal aspects), some economic growth, and yet increasing social inequalities, manifested in "growing distinctions between schooling for the poor and for the rich" (Torres and Puiggrós 1995, 22).

Filmus (1998) points out that during the 1990s the official discourse reincorporated the idea of the centrality of education and knowledge for development, as illustrated by the document of the Economic Commission for Latin America and the Caribbean (ECLAC) and UNESCO (1992), *Education and Knowledge: Basic Pillars of Changing Production Patterns with Social Equity*.

At the same time, processes of globalization and privatization have characterized the international context during the 1990s. Ball (1998) states that in the new scenario, the governments of the most developed countries experience a reduction in their ability to control national economies and turn to new forms of intervention. In education and social policy there is a combination of privatization and strategic intervention for increasing international competitiveness. This approach to social and educational policy, it is argued, disseminates even to peripheral countries through processes of "policy borrowing," cultural dependency, and the action of international organizations like the World Bank.

Neoliberalism rose as a central element of structural adjustment programs in the context of the debt crisis starting in the 1980s, and also as an alternative development model in the context of a new international political and economic scenario (Torres and Puiggrós 1995). Neoliberal policies are founded on classical economic theory, espousing the principles of the rule of the market and a change in the role of the state, where it has no longer an active role in economic production and the implementation of welfare universal programs. As Mesa Lago (1994, 1) points out, "The vast majority of countries in Latin America and the Caribbean have followed the new trend" of neoliberal policies.

The implications of neoliberalism for social policy, including education, are problematic. As Gauri (1998) notes, the new model pushes social service ministries to behave like firms. The "post-welfare" thinking implies pursuing efficiency and less politicization. At the same time, however, "social sector enhancement is required to make structural adjustment politically palatable" (9). According to Mesa Lago (1994), the neoliberal program includes, at least in theory, the development of a "long-run policy of 'investment in people' because the market alone does not generally ensure a safety net for certain parts of society (especially the poorest)," including investment in education (7). A characteristic of neoliberal governments is the implementation of targeted social programs for the poorest sectors, excluding middle classes from previous benefits (Weyland 1996, Angell and Graham 1995).

While there seems to be agreement on the deterioration of education as a result of economic adjustment programmes implemented since the 1980s, there has been a debate about the implications of long-term neoliberal reforms for education, and on whether or not educational reform has been driven mainly by the neoliberal/neoconservative ideology that inspired economic restructuring. Torres and Puiggrós (1995), for example, talk about a prevailing "neoliberal state" in Latin America whose main characteristic in terms of educational policy is the transfer of financial responsibilities to local authorities and communities. With a similar approach, Arnove et al. (1997) consider decentralization and privatization of school systems a main part of the reform agenda during the 1990s and the educational counterparts of neoliberal economic policies.[1]

Garretón (1996), by contrast, argues that, after a phase of rupture and adjustment, neoliberalism has been abandoned. He holds that educational models (and states) are in a process of redefinition in the context of globalization and the exhaustion of the traditional pattern of development and social policy. In a similar vein, Braslavsky and Cosse (1997) state that the groups that propose market approaches to education remained marginal to the processes of educational reform during the 1990s, which were conducted instead by what they call "a logic of innovation." This logic, it is argued, is based on an active state that defines priorities and produces pedagogic and institutional reforms.

A neoliberal state, however, does not necessarily imply a passive state but, as it was pointed out before, a different kind of state regulation (Ball 1998). While withdrawing from direct intervention and universal programs, the state assumes a more strategic role in trying to set priorities and in trying to manage, to the extent possible, the global forces that affect national economies and policy making.

International financial organizations are generally recognized as one of the main actors advocating educational reforms based on neoliberal models for the region (see Coraggio 1995, Puiggrós 1996) During the 1990s, international organizations like the World Bank proposed decentralization policies in order to cut fiscal deficits and increase the efficiency and quality of educational systems.[2] Such policies included the transfer of financial responsibilities to local governments and communities (Arnove et al. 1997). At the same time, school autonomy, along with the professionalization of teachers, was proposed as a necessary strategy for the improvement of education quality in Latin America. The cited document by ECLAC and UNESCO (1992) states that: "Greater autonomy for individual schools gives the faculty and director of each school the authority to define, within the framework of national policies and priorities, its own educational agenda and to assume responsibility for managing the academic, administrative and financial aspects of that agenda (136)."

Similar arguments can be found in World Bank documents. In *Priorities and Strategies for Education*, for example, it is explained that "If effective use is to be made of instructional inputs, institutions *must* be autonomous. Such a strategy is relevant in *all* contexts, even remote rural areas" (World Bank 1995, 126, my emphasis). In the view expressed in this World Bank document, school autonomy increases accountability to local communities, and should be coupled with other decentralization strategies, like local financing, the use of vouchers, and privatization of secondary schools. At some point, however, it is recognized that there are risks in school-level autonomy, which "arise particularly with regard to inequalities in educational opportunities and adherence to national standards and the curriculum" (World Bank 1995, 134).

Zibas (1996) argues that both ECLAC and the World Bank have proposed the introduction of market mechanisms in education through policies that include school decentralization. From the perspective of these international organizations, Zibas explains, the administrative, pedagogic, and financial autonomy of the school would establish a scenario in which the school's objectives and the rewards for productivity would be the source of the dynamism of the educational system. In addition, both international organizations are seen to focus on the achievement of efficiency through better coordination between the public and private sectors.

With regard to the significance of neoliberal educational reform proposals, including some forms of school decentralization, Apple (2001, 412) notes that "no matter how radical some of these proposed 'reforms' are and no matter how weak the empirical basis of their support, they have now redefined the terrain of debate of all things educational."

Historical background

During the nineteenth century and after independence, national systems of public education were created in Latin America under the leadership of central governments, establishing free and compulsory education at the primary level. The new nations were born as very centralized entities: "The Latin American countries are structured according to the French system of local government, with virtually all power concentrated in the central government and authority flowing from the top down"; nation building "was a matter of populating and thus 'civilizing' the vast empty interior and extending the central government's authority over the national territory" (Wiarda and Kline 1996, 45).[3]

In the construction of educational systems, most national governments in the region removed the control of schools from local authorities and adopted an active role in their expansion (Newland 1994). Filmus (1998) holds that two elements have contributed to centralism in Latin American education systems since the last decades of the nineteenth century:

1) The combination of the centralist tradition of colonial organization with a liberal state that "organizes" a weak civil society for capitalist development.
2) A liberal state that is also an oligarchic state, limiting participation of outside elites. Schools are designed—through centralized control—to achieve social integration and consensus in heterogeneous and unequal societies.

Despite variations among Latin American countries, centralization and uniformity continued to be widespread features of basic education systems in the region during this century.[4] Even in federal countries like Argentina, in which provinces had—according to the constitution—the main responsibility for providing elementary instruction, the central government traditionally played the most important role in the administration of schools, in the design of curriculum, and in teacher training. According to Newland (1995), centralization in the management of schools created several problems, including a high degree of rigid bureaucratization that discouraged teachers from implementing innovations and parents from participating. As early as the 1950s, governments in the region started to discuss and plan educational decentralization efforts (McGinn 1992).

In the case of Brazil, a process of educational centralization began under the government of Getulio Vargas in the 1930s, in the context of a relative consolidation of the federal state and the political inclusion of industrial elites and middle class groups (Ribeiro 1989). The general movement toward centralization, however, has not prevented the system from oscillating—through arrangements established by different constitutions and laws—between different models of relationships among the federal, state, and municipal levels (Cury 1992, Plank 1996). Moreover, the responsibility for basic education has remained almost entirely in the states and municipalities.

In response to the financial crisis of the late 1970s and the 1980s, Latin American countries established decentralization and privatization policies (Castro and Carnoy 1997, Tedesco 1994). Public expenditures in education were reduced, and many schools were transferred from the national government to provinces/states or municipalities to pursue new sources of revenue for education. During the 1970s and 1980s, Chile had the main experiences of municipalization (Newland 1995) and privatization through "financial incentives from the public sector" (Tedesco 1994).[5] According to Castro and Carnoy (1997) these "financial reforms" reduced costs for the national level, but impacted negatively on the quality of education. In the same vein, Tedesco (1994) points out that the decentralization policies of the 1980s "resulted in a deterioration in management capabilities and the quality of learning" throughout the region (809). Almost all Latin American countries experienced decreases in educational expenditures, affecting the quality of education through the decrease of teachers' salaries, outdated textbooks, and lack of teacher training (Arnove et al. 1997).[6]

The decentralization policies that prevailed during the 1970s and 1980s emphasized financial aspects while neglecting the quality of education. Although some elements of those policies have continued to be present in later reforms, during the 1990s educational decentralization assumed new forms with a redefinition of the functions of the different levels of government, including schools.

Educational decentralization policies in four countries

Argentina

After the "lost decade" of the 1980s, marked by the crisis of the external debt, economic stagnation, and hyperinflation processes, the government started a deep economic reform, including opening markets to international trade, the privatizing state-owned companies, and deregulating economic activities. Argentina experienced high rates of economic growth during the 1990s (growth averaged more than 8 percent between 1991 and 1994). On the other hand, unemployment rose to 17 percent by 1996. The influence of international lending organizations has been very important in the process of economic restructuring, and both the World Bank and the Inter-American Development Bank have participated in financing educational reform (Argentina, October 1998, Puiggrós 1996).

The reform of the educational system began in 1992 with the transfer of all of the national secondary schools and postsecondary institutes to the provinces—completing the process initiated by the military government in 1978 with the transfer of national primary schools—which was mainly driven by financial reasons (Filmus 1998, Senén González and Arango 1997).[7] Provinces agreed to receive the national secondary and post-secondary systems, but were not given specific resources to deal with the economic effort that the transfer represented.[8] In addition, many provincial administrations lacked the necessary technical expertise and resources to manage the new system (García de Fanelli 1997, Puiggrós 1997). In some provinces, decentralization was followed by an actual reduction of teachers' salaries in the context of a recurrent fiscal crisis accelerated by the burden represented by the transfer of schools (Filmus 1998, Senén González 1997).

After this provincialization, which can be seen as a continuation of the financial reforms of the 1980s, the national government moved to a comprehensive educational reform whose stated main goals were to improve the quality and the equity of the system. In 1993, the government enacted the first general law of education in the history of the country. According to the new law (Argentina 1993), the national government designs the educational policy and controls its implementation. The twenty-three provinces and the city of Buenos Aires (federal district) have the responsibilities of the funding, administration, and management of schools. The new model that emerged was one of a stronger center with few but strategic responsibilities (such as planning general policies and evaluating the system). In the new scenario, the Federal Council of Education (Consejo Federal de Educación) is the organization in which the national policy and its implementation are discussed with the provinces. The national and provincial ministries of education are part of this organization.[9]

An important element of the law was that it established a significant increase in the resources for financing education from national and provincial governments. Although the specified goal was not acheived (public educational budgets were supposed to reach a 6 percent of the GNP), educational expenditures did grow in the context of a general expansion of public expenditures.[10] The law also stressed a compensatory role for the federal government, what translated into the Social Plan, designed to directly provide federal funds for improving facilities, computers, and textbooks for the poorest schools in the country. The Social Plan reached more than 17,000 schools and around 3.6 million students during 1993–1998 (Morduchowicz 1999).

During the Menem administration (1989–1999), changes in curriculum design constituted a substantial reform related to school management and decentralization. The national Ministry and the Federal Council of Education decided to provide a general framework for all of the elementary and high schools in the country. There are three levels in the design of the new curricula. At the more general level, the Federal Council of Education sets the general objectives and guidelines (*contenidos básicos*). At the provincial level— including the city of Buenos Aires—the objectives and guidelines are more developed, taking into account the reality of each province. The final design of the curriculum at the school level implies that each school makes decisions on contents and instruction. The Federal Council of Education has stated that the school is the fundamental unit for specifying the educational project, so the provinces should leave to the schools the responsibility of developing a curriculum that responds to the local realities and needs ("Criterios para la planificación de Diseños Curriculares Compatibles en las Provincias y la MCBA, res. 37/94," in Argentina 1996a). The authentic effect of the curricular reform, however, has been controversial. The national union argues that it entailed a centralization of curriculum, since the national contents are too large and leave no room for significant contributions at provincial and school levels (CTERA 1997). In the same vein, Puiggrós (1997) characterizes the reform as neoconservative, aiming at ideological homogenization.

In addition to the structural and curricular reforms, the national government encouraged a particular school management model based on developing institutional projects at the school level. The Institutional Educational Project (IEP) became the main tool for implementing a new model of school. The IEP is a document produced by each school, including an adaptation and elaboration of the Provincial Curriculum Design as well as the instructional strategies and methods to deliver the curriculum. Each school is invited to build its own organizational and management structure based on its needs, its reality, and the people who are part of the school. These guidelines were proposed from the national level to the provinces as "basic institutional conditions" for managing all schools in the country (Argentina 1996). In 1994 the national government started the implementation of *Nueva Escuela*, a program that reached eleven hundred schools in 1995, though most of them in an indirect way (Tiramonti 1996). Each province selected a coordinator and a group of schools to participate in the program; the national government provided funds and technical assistance for the implementation.

Both national initiatives—the institutional conditions and the *Nueva Escuela* program—seemed to share the same principles. The main idea was that the application of new curricular guidelines required changes in the management and organization of schools in order to be effective and facilitate instructional innovations. This link between instructional quality and school management had been stressed by the national educational policy at least since the sanction of the new Federal Law of Education in 1993. While it was argued that curricular and instructional changes were required to improve the quality of education (Argentina 1996a), successfully implementing innovations was considered to depend on a new organizational and management model at the school level.

In a sense, the educational reforms that the Menem administration implemented seemed to be driven by the objective of building a more efficient system. The objective of granting more autonomy to the school, it was argued, was to improve quality by a more efficient use of pedagogical and economic resources. "Autonomy means greater capacity and responsibility that allows each school to decide what should be done and to manage its own resources in a better way" (Argentina 1996c, my translation). At the same time, the production of policies at the central level and a central evaluation system established limits to school autonomy and aimed at increasing general efficiency. According to Braslavsky (1998, 306) the changes introduced by the national government "make it possible once again to regulate the educational system in a manner that addresses the new challenges, attempting to correct the tendency toward fragmentation through a dual tendency to re-create an *active centre* spurred on by the federal government and to strengthen a type of *autonomy* that produces quality" (my emphasis).

A social context of increasing fragmentation and marginalization (see Minujin and Kessler 1995) is an important factor affecting policy implementation. Social segmentation and impoverishment translate into schools with different levels of resources serving different groups of students. The differences among schools in terms of cultural and material resources are a big challenge for moving toward more autonomous forms of organization and management if autonomy is expected to improve the quality of education for all. In the words of somebody who was actively involved in the analysis and planning of school reforms during the 1990s: "The main risk in the current reconversion of the educational system is that only private schools attended by the higher-income population, and public schools that participate in plans and projects for offering targeted assistance, will be able to gain the kind of autonomy needed to adopt their own proposals for restructuring the system" (Braslavsky 1998).

Evaluation of the changes has suggested that decentralization to the school level was more rhetorical than real (Experton 1999, 59), while the design of the Institutional Educational Projects at schools was done with limited participation of teachers and local communities, and lack of measurable and clear objectives (Experton 1999, 28).

In addition, it has been argued that many provinces have showed an inadequate level of financial and technical resources to implement various aspects of the reform proposed at the central level (García de Fanelli 1997, Senén González 2000). Low teachers' salaries and the unions' opposition to reforms have constituted other substantial barriers for the implementation of the new decentralization policies. Llach et al. (1999) show that teachers' average initial salary is less than 40 percent of the average salary in the Argentine formal economy. Teacher unions have strongly demanded federal intervention to improve salaries (formally a responsibility of provinces). In addition, the unions tended to see the reforms implemented during the Menem administration as part of a neoliberal policy that attacked public schools and tried to weaken unions' power (see, for example, CTERA 1997).[12]

Brazil

Brazil is probably the Latin American country with the deepest economic and social contrasts. It has the world's eighth-largest market-based economy, but more than one-third of the population is considered to live in poverty (Siqueira Wiarda 1996). The quality of education in Brazil is considered low in comparison to other Latin American countries, and access is still an important problem in the poorest regions (Guedes et al. 1997).

Brazil shifted from more statist to neoliberal policies with the election of Collor de Mello as president in 1989, after a decade marked by recession and high inflation. Franco's and Cardoso's administrations have continued the process of economic restructuring—mainly through privatization and reforming the public sector—with the objectives of reducing government expenditures and increasing the efficiency of the economy (see Purcell and Roett 1997). By 1997 the neoliberal reform process had consolidated under Cardoso's leadership (Kingstone 1999). According to some analysts (de Oliveira 1998, Sader 1998), this process has been characterized by a lack of social policies that translates into increasing social exclusion.

In Brazil, during the 1970s and 1980s, the federal level maintained a weaker role in education policy than was the case in other Latin American countries. Felix Rosar (1997) argues that adopting educational decentralization policies, particularly transfering responsibilities to the municipal level, has taken place in Brazil since the 1970s—from the point at which the Keynesian economic model began to lose credibility in the region—in the context of the globalization of the economy and with a central role of international organizations in promoting these strategies.

The 1988 constitution granted autonomy to municipal education systems. In addition, after reestablishing democracy in 1985, some states allowed the creation of school councils, composed by teachers, administrators, students, and parents, that make administrative decisions and, in some cases, select the principal. Moreover, some states and municipalities included budget and personnel administration within the responsibilities of school councils (Plank et al. 1996).

At the same time, the national government had been implementing a centralized system of evaluation since 1991, along with other measures that seem to aim at the integration of the system (Souza 1997, de la Fuente et al. 1998). A ten-year federal plan was approved in 1993 with the goals of establishing minimum curricular contents and standards for educational management, among other lines of action. In 1996, the Congress passed a law of education (*Lei de Diretrizes e Bases*) that encourages school autonomy but also establishes a more active role for the federal government.[13]

Xavier et al. (1994) analyse the decentralization policies that have created new trends in school management in Brazil from the end of the 1980s. In their view, the main elements of decentralization have been:

1. Transfering resource management from states to schools in order to gain efficiency. The authors identify the first case in 1977, but stress that it has become much more usual during the 1990s. In most cases, funds are decentralized for facilities maintenance, as well as purchasing pedagogic and other materials; in some cases funds can be used for contracting services or providing training. Usually, state governments have provided some form of training or support for resource management. This kind of innovation has faced two problems: bureaucratic barriers for effective implementation and lack of local capacities.

2. Participation mechanisms. The democratic election of principals is a new trend that appears as a consequence of the process of political democratization during the 1980s. At the same time, many states and municipalities have established school councils, with participation of parents, teachers, students, and administrators. Implementing participation mechanisms has had problems due to lack of experience with these mechanisms and authoritarian attitudes by principals (Xavier et al. 1994).

In her analysis of school management policies in eleven municipalities during the 1990s, Krawczyk (1999) notes the trend toward constituting schools as "autonomous institutions with the capacity to make their own decisions, organize tasks around institutional projects, administer economic resources in an adequate way, and select procedures," within the limits set by—and under the control of—municipal authorities (144, my translation). These policies, it is argued, have aimed at improving the quality of education, but two of their consequences have been fragmented educational systems, in which schools are "abandoned" to their own fate (ibid., 145), and the adoption—in a mechanical manner—of management models derived from the experience of business enterprises (ibid., 146).

It is noteworthy that states and municipalities in Brazil have implemented very different types of school decentralization policies. In the cities of Sao

Paulo and Porto Alegre, for example, programs have decentralized decision-making power to schools based on a radical democratization rationale.[14]

The case of Minas Gerais illustrates a more common type of reform.[15] In Minas Gerais, a comparatively rich state in Brazil, a reform started in 1991 promoting a new model of school management that encouraged school autonomy in the administrative, pedagogic, and financial aspects along with community participation. This was accompanied by a state evaluation system of student achievement (including municipal schools), as well as increases in teachers' salaries and in expenditures per student (Castro and Carnoy 1997). The reform was implemented with technical and financial support from the World Bank (Neto 1997).

According to Neto (1994), at the time state secretary of education, the reform mainly aimed at improving quality through active involvement of families and the community. Other general objectives were to increase social equity and decrease clientelistic practices. The objective of financial decentralization was to increase efficiency: "The knowledge the community has about the school reality makes the decentralized management of the available resources much more efficient" (Neto 1994, 91, my translation). From a critical point of view, Oliveira and Duarte (1997) hold that in implementing of the reform, there has been an emphasis on efficient management, which has implied neglecting quality considerations.[16]

Guedes et al. (1997) characterize the emerging system in Minas Gerais as one in which schools have autonomy for making decisions about day-to-day issues while the state government plays the role of strategic planner. About 30 percent of the content of the curriculum is established at the school level. In addition, individual schools select the texts, instructional methods, classroom organization, and evaluation methods. Schools also decide on hiring administrative personnel and temporary teachers, evaluate teachers' performance and determine the need for training, and manage the lunch program. The school community elects the principal and can ask the central office for her removal. School councils (presided by the school principal, including representatives of teachers, parents and students from age sixteen) have some responsibility in pedagogic, administrative, and financial aspects. All school-level administrative decisions need to be approved by the council. Councils participate in designing the school budget and have a say in establishing the priorities in the use of some funds that are given directly to schools. Guedes et al. (1997) point out that the transfer of administrative functions to schools implied extra work without the necessary training, and lacked the possibility of contracting additional personnel (see also Zibas 1997).

The new policies implemented in Minas Gerais included some integration of the municipal schools to the state system in the areas of evaluation and teacher training, and through the provision of technical support from the state level. However, Guedes et al. (1997) suggest that differences in the quality of education that state and municipal schools offer may be increasing as a consequence of the decentralization process that affects only state schools, resulting in the accentuation of a double system of state and municipal public schools serving two different kinds of populations. Differences among schools may also increase in a system in which the best-equipped schools are in the best position to get additional resources (Zibas 1997). Moreover, pressures resulting from the process of external evaluation and competition among schools seem to be encouraging an informal process of privatization through the imposition of registration and special fees by individual schools to students (ibid.).

Chile

Chile is considered the country in the region that adopted the most radical approach to neoliberal economic restructuring, provoking the worst social effects (Mesa Lago 1994). Under the dictatorship of Pinochet, Chile was the first country to initiate a comprehensive neoliberal program in 1975, which was pushed by the ideology of a group of economists formed in the University of Chicago rather than by international lending agencies.

In that context, an important educational reform was implemented. Its main elements were the administrative decentralization to the municipal level, competition between public and private schools, a new scheme of school financing based on the number of students, and the transfer of teachers from the public employee system to the private sector. Privatization was pursued through the establishment of private corporations that were allowed to administer municipal systems, and through a system of per-student vouchers that could be used in both public and private (subsidized) schools (Gauri 1998).[17] As Schiefelbein and Schiefelbein (2001) point out, "it was assumed that market competition would improve efficiency and even generate some additional local funding" (2). However, the financing of schools, curriculum design, student achievement evaluation, and distribution of textbooks remained centralized at the national level. There has been consensus that the privatization and municipalization policies implemented in Chile during the 1980s had negative effects for rural and poor sectors, and did not increase the general quality of the system (Arnove et al. 1997, Munín 1998, Tedesco 1994).

With the returning to democracy in 1990, the new authorities decided to maintain decentralization, but with a new role for the center of the system in order to deal with the lack of equity in the educational system (Tedesco 1994). The democratic governments reversed some of the policies implemented by the military government in a context of economic growth and stabilization. "The Aylwin government allowed unions to reorganize in the public sector, and actively consult[ed] them over future changes" (Angell and Graham 1995, 206). Educational expenditures and the salaries of teachers rose significantly since the reestablishment of democracy.

One of the main initiatives of the first democratic government was the Program for the Improvement of Educational Quality and Equity for primary and secondary schools, which started in 1992 with international assistance (World Bank) and a focus on schools serving rural and poor urban sectors. One of the components of the program was pedagogic decentralization. Each school involved in the program was supposed to produce a "Project of Educational Improvement" with the participation of directors and teachers, and with technical and financial support from the National Ministry (Cox 1995). The program espouses the idea of the improvement of quality through teacher professionalization and adaptation to the particular needs of students, innovation, and teamwork. "The objective of the Pedagogic Decentralization is to achieve the activation of the capacities of innovation and pedagogic autonomy of teachers, and a change in the organizational culture of schools, as a necessary condition for the continuous improvement in student learning" (Cox 1995, 56, my translation).

From 1996, all schools in the system have had the possibility of achieving more autonomy in curriculum design. The central government defines some national guidelines for curriculum, and at the same time offers a complete national curriculum. Each school has the chance of either defining some curricular contents (covering some 40 percent of the learning time) according to its own pedagogic project, or to adopt the national curriculum (Cox 1997, Schiefelbein and Schiefelbein 2001). Again, directors and teachers are the actors who are invited to take part in this innovation, and the main objective is to foster teacher professionalization and teamwork for improving the quality of instruction (Cox 1997).

Corvalán (2001) suggests that school decentralization has been promoted in administrative aspects and to a lesser extent in the curriculum dimension, within a policy framework that rejects the neoliberal concept of public choice and seeks a more equitable distribution of educational opportunities. In a similar vein, Cox (1995) states that the Chilean Ministry of Education adopted a more active role than during the 1980s, formulating policies and strategies for the development of the system, providing technical support to individual schools, and developing central information and evaluation systems.

It is not clear whether this shift in the role of the state represents a movement away from neoliberalism to a different model (Cox 1995) or just a correction of some imperfections of the model articulated during Pinochet's government (Munin 1998), including a component of "investment in people." The reforms implemented aiming at establishing higher salaries and better working conditions for teachers can be seen as "a requisite for improving the operation of market systems in education" (Schiefelbein and Schiefelbein 2001, 11). In addition, the introduction of policies that encourage school autonomy suggests the possibility of "further educational segmentation caused by more attractive profiling of the schools with more resources" and seems to be in line with the neoliberal idea of competition among schools (Munín 1998, 237). On the other hand, there seems to be a clear rupture in educational policy with the return of democracy, aiming at achieving more equity and a more integrated system.

Mexico

Mexico has experienced economic restructuring at least since 1985. The Salinas administration (1988–1994) moved the country to an open economy, a movement that reached a peak with the signing of the North-American Free Trade Agreement (NAFTA) with the United States and Canada in 1993.

The federalization of the Mexican education system, announced by President De la Madrid in 1982, really began in 1992 with a new law of education and agreements between the federal and state governments, as well as with the powerful teachers' union. These agreements transferred responsibilities and resources from the federal government to the states and municipalities. The reform signified a massive transfer of buildings, teachers, and students to the states, which in turn should advance in the municipalization of the system. This administrative decentralization was accompanied by the idea of social participation. The law established the creation of councils with the participation of parents and teachers at the school, municipal, and state levels.

Latapí (1996) points out that educational policies in Mexico under Presidents De la Madrid and Salinas did not have an important neoliberal component. However, he argues, education was affected by the neoliberal economic reform in three aspects: the general impoverishment of the population translated into lower attendance rates and less motivated and dedicated teachers; the instability of employment made youth question the benefits of education; and educational expenditures decreased due to the servicing of external debts.

Esteinou Madrid (1996), on the other hand, argues that the neoliberal model of development in Mexico has required important changes in the cultural area. A main aspect of these changes is the educational reform that national governments have been implementing, which aims at creating the intellectual capital necessary for the international insertion of the country and the creation of a culture of the market. In this view, the decentralization of education and curricular changes (as well as the support of privatization at the higher education level) are geared toward integration with the productive sector and the development of technical education that responds to the productive needs of the country.

According to Ornelas (1997), the reform involved centralization of power in the national ministry along with decentralization of the administration of the system. The national ministry maintained control and the evaluation of the system. It also implied an adaptation of the corporativist pact between the government and the powerful teachers' union, which responded to "the new challenges of the open economy, the international competency, and the reform of the State" (15, my translation). In another work, Ornelas (2001) suggests that the process of decentralization was pushed by several forces, including the official discourse of federalism, the efficiency argument, the government's attempts to establish more control over the national teachers' union and decentralize conflict, and the influence of the World Bank.

The educational reform designed at the national level has included the idea of decentralizing authority and/or responsibility to individual schools. The vehicle for this decentralization is the "school project," in which teachers should design curricular and organizational changes "in order to improve quality" (Ornelas 2001, 19). Several barriers for the implementation of school projects have been identified: lack of interest from state authorities given that the design and guidelines come from the national level; teachers' resistance to undertaking new roles and to the extra work that new responsibilities represent; and active opposition from teachers' unions (ibid). The Fox administration (2001–present) has recently launched a program called *Escuelas de Calidad* (Quality Schools), which employs the strategy of supporting the actions for improving quality that each school community decides through the design of a school project. The support includes financial and technical assitance as well as training of school actors. The program promotes the idea of the school as the unit of change and of school actors as responsible for student achievement (Mexico 2002).

With regard to the Councils of Social Participation, Martínez (1995) holds that the councils, given the responsibilities and resources they are assigned, might influence the management of school only at the more centralized levels (federal and state councils, and to a certain extent, municipal councils), with lack of real power for parents at the school level. Ornelas (2001) notes the resistance from the national teachers' union to parental and community participation, and points out that wider participation through the use of councils has not been achieved.

Discussion

During the 1990s, various forms of decentralization took place in the countries just discussed. Argentina completed the transfer of basic education institutions to provinces and initiated a policy of school decentralization (or autonomy) at national and provincial levels. In Brazil, there was a continuation of decentralization to the municipal level (particularly of primary schools) as well as many examples of decentralization of functions to schools. Chile started a process of school decentralization in administrative and pedagogical aspects. And Mexico carried out a major process of transferring responsibilities to the state level while proposing decentralization to individual schools.

The processes of provincialization in Argentina and municipalization in Brazil mainly responded to the financial argument or rationale. In the case of Argentina, provincialization may have also responded to the intention of diffusing conflicts with teacher unions. In most cases, these decentralization processes have not resulted in the empowerment of provinces or municipalities, due to their financial constraints and lack of technical expertise. In the case of Mexico, decentralization to states was pushed by a variety of factors, including the goals of gaining efficiency, establishing a new relationship with the teachers' union, and difussing conflict.

A common feature of the policies of the 1990s in these four countries is central governments' aim of gaining more control over the planning and evaluation of education while leaving to subnational governments and schools more space for the adaptation of central guidelines (or as Popkewitz [1996] puts it, moving from bureaucratic control to goal steering). In addition, the countries shared discourse favoring "school autonomy," which involved decentralizing some pedagogic, administrative, and financial functions to schools. The question remains whether real decision-making power is transferred to the schools or just the responsibility for implementing centrally designed policies and achieving good results (see Smyth 1993). This centralization (goals, evaluation)/decentralization (school autonomy) pattern, which has taken place in different parts of the world (see Caldwell 1990), appeared as the prevailing model of reform both at the national and state/provincial levels in Argentina and Brazil, and to some extent in Chile. Schools were granted some autonomy but within central guidelines and controls.

The similarities in these centralization/decentralization movements might be related to the similarities in the contextual factors that seem to be shaping educational policies in Latin America. During the 1990s, Argentina, Brazil, and Mexico (Chile had started the process during the 1980s) embarked on neoliberal restructuring of the state and integration to the world economy under the guidance of international financial organizations like the International Monetary Fund and the World Bank. These processes have included modernizing education and other social sectors, and have implied, in some cases, high social costs that translate into increasing social segmentation along with the pauperization of middle classes (see Minujin and Kessler 1995, Sader 1998). The impact of globalization can be considered both in terms of the influence of educational models from central countries and international organizations' prescriptions, and of the pressures (both internal and external) for adapting educational systems to the demands of the global economy.[18] Neoliberalism, on the other hand, can be seen entailing a less direct kind of state intervention, promoting competition among schools and more involvement of local communities in funding and/or administration. In Brazil, democratization demands, very explicit during the 1980s (Cunha 1991), continued to influence policies for broadening participation of teachers, parents, and students in school councils and selecting principals.

Historically, the signaled changes seem to imply that the national state adopted a new strategic position for the regulation of education during the 1990s. In Chile the central government pursued a more active role addressing quality and equity issues. Mexico implemented a reform toward a more focused and effective role in educational planning. In the case of Argentina, the state seemed to regain a strategic place while allowing a higher degree of decentralization in particular issues. Brazil, finally, experienced a process of reordering its educational system toward a clearer division of functions among the different levels of government. In this sense, the education sector is modernized, which does not necessarily mean an improvement in quality or equity.

The main justification for the policies that promoted decentralization to the school was to improve the quality of instruction. The decentralization of decision making to schools and local actors was seen to increase responsiveness to local conditions and students' particular characteristics, teacher professionalization, and the production of relevant curriculum. In the case of Minas Gerais, the involvement of local communities becomes crucial to increase the accountability of teachers and principals. In addition, school decentralization serves other objectives, like efficiency (Argentina, Brazil) and social participation (Brazil, Mexico). In the cases of Argentina and Brazil, the financial argument may have been still present in a hidden way if school decentralization was expected to encourage individuals and local communities to become more involved in the financial support of local schools. However, in both cases educational budgets increased, and in the case of Argentina, funds were directly assigned to schools in some of the most disadvantaged areas of the country.

Even for analysts who enthusiastically adhere to school decentralization (such as Winkler and Gershberg 2000), there is no clear evidence about the effects of school autonomy policies carried out during the 1990s throughout the region over the quality of education and student achievement. At the same time, in some cases like Argentina and Mexico the actual implementation of school autonomy policies at schools appeared to be very limited.

In any case, successful implementation of school decentralization (providing more learning opportunities for all students) seemed to face important barriers. McGinn and Pereira (1992) point to the need for supporting local actors with technical skills and economic means in order to avoid deepening inequalities. Some authors suggest that these kinds of supports did not take place in Latin America during the 1990s (Arnove et al. 1997, Munín 1998, Puiggrós 1996). Even in the cases where support programs were carried out there are questions about the possibility of extending those programs to all schools and about their sustainability. Morevoer, a political and socioeconomic context that did not encourage a more equitable distribution of opportunities and resources—and that in some cases tended to accentuate social disparities—could be seen as a major obstacle to advancing toward school autonomy for most schools. The low levels of material and cultural resources at most schools threaten the effectiveness of school autonomy, while current variations among regions and schools are likely to increase as a consequence of decentralization.[19]

Another aspect of the reforms that should be highlighted is the problem of participation. Some cases show a lack of effective structures for the participation of parents (Mexico), while others point to the problem of lack of ownership and motivation from the part of teachers (Argentina, Chile, Mexico).[20] These problems imply additional barriers for effectively implementing reforms. In addition, there is a lack of proposals for the internal democratization of schools. As Torres and Puiggrós (1995) argue, the present nature of state and public policy in Latin America does not seem to encourage community empowerment and democratic participation. Even when individual schools and families are given more responsibilities with regard to funding and administration, there is not evidence of more participatory and inclusive methods for decision making.

The educational changes occurring in Latin America are clearly influenced by the ideas that seem to be shaping the "new orthodoxy" of educational policies worldwide, like neoliberalism, the new managerialism (the new role of principals as managers), the demands for performativity, and the use of devolution and incentives for institutional redesign (see Ball 1998). From the point of view of the "new orthodoxy," educational systems, gaining in efficiency and quality, are expected to produce better human resources able to improve the economic competitiveness of their countries in international markets (see also Castro and Carnoy 1997). As Gentili (1994) notes, this trend may suggest subordination of education to the market, playing a role in the process of social polarization that affect Latin American countries.

Neoliberalism seems to explain, in part, the nature of educational policies that are implemented. The reforms share some characteristics of the neoliberal political style, namely the importance of policies for targeted groups and the strengthening of the apex of the state (Weyland 1996). On the other hand, the new trends do not seem to point to an extended marketization (i.e., privatization and competition among schools) of education. This might be due to the internal contradictions of the "neoliberal model," and particularly to its neoconservative elements, which can be considered to push for a more integrated and centrally controlled system (see Arnove 1997), and to the need for orienting the system toward national targets of human capital development. It might be also the case that, without escaping from the influence of globalization forces and neoliberal restructuring of the state, educational reformers do not necessarily embrace a neoliberal strategy of educational reform, attempting in some cases to find alternatives that may be seen as more democratic or more concerned with equity and the integration of the education system (as Braslavsky and Cosse [1997] suggest). As Corvalán (2001) points out, the educational policies of the 1990s hold elements from both the welfare (pre-1980s) and neoliberal state models, combining the aims of social integration and equality with a decrease of central states' functions and a reformulation of the relationships between state and society.

It is not clear whether increasing school autonomy in pedagogical and administrative aspects necessarily implies a relinquishment of the central authorities and a movement toward an educational market. According to Munín (1998), school autonomy is based on less intervention from state (deregulation); schools are responsible for results, so the state cannot be blamed for poor achievements. According to Braslavsky (1996) and Cox (1995), on the other hand, it is a different kind of intervention, where support is provided in a decentralized manner.

Conclusion

In this chapter, I have examined the educational decentralization policies implemented in Argentina, Brazil, Chile and Mexico during the 1990s, with a special focus on the new policies of school decentralization and their relationship with neoliberalism. The analysis has identified the rationales and contexts of the policies, and pointed to some implementation problems.

The general trend seems to be toward a model of "school autonomy" that promotes innovation and accountability for modernizing educational systems in the context of neoliberal restructuring of the relationships between state and society. This decentralization movement, which includes pedagogic, administrative, and financial aspects, is coupled with the centralization of evaluation and planning at the federal level and, to a lesser extent, at the state/provincial level. Both the action of international organizations promoting new models of school management and a new role for the state, as well as the pressures for adaptation to the global economy appear as important factors pushing for the implementation of this kind of educational reform. At the same time, the need for finding new mechanisms for state consolidation and for responding to internal demands regarding educational quality and efficiency also seem to be influencing the direction of policies. As Popkewitz (1996, 191) has noted, "the changes in [educational] governing have no single origin that can be reducible to ideology, economy or hegemony."

School decentralization offers many promises and has proven to be attractive—for different reasons—to governments of diverse political orientations. It is not clear what has been the authentic level of authority decentralization to schools among the different cases, and it is not clear what have been its effects on schools and classrooms either.

As Rosa María Torres (2001, 286–288) argues, an educational system that centers on learning should have the school as the key unit of operation and change. The possibility of changing schools toward more autonomous ways of organization, however, seems to depend on the existence of active support from the state and society, and on participatory policy processes that include teachers' organizations, parents, students, and community members.

Notes

1. The cases of Chile, Nicaragua, and Peru are cited as examples of privatization and community participation in the financing of education (Arnove et al. 1997, Torres and Puiggrós 1995).
2. For a discussion of the different rationales of educational decentralization, see Gorostiaga Derqui (2001).
3. Brazil, however, presented some specific features that can be traced to the Portuguese colonization as well as to the fact that political independence was obtained without fighting a war (Siqueira Wiarda 1996). The first attempts to define a national educational policy took place around 1930 (de Morais 1989). Before that time, a national system of education was virtually nonexistent (see Plank 1996, 63).
4. Tedesco (1984) states that primary schools have been characterized by a high degree of homogeneity in organization and curriculum, aiming at the integration of the population. However, he notes that, in reality, schools within each country have been organized in very different ways (e.g., the differences between urban and rural schools).
5. A different model was that of "nuclearization" (in rural districts of Bolivia, Ecuador, Honduras, Nicaragua, and Peru), in which a small network of schools organized around a well-equipped school with a degree of autonomy and integration with the local community (Newland 1995).
6. In Argentina, this type of financial reform is best illustrated by the transfer of national primary schools to the provinces that the military government implemented in 1978. It has been noted that this was not a step toward an actual decentralization of the system, even in narrow administrative terms, because the centralized management of schools had been and continued to be a feature of the provincial governments (Tenti Fanfani 1990).
7. By the end of the 1980s it was apparent that the Argentine educational system was organized in an irrational way that resulted in the anarchy of the system (Tenti Fanfani 1990). As a result of many years of political instability, authoritarian ideology, economic crisis, and a noncollaborative organizational culture, the whole educational system was informed by a management style characterized by the rejection of changes and innovations and by a focus on the bureaucratic tasks, a style which proved to be difficult to change even after the restoration of democracy in 1983 (Braslavsky and Tiramonti 1990). On the other hand, during previous years public schools had started to gain more autonomy because central bureaucracies were ineffective in controlling them (Braslavsky 1993).
8. The national government argued that from 1991 significant increases in tax collection resulted in more resources for the provinces, which allowed them to finance the administration of the transferred schools (Senén González and Arango 1997).
9. Apparently, the Federal Council of Education does not have an active role in the production of proposals, but discusses the documents produced by the ministry. The decisions of the Federal Council of Education are not compulsory for the provinces but the provinces' financial dependence on the national government—because of the tax system—and lack of expert knowledge make them follow those decisions (Tiramonti 1996).
10. The national budget for education increased about 30 percent between 1993 and 1996 (Braslavsky 1999). As Morduchowicz (1999) shows, this growth translated in an increasing transfer of funds from the national level to provinces and schools in the areas of infrastructure, equipment, scholarships and development of school institutional projects, and teacher training.
11. Tiramonti (1996), among others, questions the reforms aimed at providing quality education for all groups. She holds that one of the characteristics of the educational policy of the Menem administration was a dual political proposal that responded to the increasing dual

structure of society. It consisted of compensatory programs for the poorest sectors, like the Social Plan, and of pedagogic changes for groups that demand better education in order to improve their social status.

12. It has been recognized that national authorities failed to include nongovernmental organizations like teachers' unions in the discussion and negotiation of educational policies, and were not able to create broad public support for the proposed changes (Braslavsky 1999).

13. During the late 1990s, the Cardoso administration launched several national programs— including compensatory actions, computer training for teachers, and the provision of funds directly to schools—and established curricular guidelines for all schools in the country (Brazil 1999).

14. In both cases the PT (*Partido dos Trabalhadores*) was the dominant political force. In the City of Sao Paulo, the reform, which was lead by Paulo Freire in 1989˙1991, was replaced by a "Total Quality Control" approach when a government from a different party was elected in 1992 (O'Cadiz et al. 1998).

15. As Oliveira and Duarte (1997) note, the case of Minas Gerais has served as a model for other states and for the federal Ministry of Education in Brazil, as well as internationally.

16. Oliveira and Duarte (1997) also argue that the reform implemented in Minas Gerais has reinforced an authoritarian model of educational policy that does not include—as participants or negotiators—the different social actors.

17. The prohibitions of charging fees to students and of student selection were not respected in many cases, particularly by subsidized private schools. In 1990, a law established for all schools the possibility of charging fees not exceeding 50 percent of the voucher (Schiefelbein and Schiefelbein 2001)

18. As noted before, the World Bank, a major financial source for education reform in both countries during the 1990s, has enthusiastically promoted school decentralization. Adams et al. (2000) point to the paradox of reforms that encourage decentralization to the local level with important input from international agencies, and suggest that this kind of reform could be labeled "super-centralization."

19. Most advocates of school decentralization recognize the need for external supports to schools in the processes of gaining autonomy (Caldwell 1990, Hanson 1997, World Bank 1995). The lack of capacities at provincial/state and local levels for providing the necessary support to schools becomes a critical issue, particularly in the poorest regions of the countries.

20. Even though a lack of effective structures for the participation of parents can also be identified in Argentina and Chile, the case of Mexico is noteworthy because of the discursive emphasis placed on parental and community participation.

References

Adams, D., M. Ginsburg, T. Clayton, M. Mantilla, J. Sylvester, and Y. Wang. (2000). "Linking Research to Educational Policy and Practice: What Kind of Relationships in How (De)centralized a Context?" In B. Levinson and M. Sutton, eds. *New Approaches to Studying Educational Policy Formation and Approriation*. New York: Ablex.

Angell, A. and C. Graham. (1995). "Can Social Reform Make Adjustment Sustainable and Equitable? Lessons from Chile and Venezuela." *Journal of Latin American Studies* 27: 189–219.

Apple, M. (2001). "Comparing Neo-liberal Projetcs and Inequality in Education." *Comparative Education* 37, no. 4: 409–423.

Argentina. (1993). *Ley Federal de Educación*. Buenos Aires: Ministerio de Cultura y Educación.

Argentina (1996a). "*Condiciones básicas institucionales: Nuevos contenidos en una escuela diferente*." Buenos Aires: Ministerio de Cultura y Educación.

Argentina. (1996b). *Aspectos estructurantes de la organización y la gestión de la escuela: El tiempo, el espacio y los agrupamientos*. Buenos Aires: Ministerio de Cultura y Educación.

Argentina (1996c). Descentralización y autonomía. *Zona Educativa* 6 (Ministerio de Cultura y Educación): 10–16.

Argentina. (October 1998). Ministerio de Cultura y Educación (National Ministry of Education) web page: http://www.mcye.gov.ar

Arnove, R. F., A. Torres, S. Franz, and K. Morse. (1997). "A Political Sociology of Education and Development in Latin America." In Y. W. Bradshaw, ed. *Education in Comparative Perspective*. New York: E. J. Brill.

Arnove, R. F. (1997). "Neoliberal Education Policies in Latin America." In C. A. Torres and A. Puiggrós eds. *Latin American Education: Comparative Perspectives*. Boulder, Colo.: Westview Press.

Ball, S. J. (1998). "Big Policies/Small World: An Introduction to International Perspectives in Education Policy." *Comparative Education* 34, no. 2: 119–130

Braslavsky, C. and G. Tiramonti. (1990). *Conducción educativa y calidad de la enseñanza media*. Buenos Aires: Miño y Dávila Editores.

Braslavsky, C. (1993). *Autonomía y anomia en la educación pública argentina*. Buenos Aires: Flacso.

Braslavsky, C. and G. Cosse. (1997). *Las actuales reformas educativas en América Latina: Cuatro actores, tres lógicas y ocho tensiones*. Washington, D.C.: Inter-American Dialogue. PREAL No. 5.

Braslavsky, C. (1998). "Restructuring the Argentine Educational System, 1984–1995." In J. S. Tulchin, with A. M. Garland, eds. *Argentina: The Challenges of Modernization*. Wilmington, Dela.: Scholarly Resources, Inc.

Braslavsky, C. (1999). "La reforma educativa en la Argentina: Avances y desafíos." *Propuesta Educativa* 21: 80–88.

Brazil (1999). "Educaçao brasileira: Políticas e resultados." Available at Brazilian Ministry of Education web page, http://www.mec.gov.br/home/poleduc/default.shtm.

Caldwell, B. (1990). "School-Based Decision-Making and Management: International Developments." In J. Chapman, ed. *School-Based Decision-Making and Management*. London: Falmer Press.

Castro, C. de M. and M. Carnoy. (1997). *Como anda a reforma da educaçao na América Latina?* Rio de Janeiro: Fundaçao Getulio Vargas.

Coraggio, J. L. (1995). "Educación y modelo de desarrollo." In V. Edwards and J. Osorio, eds. *La construcción de las políticas educativas en América Latina*. Santiago: CEAAL.

Corvalán, J. (2001). *Las transformaciones educativas recientes y los cambios de la política social en Chile y América Latina: Hipótesis sobre los discursos dominantes*. Santiago: CIDE.

Cox, C. (1995). "Chile: Políticas de mejoramiento de la calidad y equidad de la educación escolar en la década de los años 90." In CORDES and BID, *Educación, crecimiento y equidad*. Quito: CORDES.

Cox, C. (1997). *La reforma de la educación chilena: Contexto, contenidos, implementación*. Santiago: PREAL.

CTERA. (1997). "Situación de la educación en Argentina. Diagnóstico." Available at CTERA web page http://www.wami.apc.org/ctera/diagno.html.

Cunha, L. A. (1991). *Educaçao, estado e democracia no Brasil*. Sao Paulo: Cortes Editora.

Cury, C. R. J. (1992). "A nova lei de Diretrizes e Bases e suas implicaçoes nos estados e municipios: O Sistema Nacional de Educaçao." *Educaçao & Sociedade* 41: 186–201.

de la Fuente, M. T., E. Luck, and C. Ramos. (1998). "Monitoring and Evaluation of Educational Reform Initiatives in the State of Paraná, Brazil." In B. Alvarez H. and M. Ruiz-Casares, eds. *Evaluation and Educational Reform: Policy Options*. Washington, D.C.: Academy for Educational Development.

de Morais, R. (1989). *Cultura brasileira e educaçao*. Campinas, SP: Papirus.

de Oliveira, F. (1998). "Vanguardia del atraso y atraso de la vanguardia: Globalización y neoliberalismo en América Latina." In E. Sader, ed. *Democracia sin exclusiones ni excluidos*. Caracas: ALAS, CLACSO, UNESCO, Editorial Nueva Sociedad.

ECLAC and UNESCO. (1992). *Education and Knowledge: Basic Pillars of Changing Production Patterns with Social Equity*. Santiago: UNESCO.

Esteinou Madrid, J. (1996). "Contexto sociopolítico de la modernidad en educación." In J. Esteinou M. et al., *Modernización de la educación en México*. Mexico, D.F.: Universidad Autónoma Metropolitana.

Experton, W. (1999). *Desafíos para la nueva etapa de la reforma educativa en Argentina*. Washington, D.C.: The World Bank. LCSHD Paper Series No. 46.

Felix Rosar, M. (1997). "A municipalizaçao como estratégia de descentralizaçao e de desconstruçao do sistema brasileiro." In D. A. Oliveira, ed. *Gestao democratica da educacao*. Petropolis: Vozes.

Filmus, D. (1998). "La descentralización educativa en el centro del debate." In D. Filmus and A. Isuani, eds. *La Argentina que viene*. Buenos Aires: Norma.

García de Fanelli, A. M. (1997). "Reformas en la educación básica y superior en la Argentina: Avances y restricciones en su implementación." In CEPAS, ed. *Los desafíos para el estado en la Argentina actual*. Buenos Aires: Universidad de Buenos Aires.

Garretón, M. A. (1996). "Citizenship, National Integration and Education: Ideology and Consensus in Latin America." *Prospects* 26, no. 4: 683–94.

Gauri, V. (1998). *School Choice in Chile: Two Decades of Educational Reform.* Pittsburgh, Pa.: University of Pittsburgh Press.

Gentili, P. (1994). "El discurso del la "calidad" como nueva retórica conservadora en el campo educativo." In *Proyecto neoconservador y crisis educativa.* Buenos Aires: Centro Editor de América Latina.

Gorostiaga Derqui, J. (2001). "Educational Decentralization Policies in Argentina and Brazil: Exploring the New Trends." *Journal of Education Policy* 16, no. 6: 561–583.

Guedes, A., T. Lobo, R. Walker, and A. Amaral. (1997). "Gestión descentralizada de la educación en el Estado de Minas Gerais, Brasil." LSCHD Paper Series 11. Washington, D.C.: World Bank.

Hanson, M. (1997). *Educational decentralization: Issues and challenges.* Washington, D.C.: Inter-American Dialogue. PREAL, No. 9.

Kingstone, P. R. (1999). *Crafting Coalitions for Reform: Business Preferences, Political Institutions and Neoliberal Reform in Brazil.* University Park, Pa.: The Pennsylvania State University Press.

Krawczyk, N. (1999). "A gestao escolar: Um campo minado . . . Análise das propostas de 11 municipios brasileiros." *Educaçao & Sociedade,* ano 20 (67): 112–149.

Latapí, P. (1996). "Neoliberalismo y educación." *Tiempo Educativo Mexicano* 4: 15–18. Aguascalientes: Universidad Autónoma de Aguascalientes.

Llach, J. J., S. Montoya, and F. Roldán. (1999). *Educación para todos.* Córdoba: IERAL.

Martínez P., J. L. (1995). *Reformas educativas comparadas: Los casos de Bolivia, México, Chile y España.* La Paz, Bolivia: CEBIAE.

McGinn, N. and L. Pereira. (1992). "Why States Change the Governance of Education: An Historical Comparison of Brazil and the United States." *Comparative Education* 28, no. 2: 167–80.

McGinn, N. (1992). "Reforming educational governance: Centralization/decentralization." In R. F. Arnove, P. G. Altbach, and G. P. Kelly, Eds. *Emergent Issues in Education: Comparative Perspectives.* Albany, N.Y.: State University of New York Press.

Mesa Lago, C. (1994). *Changing Social Security in Latin America: Toward Alleviating the Social Costs of Economic Reform.* Boulder, Colo.: Rienner.

Mexico (2002). "Reglas de operación e indicadores de gestión y evaluación del Programa de Escuelas de Calidad." Available at http://www.sep.gob.mx. May 2002.

Minujin, A. and G. Kessler. (1995). *La nueva pobreza en la Argentina.* Buenos Aires: Editorial Planeta.

Morduchowicz, A. (1999). *Una mirada desde los costos del sistema educativo argentino.* Buenos Aires: Ministerio de Cultura y Educación.

Munín, H. (1998). "'Freer' Forms of Organization and Financing and the Effects of Inequality in Latin American Educational Systems: Two Countries in Comparison. *Compare* 28, no. 3: 229–244.

Neto, W. S. dos Mares Guia. (1994). "Repasse de recursos para a escola: Critérios, mecanismos e tendencias—A experiencia de Minas Gerais." In C. da R. Xavier, J. A. Sobrinho, and F. Marra, eds. *Gestao Escolar: Desafios e Tendencias.* Brasilia: IPEA.

Neto, W. S. dos Mares Guia (1997). "A reforma educativa em Minas Gerais." In C. de M. Castro and M. Carnoy, eds. *Como anda a reforma da educaçao na América Latina?* Rio de Janeiro: Fundaçao Getulio Vargas.

Newland, C. (1994). "The *Estado Docente* and Its Expansion: Spanish American Elementary Education 1900–1950." *Journal of Latin American Studies* 26: 449–467.

Newland, C. (1995). "Spanish American Elementary Education 1950–1992: Bureaucracy, Growth and Decentralization." *International Journal of Educational Development* 15, no. 2: 103–114.

O'Cadiz, M., P. Lindquist Wong, and C. A. Torres. (1998). *Education and Democracy: Paulo Freire, Social Movements, and Educational Reform in Sao Paulo.* Boulder, Colo.: Westview Press.

Oliveira, D. A. and M. R. T. Duarte. (1997). "Política e administraçao da educaçao: Um estudo de algumas reformas recentes implementadas no estado de Minas Gerais." *Educaçao & Sociedade,* ano 18 (58): 123–139.

Ornelas, C. (1997). *La descentralización de la educación en México: Un estudio preliminar.* Documento de Trabajo no. 35. México: CIDE.

Ornelas, C. (2001). "The Politics of the Educational Decentralization in Mexico." Available at http://www1.worldbank.org/education. Feb. 2002.

Plank, D. (1996). *The Means of our Salvation: Public Education in Brazil, 1930–1995.* Boulder, Colo.: Westview Press.

Plank, D. N., J. A. Sobrinho, and A. C. Xavier. (1996). "Why Brazil Lags Behind in Educational Development." In N. Birdsall and R. H. Sabot, eds. *Opportunity Foregone: Education in Brazil.* Washington, D.C.: Inter-American Development Bank.

Popkewitz, T. S. (1996). "Rethinking Decentralization and the State/Civil Society Distinctions: The State as a Problematic of Governing." *Journal of Education Policy* 11, no. 1: 25–48.

Porto Alegre. (1999). *Cycles of Formation: Politic-Pedagogical Proposal for the Citizen's School.* Porto Alegre, Rio Grande do Sul: City Secretariat of Education.

Puiggrós, A. (1996) "World Bank Education Policy: Market Liberalism Meets Ideological Conservatism." *NACLA Report on the Americas* 29, no. 6.

Puiggrós, A. (1997). *La otra reforma: Desde la educación menemista hasta el fin de siglo.* Buenos Aires: Galerna.

Purcell, S. K., and R. Roett, eds. (1997). *Brazil under Cardoso.* Boulder, Colo.: Lynne Rienner.

Ribeiro, M. L. S. (1989). *Historia da educaçao brasileira: A organizaçao escolar.* Sao Paulo: Cortez Editora/Autores Asociados.

Sader, E. (1998). "Brasil: Una cartografía de la injusticia." In E. Sader, ed. *Democracia sin exclusiones ni excluidos.* Caracas: ALAS, CLACSO, UNESCO, Editorial Nueva Sociedad.

Schiefelbein, E. and P. Schiefelbein. (2001). "Three decentralization strategies in two decades: Chile 1981–2000." Available at: http://www1.worldbank.org/education/globaleducation reform. Feb. 2002.

Senén González, S. and A. Arango. (1997). "La descentralización educativa ¿Política educativa o política fiscal?." In O. Oszlak, ed. *Estado y sociedad: las nuevs reglas del juego,* vol. 1. Buenos Aires: CBC-CEA,.

Senén González, S., with the collaboration of M. A. Sendón. (1997). *Ajuste y reforma educativa: dos lógicas en pugna.* Third Congreso Latinoamericano de Administración de la Educación, UNICAMP, Campinas, Brazil.

Senén González, S. (2000). "Argentina: Actores e instrumentos de la reforma educativa. Propuestas del centro y respuestas de la periferia." *Revista Alternativas,* Universidad Nacional de San Luis.

Siqueira Wiarda, I. (1996). "Brazil: The politics of "order and progress" or chaos and regression?" In H. Wiarda and H. Kline, eds. *Latin American Politics and Development.* Boulder, Colo.: Westview Press.

Souza, M. Z. (1997). "Avaliaçao do rendimento escolar como instrumento de gestao educacional." In D. A. Oliveira, ed. *Gestao democratica da educaçao.* Petropolis: Vozes.

Tedesco, J. C. (1984). "Elementos para un diagnóstico del sistema educativo tradicional en América Latina. In R. Nassif, G. W. Rama, and J. C. Tedesco, eds. *El sistema educativo en América Latina.* Buenos Aires: UNESCO-CEPAL-PNUD / Kapelusz.

Tedesco, J. C. (1994). "Changes in managing education: The case of Latin American countries." *International Journal of Educational Research* 21, no. 8: 809–815.

Tenti Fanfani, E. (1990). *Descentralizar la educación.* Buenos Aires: CIEPP.

Tiramonti, G. (1996). *Los nuevos modelos de gestion educativa y su incidencia sobre la calidad de la educacion.* Buenos Aires: Flacso/Serie Documentos e Informes de Investigación, No. 211.

Torres, C. A. and A. Puiggrós. (1995). "The State and Public Education in Latin America." *Comparative Education Review* 39 (1).

Torres, R. M. (2000). "Reformadores y docentes: El cambio educativo atrapado entre dos lógicas." In A. L. Cárdenas Colmenter, A. Rodríguez Céspedes, and R. M. Torres, eds. *El maestro protagonista del cambio educativo.* Bogotá: Cooperativa Editorial Magisterio.

Weyland, K. (1996). "Neopopulism and Neoliberalism in Latin America: Unexpected Affinities." *Studies in Comparative International Development* 31, no. 3: 3–31.

Wiarda, H. and Kline, H., eds. (1996). *Latin American Politics and Development.* Boulder, Colo.: Westview Press.

Winkler, D. and A. Gershberg. (2000). *Los efectos de la descentralización del sistema educacional sobre al calidad de la educación en América Latina.* PREAL, no. 17.

World Bank. (1995). *Priorities and Strategies for Education.* Washington, D.C.: The World Bank.

Xavier, C. da R., J. A. Sobrinho, and F. Marra. (1994). "Gestao da escola fundamental: situaçao atual e tendencias." In *Gestao Escolar: Desafios e Tendencias.* Brasilia: IPEA.

Zibas, D. (1996). "La agenda latinoamericana de modernización educativa y la privatización de la enseñanza media." *Propuesta Educativa,* no. 14: 32–39.

Zibas, D. (1997). "As diretrizes basicas das políticas educacionais na América Latina e algumas de suas contradiçoes." In G. Frigerio, M. Poggi, and M. Giannoni, eds. *Políticas, instituciones y actores en educación.* Buenos Aires: Novedades Educativas.

6

Searching for "Neoliberal" Education Policies

A Comparative Analysis of Argentina and Chile

MARIANO NARODOWSKI
MILAGROS NORES

The term "neoliberalism" has a specific meaning concerning a particular group of economic recipes and policy programs that were first proposed in the seventies. . . . However, and concomitantly, at the world level an historical change has occurred in the institutional relations between market and state and between businesses and markets. This change has not been the output of the neoliberal project; it cannot be reduced to a mere policy output of these regimes; neither is it the effect of a single determined economic ideology. It is a change that has behind it the strength of a much more complex configuration.

Göran Therborn (in Sader and Gentili 2001, 92, my translation)

Originating in the north—North America and Europe—a tidal wave of thinking about the downfall of the welfare state swept over Latin America in the 1980s, and consequently, some education policies were "dramatically altered to reflect changed economic policies" (Arnove 1997, 79). In this context, the denominated neoliberal trend toward "increasing decentralized markets" and away from "centralized decision-making" (Roxborough 1997, 64) has had a significance influence on Latin American economies. As a general term, Neoliberalism is related to a series of measures toward opening and deregulating the economy, deregulating the labor market, restricting union activities, and allowing a more inflexible use of the labor force within a competitive arena. Such a term has been widely and generally applied when describing the last two decades of education reforms in Latin America (Arnove 1997, Gorostiaga 2001, Casassus undated, Puiggrós 1996).

Although the term is widely accepted, it is difficult to find a unique, formal definition of neoliberalism in academia. Most especially, it is impossible to find authors who identify themselves as "neoliberals." Neoliberalism is most frequently identified with a minimalist state and the market as center stage, based on the belief that it is the "most effective transformative force," and that "the less constraints that are put on free operation of the market the better for the national economy, society and polity" (Gwynne and Kay 2000). However, whilst neoliberalism is characterized as having a series of features, basically summarized by the market approach, there is no standing accepted definition upon which arguments in favor and against are built.[1]

In the education arena, most reforms in Latin America have tended toward decentralization of education, but rarely toward a market-oriented provision of services. In an intent of improving administrative efficiency, school quality, and/or school equity in education, the reform trend has been toward an important transformation of the national state's role in education. However, while as an international trend education decentralization has been widely recognized (Rondinelli, Middleton, and Verspoor 1990, Rideout and Ural 1993, Prawda 1993, Bullock and Thomas 1997, Cummings 1997, Welsh and McGinn 1998, Ball 2002, and others), its uncritical acceptance as a concept in itself can fail to appreciate its variety within the different educational systems (Bullock and Thomas 1997). As Whitty, Power, and Halpin (1998, 34) describe in their study of the redistribution of powers in England and Wales, Sweden, New Zealand, Australia, and the United States, the complexity of the problem derives from the many shades of meaning behind the concept. These authors agree with Lauglo (1996, as cited in Whitty et al.), in that decentralization should not be thought as a unitary concept. Furthermore, they recognize a "definition" of neoliberalism in education in Lauglo's work, relating this term to an emphasis on the wide dispersal of decision-making authority (strong local government, private provision, market mechanism, etc.) and to evaluation schemes through the market forces or professional state regulation and weak state control.

On the other hand, Welsh and McGinn (1998, 3) define decentralization in education as being "about shifts in the location of those who govern, about transfers of authority from those in one location or level vis-à-vis educational organizations, to those in another level." Additionally, they recognize three major positions in the conflict about who should govern education: political legitimacy, professional expertise, and market efficiency. The authors state that the fundamental difference between these three issues is in terms of the justification for holding authority. Political legitimacy is about governance of education legitimated by individuals who have been selected through a political process; professional expertise in governance refers to authority assigned primarily to those with technical expertise; and the market efficiency position recognizes the market as the best allocation mechanism. This last one can be understood as a shift toward neoliberalism in education.

For the purposes of this chapter, it is also important to distinguish neoliberal economic reforms, which are those most basically attributed to the Washington Consensus (Gentili 2001, Torre 1997), from what is understood by neoliberal education policies. Certainly, economic reforms have effects over wealth distribution and, therefore, over those who have access to (can afford) different goods and services (such as education), and to differing qualities within these. Although the effects of such reforms can have a visible impact on education, it is fundamental not to confuse such reforms with neoliberal education reforms—those reforms that give a higher predominance to the market, introduce competition in the system, place the interaction between consumers and producers at the center (price systems), introduce accountability through incentive-based schemes (such as the League Tables in England and Wales), broach higher labor flexibility, promote school-based management, etc.

As Phillips (1998, xvii) states, "[m]uch of the appeal of neoliberalism is its emphasis on individual autonomy, flexibility, and choice within the general context of protecting law and order, private property, and family life." It is because of a higher predominance of such values in Latin American education reforms that such reforms tend to be denominated as neoliberal, notwithstanding the lack of market oriented reforms. This chapter intends to provide evidence on the complexity of the problem, and to how the concept of "neoliberalism" contributes little to the understanding of education reforms, especially in the cases of Argentina and Chile.

A comparative analysis of Argentina and Chile implies a comparison of two countries that have faced very different decentralization reforms with differing shifts in the locus of educational governance: in Argentina, a decentralization reform in which the locus is still mostly related to the political legitimacy position at the intermediate levels of government, and in Chile, a mixed shift towards the political legitimacy position and the market efficiency one. However, both countries present highly similar patterns in terms of their enrollments' socioeconomic segregation (Narodowski and Nores 2002), together with increasing state expenditures in education. In short, notwithstanding the differing models of schooling provision, and the differing sets of regulations and market settings, these two do not appear to have highly differing patterns in terms of the distribution of education, and evidence a "growing" state rather than a diminishing one.

In particular, the model of education provision and administration in place in Chile is one of a quasi market. The general characteristic of such a market is public finance of education together with public and private competitive provision of it.[2] In contrast, Argentina represents a model of public provision of schooling inherited from a strong welfare state that faced a series of national state reduction reforms during the 1990s over the basis of issues of efficiency and federal legitimacy. In education, such national state reduction reforms have implied an increased presence of the provincial states—in accordance with the constitutional principle of "federalism." This system of quasi monopoly (Narodowski and Nores 2001), provides an exit option to private schools, only to a portion of its school population, and furthermore promotes such an exit through public financing of private schools.[3] Within such a system, the reforms introduced in the last decade have been characterized as "neoliberal" by no few authors (Paviglianiti 1991, Casassus undated, Puiggros 1996, and others).

While the origin of the reforms do not differ significantly and they have been introduced in parallel with a series of denominated "neoliberal reforms" in the economic arena, the neoliberalism label attached to these education reforms needs to be revised. This is what this chapter intends to do in a comparative perspective—as, notwithstanding the nonexistence of vouchers or any similar form of competitive model of education provision in Argentina—some of the most important criticisms to market-oriented policies are present, particularly, the strong patterns of socioeconomic enrollment segregation described by Narodowski and Andrada (2001), Narodowski (2002), and Narodowski and Nores (2002).

Underlying Theoretical Approach

The quasi monopoly definition hereby considered is based on a previous work of ours (Narodowski and Nores 2001) created on the basis of Herbert Gintis's work (1994). As mentioned before, this work elaborates a taxonomy of education provision models and differentiates pure monopolies from quasi monopolies. Its contribution is the differentiation of pure monopolies from quasi monopolies, that is, models of state provision that have embedded "exit" options but that do not contemplate the promotion of supply competition or market-oriented provision as quasi markets do. Explicitly, if a monopoly and a market model could be thought of as linear opposites and the distance between these two a continuum, a quasi monopoly system of education provision would be somewhere between a pure monopoly and a quasi market.

Although in this previous work we did not intend to determine (or measure) categorical distances between what is a quasi monopoly and what is a quasi market, it definitely intended to provide some kind of order based on a normative categorization of the differences in the systems—that is, by ordering the systems on the basis of categories through which the regulations in each system are characterized and analyzed.

On the basis of their linear approach, the denominated "neoliberal" reforms, as they are related to the operation of free markets, define systems on the right-hand side of the relationship. On the other hand, decentralization or school-based management reforms, which are intended to make the system more responsive to the local needs, are not necessarily market-oriented reforms. Basically, this derives from the difference between decentralization reforms and market reforms—the later usually considered a form of decentralization. Welsh and McGinn's (1998) distinction between the three positions on who should govern education, as well as Lauglo's (1996 as cited in Whitty et al. 1998) characterization of the implications of the different forms of decentralization give further insight to this matter.[4]

Consequently, a comparative analysis of the reforms introduced in Argentina and Chile at the end of the twentieth century is pertinent for two main reasons. First of all, it differentiates market-oriented reforms from other types

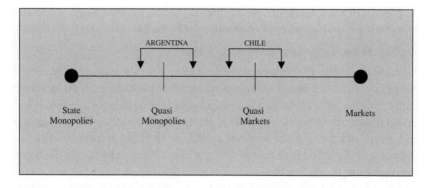

Figure 1. A Linear Approach to the Distribution of Education Systems. Source: Narodowski and Nores 2001.

of decentralization reforms. Second, it adds to the debate about what type of reforms where introduced in the education arena in these two countries. Behind this second question lies the presumption that in the provision of certain services, such as education, strong centralization has prevailed, and the systems as a whole have successfully contested neoliberal education reform initiatives (or even assimilated its underlying concepts into the centralized predominant mode of decision making).

The governance of education in Argentina and Chile

The differing decentralization reforms that took place in Argentina and Chile have defined in each a very different institutional framework, understanding such as the set of regulatory and finance rules under which the service is provided. In the state-provided schooling in Argentina, the education system is presently administered in a very similar way to how it was administered before the reform, but with a change in the location of such administrative institutions—from the federal to the provincial government. On the other hand, in Chile, the reforms introduced in the early eighties has meant a shift toward market competition between locally administered municipal schools and a per-capita subsidized private sector.

Such differing governance frameworks were compared in our previous work (Narodowski and Nores 2002), which examines the decisions made at each level, on the basis of a series of decision-making areas defined for this purpose: policy planning, school supply, school organization, financing, personnel, curriculum and instruction, monitoring and evaluation, and student choice regulation.[5] We found that, while in Argentina 88 percent of these decisions for public schools are wholly or partially a responsibility of the provincial education authorities, in Chile, municipal governments are responsible for

46 percent of such decisions, preserving, at the central level, supervising and monitoring responsibilities (59 percent) (see figure 2).

Argentina's quasi monopoly provision of education

Up until the 1980s, the history of the Argentine education system had several similarities with Chile's. However, Argentina's education reforms occurred mainly in the early 1990s and are still in process.[6] Such reforms have introduced important changes, especially in the ordination of the education grades and levels and curriculum content, as well as specified responsibilities.[7] At present it is not evident that such reforms have implied any strong deviation from previous policy trends.

The decentralization reforms of 1978 and 1992 (correspondingly, transference of primary national schools and middle schools to the provincial authorities) dismantled the national system of schools on the basis of financial and economic needs. Such transference meant a devolution of authority to the government level ultimately responsible for education as established by the constitution.[8] However, this decentralization has not meant increased school autonomy, but a mere shifting from federal to provincial bureaucracies. No major novelties appeared in terms of strategic state prevalence (Narodowski 1998), except at most for the curricular component of the Federal Education Law. As a consequence, the last thirty years of education policy have resulted in a hyperregulated impoverished state system coexistent with a highly autonomous and expanded private sector.[9] In short, the present public education system has the particularity of being a mix between the strong welfare state inherited from the post–World War II era, with reforms based on efficiency and federal legitimacy principles. The present regulatory frameworks have been construed over the former existing one instead of replacing it.

As a consequence, Argentina has preserved its quasi monopoly configuration—that is, main form of education provision being that of public schools centrally administered and financed—by provincial governments now—with a state-financed exit option. Such exit alternative, in place since 1947 (Morduchowicz et al. 2000) is the subsidized private sector. The decentralization of the system did not establish any competitive and/or market setting for schools. Therefore, at present, only the long-existing subsidized private sector is part of a competitive market (together with nonsubsidized private schools).

From the national perspective, the major reforms and programs under the different federal administrations (summarized in table 2) do not evidence market-oriented trends. The national assessment system introduced during the mid-nineties, and financed by World Bank funds (Prodymes I-Program for the Decentralization and Improvement of Secondary Education), is probably the only program that could be denominated "neoliberal." However, while in form and shape the program does not differ from other educational assessment experiences in the world, including Chile's, the elaboration of rankings

Table 1. The Governance of Education in Argentina by Major Components

Components	Central	Provincial	School
Governance			
Policy planning	X	X	
Implementation	X	X	
School supply			
Official authorization		X	
School opening and closure		P	S
School organization			
Structure		P	S
Minimum Requirements	X		
Financing			
Recurrent funding		X[a]	
Capital funding		P	
Compensatory funding	X	X	
School budget administration		X	S
Private funding			S[b]
Personnel			
Hiring and firing		P	S[c]
In-service training	X	X	S
Salary determination		P	S[d]
Qualification standards		X[e]	
Curriculum and instruction			
Curriculum content[f]	X	X	S
Choosing textbooks		P	S
Textbook provision	X	P	
Didactic methods		P	X
Student evaluation		P	X
Monitoring and evaluation			
Monitoring/supervision			
Accreditation		X	
Promotions			X
Discipline			X
Student/Schools Assessment	X	X	
Students			
Admissions		P	S

Note: X = all schools, P = public schools only, S = private schools only.

a) Subsidies to private schools are only given to cover teacher salaries.

b) Schools that are granted subsidy are done so at different percentages on the basis of their "main ground personnel" (*planta orgánica funcional*).

c) The province of Jujuy however, establishes that private schools have the possibility of receiving financial support under the condition that they comply with the provincial teacher statute in terms of job stability and labor conditions.

d) As stated in the Federal Law of Education, teachers in private institutions have the right to earn a minimum wage of at least as much as teachers in the public sector.

e) The requirement of the Federal Law of Education on teacher certification is that it complies with each jurisdiction's requirements.

f) Schools have to comply with study plans and programs, either general ones dictated by the central government or their own after the National Ministry's approval.

Source: Taken from Narodowski and Nores, 2002. Socioeconomic segregation with (without) competitive education policies. A comparative analysis of Argentina and Chile. *Comparative Education*, special edition., (38) 4. London.

Table 2. Major Reforms and Programs in Argentina under the Different Presidential Periods, from Alfonsín (1983) to Duhalde (2002)

President	Dates Appointed	Minister of Education	Laws or Programs
R. Alfonsín	December 1983	R. S. Alconada Aramburú	Summon of the Second National Pedagogical Congress: Law 23.114
	July 1986	J. Rajneri	Summon of the Second National Pedagogical Congress: Decree 432/86 Second National Pedagogical Congress: February/March 1987
	September 1987	J. F. Sábato	
	May 1989	J. G. Dumón	
	July 1989	A. F. Salonia	Transference Law: Law 29.049 (December 1991)
C. S. Menem 1st and 2nd	December 1992	J. A. Rodriguez	Federal Law of Education: Law 24.195 (April 1993) National Teachers and Schools' Census: Law 1521 (August 1994) Higher Education Law: Law 24.521 (August 1995)
C. S. Menem 2nd	April 1996	S. B. Decibe	National Secondary Scholarships Program is created: Decree 851/96 Prodymes I: Decree 288/94 and 794/96. Federal Education Pact: Law 24.856 (August 1997) Social Education Plan: Ministry Resolution 515/96 National Teachers' Incentive Fund (FNID): Law 25.053 (November 1998) and Decree 1451/98.** Monitoring of Education Policy Law: Law 25.030 (October 1998) and Decree 1283/98.**
	May 1999	M. García Solá	
F. De la Rúa	December 1999	J. J. Llach	Reestablishment of the FNID Creation of the Institute of Education Financing (private resources to finance school projects) Participation of Argentina on International Assessments Promotion of the Second Federal Education Pact: Unsuccessful
	September 2000	H. Juri	
	March 2001	A. G. Delich	Creation of IDECE: Institute for the Development of Education Quality
R. Puerta*	December 2001	—	—
R. Saá*	December 2001	—	—
E. Camaño*	January 2002	—	—
E. G. Duhalde	January 2002	G. Giannettasio	

*There was no Minister of Education from December 20th, 2001 (when De la Rúa left office) until January 2nd, 2002 (when Duhalde took office).

**The FNID is the result of a conflict with the teachers unions (known as the *Carpa Blanca*), who should negotiate with their provincial administrations, but nationalized the conflict and therefore managed for central state intervention so as to provide teachers with a plus.

***This law, which actually shows little abidance, refers to a request of Congress that a yearly report be sent to the education commission in both the Senate and the House of Representatives in relation to education policies, programs, and results.

Note: The reforms and activities hereby included are definitely not of the same level of importance. While the early 1990s were marked by systemic reforms, the activities of the late 1990s and the present decade are programs more than systemic specific policies reforms.

has been explicitly avoided, the information has not been transparently and openly provided, there are no "sticks and carrots" attached to the results, and there are no signs of beneficial uses of the information for more than some compensatory initiatives (Narodowski, Nores, and Andrada 2002). The rest of the programs, even those promoted by international funding agencies such as the World Bank (Prodymes I & Prodymes II) and the IDB (Prise-Project for the Reform and Investment in Education) have attended basic needs such as institutional strengthening and modernization of provincial education administrations, as well as compensatory needs (as the Scholarships program, the Institute of Education Finance, the infrastructure components of the international loan programs, and the Social Education Plan). This is related to a national state receding as little as possible, and strengthening provincial administrations, rather than diminishing states.[10]

Similarly, even though a trend toward state reduction and dismantling social policies is attributed to the neoliberal paradigm (Roxborough 1997, 62), public expenditure in education in Argentina has increased over the decade not only in real terms, but as a percentage of GDP and as a percentage of total public expenditure.[11]

Even more, just in the City of Buenos Aires, the size of the public sector is even more evident.[12] Between 1998–2000, over thirteen hundred educational regulations and norms (National Laws, National Decrees, Provincial Laws, Provincial Decrees, and Ministerial Resolutions) have been passed. This figure doesn't include lower-level regulations such as *circulares* and *disposiciones* from the directorates of either primary education, middle education, or private education, which is estimated to exceed other higher-level regulations in number).[13] These hyperregulative trends appear to have little to do with the ideals of "neoliberalism" of wild deregulation of the public sector.

Chile's quasi market in education

Chile's educational history in the early twentieth century is not that much different than what has been said for Argentina. It went through a similar centralization of education with an increased state involvement, therefore denominating it the "Teaching State" (Matte and Sancho 1991). Schooling was as a result provided by the state, which also subsidized private schools, and most responsibilities for basic education were held at the center.[14] Similar to Argentina, even teacher resources were centralized, with national salary scales and centralized school appointment.

In the series of reforms introduced during the 1980s, the underlying concept was that of public funding of schooling as separate from the production function. Panadeiros et. al. (1998) describe three main reform components: (1) transference of public education establishments to the municipal level; (2) transference of middle technical-professional schools to nonprofit business organizations; and (3) replacement of the existing supply-based funding

Table 3. Public Expenditure on Basic Education in Argentina*

Years	Trends in Total education expenditure	As % of GDP	Per student	As % of public expenditure
1980	100.0%	3.00%	1,010	7.80%
1989	93.2%	3.00%	711	8.70%
1991	103.1%	3.00%	n/a	9.10%
1992	122.7%	3.30%	n/a	9.60%
1993	138.4%	3.60%	n/a	10.20%
1994	149.3%	3.50%	1,077	10.30%
1995	144.0%	3.40%	n/a	10.20%
1996	142.3%	3.20%	924	10.40%
1997	163.2%	3.40%	1,022	11.20%
1998	168.1%	3.40%	1,025	11.00%
1999	178.0%	3.80%	1,086	11.10%
Variance % *1999/1980*	78.0%	26.7%	7.5%*	42.3%
Variance % *1999/1991*	72.6%	26.7%	52.7%	22.0%

*Excludes university level.
**Calculated on the basis of 1989.
Source: J. P. Nicolini, P. Sanguinetti, and J. Sanguinetti 2000.

mechanism to a demand-side funding scheme accessible to private nonprofit schools. Basically, a per student funding scheme was established for students of public schools (administered by the municipalities) and private incorporated schools, with the amount of the per student subsidy varying by education level (Matte and Sancho 1991).

In addition to the mentioned reforms, during the 1990s, two sets of policies were put in place that evidence a stronger rather than weaker state. On the one hand, proactive initiatives of positive discrimination and initiatives to strengthen the educational system's institutional capacities were dominant (P900, MECE-Básica, and MECE-Media). Additionally, a teacher statute was legislated.[15] Since this law was actually highly regulatory, it was even considered a step back on the existing decentralization policies. It imposed on schools rigidity in terms of teacher mobility. However, this rigidity was then partially reduced by Law of Teacher Statute Reform of 1995.

Consequently, the Chilean model implemented since the 1980s allows access to public resources for both public and private schools; includes regulatory curriculum components and infrastructure requirements; has since the 1990s a finance component allowing for parental funding in addition to the subsidy amount; and has an information component that includes assessment of student's results and publicly disseminated rankings (Narodowski and Nores 2002).[16] Therefore, control over output and content rather than over inputs, is emphasized—except minimum infrastructure requirements and the teacher statute regulating working conditions.

Chile is frequently posed as the Latin American example of neoliberal reforms in education. As such it has been widely studied (Viola Espinola 1992 and undated, Aedo and Larrañaga 1994, West 1996, Parry 1997a and 1997b, Bullock and Thomas 1997, Carnoy 1997 and 1998, Patrinos and Ariasingman 1998, Rodriguez 1988, Welsh and McGinn 1998, Carnoy and McEwan 1998 and 2000, Gauri 1999, McEwan 2000a and 2000b, Belfield 2001, Bravo, Contreras, and Sanhueza 1999, Mizala and Romaguera 1998 and 2000, Contreras 2001, Narodowski and Nores 2002, and others) because of the decentralization and market reforms introduced at this time in its education system. The model integrates into a single market traditional public schools and private subsidized schools with an explicit intention of making all public schooling subject to market rules, which is why it can be characterized as a quasi market of education.[17]

As a consequence of these reforms, private subsidized enrollment grew enormously in Chile, mostly because of the market-entry incentives for privately administered schools (Narodowski and Nores 2002). The main criticisms of the existing model have concentrated on the issues of socioeconomic segmentation and a lack of evidence of private school effectiveness under this school choice scheme. The work of Viola Espínola (1992) describes the enrollment segmentation—that higher income groups, urban and rural, have chosen the private system while lower-income households still attend municipal schools.[18] Similar results are shown in studies done by the Chilean Ministry of Planning and Cooperation (1999a, 1999b, and 1999c). On the other hand, the various econometric studies of the Chilean system agree on the existence of a rough gap in student achievement test scores, between public and private subsidized schools, which is strongly determined by differences in students' socioeconomic background (Parry 1997, Mizala and Romaguera 1998 and 2000, Bravo et al. 1999, Carnoy and McEwan 1998 and 2000, McEwan 2000). However, as analyzed by Narodowski and Nores (2002), the gap between public and private subsidized schools has narrowed or disappeared in the 1990s.

In addition, expenditure in education has also increased (see table 4). Therefore, notwithstanding the existence of the denominated "neoliberal" education policies, Chile's state does not show evidence of reducing or minimizing its role in education. And while it has decentralized several functions, it remains strong and active at the center.

Conclusions

Basically, two fundamental issues must be taken into account when thinking and analyzing education policies in Argentina and Chile: first, the definition of a "neoliberal" education policy, and second, that such definition needs to be different from what is known as "neoliberal" economic reforms. That is, it is

Table 4. Public Expenditure on Basic Education in Chile

Years	Trends in total education expenditure	As % of GDP*	Per student —primary Education— as % GDP	As % of public expenditure
1970	100.0%	5.10%	n/a	22.00%
1975	76.8%	4.10%	9.58	12.00%
1980	123.3%	4.60%	13	11.90%
1985	110.5%	4.40%	8.89	15.30%
1991	108.6%	2.70%	8.42	10.00%
1992	123.8%	2.80%	8.9	12.90%
1993	129.3%	2.80%	n/a	n/a
1994	147.4%	3.10%	9.57	13.40%
1995	162.5%	3.10%	10.44	14.00%
1996	183.5%	3.40%	10.88	14.80%
1997**	204.3%	3.60%	n/a	15.50%
Var. % 1997/1970	*104.32%*	*−29.41%*	*n/a*	*−29.55%*
Var. % 1997/1980	*65.72%*	*−21.74%*	*−16.31%*	*30.25%*
Var. % 1997/1985	*65.72%*	*−21.74%*	*−16.31%*	*30.25%*
	65.72%	*−21.74%*	*−16.31%*	*30.25%*
Var. % 1997/1991	*88.16%*	*33.33%*	*29.22%*	*55.00%*

*Variances calculated on the basis of 1996.
**Own estimation.
Source: Unesco Indicators, Global Education Database.

fundamental to recognize that the introduction of neoliberal economic poli-cies does not necessarily bring about neoliberal education policies. And if, as in the economic arena, education policies are to be neoliberal when they are market-oriented, then finding such policies in Argentina is not an easy task.

In the analysis of Latin American education policies it becomes important to avoid reducing the existing complexities to labels such as neoliberalism. Such labels diminish not only the possibilities for generating viable alter-natives, but also limits the extent of the analysis. Fundamentally, the catego-rization of Latin American reforms as "neoliberal" needs be revised. Most importantly, since neoliberal reforms in the social areas have been highly con-tested by the existing welfare states, neoliberal initiatives have barely touched the system—or, more specifically, the existing resource distribution schemes (economic and human), the accountability mechanisms, the state-centered strategic stand, and so on.

Second, the provincial states in Argentina have continued as the predomi-nant decision makers in education issues. These have protected the state monopoly through subsidies, price controls, minimum teacher wages, requirements for the entry of new private schools, and centralized decision-making power over the opening of new public schools, among others. In short, the regulatory weight of the bureaucracy has not diminished.[19] Notwithstanding, it cannot be denied that a significant and relevant shift has been done toward rethinking such hierarchical modes of provision.

It is therefore true that the worldwide trend toward increasing administrative efficiency and quality and equity in education has meant important reforms aimed at increasing the roles of lower government in both Chile and Argentina. However, there is little in common between these reforms besides a general concept of decentralization. Chile introduced reforms with specific competition and efficiency components, and Argentina has stayed in the decentralization discourse, having introduced limited real changes in the predominant role of the state. However, in both cases little of a "minimalist state" can be observed. In any case, what should be analyzed and researched are in-depth changes in the modes of governance of education systems (Ball 2002). Apparently, the general construction of the "neoliberal" perspective in comparative education emphasizes an analysis of the similarities between worldwide implemented policies, rather than an analysis of the changes these policies in fact promote (or do not promote) in each particular case.

In Argentina, the transfer of authority from those on one level of educational organizations to those on another has not meant a change in the rules of the game from the schools' perspective, which continue to educate within hyperregulated environments. In short, Argentina—a quasi monopoly education system—has preserved a highly centralized system at the provincial level, and a state-subsidized exit option. On the other hand, Chile introduced strong decentralization and market reforms during the 1980s and evolved into a quasi market model of education provision in which the decision-making power over the aspects of finance, monitoring, assessment, and curriculum have been preserved at the centralized level. Although these two countries present different sets of regulatory frameworks, they have similar patterns of enrollment, socioeconomic segmentation, and increased educational expenditure. Does it sound as if they both have unquestionably implemented "neoliberal" educational reforms?

Notes

1. We can backtrack to the origins of what is known as neoliberalism, and its fundamental proponent Friedrich Von Hayek (Gentili 2001). "Our freedom of choice in a competitive society rests on the fact that, if on a person refuses to satisfy our wishes, we can turn to another. But if we face a monopolist we are at his mercy. And an authority directing the whole economic system would be the most powerful monopolist conceivable. . . . It would not only decide what commodities and services where to be available and in what quantities; it would be able to direct their distribution between district and groups and could, if wished, discriminate between persons to any degree it liked" (Von Hayek 1944, 93, as cited in Gentili 2001).

Among others, Oxhorn and Ducatenzeiler (1998, 8) define the new neoliberal economic reform policies as those that "presuppose the existence of a market that must regulate the behavior of all economic actors, a role played fundamentally up until now by the state." Phillips (1998, xi) defines neoliberalism as involving "a shift from 'inward-oriented' strategies of development promoting national self-sufficiency to 'outward-oriented' free trade aimed at total integration into the world market." Smith and Korzeniewicz (1997, 1) state that advocates of neoliberalism talk of "extending the reach of the markets and shifting responsibility for the allocation of resources away from state elites." Roxborough (1997, 57) remarks that "neoliberalism increases the role of the market and decreases, or at least redefines, the role of the market." Przeworski (1992, 46) talks of neoliberal ideology and market ideology basically as synonyms.

2. For further definition of quasi markets, refer to Cullis and Jones (1998). They differentiate such markets in their recognition that they are the result of a world trend for lower levels of public provision and higher market levels.

3. We make reference to the concept of "Exit" as developed by A. Hirschman (1969).

4. Similarly, the concept of privatization (a neoliberal concept in itself) comprises part of the literature on market oriented reforms in education (see Levin 2001).

5. A total of twenty-five decision-making categories within these areas.

6. The Federal Education Law (*Ley Federal de Educación*), puts into place a different configuration of education levels. However, because of the crisis and the cost of this reform, it has not been implemented by all provinces, and for the moment all initiatives of doing so have frozen.

7. All through the twentieth century and up until the Federal Education Law, the state's provision and regulation of education was founded on very few parliamentary laws.

8. Both a national system of schools and provincial systems of schools coexisted all through the twentieth century, but the National Constitution of 1853 already specified that basic education was a responsibility of the provinces.

9. This trend has apparently changed in Argentina in the years 2001 and 2002 due to the economic crises.

10. Only in the province of San Luis, where the supply need for ten new public schools was chartered in terms of their administration in 1999 so as to start in the year 2000, can one distinguish "neoliberal" policies in the public provision of education. However, even this program does not introduce competition between schools to attract demand, nor for profits. More so, it explicitly forbids any association between these schools and education for profit corporations. The decision-making and management space these schools actually have is highly similar to traditional public schools in the United States (Narodowski 1999).

11. However, it can be argued that the consequences of neoliberalism on income inequality demands for increased social expenditure (Gwynne and Kay 2000, Roxborough 1997).

12. The City of Buenos Aires is presently equivalent to a province, with the same jurisdictional responsibilities.

13. This data has been collected as part of an ongoing project on the City of Buenos Aires administered by the Center for Education Policies (*Fundación Gobierno y Sociedad*) and funded by the Tinker Foundation. It includes all published regulations and norms.

14. The traditional subsidized supply was mainly urban primary schools serving middle/low-income families, half of which were catholic and received an average subsidy of around 60–65% on their expenses (Viola Espinola, 1992), which meant a funding of 25% of the per student cost at public schools (Panadeiros, Susmel & Nores, 1998).

15. Law 19.070 and Law 19.410.

16. La Segunda. Wednesday, December 5, 2001. *Mejores Colegios del País.* Santiago de Chile.

17. Levacic (1995), cited in Gordon and Whitty 1997, describes as the salient characteristic of such a market the separation between schooling provider and producer, with the simultaneous introduction of consumer choice elements. Additionally, Vandenberghe (1999, 273) states that quasi markets form a subtle combination of the principle of public funding with the corresponding bureaucratic controls, and the "market-oriented, competition-driven approach of education."

18. The author also found a higher compensatory ability of private subsidized schools.

19. "In general, the Welfare State has been the object of strong criticism because of its crisis state and for being wholly and inevitably subject to certain internal unsolvable contradictions, etc. Analyzed from an historical point of view, this is simply not true. The balance

shows that this type of state constituted itself into a very robust institution that has managed to preserve itself surprisingly well. The most dramatic evidence of this can be found in Latin America: by the end of the Pinochet era Chile still preserved the most organized and efficient Welfare State in the region" (GöranTherborn, in Sader and Gentili 2001, 92–93, my translation).

References

Aedo, C. and O. Larrañaga. (1994). "Sistemas de Entrega de los Servicios Sociales: La Experiencia Chilena." In C. Aedo and O. Larrañaga, *Sistemas de Entrega de los Servicios Sociales: Una Agenda para la Reforma.* Washington D.C.: Inter-american Development Bank, 33–74.

Arnove, R. F. (1997). "Neoliberal Education Policies in Latin America: Arguments in Favor and Against." In C. A. Torres, A. Puiggrós, eds. *Latin American Education* Westview Press, Boulder, Colo.: 79–100.

Ball, S. (2002). "Bog policies/Small world: An Introduction to International Perspectives in Education Policy." *Comparative Education* 34, no. 2, 119–130.

Belfield, C. R. (2001). *International Experience with Demand-led Financing: Education Vouchers in the USA, Great Britain, and Chile.* Occasional Paper No. 23, NCSPE. New York: Teachers College, Columbia University.

Bravo, D., D. Contreras, and C. Sanhueza. (1999). *Educational Achievement, Inequalities and Private/Public Gap: Chile 1982–1997.* Chile: Universidad de Chile.

Bullock, A. and H. Thomas. (1997). *Schools at the Centre? A Study of Decentralisation* New York: Routledge.

Carnoy, M. (1997). "Is Privatization through Education Vouchers Really the Answer? A Comment on West." *The World Bank Research Observe* 12, no. 1: 105–116.

Carnoy, M. (1998). "National Voucher Plans in Chile and Sweden: Did Privatization Reforms Make for Better Education?" *Comparative Education Review,* 42, no. 3: 309–337.

Carnoy, M. and P. McEwan. (1998). *Is Privatization More Effective and Cost-Effective than the Public? The Case of Chile.* Draft. Palo Alto: Stanford University.

Carnoy, M. and P. McEwan. (2000). "The Effectiveness and Efficiency of Private Schools in Chile's Voucher System." *Educational Evaluation and Policy Analysis* 22, no. 3: 213–239.

Casassus, J. (undated). "¿Debe el estado ocuparse aun de la educacion? Un analisis desde las dimensiones de la regulacion y la legitimacion." Santiago de Chile: OREALC.

Chilean Ministry of Planning and Cooperation. (1999a). *Impacto de la Política Educacional, 1990–1996.* Chile: División Social.

Chilean Ministry of Planning and Cooperation. (1999b). *Resultados de la VII Encuesta de Caracterización Socioeconómica Nacional (CASEN 1998). Situación de la Educación en Chile.* Documento No. 5. Chile: División Social.

Chilean Ministry of Planning and Cooperation. (1999c). *Resultados de la VII Encuesta de Caracterización Socioeconómica Nacional (CASEN 1998). Situación de la Infancia en Chile.* Documento No. 8. Chile: División Social.

Contreras, D. (2001). "Evaluating a Voucher system in Chile. Individual, Family, and School Characteristics." Working Paper No. 175 Chile: Economics Department, Universidad de Chile.

Cox, C. (1997). *La Reforma de la Educación Chilena.* No. 8. Chile: PREAL.

Cullis, J. G. and P. Jones. (1998). *Public Finance and Public Choice.* 2d ed. Oxford and New York: Oxford University Press.

Cummings, W. K. (1997). "Patterns of Modern Education." In W. K. Cummings and N. F. McGinn, eds. *Handbook of Modern Education and its Alternatives.* Oxford, Elsevier Science, 63–86.

Foucault, M. (1990). "Fobia al estado." In *La vida de los hombres infames.* Madrid, Ed: La Piqueta.

Gauri, V. (1999). *School of Choice in Chile: Two Decades of Educational Reform.* Pittsburgh: University of Pittsburgh Press.

Gentili, P. A. (2001). *Falsificaçao do consenso. Simulacro e imposição na reforma educacional do neoliberalismo.* Petrópolis, Brazil: Vozes.

Gintis, H. (1994). "School Choice: A discussion with Herbert Gintis." *Education Policy Analysis Archives* 2, no. 6. Available at http://olam.ed.asu.edu/epaa/v2n6.html.

Gordon, L. and G. Whitty. (1997). "Giving the Hidden Hand a Helping Hand?" *Comparative Education* 33, no. 3: 453–467.

Gorostiaga Derqui, J. M. (2001). "Education Decentralization Policies in Argentina and Brazil: Exploring the New Trends. *Journal of Education Policy* 16, no. 6: 561–583.

Gwynne, R. N. and C. Kay. (2000). "Views from the Periphery: Futures of Neoliberalism in Latin America." *Third World Quarterly,* 21, no. 1: 141–156.

Hirschmann, A. (1969). *Exist, Voice and Loyalty.* Cambridge: Harvard University Press.

La Segunda. Wednesday, December 5, 2001. *Mejores Colegios del País.* Santiago de Chile.

Levin, H. M., ed. (2001). *Privatizing Education. Can the Marketplace Deliver Choice, Efficiency, Equity, and Social Cohesion?* Boulder, Colo.: Westview Press.

Matte, P. and A. Sancho. (1991). "Primary and Secondary School Education. In C. Larroulet, ed. *Private Solutions to Social Problems,* Chile: Libertad y Desarrollo. Available at: http://www. lyd.com/biblioteca/libros/private/school.html.

McEwan, P. (2000a). "Private and Public Schooling in the Southern Cone: A Comparative Analysis of Argentina and Chile." Occasional Paper No. 11, NCSPE. New York: Teachers College, Columbia University.

McEwan, P. (2000b). "The Potential Impact of Large-Scale Voucher Programs." Occasional Paper No. 2, NCSPE. New York: Teachers College, Columbia University.

Mizala, A. and P. Romaguera. (1998). *Desempeño escolar y eleccion de colegios: La experiencia chilena.* Chile: Center of Applied Economics, Universidad de Chile.

Mizala, A. and P. Romaguera. (2000). *Determinación de factores explicativos de los resultados escolares en educación media en Chile.* Chile: Center of Applied Economics, Universidad de Chile.

Morduchowicz, A., A. Marcon, G. Iglesias, M. Andrada, J. Perez, A. Victoria and L. Duro. (2000). *La educación privada en la Argentina: Historia, Regulaciones, y Asignación de Recursos Públicos.* Serie Documentos de Trabajo, Documento 38. Buenos Aires, Fundación Gobierno y Sociedad.

Narodowski, and M. Andrada. (2001). The Privatization of Education in Argentina. *Journal of Education Policy* 16, no. 6: 585–595.

Narodowski, M. and M. Nores. (2001). "A Taxonomy of Models for the Provision of Education: Theory about Competition and Cooperation." Unpublished. Buenos Aires: Fundación Gobierno y Sociedad.

Narodowski, M. and M. Nores. (2002). "Socioeconomic Segregation With (Without) Competitive Education Policies. A Comparative Analysis of Argentina and Chile." *Comparative Education* 38, no. 4: 429–451.

Narodowski, M. (1998). "Hacen falta políticas educativas de estado en la argentina?" *Punto de vista* 58.

Narodowski, M. (1999) *"Varias respuestas a diez objeciones a las escuelas públicas autogestionadas. Un aporte al debate en la Argentina."* Serie Cuadernos de Opinión, Documento 6. Buenos Aires: Fundación Gobierno y Sociedad.

Narodowski, M. (2002). "Socioeconomic Segregation in the Argentine Education System. School Choice without Vouchers." *Compare* 32, no. 2: 181–191.

Narodowski, M., M. Nores, and M. Andrada. (2002). *Desde los Operativos Nacionales hasta los Boletines Escolarwa. La evaluación educativa en la Argentina, (1993–2001).* Buenos Aires, Editorial Prometeo.

Nicolini, J. P., P. Sanguinetti, and J. Sanguinetti. (2000). *Análisis de alternativas de financiamiento de la educación básica en Argentina en el marco de las instituciones fiscales federales.* Agreement between Torcuato Di Tella University-National Ministry of Education and Culture. Buenos Aires: UTDT.

Oxhorn, P. D. and G. Ducatenzeiler. Economic Reform and Democratization in Latin America. In Oxhorn, P. D. and G. Ducatenzeiler, eds. (1998). *What Kind of Democracy? What Kind of Market? Latin America in the Age of Neoliberalism.* University Park, PA: The Pennsylvania University Press.

Panadeiros, M., N. Susmel, and M. Nores. (1998). "La Experiencia Internacional." In FIEL/CEP, *Una Educación para el Siglo XXI. El Caso Argentino y Otras Experiencias Internacionales.* Buenos Aires: Fundación de Investigaciones Económicas Latinoamericanas.

Parry, T. (1997a). "Theory Meets Reality in the Education Voucher Debate: Some Evidence from Chile." *Education Economics,* 5, no. 3: 307–331.

Parry, T. (1997b). "How will Schools Respond to Incentives of Privatization? Evidence from Chile and Implications for the United States." *American Review of Public Administration* 27, no. 3: 248–269.

Patrinos, H. A. and D. L. Ariasingman. (1998). *Decentralization of Education. Demand-Side Financing.* Washington, D.C.: World Bank.

Paviglianiti, N. (1991). *Neoconservadurismo y educación. Un debate silenciado en la Argentina.* Buenos Aires: Colihue.

Phillips, L. (1998). *The Third Wave of Modernization in Latin America: Cultural Perspectives on Neoliberalism.* Jaguar books on Latin America, Number 16. Delaware: Scholarly Resources Inc.

Prawda, J. (1993). "Educational Decentralization in Latin America: Lessons Learned." *International Journal of Educational Development,* 13, no. 3: 253–264.

Przeworski, A. (1992). "The Neoliberal Fallacy." *Journal of Democracy,* 3, no. 3: 45–59.

Puiggros, A. (1996). "World Bank Education Policy: Market Liberalism Meets Ideological Conservatism." In NACLA Report on the Americas, May/June.

Rideout, W. M., and I. Ural. (1993). *Centralized and Decentralized Models of Education: Comparative Studies.* Capetown: Development Bank of Southern Africa, Centre for Policy Analysis.

Rodriguez, J. (1988). *School Achievement and Decentralization Policy: the Chilean Case.* Draft. Chile: ILADES.

Rondinelli, D. A., J. Middleton, and A. M. Verspoor. (1990). *Planning Education Reforms in Developing Countries: The Contingency Approach.* Durham, N.C.: and London: Duke University Press.

Roxborough, I. (1997). "Citizenship and Social Movements under Neoliberalism." In W. C. Smith and R. P. Korzeniewicz, eds. *Politics, Social Change, and Economic Restructuring in Latin America.* Florida: North-South Center Press.

Sader, E. and P. Gentili, eds. (2001). *La trama del Neoliberalismo: Mercado, crisis, y exclusión social.* EUDEBA: CLACSO.

Smith, W. C. and R. P. Korzeniewicz. (1997). "Latin America and the Second Great Transformation." In W. C. Smith and R. P. Korzeniewicz, eds. *Politics, Social Change, and Economic Restructuring in Latin America.* Florida: North-South Center Press.

Torre, J. C. (1997). "The Politics of Transformation in Historical Perspective." In W. C. Smith and R. P. Korzeniewicz, eds. *Politics, Social Change, and Economic Restructuring in Latin America.* Florida: North-South Center Press.

UNESCO Institute for Statistics. *Unesco Indicators.* http://www.unesco.org. Cited March 1st, 2002.

Vandenberghe, V. (1999). "Combining Market and Bureaucratic Control in Education: An Answer to Market and Bureaucratic Failure?" *Comparative Education* 35, no. 3: 271–282.

Viola Espínola, H. (undated). *Revisión de Quince Años de Política Educativa en Chile: Ajustes en Función de la Equidad.* Washington, D.C.: BID.

Viola Espínola, H. (1992). *Decentralization of the Education System and the Introduction of Market Rules in the Regulation of Schooling. The case of Chile.* Santiago: Centro de Investigación y Desarrollo de la Educación.

Welsh, T. and N. F. McGinn. (1998). *Decentralization of Education: What and How?* Draft. Cambridge: Harvard University.

West, E. G. (1996). *Education Vouchers in Practice and Principle: A World Survey.* Human Capital Development and Operations Policy Working Papers. Washington, D.C.: World Bank.

Whitty, G. Power, S. and D. Halpin. (1988). *Devolution and Choice in Education. The School, the State and the Market.* Buckingham and Philadelphia: Open University Press.

7

Beyond Neoliberalism in Education

The Citizen School and the Struggle
for Democracy in Porto Alegre, Brazil

LUÍS ARMANDO GANDIN
MICHAEL W. APPLE

In this chapter, we want to situate the processes of educational policy and re-form into their larger sociopolitical context. We discuss the ways in which a set of policies has had what seem to be extensive and long-lasting effects. This is due to the fact that the policies are coherently linked to larger dynamics of so-cial transformation and to a coherent strategy that aims to change the mecha-nisms of the state and the rules of participation in the formation of state policies. We describe and analyze the policies of the "Popular Administration" in Porto Alegre, Brazil. We specifically focus on the "Citizen School" and on proposals that are explicitly designed to radically change both the municipal schools and the relationship between communities, the state, and education. This set of polices and the accompanying processes of implementation are constitutive parts of a clear and explicit project aimed at constructing not only a better school for the excluded, but also a larger project of radical democracy. The reforms Porto Alegre is building are still in formation, but we argue that they have crucial implications for how we might think about the politics of ed-ucation policy and its dialectical role in social transformation.

In this period of crisis we are living in, what has been called "conservative modernization" (Apple 2001), there have been conscious attempts to radically transform our common sense about the legitimate ways to solve our pressing educational and social problems. We are told by neoliberals that only by turn-ing our schools, teachers, and children over to the competitive market will we find a solution. We are told by neoconservatives that the only way out is to re-turn to "real knowledge." Popular knowledge, knowledge that is connected to and organized around the lives of the most disadvantaged members of our communities, is not legitimate. But are the neoliberal and neoconservative po-sitions the only alternatives? We do not think so.

While it is crucial to recognize and analyze the strength and the real conse-quences of neoliberal and neoconservative policies (something both of us have been engaged in over the past decade; see for example Apple 1996, 2000, 2001 and Gandin 1994, 1998, 1999), it is also essential to understand the renegotiations that are made at the regional and municipal levels. As Ball emphasizes, "policy is . . . a set of technologies and practices which are realized and struggled over in local settings" (Ball 1994, 10). Hence, rather than assuming that neoliberal and neoconservative policies dictate exactly what occurs at the local level, we have to study the *rearticulations* that occur on this level to be able to map out the creation of alternatives.

This is one of the major reasons a focus on the Citizen School in Porto Alegre is so important. What is forming there may be crucial not only for Brazil, but for all of us in so many nations who are struggling in classrooms and schools to create an education that serves *all* of our children and communities.

Porto Alegre and the "Popular Administration"

Porto Alegre is a city of 1.3 million people, situated in the southern region of Brazil. It is the capital of the state of Rio Grande do Sul, and the largest city of the region. Since 1989, it has been governed by a coalition of leftist parties, under the general leadership of the Workers' Party (Partido dos Trabalhadores, PT, formed in 1979 by a coalition of unions, social movements, and other leftist organizations). PT has been reelected three consecutive times, thus giving it and its policies even greater legitimacy.

According to one of Porto Alegre's former mayors (a nationally respected member of the Workers' Party), the purpose of government is to "recuperate the utopian energies," to "create a movement which contains, as a real social process, the origins of a new way of life, constructing a 'new moral life' (Gramsci) and a new articulation between state and society . . . that could lead social activity and citizenship consciousness to a new order" (Silva 1999b, 9).

The municipal administration, the Popular Administration, has brought significant material improvements to the most impoverished citizens of the city. To give just an example, as Santos points out, "as regards basic sanitation (water and sewage), in 1989, only 49 percent of the population was covered. By the end of 1996, 98 percent of the households had water and 85 percent were served by the sewage system" (Santos 1998, 485). In terms of education, the number of schools has more than doubled since the Popular Administration took office.

One particular measure adopted by the Popular Administration, "Participatory Budgeting" (Orçamento Participativo, or OP), is credited with the reallocation of resources to the impoverished neighborhoods. The OP is a mechanism that guarantees active popular participation and deliberation in the decision-making process for the allocation of resources for investment in the city. In Santos' words,

> The participatory budget promoted by the Prefeitura of Porto Alegre is a form of public government that tries to break away from the authoritar-

ian and patrimonialist tradition of public policies, resorting to the direct participation of the population in the different phases of budget preparation and implementation, with special concern for the definition of priorities for the distribution of investment resources. (Santos 1998, 467)

Santos' points are important. Politics in Brazil have been historically characterized by patrimonialism and clientelism. The government of the Popular Administration was able to break with this tradition; and active popular participation in the construction of policy and allocation of resources has been part of its success. The OP is at the core of the project of transforming the city of Porto Alegre and incorporating an historically excluded impoverished population into the processes of decision making. Just as important, as a number of researchers have shown (Baiocchi 1999, Santos 1998, Abbers 1998, Avritzer 1999), not only have the material conditions of the impoverished population changed, but also the OP has generated an educative process that has forged new organizations and associations in the neighborhoods. The citizenry of the city has been engaged in an extensive pedagogic project involving their own empowerment. There has been a process of political learning through the construction of organizations that enable full participation in the OP. In essence, the OP can be considered a "school of democracy." The learning acquired within the OP is transferred to other spheres of social life (for this see Baiocchi 1999; see also Bowles and Gintis 1986). Yet, there may be an even more significant educational aspect in the OP. The government agencies themselves are engaged in being "re-educated." Popular participation "teaches" the state to better serve the population. This is a crucial point that is often forgotten in our discussion of the role of democracy in state policy formation and in bureaucratic institutions.

Working in tandem with the OP, there is another more specifically educational project for the city, the Citizen School, implemented by the Municipal Secretariat of Education (Secretaria Municipal de Educação, or SMED). The Citizen School is pushing in the same direction and aims to initiate a "thick" version of education for citizenship very early in the formal education process. Like the Participatory Budgeting, through clear normative goals and innovative institutional design, the Citizen School project has been transforming formal education in Porto Alegre.

Before we describe some of the mechanisms created by the Citizen School project, we want to situate this initiative within the global context of predominantly neoliberal reforms. If we are to understand the case of the Citizen School, we have to investigate the particular rearticulations forged at this locale, since part of the political/ethical/educational project that is going on here is both to counter the neoliberal and neoconservative attempts at transforming our common sense and to build a new one based on much more participatory principles.

The concept we used in the prior paragraph, *articulation*, is central here. It helps us to understand the ideological "work" that has do be done to disconnect ideas and practices about what our educational and social institutions should do and how these goals should be talked about and evaluated from one set of historical causes and movements and reconnect them to another set that has very different ideological commitments. To disarticulate a concept historically associated with counterhegemonic movements and rearticulate it to the hegemonic discourse actually requires heavy lifting. Yet this is exactly what neoliberals, for instance, have done when they have reappropriated the traditional language of protest movements (democracy, choice, autonomy, local power, and decentralization are prime examples) for their own purposes. To disarticulate these concepts from hegemonic discourse and rearticulate them back to progressive and counterhegemonic initiatives is an even tougher job. As Hall states, "an articulation is . . . the form of the connection that *can* make a unity of two different elements, under certain conditions. It is a linkage which is not necessary, determined, absolute, and essential for all time" (Hall 1996, 141). This is a key to our analysis in this chapter.

The concept of articulation provides us with a tool to understand that the apparent homogeneity and solidness of a given discourse actually is a historical construction, one that has to be constantly renovated. Connections that are established between groups and specific ideologies are not "necessary" or given; they cannot be easily deduced from a central dominant ideology. They are better understood as an articulation, a non-necessary and more or less contingent connection made possible in a specific context and in a specific historical moment.

How does that help us to better understand the case of Porto Alegre? As we noted, there is a process of conservative modernization going on in education throughout the world. One of the key ideas associated with this is the claim that education is both the blame for and a major solution to the economic and cultural dilemmas "we" are experiencing. Thus, the dominant rhetorical claim is that if "we" prepare our students for the increasingly competitive world of new capitalism, "our" nation and our people will be better prepared to excel in the globalized market. Education is stressed as a privileged site in this hegemonic discourse.

While this set of claims has become truly international, its effects need to be seen in a nonreductive, conjunctural way. When this discourse reaches Brazil, and more specifically the city of Porto Alegre, some interesting rearticulations are forged. In this transnational hegemonic discourse, the stress on education and its relationship to the economy is related to the aim of dominant economic and cultural forces to colonize the space of educational policy and practice and produce an educational environment more in tune with the economic needs of the market. But "message sent" may not always be "message received."

When this global process reaches Brazil, contradictions are created and a hybrid product is formed. If it is true that the hegemonic discourse tries to colonize the educational sphere, it is also true that it creates unintended spaces for alternative experiences and interventions. Hegemonic discourses cannot totally contain the ways in which these unintended spaces are reoccupied and used for counterhegemonic purposes. Thus, for example, the idea that education will solve the problems of the country allows for and legitimates real investment in education *for everyone*. The Popular Administration uses this space to prioritize education in a country where education for the poor has been neglected. Once the space is occupied by the rhetoric of more investment in education, the Citizen School can deploy its alternative project, its transformation of priorities, and invest in an emancipatory project of education for the excluded. In the process, the Popular Administration can also start to recuperate and, at the same time, reinvent concepts such as "autonomy," "decentralization," and "collaboration" that are currently articulated by neoliberals. In the popular movements of Brazil, historically these concepts had a meaning that was very different than that attached to them by neoliberal positions. This very history provides a basis for action. The concepts now have to be disarticulated from neoliberal discourse and rearticulated to the Citizen School project. They can then be reattached to and used to justify more fully participatory movements for social justice. This creative reappropriation is exactly what the Popular Administration has done.

However, the fact that these rearticulations are happening does not mean that the Popular Administration has won the battle. Hegemonic groups themselves constantly attempt to forge new articulations and win back the space for their own use. Thus, education remains a site of struggle. But the important point is that no hegemonic action can block all spaces simultaneously, and even its own discourse can be rearticulated to favor counterhegemonic purposes.

This can be seen, for instance, in another very important example of articulation, the creative use of the concept of citizenship in the programs forming in this part of Brazil. This concept, central to the political and educational project in Porto Alegre, has a very specific meaning in contemporary Brazil. "Education for citizenship" is a sliding signifier. It can have multiple meanings, sometimes very conservative ones. However, in this case it is not a random category; it symbolizes the struggles against the attempts to introduce market logics into the very core of public sites such as education. The focus on the formation of citizens inside public schools has to be read within the context of this discursive struggle. The category of "citizenship" serves as a discursive weapon against the possessive individualism embodied in the rival notions of "client" or "customer" fostered by neoliberal discourse. It provides very different subject positions for agency than those offered by the idea of the consumer in a set of market relations. The political meaning of citizenship has been rearticulated to a set of more socially critical ideas and practices, one that intends to construct a new common sense that is truly focused on collective as well as individual empowerment.

This is not a simple task, though. Certain discourses more easily gain the effects of truth. Others do not have access to the channels of distribution; when they do have access, they have to struggle to rearticulate concepts that have already been framed in dominant ways. The fact that the municipal government has access to a large number of schools, and that the schools themselves are sanctioned by the municipal level of the state, does not mean that the rearticulation goes smoothly. The Popular Administration must constantly struggle against dominant groups' ability to sustain hegemonic control by their power to restrain the spaces of visibility of alternatives, to use the media to circulate negative readings of the educational and social transformations in which the Popular Administration is engaged, and to win back the discursive spaces that have been successfully reoccupied by progressive groups and governments.

Because of this, it is important to realize that the discursive struggles about both education and its major goals that are taking place in Porto Alegre are significant. They are not epiphenomenal, but have real and material effects. As we mentioned above, the language of "citizenship" is used in a way that tries to "accent" it in the struggles over meaning. Again, talking about "citizenship" in opposition to "client" or "consumer" is a conscious move to bring "political" words into the arena of discussion. Part of the project is to bring to the very center of the debate alternatives that have been marginalized. Thus, as we shall see in the next section, there is an attempt to bring the idea—contrary to what many "experts" would say—that impoverished communities, say, can participate in the definition of their social destiny through the channels created by the Citizen School to the very core of political practice. Not only are concepts that were relegated to the margins brought back to the center of public discussion, but even more importantly, a entire group of people who were marginalized and excluded from the economic, social, and political goods of the society are affirmed as having the right to space, to voice, to social existence. In order to accomplish all of this, there is a constant struggle to legitimize the experience of the Citizen School, to make it socially visible, to pose the discussion over education in terms other than those of neoliberalism, to pull education from the technical economistic realm and push it to a more politicized one that has as its basic concern the role of education in social emancipation.

These successful struggles have indeed had an affect on the common sense of the people who are most marginalized in Porto Alegre. The Popular Administration has been reelected a number of times and, at the time of our writing, the polls for this year's elections indicate overwhelming popular support. That this support has had lasting effects can be seen in the fact that certain issues and policies are already established as givens in the conversation about elections in the city of Porto Alegre. No political party can win the election in

Porto Alegre if it do not guarantee that certain elements created by the Popular Administration—such as direct participation of the communities in the decisions of the municipal schools—will be maintained. A new common sense and a new set of expectations have been created about the relationship between communities and the municipal government.

This has occurred in large part as well because there has been a recognition that counterhegemonic struggles must be able to connect with popular memory, with the residual idea that there is a more than just way to structure social life, where social exclusion is not a daily reality. In the case of Porto Alegre, where a strong history of popular organization and politicization of daily life is part of this popular memory, latent in the local common sense, the project of the Citizen School and its repoliticization of the educational arena, along with the activation of community participation, does exactly that. The project was able to connect with this residual element already present in common sense and not totally expunged from popular consciousness by the experiences of neoliberal economic and social policies. By constructing social relations that actually recuperate this popular participation in reality, it has created a new common sense. High levels of participation by the people are now considered a new minimum for the relationship between state and communities.

So far we have talked rather generally about the overall political, ideological, and educational aims and processes of the counterhegemonic movements in Porto Alegre, claiming that part of the program's power lies in its ability to disarticulate and rearticulate the parts of the neoliberal agenda in creative ways. Yet, we cannot remain at this level if we are to more fully understand what has happened there. It is important to get more specific. We can now examine some of the institutional mechanisms created to implement the Citizen School project in the reality of the broader school system and in the daily life of the schools themselves.

Creating the Citizen School

Education in Brazil, as a rule, is centralized. In the majority of states and cities there are no elections for the city or state council of education (traditionally a bureaucratic structure, with members appointed by the executive), let alone for principals in schools. The curriculum is usually defined by the secretariats of education of the cities and states. Since the resources are administered by the centralized state agencies, schools usually have very little or no autonomy.

Although recently Brazil has achieved a very high level of initial access to schools (close to 99 percent), the indexes of failures and dropouts are frightening. Brazilian data have consistently shown over many years that less than 50 percent of the students in first grade passed to second grade in their first attempt. Hence, although initial access is granted, the chance of a poor child passing to second grade is very low. Furthermore, the dropout rate is extremely high, close to 20 percent in fourth grade. These data show clearly the exclusion reproduced in the Brazilian educational system.

This brief description represents a sharp contrast with the Citizen School project of the Popular Administration. As we noted, through the OP the Popular Administration wishes to engage in the transformation of the relationship of the state with civil society. The field of education has become central to its project of constructing new relations between state, schools, and communities. The Citizen School is organically linked to and considered part of the larger process of transforming the whole city.

The municipal schools of Porto Alegre are all situated in the most impoverished neighborhoods of the city—in *favelas*, or shantytowns. This is because the expansion of the system occurred recently (since the Popular Administration took office in 1989) and the schools were built in the zones where there was a deficit of educational offering. In fact, many of the schools were constructed as a concrete result of the *OP*, because some regions of the city prioritized education and, specifically, a school in their assemblies.

Dealing with the excluded of Brazilian society, the Citizen School has a clear and explicit project of transformation. It "institutes the possibility for citizens to recognize themselves as bearers of dignity, to rebel against the 'commodification' of life. . . . In the Citizen School, the conformist and alienated pedagogy that sustains the idea that history is a movement rigorously pre-organized of realization of capital needs is denied" (Silva 1999a, 10, our translation).

The grounding of the SMED proposals can be seen in the words of one of the most recent secretaries of education in Porto Alegre.

> The Citizen School is not a product of a group of enlightened administrators that had formulated and executed a "new proposal." It is not, as well, a spontaneous construction, without intentionality. . . . The Citizen School nourished itself from and was inspired by theoretic-practical contributions of academic progressive educators, by contributors in the public schools, and by the experiences of democratic and transformative struggle of social movements. Many of the builders of the Citizen School were actors of the movements in unions, communities, and in the popular trenches of the struggle for redemocratization of the country. (Silva 1999a, 12–13, our translation)

This political origin of the coordinators of the Citizen School is an important factor in the democratic component of the proposal. It constitutes one of the reasons that there is a clear political will for constructing participatory and democratic alternatives. In fact, although the SMED plays an essential role in coordinating the actions of the schools and pushing a democratic agenda, the principles that officially guide SMED's actions were created collectively, with active participation of teachers, school administrators and staff, students, and parents in institutionalized forums of democratic decision-making.

In order to construct the principles that would guide the actions of the Citizen School, a democratic, deliberative, and participatory forum was created—

the Constituent Congress of Education. Through a long process of mobilization of the school communities (using the invaluable lessons learned in the mobilization for the OP), a Congress was constructed whose objective was to constitute the organizing principles that would guide the policy for schools in Porto Alegre.

From the Constituent Congress, the main normative goal for education was defined as a radical democratization in the municipal schools along three dimensions: democratization of management, democratization of access to the school, and democratization of access to knowledge.

For the Popular Administration, democratization of management is not simply a "technical," but a political and ethical issue. It involves the democratization of the relationships inside the schools, between the school and the community, and between the school and the central administration (SMED). It requires the creation both of mechanisms that enable the full participation of teachers, staff, parents, teachers, and administrators in the construction of democratic decisions about education in Porto Alegre, and of a system of monitoring that guarantees that the collectively constructed decisions are being implemented. It is also grounded in the recognition of the centrality of the culture of the community as part of the educational and administrative spheres of the school and school system. In this sense, the democratization of management involves a clear educational process, because both the state agencies and the communities learn together to construct new mechanisms that represent the will of the communities.

The decision-making and monitoring processes in education occur at various levels: the establishment of a larger policy for education in the city and a constant evaluation of it; deliberations about how to invest the money allocated by the central administration to the school; and decisions about creating mechanisms of inclusion that are overtly linked to the ongoing struggle against a society that marginalizes impoverished students and denies knowledge to them.

The task that the SMED had to engage in, hence, was complex, but the basic question was simple: "How [do we] develop a transformative and democratic project inside a state apparatus that has a logic that goes in the opposite direction of democracy and transformation?" (Azevedo 1998, 309, our translation). In order to implement the principle of democratization of management in the educational system of Porto Alegre, the SMED and the Popular Administration created several mechanisms designed to achieve this goal. The following sections examine some of these mechanisms.

The new school configuration

The first transformation involved one of the most pressing issues facing schooling throughout Brazil—the terrible exclusion of students. It was aimed at abolishing the existing year-long grade structure. Instead, it established schools that had three "cycles." In the municipal elementary schools of Porto Alegre, there are three cycles, each one three years long, and thus totaling nine years of education. The establishment of such cycles is a conscious attempt to eliminate the mechanisms in schools that perpetuate exclusion, failure, and dropouts. In the cycle plan, students progress from one year to another within one cycle; the notion of "failure" is eliminated. In the traditional school, the very idea of failure creates a situation in which the student is the one to blame for her or his problems. The responsibilities of the school itself are marginalized in such policies. Yet the SMED understood that the elimination of mechanisms of exclusion was not enough. Because of this, the Citizen School created several mechanisms that guaranteed the inclusion of students. It established "progression groups" in which students who come from other school systems (from other cities, for example) and have experienced multiple failures are given close attention so that they are ultimately integrated into the cycle. The policies include a learning laboratory, a space where students with special needs are helped, but also a place where teachers conduct research in order to improve the quality of the regular classes. Each of these has proven crucial to the Citizen Schools' success. But among all of the changes, it is the integration within the Citizen School of a new conception of knowledge that is perhaps the most important, since cycles must teach something that does not itself cause exclusion.

Transforming "official" knowledge

Curriculum transformation is a crucial part of Porto Alegre's project to build "thick democracy." It is important to say that this dimension is not limited to access to traditional knowledge. What is constructed is a new epistemological understanding about what counts as knowledge as well. It is not based on a mere incorporation of new knowledge within the margins of an intact "core of humankind's wisdom," but a radical transformation. The Citizen School project goes beyond the mere episodic mentioning of race, class, gender, and sexual oppression. It includes these themes as an *essential* part of the process of the construction of knowledge.

In the Citizen School, the notion of "core" and "periphery" in knowledge is made problematic. The starting point for the construction of curricular knowledge is the culture(s) of the communities themselves, not only in terms of content but in perspective as well. The whole educational process is aimed at inverting previous priorities and instead serving the historically oppressed and excluded groups.

The starting point for this new process of knowledge construction is the idea of "thematic complexes." Through action research (one that the teachers do in the communities where they work, involving students, parents, and the whole community), the main themes from the interests or worries of the community are listed. Then the most significant ones are constructed in the thematic complex that will guide the action of the classroom, in an interdisciplinary form, during a period of time. The traditional rigid disciplinary structure is broken and general interdisciplinary areas are created. These areas of study are given the names of social expression, biological, chemical and physical sciences, sociohistoric, and logic-mathematical.

To give a concrete example of how this works, one of the schools organized its thematic complex in the sociohistoric area in order to examine questions directly linked to the interests and problems of the community. At the center of the complex was the issue of the community's standard of living. Three sub-themes were listed: rural exodus, social organization, and property. In the rural exodus subthemes, the issues reflected the origin of the community—living now in a *favela*, but originally from the rural areas. This is a common story in the *favelas* where people who had nothing in the rural areas came to the cities only to find more exclusion. In these subthemes, the issues discussed were migration movements, overpopulation of the cities, "disqualification" of the working force, and marginalization. In the subtheme of social organization, the issues are distributed in terms of temporal, political, spatial, and sociocultural relations. The issues, again, represent important questions in the organization of the community: the excessive and uncritical pragmatism of some in the associations, the connections with the neighborhood associations and the OP, and cultural issues such as religiosity, bodily expression, African origins, dance groups, and "samba schools." In the third subtheme—property—the issues were literally linked to the situation of the families in the *favela*, living in illegal lots with no title, having to cope with the lack of infrastructure, and at the same time fighting for their rights as citizens.

This example shows the real transformation that is occurring in the curriculum of the schools in Porto Alegre. The students are not studying history or social and cultural studies through books that never address the real problems and interests they have. Through the thematic complexes, the students learn history by beginning with the historical experience of their families. They study important social and cultural content by focusing on and valorizing their own cultural manifestations. A real shift is occurring because the focus is not on the "core/official" knowledge organized around dominant class and race visions of the world, but on the real problems and interests of the students and the community. It is important to note that these students will ultimately still learn the history of Brazil and the world, "high" culture, and so on, but this will be seen through different lenses. Their culture will not be forgotten in order for them to learn "high status" culture. Rather, by understanding their situation and their culture and valuing it, these students will be able to simultaneously learn *and* will have the chance to transform their situation of exclusion. By studying the problems (rural exodus, living in illegal lots, etc.) and not stopping there, but studying the strengths of self-organization (in the OP, in neighborhood associations, in cultural activities and groups), the Citizen

School helps to construct alternatives for the communities living in such terrible conditions.

We also can see in this example that the historic silence about race in Brazil is being challenged. Bringing the African origins of the music (samba), of the religion (candomble), and openly discussing racist practices in Brazil in the process of constructing critical knowledge teachers and students are learning that the silences about oppression only help the reproduction of exclusion and racism. Thus, the Citizen School has embarked on a dual path. It has recognized the necessity of creating empowered channels in which people can speak openly, but it also knows that at the same time one must unveil the meanings behind these voices, question their hidden presuppositions, and construct new knowledge. Beginning from the insights of the community, it is necessary not to stop there, but rather to construct knowledge that fights discrimination, racism, and exclusion. This experience overcomes the limited forms of multiculturalism that have dominated education. Not only does it incorporate elements of "ethnic information," but it also aims at constructing a new form of knowledge by shifting the center of discussion.

This shift of what is considered the core or the center of knowledge should affect not only the pedagogical conception that guides the daily life in the classrooms. It should also transform how the school itself functions as a whole. One of the major achievements of the Citizen School is the fact that this conception of knowledge is spreading throughout the entire school system. The project not only serves the "excluded" by generating a different formal education for students, but by creating an innovative structure that makes it possible for the community of those who have historically been excluded to regain their dignity (both material and symbolic).

School councils

School councils, the product of the political efforts of the popular administration and of a number of social movements involved with education in the city, are the most central part of the democratization of the decision-making process in education in Porto Alegre. They are composed of teachers, school staff, parents, students, and one member of the administration.

Each school council has 50 percent of the seats for teachers and staff and 50 percent for parents and students. One seat is guaranteed to the administration of the school, usually the principal (elected her/himself by all members of the school), something to which we shall return shortly.

The rules concerning parents and students are strikingly democratic. Students who are twelve years old or more and parents or legal guardians of students who are less than sixteen years old can vote and be elected. When the number of parents or students cannot be reached because of these legal conditions, more students or parents (depending on the specific case) are added until the percentage of 50 percent for the parents/students segment is reached.

The task of the school councils is to deliberate about the global projects for the school, the basic principles of administration, and the allocation of economic resources, and also to monitor the implementation of these decisions. The principal and her/his team are responsible for the implementation of the policies defined by the school council.

In terms of resources, it is important to say that, before the Popular Administration took office, there was a practice (common throughout in Brazil) of centralized budgeting. Every expense (even small daily ones) had to be sent to the central administration before it was approved and then the money was sent to the school, or a central agency would purchase the necessary product or service. With such a structure, school councils had their hands tied, possessing no autonomy at all. The SMED changed this structure and established a new policy of making the resources allocated to each school available every three months. This measure instituted financial autonomy for the schools, and allowed schools to manage their expenditures according to the goals and priorities established by the school council. At the same time, such autonomy gives parents, students, teachers, and staff present in the council a notion of social responsibility in administering public money. It also teaches them to prioritize their spending priorities with solidarity in mind (SMED 1999b).

Decisions about the curriculum are also part of the council's deliberations. The inclusion of parents, students, support staff, and teachers in this process is one of the most innovative aspects of the model. Because the school has relative autonomy (decisions of the Congress of Education must be implemented in the schools, but these are general guidelines, not content-specific), this opens up the boundaries for "thick" democracy.

It is important to realize that participation in the school council demands a certain level of technical knowledge. Because of this, in order to enhance the participation of parents the SMED has been promoting municipal meetings of the school councils (six, so far). This is a space where parents, students, teachers, and staff acquire the tools and construct the necessary knowledge to administer the schools. It also generates an arena where the individual councils meet to share their knowledge and their doubts, allowing for a larger perspective beyond a corporatist or a "localist" view. Furthermore, the SMED has a permanent program of "formation" (continuing education of all the participants) inside the schools. This provides an additional space for the education of the councilors. Finally, in order to make participation truly substantive, the SMED has been stimulating the connections between councils and local associations or unions. This gives the councilors more representativeness. In short, the process of education is not only happening inside the classrooms of the schools, but in every instance of the school that involves democratic participation.

Although the school council is a remarkably democratic institution, there is another structure that guarantees representativeness. In the schools of Porto Alegre, the whole school community elects the principal by direct vote. Thus, the one responsible for the implementation of the decisions of the school council is her/himself elected, based on the program that she or he articulates. This enhances administrative legitimacy in the community. The principal, hence, is not someone who represents the interests of the central administration inside the school councils, but someone with a majority of supporters inside that particular educational community. But the responsibility of the community does not stop with the election; through the school council, the school community also monitors the activities of the principal and holds her/him accountable.

The process of direct election of principals by the whole educational community seems to produce a considerable level of mobilization. In the 1998 elections for principals, data from the Popular Administration indicate that almost thirty thousand people voted. Once again, this provides an important part of the democratic learning of the communities, especially because the very process provokes a good deal of debate about the varying proposals for managing the school. The direct election of the one responsible to implement the directives created by the school council, and a school council that is elected directly by the school community, together represent a pedagogic mechanism that aims at both generating and teaching the principles of democratic management at the local level of the school.

Judging success

Up to this point, our focus has been on the processes and mechanisms that have been put in place in Porto Alegre. Yet, a final question remains. Are the mechanisms created capable of realizing the goals? Here we can only offer some tentative conclusions, since the reforms in Porto Alegre are ongoing and still in formation.

Obviously, we have already offered some elements of an evaluation throughout this chapter. The Citizen School, through the collective creation of goals and mechanisms that generate active involvement of the communities, so far seems to be a genuinely transformative experience. The Citizen School has broken with the separation between the ones who "know" and "educate" (the administration) and the ones who "don't know" and need to be "educated." A new form of thinking not only about education, but also about the whole society, seems to be in gestation. Here the project reflects Paulo Freire's (himself a member of the Workers' Party) dictum that "the Workers" Party cannot be the educator that already knows everything, that already has an unquestionable truth, in relation with an incompetent popular mass needing to be rescued and saved (Freire 1988, 17).

The epistemological rupture that plays such a major role in the experiment also allows for optimism. The challenge to what counts as knowledge, to what counts as core and periphery, represents the essence of the educational proposal. Instead of creating isolated multicultural programs or content that have little efficacy in the context of a largely dominant whole structure, the Popular

Administration has been creating a structure, with popular participation, in which the question of diversity of cultures has space to flourish. The Citizen School created spaces in which multicultural practices are organically integrated, not only added artificially to a bureaucratically determined structure that is averse to "difference." To construct a powerful and democratic set of multicultural experiences, the whole institutional structure had to be changed. An important example is the fact that the SMED has been acting to create a context in which the problems of racism can surface and be treated seriously. At the same time, the SMED is acting proactively by establishing advisory boards that can quickly discuss with the community and incorporate new agendas in the curriculum and in the relationship of the school with the community. This is enhanced by the establishment of and participation by popular organizations that are organized around the powerful issues of race, gender, and sexuality. Local knowledge is valorized and considered essential to the educational and democratic quality of the project. This vision of "thick" democracy is crucial. As we argued earlier, the project of the Citizen School has also radically challenged the roles of the traditional school. In these transformed schools, all of the segments of the educational community collectively construct the principles that guide their daily action. But the project not only constructs this as a goal; it also consciously takes up the task of *creating* concrete participatory mechanisms to implement these goals. In the process, a new conception of respect for the diversity of cultures is generated. Challenging the elitist belief that impoverished people from poor neighborhoods or slums cannot participate because they are "ignorant," the Citizen School inverts this logic, placing the ones who live with the problems at the center as the people in a privileged position to construct alternatives. The "local" and "decentralization" here take on a distinctly non-neoliberal cast.

In this sense, the Citizen School contains major advances in relation to the "mainstream" notion of multiculturalism. The project seems to perfectly fit what Giroux calls an "insurgent multiculturalism," one in which "all participants play a formative role in crucial decisions about what is taught, who is hired, and how the school can become a laboratory for learning that nurtures critical citizenship and civic courage" (Giroux 1993, 340–341).

A major difference here is the fact that the objectives are not simply the formulations of a team of experts in the SMED, but a democratic and collective construction with the participation of all of the segments involved in education (including especially those people historically excluded from nearly all of the processes). The very fact that what is evaluated are normative goals that were not created by bureaucrats, but ones that are the fruit of participatory collective creation, means that the expectations are already high in terms of participation and democracy. As we showed, taken in their entirety, the participatory mechanisms created as part of the whole design for reform by the Popular Administration are powerful ways of implementing the goal of democratization of decision making and of implementing and monitoring processes in the schools and in the educational life of the city. This is a strikingly different vision of collective democracy than the "thin" model of democracy based on possessive individualism found in neoliberalism (Apple 2001).

The SMED clearly wants the decentralized local School Councils to achieve the larger goals for the education of the city; but these larger goals were themselves forged through a democratic process. In this sense, what the Popular Administration is avoiding is a common practice in Brazil and in many other countries in which power is devolved to local units, but these are held accountable by criteria not based on democratic decisions.

The SMED understood that participation is a process that had to be *constructed*. Therefore, it consciously launched a program of providing advice and education so that people could participate knowledgeably in the OP, in the school councils, and elsewhere. Thus, the transfer of technical knowledge has been an important part of the process. But perhaps the most significant element in the education of the formerly excluded participants has been the very openness of the process that permits constant evaluation and transformation of the mechanisms themselves. This environment of deliberation transforms the participants into co-constructors of the mechanisms and the rules. It reconstitutes them as subjects, as historical actors. Participants are not only implementing rules, but are part of an historical experiment of reconstructing the structure of the municipal state.

This can be seen in the fact that the school community gets to decide the allocation of economic resources. The schools are granted autonomy in the management of their share. This has had a significant impact on the reality of the schools themselves. Of just as much import, unlike many other parts of Brazil where decentralization has actually meant a decline in real resources, the decentralization that has occurred in Porto Alegre has not been accompanied by an allocation of fewer resources. This process has produced a real empowerment of the school councils and not—as in the majority of the cases in the rest of the country—a mere formal transfer of responsibility from the centralized agencies to the local units, a transfer whose ultimate effect has all too often simply meant that local units have been forced to cut needed programs. Such decentralization is usually merely part of the legitimacy strategies of the regional or national state as the state exports the fiscal crisis downward (Apple 1995, 2000).

We still need to ask, however, whether such participatory processes and the changed curricula have had real and substantial effects on issues such as exclusion in schools. While data are limited, they do seem to show significant improvement in terms of quality. Since it took office in 1989, the Popular Administration has increased the number of schools by more than 220 percent. The number of students enrolled has risen from 24,332 in 1989 to more than 50,000 in 1999. But without any doubt, the success of the Citizen School can be measured by the sharp decrease in the number of student dropouts. In 1989, when it took office, the percentage of dropouts (and remember that we are talking about *elementary* schools) was a frightening figure of nearly 10 percent. The consequences of this for already disadvantaged and excluded children were truly horrible. Through the Citizen School's emphasis on parental and student involvement, curriculum transformation, teacher education, and other similar mechanisms, the SMED reduced this dropout rate to 0.97 percent in 1998. This is clearly one of the most important educational achievements of the project. If the children stay in school, then clearly the new curricular proposals can actually affect them (SMED 1999a).

Another telling fact is the virtual nonexistence of vandalism against the majority of the municipal schools. School vandalism used to be a serious problem in public schools (and still is in the state schools). The fact that the community actively participates in the governance of the schools and uses them as a space for the community (for sports, cultural activities, etc.) creates a sense of responsibility and enhances the notion that public goods are the property of all. That many of the new schools are fruits of the OP makes the school "theirs" as well.

Potential problems

While we have been very positive in our evaluation of the project here, we do not want to be romantic. Although the mechanisms and the curriculum constructed by the Citizen School have a good deal of potential to construct an education that helps to include the historically excluded, there are a number of potential problems that need to be carefully examined.

One potential issue is the possibility of a recreation of hierarchies within the cycles. The cycles represent a very thoughtful innovation. They allow students to stay in school, thereby combating the serious problem of dropouts. The overall structure also allows a more integrated construction of knowledge, which valorizes the knowledge that the students bring from their community. Yet we need to step back and ask whether parts of this structure could ultimately lead to the production of new hierarchies of students within the cycle. Even though they are seen as temporary, the progression groups have the risk of creating a "second class" group of students.

Another potential problem of the Citizen School project is related to the issue of class. The Workers' Party has historically had its roots in a Marxist understanding of the primacy of class. Parts of the Marxist tradition have been accused (correctly, we think, in many cases) of choosing class as not just the central, but often only, category of analysis, thus subordinating other forms of oppression to class (See Apple and Weis 1983, Apple 1988). A conception based on steps, where fighting class oppression is the most important step and the other oppressions are to be fought "later on," can be problematic, since in the real world in very many instances there is no way of fighting one set of oppressive relations without fighting all. Thus, in the material produced by the

Popular Administration, there are several explicit references to class oppression, and rightly so; but there are fewer references to racial oppression or gender oppression. This could potentially lead to a position that ignores the specificities of oppressions other than the class-based.

It is to the SMED's credit that these potential problems are not unrecognized. As we demonstrated, there is some evidence that the practical experiments of the Citizen School are incorporating race issues into their thematic complexes. In addition, the various mechanisms of continuous education of teachers in the Citizen Schools do provide sites in which explicit discussions of race, gender, and sexuality are brought up, thereby creating theoretical spaces for the construction of new practices that challenge the silences about these themes. These movements represent positive signs, in the sense that the members of the school communities are using the open channels to problematize the issues of daily life, issues that certainly include moments of prejudice and racism. It is also true that the Popular Administration has several advisory boards (with both budget and structure, and the power to act) that have the explicit task of bringing up the themes of gender, race, sexuality, and religiosity.

Hence, although the potential problems should not be ruled out, there are reasons to believe that there are open spaces for popular organizations, such as the growing activist movement among Afro-Brazilians, women's social movements, and gay and lesbian organizations, to operate and demand from the state agencies the inclusion of issues that we believe should be part of the agenda of every citizen who fights oppression.

Of equal significance, however, is another possible problem for the project. This is the possibility that participants who have historically had more power will dominate the school councils and the other mechanisms of popular participation. This is a serious issue that should not be pushed into the background, given the experiences of such experiments elsewhere. However, we think that the case of Porto Alegre has some specific attributes that can lessen the probability that this will occur. First, the municipal schools are all situated in the most impoverished areas of Porto Alegre. Therefore, the classical cases of middle-class people dominating the discussions (see McGrath and Kuriloff 1999) are avoided because, as a rule, there are no middle-class people in the regions where the schools are situated. Two recent studies of the OP in Porto Alegre offer some indirect evidence (Santos 1998, Abbers 1998) and one study offers direct empirical evidence (Baiocchi 1999) that show that there is no domination by powerful groups in the deliberative processes. In the OP, there is gender parity among the participants of the meetings and the proportion of "less educated" people corresponds to the city average (Baiocchi 1999, 7). While it is true that there are more men and educated people speaking at the meetings, the research has also shown that the main factor is the number of years of participation. There is a learning curve that encourages people with more years of participation to speak. In fact "participation over time seems to increase participation parity" (Baiocchi 1999, 10). This is a very encouraging conclusion, which leads us to be optimistic about the process, especially given its conscious pedagogic aims.

This said, no data about the composition of the various mechanisms of the Citizen School itself are yet available and therefore we cannot evaluate whether this potential problem has surfaced in the specifically school-related parts of the experiment of Porto Alegre. There are no data about the race of the participants, or whether teachers—because of their more technical "insiders" knowledge—play more dominant roles in the various forums and councils. This clearly is worth further research.

One final potential issue needs to be mentioned. The very fact that the entire project is based on an active engagement of the citizenry could have serious consequences in terms of sustainability. Because the city administration is using citizen participation in all sites where a process of policy decision-making is necessary, the requirement for active engagement of the members of the communities is multiplying. There are dozens of sites where an active and involved citizen or activist is asked to contribute with her/his perspective. This could generate an "overload" for those who are already integrated into other sites of deliberation. How many hours can a working class person, with two or three jobs necessary to feed her/his family, allocate to deliberative instances? Can the levels of active engagement with the participatory institutions be maintained over the time? Our own involvement in political/educational work of this type, and the intense time commitments this requires, leads us to worry about whether such involvement can be maintained.

Yet, once again, our worries are lessened by the fact that the *SMED* seems to be trying to deal with these potential problems proactively. We are witnessing an *increase*, not a decrease, in participation in the democratic mechanisms that have been put in place by the Popular Administration. The community agents of the city administration are constantly stimulating the involvement of individuals and neighborhood associations. Because the idea of participation is not isolated in the action of one secretariat, but is something incorporated in the daily practices of the city administration as a whole, we can see an integrated effort to generate active involvement of the communities in the definitions of the directions that the city will chose to go. If it is true that this could demand too much from communities accustomed to only being the recipients of policies, and especially could overload activists already involved in the existing sites of decision making, it is also true that the city administration has an aggressive policy of actively involving and educating new participants. This policy has been more than a little successful so far. The visible results of participation—translated in the extremely lower dropout rate and better education for the community's children, as in the case of school councils—are the best guarantees both of maintainability and of the creation of new generations of participants.

Finally, as an ongoing project, the Citizen School is constantly evaluated in order to construct new mechanisms and revise the existing ones to create a democratic structure of decision making, implementation, and monitoring for education in Porto Alegre. There are reasons to believe that the *SMED* and the organized communities are learning from their mistakes and successes. The constant evaluation of the reforms and their improvement are signs that this learning process is having effects on daily policy and practice.

Yet, this should not make us overly sanguine. It is important to point out that because of the electoral success of the Popular Administration—currently in its fourth term—the previously hegemonic conservative forces have responded with renewed vigor. There has been a major reorganization of the center-right forces in the city to challenge the policies of the Workers' Party. So far, these attempts have been unsuccessful. Up to this point, the left government of Porto Alegre has been able to stimulate independent social movements and create real channels for these movements to operate. The fact that in 1986 Porto Alegre had 180 neighborhood associations and in 1998 this number had increased to 540 suggests that it will not be easy for conservative forces to regain their dominance (Baiocchi 1999). Nevertheless, one should not minimize the strength of the possible center-right coalitions that are being formed to defeat the Popular Administration and its comprehensive program of reforms. As we have seen repeatedly in other contexts, rightist movements have been able to successfully mobilize around issues of racial backlash, economic worries, and antigovernment sentiment (Apple 1996, 2001). Such movements are themselves part of ongoing attempts by neoliberal and neoconservative forces to disarticulate and rearticulate the ideas surrounding democracy once again. The creation of and challenges to hegemonic relations are always involved in ongoing processes. Hegemony and counterhegemony are not stable. Gains can be taken back as well as move forward. It remains to be seen whether such mobilizations will have any marked effect in Porto Alegre.

Conclusion

In this chapter, we have sought to situate the processes of educational policy and reform into their larger sociopolitical context. We have described the ways in which a set of educational policies has had what seem to be extensive and long lasting effects *because* these polices are coherently linked to larger dynamics of social transformation and to a coherent set of polices and practices that aim to change the mechanisms of the state and the rules of participation in the formation of state policies. All of this has crucial implications for how we might think about the politics of education policy and its dialectical role in social transformation (see also Wong and Apple, in press).

The Citizen School has been important not only as a way of giving an impoverished population a quality education that will enable them to have better chances in the paid labor market and at the same time operate as empowered citizens. It is important because, in challenging neoliberal assumptions and in using the spaces they unintentionally provided, it has generated structured forms of "educating" the communities—both for organizing around and discussing their problems *and* for acting on their own behalf through the channels of participation and deliberation. In the process, it has "educated" the state agencies as well. The OP, the Municipal Congress of Education, the New Educational Configuration of the Schools, and the school councils have—together—helped create the beginnings of a new reality for the excluded. They have forged new leadership, brought about the active engagement of the communities with their own situations, and led to much more active participation in the construction of solutions to these problems.

In spite of the potential problems we discussed above, we are optimistic about the lasting impact of the Citizen School's democratizing initiatives and its construction of a more diverse and inclusive education. By itself, the Citizen School has been very successful in including an entire population that, if it were not for this project, would be out of the schools and even further excluded in an already actively excluding society. But the larger educative aspect of the Citizen School—empowering impoverished communities where they are situated and transforming both the schools and what counts as "official knowledge" there—is also of significant moment. Together with the OP (with its own cumulative effects), they represent new alternatives in the creation of an active citizenry—one that learns from its own experiences and culture—not just for now, but also for future generations. For these very reasons, we believe that the experiences of Porto Alegre have considerable importance not only for Brazil, but also for all of us who are deeply concerned about the effects of the neoliberal and neoconservative restructuring of education and of the public sphere in general. There is much to learn from the successful struggles there.

Note

This study was made possible, in part, with funding provided by the Brazilian National Council for Scientific and Technological Development (CNPq). A briefer version of this chapter appeared in the *Journal of Education Policy*.

References

Abers, R. (1998). "From Clientelism to Cooperation: Local Government, Participatory Policy and Civic Organizing in Porto Alegre, Brazil." *Politics & Society* 26, no. 4: 511–537.

Apple, M. W. (1988). *Teachers and Texts.* New York: Routledge.

Apple, M. W. (1995). *Education and Power,* 2nd ed. New York: Routledge.

Apple, M. W. (1996). *Cultural Politics and Education.* New York: Teacher College Press.

Apple, M. W. (1999). *Power, Meaning, and Identity.* New York: Peter Lang.

Apple, M. W. (2000). *Official Knowledge,* 2nd ed. New York: Routledge.

Apple, M. W. (2001). *Educating the "Right" Way: Markets, Standards, God, and Inequality.* New York: Routledge.

Apple, M. W. and J. A. Beane, eds. (1998). *Democratic Schools: Lessons From the Chalk Face.* Buckingham: Open University Press.

Apple, M. W. and L. Weis, eds. (1983). *Ideology and Practice in Schooling.* Philadelphia: Temple University Press.

Avritzer, L. (1999). Public Deliberation at the Local Level: Participatory Budgeting in Brazil. Mimeo

Azevedo, J. C. (1998). "Escola Cidadã: Construção coletiva e participação popular." In L. H. Silva, ed. *A Escola Cidadã no contexto da globalização*. Petrópolis: Vozes, 308–319.

Baiocchi, G. (1999). Participation, Activism, and Politics: The Porto Alegre Experiment and Deliberative Democratic Theory. Mimeo.

Ball, S. J. (1994). *Education Reform: A Critical and Post-Structural Approach*. Buckingham: Open University Press.

Bowles, S. and H. Gintis. (1986). *Democracy and Capitalism*. New York: Basic Books.

Connell, R. W. (1995). *Masculinities*. Berkeley: University of California Press.

Dyer, R. (1997). *White*. New York: Routledge.

Fine, M., L. Weis, L. Powell, and L. M. Wong, eds. (1997). *Off White*. New York: Routledge.

Freire, P. (1988). "O partido como educador-educando." In A. Damasceno, et al. *A Educação Como Ato Político Partidário*. São Paulo: Cortez.

Freitas, A. L. S. (1999). "Projeto constituinte escolar: A vivência da 'reinvenção da escola' na rede municipal de Porto Alegre." In L. H. Silva, ed. *Escola Cidadã: Teoria e Prática*. Petrópolis: Vozes, 31–45.

Gandin, L. A. (1994). "Qualidade Total Em Educação: A Fala Mansa do Neoliberalismo." *Revista de Educação—AEC* 23, no. 92: 75–80.

Gandin, L. A. (1998). "Para Onde a Escola Está Sendo Levada? (ou a Escola Pode ser Levada para Algum Lugar Diferente Daquele que o Projeto Hegemônico Quer?)." *Revista de Educação— AEC*. 27 (107), 9–16.

Gandin, L. A. (1999). A Educação Escolar como Produto de Marketing: Processo Natural? *Revista de Educação—AEC* 28, no. 112: 33–39.

Garcia, R. L. (1995). "A educação na virada do século." In M. C. V. Costa, ed. *Escola Básica na Virada do Século: Cultura, Política e Currículo*. Porto Alegre: FACED/UFRGS, 78–91.

Giroux, H. (1995). "Insurgent Multiculturalism and the Promise of Pedagogy." In D. T. Goldberg, ed. *Multiculturalism: A Critical Reader*. Cambridge, Mass.: Blackwell, 325–343.

Hall, S. (1996). "On Postmodernism and Articulation: An interview with Stuart Hall." Edited by Lawrence Grossberg. In D. Morley, and K. Chen. *Stuart Hall—Critical Dialogues in Cultural Studies*. London: Routledge, 131–150.

McGraith, D. J. and P. J. Kuriloff. (1999). "They're Going to Tear the Doors Off This Place: Upper-Middle-Class Parent School Involvement and the Educational Opportunities of Other People's Children." *Educational Policy* 13, no. 5: 603–629.

McLaren, P. (1995). "White Terror and Oppositional Agency: Towards a Critical Multiculturalism." In D. T. Goldberg, ed. *Multiculturalism: A Critical Reader*. Cambridge, Mass.: Blackwell, 45–74.

Mills, C. (1997). *The Racial Contract*. Ithaca, N.Y.: Cornell University Press.

Offe, C. (1995). "Some Skeptical Considerations on the Malleability of Representative Institutions." In J. Cohen and J. Rogers, eds. *Associations and Democracy*. London: Verso, 114–132.

Omi, M. and H. Winant. (1994). *Racial Formation in the United States*. New York: Routledge.

Pagenhart, P. (1994). "Queerly Defined Multiculturalism." In L. Garber, ed. *Tilting the Tower*. New York: Routledge.

Porto Alegre City Secretariat of Education. (1999). Cycles of Formation: Politic-Pedagogical Proposal for the Citizen's School. *Cadernos Pedagogicos* 9, no. 1: 1–111.

Santos, B. S. (1998). Participatory Budgeting in Porto Alegre: Toward a Distributive Democracy. *Politics and Society* 26, no. 4: 461–510.

Silva, L. H. (ed.) (1998). *A Escola Cidadã no Contexto da Globalização*. Petrópolis: Vozes.

Silva, L. H. (ed.) (1999a). *Escola Cidadã: Teoria e Prática*. Petrópolis: Vozes.

Silva, L. H. (ed.) (1999b). *Século XXI: Qual conhecimento? Qual currículo*. Petrópolis: Vozes.

SMED (1993). Projeto Gestão Democrática—Lei Complementar no. 292.

SMED (1998). Regimento Interno do Planejamento e Orçamento Participativo na Escola Cidadã.

SMED (1999a). *Boletim Informativo—Informações Educacionais*. Ano 2, Número 5.

SMED (1999b). Official Homepage of the SMED. http://www.portoalegre.rs.gov.br/smed

Wong, T. H. and M. W. Apple. (in press). "Rethinking the Education/State Formation Connection." *Comparative Education Review*.

8

Teachers' Work Revisited

Mexican Teachers' Struggle for Democracy and the Anti-Neoliberal Alternative

SUSAN STREET

History teaches us that there can be no social policy
without a social movement capable of imposing it.
Pierre Bourdieu +, *Clarín,* 1999

The legacy of neo-liberalism in Mexican education thus far can be best understood as a shift in the terrain from whence educational issues are discussed, disputed, and resolved or transformed. Unfortunately, this shift has occurred in the direction anticipated by the very nature of neoliberalism as a phase in capitalist development: Everything becomes subordinated to the macroeconomy at the same time as the economic (political) decisions become abstracted out of sight of mortal men and women. For Mexican education, this has meant that educational problems are being defined, negotiated, and interpreted in novel ways. Twenty years ago debates about education appeared as explicitly political issues: modernization (as administrative rationalization for improved efficiency of state institutions) confronted democratization (as extension of labor and union rights for teachers as state workers) while social consensus and state legitimacy presupposed the expansion of public education as a social good. Today, a couple of years into the twenty-first century, issues seem no longer political in the sense of continually contesting the existing power arrangements; problems are couched in either/or options that assume the form of local-level, apolitical (mostly expertise) interpretations: successful or unsuccessful schools; effective or ineffective teachers; good or bad education; improved retention rates; or declining demand for public schools.

If the educational system has been perceived to be excessively politicized by virtue of conflicts involving major, national-level political actors, now education has seemingly come unto itself and embraced its "true" nature as pedagogy, as the means for producing school-based learning. During the seventies and eighties, educational reform was depicted by researchers as a scramble for control of state educational institutions and bureaucracy between two major groups: the technocratic *profesionistas* articulated to the Mexican state's initial administrative reforms and the patrimonial *sindicalistas* linked to the dominant party's way of playing politics (state power was equivalent to the PRI-government, Partido Revolucionario Institucional.) Education was the arena for asserting social and political positions of power; many researchers lamented the subordination of educational decision making to *politics*.

The possibility of democratizing the authoritarian political regime—made real by the teachers' struggles organized under the umbrella organization of the Coordinadora Nacional de los Trabajadores de la Educación (CNTE)—complicated the conflicts about "who controls education." By eliminating clientelistic and elitist practices in some union locals of the national teachers union—the Sindicato Nacional de Trabajadores de la Educación (SNTE)—CNTE's challenge to SNTE intensified the political nature of the educational field and diverted attention from students and teachers as pedagogical subjects to labor and political issues. As it was, during the decades of the Mexican miracle, the state was assumed to be *the* pedagogical subject, not students or teachers. In a discursive sense at least, neoliberalism (as historical period in global capitalism and as a series of nation-state policies) has performed an about-face: the Mexican state has been decentered as the uncontested source of a pedagogical project, notwithstanding the (low-key) maintenance of state-funded teacher-training institutions (*las escuelas normales*) and continued (though declining) state funding of basic education.

The nineties proved to be the transitional years toward centering pedagogical discourse—a particular body of ideas for *improving educational quality*—as the discourse within which educational debates are ordered and carried out. While many educators and researchers seem to have swallowed whole the idea that pedagogy finally rules, with teachers as privileged protagonists, others are quickly discovering the *hidden curriculum:* pedagogical practices can no longer be separated from a new labor regime in which teaching is much more restructured work than pedagogical knowledge. Pedagogy does not tend to be a theoretical or practical space for creative teacher-student interaction and learning, but instead a predetermined field of external, top-down evaluation criteria that serve as incentives for improved teacher performance ("mejoras en el desempeño docente").

In this chapter, I address this new centrality of schools—and teacher actions within them—but I choose to do this not by virtue of presupposing schools' place within the neoliberal program (to which the policy of self-managing or autonomous schools surely belongs; see Smyth 1993). Instead, I address the school reform issue as it has evolved in Mexico from the perspective of a subaltern actor—the teachers' dissident movement—and this actor's current efforts to disengage its struggle for democracy from the traditional leftist posture of *taking over state power* (democratizing the teachers' union), so that it may develop a pedagogical movement deemed necessary to revolutionize teaching and schooling at the community level, as the struggle for popular or radical democracy continues and deepens. I refer mainly to a specific sector of the Mexican teachers' democratic movement—namely, the SNTE Section 18 in the state of Michoacan, because it is here that this effort originated, consolidated, and has become a political project vying for recognition among teachers.[1]

My purpose in this approach is not so much to theorize teachers as policy makers (Street 2001a), nor do I intend to document the implementation process of official policy so as to argue Mexico's place on the map of neoliberal reforms worldwide. While some research is available on results of the decentralization process as organizational change (Pardo 1999; Ornelas 1995), too little is known about local level school reforms from a sociological (political) perspective. Practically no research has been done to reveal the effects of such macro "globalization" trends as privatization, productive restructuring, and flexibilization on teachers in schools. Instead, I wish to make problematic what many accept as *the new educational reality*, what is appearing to teachers as new opportunities, what Andy Hargreaves has labeled "the new orthodoxy for teachers."[2]

Given the emerging hegemony of the discourse of educational quality (Angulo Rasco 1999; Fernández Enguita 1999), it becomes imperative to move outside this terrain to a different social territory, to a project whose subjects oppose practically and theoretically the neoliberal ideology as it appears in social consciousness. It is necessary to inhabit an alternative field of thought and action (alternative to that of *el pensamiento único*) in order to put into perspective the problems at hand and enable us to rescue and reconceptualize teachers' work in public schools. SNTE Section 18, or the Michoacan democratic teachers' movement, is important because its discourse is grounded in material practice to a degree other democratic activists can only envy: The movement controls the state-level union section (democratized since 1994) and, from there, attempts to construct an anti-neoliberal alternative. These democratic teachers are disbelievers of the dominant claim that neoliberalism is invincible and inevitable. Their problems, their search, and their hope need to be known and appreciated, for it is still true that some of us continue to aspire to control our lives and emancipate humanity.

Teachers' work (partially) researched

I am careful to refer to neoliberal gains in Mexico in terms of the gradual rise of a dominant discourse in order to distinguish between discourse and reality. Mexican research has not generated a body of results that can speak to school reform processes in terms other than those of traditional school ethnography.[3] This new field of educational ethnography has blossomed over the past fifteen years, yet is still incapable of offering a clear and general vision of tendencies that could be compared with results in other countries. With the election of Vicente Fox as president, and his appointment of a team of private entrepreneurs as top-level Cabinet members, it would be tempting—yet premature—

to speak of the deepening of the Right's educational project, notwithstanding many indicators from within and from without the educational system (Street 2001a). School ethnography reminds us also that schools, in particular, are resistant to change; Mexican research tells us teachers "obey commands, but do not comply with top-down directives," as the saying goes.

Susan L. Robertson's summary of results of educational restructuring in countries such as Australia, England, and Spain provides a reference point for interrogating what little we know about recent school transformation in Mexico.

> The outcome of the reorganization of teachers' work is increased segmentation for the purposes of organizational flexibility, pedagogical deskilling, a new conception of professionalism linked to managerial activity, the reconstruction of the teacher as learner-manager, an expansion of tasks to include management activity, and tighter exernal controls. These developments create a qualitatively different terrain on which teachers must work. . . . Teachers' workplace is also now a marketplace. . . . Teachers are the new saleswomen and salesmen for the economy. (1996, 50)

One ethnographic study based on four urban public schools in the city of Torreón concludes that the Coahuila version of the Acuerdo Nacional para la Modernización de la Educación Básica (ANMEB) was pushing teachers to new levels of involvement with school directors in order to safeguard their school's successful public image. By using a theoretical approach based on many of Thomas Popkewitz' (1997) contributions to the political sociology of educational reform, María de la Luz Jiménez was able to document changing internal political alliances and varied responses by teachers, mainly to the new evaluation procedures of *Carrera Magisterial* (CM), representing a pattern of work intensification and loss of time for students. She also detected new practices pointing in the direction of privatization: teachers paying for substitutes; teachers contracting computer and English-language specialists; teachers purchasing premade standardized tests and workbooks to substitute official textbooks; schools expelling students whose families are unable to pay higher school-maintenance quotas. Here is an excerpt from her conclusions.

> The government proposal for a new school management based on school quality, in order to strengthen competition among schools, is intertwining with and matching the more local concerns about each school's public image and about teachers' beliefs about themselves (as professionals, not as workers). In these articulations, we may begin to find an incipient rationality that normalizes teacher responses in accord with market criteria and strategies. (2001, 337)

Sergio Lorenzo Sandoval has investigated the evolution of the notion, borrowed from critical pedagogy, of "teachers as researchers" as it has been applied in postgraduate programs for teachers in the state of Jalisco. Besides generating an elite teaching force, these mostly master-level programs represent a new discourse for teaching—one that, Sandoval demonstrates, urges teachers to individually transform their teaching practice by performing self-critical, auto-ethnographic observation, using as a referrent the theoretical body of critical pedagogy previously purged of any critical, social commentary. In analyzing a number of masters' theses, Sandoval finds an abundance of tales about teachers' almost religious transformation from bad and mediocre pedagogical practices to good and excellent ones, thanks to their appropiation of the theoretical materials elaborated by the programs' intellectual leaders. He pays special attention to the way the students (who are mostly experienced teachers training other teachers) have appropriated the discourse of educational quality as it makes teachers responsible for student results.

> We know from many studies that the new conception of teaching gives control to the teacher over his or her professional practice—control and authority are "devolved"—and in this way, the teacher is made responsible for the quality of education. This study shows that teachers are perfectly predisposed to accept and subjectively experience this responsibility as personal guilt. Government policy and institutional practice are demanding that teachers resolve such urgent and complex problems as social and economic crises; this social pressure deepens professors' feelings of being responsible, of being guilty, regarding what are really complex institutional and social problems. (2001, 257)

I have reported my research elsewhere regarding democratic activists' interpretations of the effects of Carrera Magisterial on teachers' work and on teachers' involvement in the democratic teachers' movement (Street 1998, 2000) Based on CNTE activists' testimonies and theorizing, I conclude that many teachers' basic concepts concerning teaching and schooling are in a process of being deconstructed ("conceptual destructuring," to use María Rosa Neufeld's term [Grassi et al., 1996]). That is to say, teachers are (or are seen by their union leaders to be) abandoning collective rationalities, and reaffirming an individualism with an historical basis in the teaching field, and produces other effects when combined with the notions and pressures of competition among teachers for positions and economic rewards and among schools for student populations and government stipends.

Whatever the case, schools and teachers are in the middle of the ring, fighting it out among themselves. Perhaps the ring is bigger—allowing for more participants to join in the punches—though surely no winner has been declared. Whether teachers will become adept at improving their pedagogical practice as a function of school-based student learning (at the cost of ignoring the deterioration in their working conditions), whether they will cling to the patrimonial sense of their work as a life-long job (*la definitividad de la plaza docente*) to be defended at any cost, or whether they will embrace their new status as symbolic professionals and adopt the new technologies so as to be integrated into post modern society is uncertain. Will any or all of these possibilities be resisted by teachers and turned into a viable political project by collective subjects? My brief look at the Michoacan experience is meant to provide a different analytical window on the issue of teachers' work. It is meant to express what democratic teachers portray in their critical thinking: There is another way. Before exploring this other way, I first recall the times when democratic teachers had no particular pedagogical component to their political project, years before pedagogy became submitted to flexible work.

From the inseparable economic and political demands of teachers upon the state to the fusion of the pedagogical subject with the flexible labor regime

The novelty of the inseparability of *lo pedagógico* and *lo laboral* for teachers can be best appreciated by remembering when these two fields were perceived to be completely unrelated. Teachers' struggles for union democracy in the late seventies and early eighties suffered from the divorce between educational practice and labor demands. Back then, teachers' mobilizations for increased salary and improved state benefits became political issues as soon as union leaders resisted pushing teachers' demands through the proper governmental channels. In response, local activists and rank-and-file teachers organized parallel union structures—employing the procedures of direct democracy—in order to delegitimize the entrenched union leaders (linked to the national SNTE leader Carlos Jonguitud Barrios and and his group Vanguardia Revolucionaria.) Union democratization in several state-level sections of the SNTE (Chiapas, Oaxaca, Morelos, Hidalgo, State de México, and Zacatecas) proceeded quickly in the early years of the movement (1979–1982), to a great extent because of the inseparability of political and economic demands (Cook 1996). Improving teachers' benefits as state workers was essentially a political problem related directly to the corporatist nature of the Mexican state, a problem that historically had been sustained by incorporating worker (and also peasant and the popular) sectors into state institutions. Teachers joining the protests for economic and political demands and those participating in the resulting mass movements (in large part because repression was more frequent than concession) became union dissidents and political opponents, notwithstanding the success of several regional movements in obtaining formal recognition in SNTE union sections.

Contestation and opposition have marked democratic teacher identity ever since; union democratization came to be understood as a process of substituting leadership governed by a democratic code of ethics, a process that operated upon SNTE's vertical, centralized union structures and practices. Certainly not unrelated to the then-predominant conception of leftist militancy as a struggle for state power, democratic teachers and activists were concerned with control of union positions, an issue that was seen to depend on the degree of movement unity as a social force and political actor. The objective of "occupying the union" came to include schools as centers of workers (who were either with the democratic project or against it), but not as places of teaching and learning. Democratization did revolve around teachers' rights as workers; what was missing from these struggles was recognition of the specificity of teachers as workers—their particular training by the state as ideological workers, namely as state agents for transmitting a nationalistic, racially homogeneous (mestizo) educational project pursuing passive citizenship (in correspondence with the authoritarian political regime.)

While many CNTE activists were theoretically aware that teachers were trained to be social reproducers (Althusser and Gramsci were often quoted), the democratic project seemed incapable of overcoming the limitations of a perenially inconclusive alternative educational project, whose documents were revised in endless committee discussions (normally interrupted by more compelling political needs) or discussed at an educational forum only attended by dissident teachers. Teachers were simply not thought of as educators; teachers' work—teaching in schools—was seen as unproblematic, in part because the doctrine of teachers' rights, the core concept of the democratic ethic, was a labor issue to be forced upon the national political arena under adverse conditions as opponents and dissidents. The schools were imagined as prizes or punishments along the various routes (*rutas escalafonarias*) of teacher mobility, preferably from rural to urban schools and school zones and from the classroom to union and administrative positions (school directors, supervisors, district boss, etc.), a labor mobility structure mediated by SNTE (PRI) leadership practices. Teachers' pedagogical practices went unappreciated by movement activists as a constituent part of teacher identities because such practices were abstracted into labor demands made upon the state for improved and expanded access for teachers, for the *gremio magisterial:* more teacher-training opportunities, more teacher positions (*plazas*), increased enrollment at *normalista* institutions, and so on. The change in activists' thinking, then, has to do with the failure of this strategy of quantitative demands on the state and the recognition that democratic teachers must develop their own discourse about schooling and rearticulate their work in the light of global changes implied by post-Fordist labor regimes.

Technocratic policymaking continuity versus market-oriented education as a *ruptura neoliberal*

Before looking directly at teachers' work in Michoacan, it is important to contextualize Mexican actors' appreciation of neoliberalism in the light of recent policy.

For those working in the educational field in Mexico, there is generalized resistance to the use of the term "neoliberal" to talk about Mexican education. The neoliberal program as such and as it has been developed in education across many countries is well known, or so it seems, perhaps everywhere except Mexico. The few who do deploy the term tend to be identified as critics of government policies, leftist-oriented activists in the Partido de la Revolución Democrática (PRD) or teachers connected to the CNTE. From this I infer that education is still viewed very much as a product of the nation-state, hardly affected by globalization processes. At issue here is the posture people take regarding the continuity—or the discontinuity—of educational policy. Many educational researchers, I find, presume the continuity of state educational policy, underrating, probably, the current phase in capitalist development and its eroding effect on a once-autonomous educational system.

Technocratic educational policy making, from the initial adminstrative de-concentration policy in 1978 (Street 1992) to the more recent educational decentralization policies (Arnaut 1998, Noriega 2000), revolves around an assumed legitimate need of the government to allocate limited resources efficiently and effectively. Rarely do analysts in education link this need to the International Monetary Funds (IMF) Structural Adjustment Programs (SAP) that put the modern dependencies of the periphery (the public debt, austerity regime for wages, multiple financial adjustments, pressures to reduce funding for social policy, etc.) on the agenda for minimizing the state. Once this "international" factor is acknowledged, it becomes more difficult to reduce the multiple educational crises—often subsumed under the rubric of poor quality public schools—to the question of student and teacher performance.

The maintenance of the Mexican state's educational policy's formal principles, in addition to the technocratic group's resource allocation policy provides a base for the continuity thesis. Formally, policy makers have continued to uphold the same policy of providing basic education to all; each new policy is presented as an improvement on the traditional state commitments. People's rights to education appeared to be fulfilled, for example, when secondary education became compulsory in 1993, when three years of preschool became mandatory in 2001 (without the corresponding infrastructure or budget), when every May of every year teachers' salaries are increased (according to the official minimum salary hike), when the *Consejos Sociales de Participación* were legalized (1993). The Secretaría de Educación Pública (SEP) continues to determine the educational budget, though in recent years, public and congressional discussion of budget reductions has been controversially debated and opened to public opinion, in contrast with the historical practice of bureaucratic secrecy surrounding the federal budget.

The 1992 ANMEB—which obtained SNTE-leadership compliance with the decision to delegate educational administration to state-level governments, at the same time as guaranteeing central, mainly executive powers over finances, the curriculum, and a newly-appropiated duty of evaluation—was applauded by most researchers as a serious effort to ameliorate the educational crisis. Decentralization, or educational federalization, carried out via ANMEB, is generally viewed as an organizational transformation—in part because it does not go far enough as both a mechanism to redistribute financial responsibilities (among different governmental levels) and as a fiscal reform measure (Latapí and Ulloa 2000), and in part because, defined as a delegation of authority within governmental structures, it is theoretically disconnected from related state-initiated privatization policies. Analysis of privatization policies in education tends to be constrained to higher education institutions, where governmental rationalization policies have forced public universities to implement a number of meritocratic policies based on standardized examinations for entrance and exit selection (Ibarra 2001, Aboites 1999).

By viewing decentralization as a technical, legal, intragovernmental (top-down) process, analysts fail to conceive of this policy as part and parcel of overall restructuring processes affecting the state–society relationship. In the field of education, and as Chilean and Argentinean researchers have documented (Almonacid 2000, Birgin 1999), situating descentralization in the current globalization trends involves thinking mostly in terms of multiple and complementary privatization policies, which include the following: state subsidies to private schools; state initiatives creating private evaluation organizations (such as the Consejo Nacional de Evaluación, [CENEVAL] in Mexico) later funded with public subsidies; state-initiated compensatory programs later taken over by private organizations; state promotion of combined private-public financing for selected schools; and extragovernmental municipalization processes. Public–private cofinancing of scholarships and schools (and perhaps not so distant in Mexico's future, teachers' salaries); public–private cooperation in designing and applying standardized tests from grade one to postgraduate work; and a government-run incentive system for teachers are currently underway in Mexico, as they are in most of Latin America (Gentili 1994).

Hugo Aboites (1997) was among the few that analyzed Carlos Salinas de Gortari's policy (ANMEB) in terms of the state's withdrawal from of its historical, social, and constitutional mandate of offering free education to all. Based on an in-depth analysis of the North American Free Trade Agreement (NAFTA—Tratado de Libre Comercio [TLC] in Mexico) and its impact on education, he interpreted the policy, and the constitutional amendments that accompanied it, as the destruction of the social pact between the government and civil society, a pact underlying the official policy of expansion of educational opportunities for all. Aboites saw NAFTA as having four important effects on Mexican education. First, the agreement between governments created commitments that excluded the participation of normal citizens and schooling agents. Second, education was to become a development strategy subordinated to Mexico's overall (neoclassical) economic model. Third, education would become a market-place: The educational system was defined as part of a trinational market, as a service without borders where state intervention was interpreted as unwanted, inefficient monopoly. And fourth, educational services were to be commercialized and led by "knowledge brokers and managers" to the detriment of social actors who could exercise some public control over schools.

Aboites' work pointed to the essence of what Brazilian academic Gaudencio Frigotto (1998) has called "neoliberal rupture": the shift in the state's orientation away from considering education as a right of all citizens guaranteed by the state (and thereby abandoning a preoccupation to erradicate inequalities in access and results) toward assuming education to be the responsibility of every individual and of every family, while education's social utility is reduced to a manpower function reminiscent of the theory of human capital popular decades ago in the United States. In Mexico, the nineties was a decade of, on the one hand, state-dominated destruction of its own institutional capabilities for enacting a regime based on citizens' and workers' rights and, on the other, of construction of the evaluation state focusing on learning results (measured by standardized tests) rather than on educational processes. Since Mexican education historically has been dominated by the state, it might seem easy to view a state-led process of overall radical restructuring of itself as simply more of the same. To emphasize the rupture is to recognize, along with Marcos Roitman (2000), that neoliberalism also refers to societal transformations whereby much of collective life, subject to market forces and traditional political forms of representation, loses its centrality to *economics*.

Democratic teachers' representations of "neoliberalism": An attack on unionism, an offensive against SNTE and CNTE

Unionists have become accustomed to being on the defensive in a field typically depicted as a technical field requiring special knowledge. The long-term process of decentralization itself exacerbated the attack on union power stemming from global productive restructuring. Decentralization became the means for both recolonizing the educational bureaucracy with university-prepared *técnicos* operating federal programs in the states, and municipalities and marginalizing union criteria and logic. A process originating in 1989, and directly related to the threat the teachers' democratic movement represented for the state when at the height of its power as a national political actor, refers to the modernization of SNTE leadership led by Elba Esther Gordillo, appointed by President Salinas to replace *cacique*-type leader Carlos Jonguitud Barrios. Gordillo pushed through a political liberalization program in order to delink SNTE structures and practices from those of the PRI-government. These limited reforms within SNTE are now seen to have created the conditions for modifying SEP–SNTE conflicts (over control of educational bureaucracy), which were behind the historical pattern of SNTE vetoing SEP "innovations" (i.e., technocratic planning policy). SEP–SNTE confrontations slipped into a slightly different mode that could be defined as SEP–SNTE coordination and comanagement of educational policy overall, as corporativist interests were (and continue to be) accommodated to the state's self-transformation process. SEP–SNTE coordination from within SEP was first observed with the implementation of the incentive system applied to basic education teachers, the *Carrera Magisterial* program. More recently, the creation of a purportedly autonomous national evaluation system or institute has been allegedly blocked by top SNTE leadership; it is assumed by many that (secret) negotiations will produce a working agreement that will expand the state's new evaluation function beyond its current use as a selection mechanism in middle and higher education.

Whereas researchers tend to pay little attention to global forces operating within the educational system and "institutional" SNTE unionists rapidly adopt the latest globalization jargon, Mexican teachers socialized in struggles for union democracy tend to overextend their use of "neoliberalism," envisioning in the term all the attributes of the (class) enemy. Initial reactions to decentralization saw this policy as directly undermining the national character of the union, a threat that CNTE activists were sure would be the first step in dismantling the regime of teachers' rights that the SNTE had been pushed to defend since the early forties. More recently, the municipalization stage of decentralization has been contested based on insights from the Chilean process under Pinochet, where municipalization was the means for turning over teacher salaries to municipal governments and private associations, including parents. Now it seems clear to teachers participating in the democratic movement that "neoliberalism" has succeeded—if not in dismembering SNTE as a national-level political actor, it has been able to separate many teachers from the democratic movement and its cause. Some have succumbed to the attractions of *new professionalism* by pursuing postgraduate studies designed especially for teachers, by participating in CM or by getting actively involved in the school-level projects supported by government funds.

"Regulated Autonomy": Restructured controls in schools and teachers' reactions

In any case, dissident teachers are saying that the state has effectively restructured teacher controls in the schools. Central to this affirmation is the empirically well-founded argument that the government improved its direct control of the operating hierarchy (supervisors, directors, and teachers) precisely by subverting many of the mediations earlier carried out by school authorities turned union agents (mainly by supervisors loyal to SNTE). Improved administrative controls of teacher assistance make it more difficult for teachers to participate in CNTE mobilizations, for example. CM has been the major means for introducing technocratic controls into the schools. This incentive program, placing economic value on different aspects of teachers' careers (years worked; test scores; teacher training and actualization; student scores; school evaluations), has implied submitting teacher behavior to criteria designed from central offices and applied by local school agents. This widespread trend has been called "regulated autonomy" by José Contreras (1997), who distinguishes it from the earlier scheme of professional autonomy based on the teacher's perogatives regarding the use of teaching methods in the classroom. The adjective "regulated" is meant to communicate the idea that external criteria are linked to system directives and policies, providing the government with a new set of controls linked to its resource allocation process.

Democratic teachers have systematically resisted CM—entering into the program is voluntary—but admit to fighting a losing battle because of the difficulty of imagining and offering a concrete alternative, going beyond that of simply participating in "the struggle" as *maestros democráticos*. This merit-pay system, similar to those recommended by international agencies (UNESCO 1992), was received by dissident teachers with mixed feelings: on the one hand, as union activists they felt they could not deny rank-and-file teachers access to a system meant to compensate a twenty-year loss of salary's purchasing power, and, on the other hand, they witnessed the resulting divisions in schools between good and bad teachers and between the best and worst schools, as well as the incorporation of school-level union representatives into the evaluation procedures set up by CM. CNTE activists consider CM to be the right's proposal for refunctionalizing the corporatist nature of state controls of workers. One leader from Michoacan told me that CM represented "the substitute of *charrismo*": it led teachers into a direct relationship with the government (operated by shared union and government bureaucratic instances), a relationship that teachers feared would lead to major reversals in the union's ability to defend worker rights. ("How can the union be *juez y parte* at the same time?")

Michoacan union leaders have had to admit that almost 60 percent of Section 18 teachers currently are receiving the CM stipend; the program has indeed become part of daily working conditions. Section 18 policy vis-á-vis CM has been to develop and socialize among the rank and file a critique of the origins and possibilities of CM based on their analysis of the program as a trick (*trampa del Estado*), a cost-reducing means to induce teachers into an individualized labor relationship seen to have little to do with improving teaching or learning (Street 2000). They insist that most teachers appreciate the program only to earn more money, clearly realizing that the program's educational objectives are irrelevant and unrealizable. Here is one activist's account of the dilemmas teachers face when attempting to construct an alternative to CM.[4]

> In Michocan we see *Carrera Magisterial* as a career of obstacles; it is a pyramid because the majority of teachers remain at the bottom. Its entire logic is to impede accumulating points. Recently, official policy discards the col-

lective participatory body evaluating teachers (because they give too many perfect scores) and place more emphasis on the supposedly more objective standardized tests judging student learning. In Michoacan, being in *Carrera* almost means not participating in union affairs, which leads us to believe that CM is leading to the union's disappearance, to its atomization. We have spent hours and hours discussing what to do and have decided not to demand its cancellation so as not to convert half our members into internal enemies. Nor would it be a good idea to push to generalize the program when that effort would deny its true nature as a control system whose entire purpose is to create an elite and to select "the best" teachers. We believe that we must imagine a completely different school organization, one that includes an eight-hour day with time for planning and training within the school day, one that would allow recovering the humanistic parts of the curricula sacrificed by neoliberalism (the arts, sports, the humanities and special education), along with a professional salary that should represent 9.6 times the official minimum salary (the current rate is under 4 percent), and which would also include an incentives program linked to improvement of teaching and educational levels of teachers.

At the same meeting, another Section 18 leader added his own interpretation; it underlines the radical nature of the transformation they are pushing.

This proposal arises in a particular historical moment: either we go for it all, or we play the game of always accommodating ourselves to what the government says and wants. Our idea is to not confront those teachers who are in *Carrera;* instead, we want to start building consensus among those who say no to CM. With them we need to develop an entirely new educational model that agrees with what we want for ourselves as workers, as educators of the Mexican masses. This means that we must create a new school out of the ruins of the old.

Michoacan's alternative: Trials and tribulations with schools and pedagogical thinking

The school—and how to transform it—has become an uncomfortable enigma for the Michoacan teachers; activists openly recognize that they do not know how to even think about the issue. On the one hand, they realize that rank-and-file teachers are completely absorbed with daily routines, especially the many who have a double shift (*doble plaza*), and on the other, they are beginning to admit that political awareness is not the sole element needed for school reform to unfold. Other than the general idea that schools need to be reorganized around an integral notion of education that recovers its humanistic potential in relation to the real social needs of the community (as determined by those communities transformed into a new popular democratic subject)

Section 18 has no formal school reform policy, though it does have educational plans and position papers used for negotiating with state-level educational officials.[5] It also has an ongoing system of seminars and training courses on explicitly pedagogical topics, as well as a whole series of special projects coordinated by union leaders and implemented in various regions of Michoacan. One such project, for example, is the "improvement of reading and writing" project, which prepares teachers to learn a new reading and writing method (based on Vigotsky) that was developed originally by local teachers in the Michoacan town of Maravatío. The training sessions are lessons in critiquing the Piagetian-based model the SEP has developed, at the same time that teachers discuss the problems in the schools confronting teachers attempting to innovate the curricula.

It would be difficult to say just how much this new priority of school reform is due to democratization's own limitations or to the state's success in penetrating the schools (which is also attributed to the Mexican workers' overall defeat). Teachers were first aware of the significance of "educational modernization" when the government withheld funds for school maintenance; more recent privatization policies and the resulting rise in private enrollments have contributed to a generalized sense among teachers of state abandonment of public schooling. While teachers are still reluctant to question their position as state workers, and SNTE and CNTE coincide in demanding that education be organized by the state, the concept of "public" education has—inevitably, it seems—been subverted and relativized. Once the state has been displaced from its historical site as educator state, who is there to occupy the space?

Here Emir Sader's notion of public space is helpful for understanding the concept currently discussed in the democratic teachers' movement. This Brazilian thinker defines public space as that corresponding neither to state nor market, but instead to the multiple ways of giving public solutions to social needs in order to "move the citizens." Michoacan activists realize that their earlier thinking enclosed the teacher within the four walls of the classroom: "Now we are thinking of the teacher more as a social militant, an idea that incorporates other social roles—namely citizen and educator—besides that of State worker" (2000, 244).

From one document discussed among teachers, we can learn about the following idea meant to go beyond the currently dominant notion that schooling's value depends on the labor market.

> The most general characteristics of our proposal have to do with the destruction of the school as a closed space . . . and the construction of a space open for the satisfaction of needs of all kinds of a community that builds its culture as it solves its vital necessities. . . . We propose to con-

vert the school into a center for community organizing at the same time as we work to destroy the school's deeply entrenched myths. By myths, we mean those ideas hardly ever expressed or discussed: the school as a "temple of knowledge," the teachers as the "apostles of education," and the school as a place where only winners' futures are imagined.[6]

The current dilemma for these teachers could be described as the emergence of an incipient consciousness of the vulnerability of their inherited social definition as transmitters of official state curriculum. At all costs, they sustain the centrality of being workers; at issue, then, is the question of workers for whom? Disputes are beginning to arise over just what is and should be the identity of the teacher, a teacher the dominant discourse argues needs to disinherit his or her own social and institutional production and take personal responsibility for teaching and learning within the schools. For democratic leaders seeking to deepen teachers' anti-neoliberal consciousness, the problem has become one of ridding the teachers of their (excessively conservative) cultural baggage. *Gremialismo* is thought to impede solidarity with other social sectors so necessary for political alliances as well as inhibit rethinking teacher rights in the light of those groups without rights (the unemployed, subemployed, exploited, and marginalized populations) who also need organizing.

Curiously enough, those activists working directly on pedagogical questions—the most theoretically aware of pedagogical and educational trends—are beginning to place teachers' schooling categories (*pensamiento escolarizado*) at the center of their critiques. For the most part, even politically aware teachers who participated actively in the union democratization process are reluctant to question the traditional teacher–parent relationship based on teacher authority and parent submission to school requisites. The popular democratic project to which Section 18 is committed calls for breaking down these barriers, but traditional organizing based on building parents' associations to support the democratic union in its demands on the state has not yet lent itself to addressing pedagogical issues, including current discussions on teacher role and identity. Activists see conservative teacher subjectivity as the major obstacle toward moving teachers to understand school reform, whether it be top-down or bottom-up.

The major "problem" with "conservative teachers" relates to three ideas that provoke heated discussions among activists as they review the degree to which teachers are appropriating governmental programs such as *Carrera Magisterial*, and in particular, the recent "Schools of Quality" program.[7] First is the idea of the teacher as "the great simulator," as someone who simply recycles dominant ideology about being responsible for the poor quality of education. Second is the idea of the teacher as lacking solid training in pedagogy. A third idea is that the teacher's interest is only in obtaining more money; teachers' ingrained personal interests are said to fit perfectly with all the new talk about competency for competitive reasons. The critique of teacher identity circulating in Michoacan and among other democratic teachers sympathizing with Section 18 (in Tlaxcala, Guerrero, and Zacatecas) refers to those teachers who believe, still today, that democratic struggle can be compatible with mindless teaching. For example, one activist recently complained that many teachers in Michoacan still imagine their union participation as completely isolated from classroom activities, unaware that the whole point is to rethink the struggle itself as radiating fundamentally from within the schools as they open to community needs. She sees teachers as having an either-or conception of their duty, in part toward their work and in part toward the union. She quoted teachers as still saying things such as the following: "I just completed the stipulated sections of the study plan, now I can join our mobilizations for more salary."

Key to Section 18's efforts to create a pedagogical movement, besides the basic push to uphold teachers' rights as workers, is the argument that teaching is a social service that must be provided for the welfare of the general population. Teachers' negative reactions to the tests they must take in order to receive government stipends (in CM) are believed by activists to actually facilitate challenging some of the teachers' blind faith in the government-defined curriculum and their overdependence on the textbook. Michoacan's educational project is beginning to reconceptualize education outside the state's institutional field and inside a specifically class-based, popular cultural field. This important shift is performed by stressing financial capital's use of the state (i.e., neoliberalism) and therefore its educational policy's economistic orientation that has teachers preparing students for jobs in the sweat shops (*maquiladoras*), on the one hand, and, on the other, by reconceptualizing the teacher as a producer of culture *al servicio del pueblo*. This in turn leads to conceiving of the school as a social space marked by cultural practices, a very novel idea for teachers who have historically appropriated state-dominated nation-building ideology about equal citizens based on the unity of the *mestizo* race (Levinson 2001). After critiquing most school reform proposals because they assume that improvement can happen simply based on a new instrumentality of given inputs, one CNTE activist wrote the following:

> In all these attempts, there is a one thing that is always missing and that is the analysis of the ways the production and reproduction of culture contributes to maintaining the predominant power structure. The absence of a profound critique of the transmission and creation of culture has allowed official discourse to invade the schools.[8]

So far, this critique has not been socially developed in Section 18's political project in the sense that some researchers argue schools should be moving: toward making discrimination of any kind inacceptable in order to promote intercultural practices that would better respect Mexico's ethnic diversity.[9]

Conclusion

Neoliberalism's legacy, then, is to have opened the black box of classroom teaching to scrutiny by educational actors previously only interested in affecting educational policy by accumulating enough power "at the top." The teachers' movement has been profoundly shaken because its only alliances were other national-level political actors pursuing regime democratization after a century of authoritarianism. Not all democratic sections of SNTE have been able to trascend the initial conceptions of democratization as a phenomenon internal to union structures. Schools themselves, and teaching within them, became an enormous black box for democratic teachers whose major priority had been to control the union as a function of rank-and-file interests for access to state benefits. Michoacan teachers have learned that, if democracy is to be made real as a social project that allows *politics* to be recentered as a function of majority needs, it is not enough to democratize the school as an institution (by taking over directorships, for example), nor is it enough to posit alternative educational principles mirroring state policy. If the teachers' democratic movement led teachers to appropriate their social definition as worker, and if current teacher mobilizations respond to a defensive position to reduce the loss of their rights implied by neoliberal policies, then ways must be found to transform teacher identity away from its historical state-formation determinations.

What Michocan teachers call their pedagogical movement is really a new territory for struggle because teachers are confronting other teachers within schools over pedagogy and its ever-more restricted possibility for guiding teaching and learning. In this battle over teachers' work (as pedagogically informed or as restructured work), their status as state workers is being undermined, on the one hand by peer pressure to *professionalize*, and, on the other, by social pressures (augmented by Section 18 union leaders) to become public intellectuals, leading popular organizations to construct collective, autonomous social subjects. This dilemma indeed parallels earlier debates over the contradictory class location of teachers as workers and professionals. But perhaps neoliberalism has managed to externalize this contradiction from a realm of teacher subjectivity to that of public schools, whose very survival is more dependent now then ever on consumer/clients (students and parents). This is to say that neoliberalism constructs a social denial of teachers' worker status (by diversifying the function of the boss), and thereby upsets or removes the contradiction that once opened space for teachers to choose their social position in accord with their ideological preference. The Mexican experience suggests that the only way that teachers may, today, recover that fundamental choice is to put themselves, and schools as social and cultural practices, into an anti-neoliberal perspective materialized in collective subjects organizing the struggle for radical democracy.

Notes

1. My research has been directed toward three problematic fields in Mexican education since the early eighties: educational policy making (decentralization) as state practices; teachers' national movement as a democratic subject (specifically in Chiapas, later in Michoacan) and teachers' work and school reform. Ongoing seminars since 1993 to discuss teachers' work and the democratic movement with researchers, activists, and teachers from different parts of the country, in addition to a more ethnographic, in-depth approach to studying the Michoacan democratic movement's educational project, have provided the empirical basis for this chapter. The citations of teacher testimonies come from my interviews with teachers, from seminar discussions, and from my participatory observation of collective discussions at public events. (For some research results presented in English, see Street 1996 and 2001.)

2. Andy Hargreaves used this term while addressing educators at a University of Barcelona event, Simposi Itineraris de Canvi en L'educació, in Cataluña, Spain, March 15–16, 2001. He introduced this (World Bank) *new orthodoxy* by a question: "Does this country want a reform that builds low-capacity, low-cost, poorly-trained teachers?" The new discourse implies high standards for all; an emphasis on (packaged) basic literacy and mathematics; a national curriculum as increasingly prescribed, with clearer standards to ensure teacher compliance; assessment procedures linked to national standards; and increased accountability in the form of rewards for successful people and schools and punishments for poor performers.

3. I refer here to the research tradition established first in the Departamento de Investigaciones Educativas (DIE-CINVESTAV) of the National Polytechnical Institute in Mexico City. Elsie Rockwell (1986) and Justa Ezpeleta (1992) led many masters' students through theses using a school ethnography approach; some of these researchers currently participate in the yearly InterAmerican Simposium on Educational Ethnography.

4. My ethnographic registration of the Primer Encuentro Pedagógico Nacional "Por la construcción de un proyecto democrático popular" in Zacatecas, July 7–8, 2001.

5. Section 18 has a journal entitled *Educación y Cultura* that may be consulted, along with other documents, on its web page http://www.seccion18.homepage.com.

6. "*Propuesta de construcción escolar,*" unpublished manuscript, 1999.

7. *Escuelas de calidad* is a government project recently begun by President Fox; it aims to assign funds to the schools whose proposal for development best correspond's with government criteria. An earlier project (*Proyecto Escolar*) was promoted by President Zedillo; without involving extra funds, it established that all schools, via the technical council including school director and teachers, must develop a pedagogical proposal for school improvement.

8. See note 6.

9. Critiques of teachers and public schooling have come from the field of indigenous education, both as academia and as social movement, namely the zapatista movement initiated in 1994 by the Ejército Zapatista de Liberación Nacional. The question of whether an intercultural curriculum is possible in public schools is just beginning to penetrate the teachers associations and public discussion in general.

References

Aboites, Hugo. (1997). *Viento del Norte: TLC y privatización de la educación superior en México.* Mexico City: Universidad Autónoma Metropolitana-Xochimilco and Plaza y Valdes.

Aboites, Hugo. (1999). La batalla por el financiamiento de la educación superior en los años noventa. *El Cotidiano* (Universidad Autónoma Metropolitana Atzcapotzalco) 15 no. 95: 35–48.

Almoncid, Claudio. (2000). "Educación y exclusión social: Una mirada desde la experiencia educacional chilena." In Pablo Gentili and Gaudencio Frigotto, eds. *A cidadania negada; políticas de exclusao na educaçao e no trabalho.* Buenos Aires: Consejo Latinoamericano de Ciencias Sociales, Grupo de trabajo Educación, Trabajo y Exclusión Social, y Agencia Sueca de Desarrollo Internacional, 259–65.

Angulo Rasco, J. Féliz. (1999). "El neoliberalismo o el surgimiento del mercado educativo." In Pablo Gentili, ed. *Escuela pública y sociedad neoliberal.* Buenos Aires: Niño y Dávila Editores, 17–38.

Arnaut, Alberto. (1998). *La federalización educativa en México; Historia del debate sobre la centralización y la descentralización educativa (1889–1994).* México: El Colegio de México y el Çentro de Investigación y Docencia Económicas, CIDE.

Birgin, Alejandra. (1999). *El trabajo de enseñar; Entre la vocación y el mercado: las nuevas reglas del juego.* Buenos Aires: Editorial Troquel.

Cook, María. (1996). *Organizing Dissent: The Unions, the State and the Democratic Teachers' Movement in Mexico.* University Park, Pa.: Penn State Press.

Contreras, José. (1997). *La autonomía del profesorado.* Madrid: Morata.

Ezpeleta, Justa. (1992). *Escuelas y maestros; condiciones de trabajo en Argentina.* Buenos Aires: Centro Editor de América Latina.

Fernández Enguita, Mariano. (1999). "O discurso da qualidade e a qualidade do discurso." In Pablo Gentili and Tomaz Tadeu da Silva, eds. *Neoliberalismo, qualidade total e educaçao; visoes críticas.* Petropolis, Brazil: Editora Vozes, 93–111.

Frigotto, Gaudencio. (1998). "Educaçao, crise do trabalho assalariado e do desenvolvimento: teorías em conflito." In Gaudencio Frigotto, ed. *Educaçao e Crise do trabalho: Perspectivas de final de século.* Petropolis, Brasil: Editora Vozes, 25–54.

Gentili, Pablo. (1994). "O discurso da 'qualidade' como nova retórica conservadora no campo educacional." In Pablo Gentili and Tomaz Tadeu da Silva, Eds. *Neoliberalismo, qualidade total e educaçao; visoes críticas.* Petrópolis, Brazil: Editora Vozes, 111–79.

Ibarra, Eduardo. (2001). *La universidad en México hoy: Gubernamentalidad y modernización.* México: UNAM, UAM, ANUIES.

Jiménez, Maria de la Luz. (2001). "La gestión escolar y la profesionalidad docente; un estudio etnográfico en cuatro escuelas primarias en Torreón, Coahuila." Draft of doctoral thesis, Universidad Autónoma de Aguascalientes.

Latapí Sarre, Pablo and Manuel I. Ulloa. (2000). "El financiamiento de la educación básica en el marco del federalismo." Unpublished manuscript.

Levinson, Bradley. (2001). *We are All Equal: The Play of Student Culture at a Mexican Secondary School and Beyond.* Durham, N.C.: Duke University Press.

Neufeld, María Rosa. (1996). "Educación, las crisis, y el sistema educativo en la Argentina." In Estela Grassi, Susana Hintze, and María Rosa Neufeld, eds. *Políticas Sociales: Crisis y ajuste estructural.* Buenos Aires: Espacio Editorial, 61–112.

Noriega, Margarita. (2000). *Las reformas educativas y su financiamiento en el contexto de la globalización: El caso de México, 1982–1994.* México: Universidad Pedagogica Nacional and Plaza y Valdes.

Ornelas, Carlos. (1995). *El sistema educativo mexicano; la transición de fin de siglo.* México: Centro de Investigación y Docencia Económicas, Nacional Financiera, Fondo de Cultura Económica.

Pardo, María del Carmen, ed. (1999). *Federalización e innovación educativa en México.* México: El Colegio de México.

Popkewitz, Thomas. (1997). *Sociología política de las reformas educativas.* Madrid: Morata.

Robertson, Susan L. (1996). "Teachers' Work, Restructuring and Postfordism: Constructing the New 'Professionalism.'" In Ivor Goodson and Andy Hargreaves, *Teachers' Professional Lives.* Washington, D.C.: The Falmer Press, 28–55.

Rockwell, Elsie. (1986). *De huellas, bardas, y veredas.* México: Departamento de Investigaciones Educativas del CINVESTAV, IPN.

Roitman, Marcos. (2000). "Política y sociedad en el neoliberalismo." Paper presented at the Second Reunion of CLACSO Grupo de Trabajo, Educación Trabajo y Exclusión Social, Buenos Aires, November, 2000.

Sader, Emir. (2000). La Dimensión pública: el Estado y la política, in Claudio Lozano, *Democracia, Estado y desiqualdad.* Buenos Aires: Eudeba, Universidad de Buenos Aires, Instituto de Estudios y Formación CTA, 239–242.

Sandoval, Sergio Lorenzo. (2001). "Los programas de postgrado para el magisterio en jalisco y las nuevas formas de dominación en el campo educativo." Draft of doctoral thesis, doctorado en ciencias sociales, CIESAS-Universidad de Guadalajara.

Smyth, John Ed. (1993). *A Socially Critical View of the Self-Managing School.* Washington, D.C.: The Falmer Press.

198 • Susan Street

Street, Susan. (1996). "Democratization 'from Below' and Popular Culture: Teachers from Chiapas, Mexico." *Studies in Latin American Popular Culture* 15: 261–78.

Street, Susan. (1998). El movimiento magisterial como sujeto democrático ¿autonomización de los educadores o ciudadanización de la educación? *El Cotidiano* (UAM-Azcapotzalco) 14, no. 87: 7–15.

Street, Susan. (2000). "Trabajo docente y poder de base en el sindicalismo democrático magisterial en México; entre reestructuraciones productivas y resignificaciones pedagógicas." In Pablo Gentili and Gaudencio Frigotto, eds. *A cidadania negada; políticas de exclusao na educaçao e no trabalho.* Buenos Aires: CLACSO and ASDI, 177–212.

Street, Susan. (2001a). "Magisterio y escuela pública: Repensando los compromisos ante la agenda conservadora." In Esmeralda Matute and Rosa Martha Romo Beltrán, eds. *Los retos en la educación del siglo XXI.* Guadalajara: Universidad de Guadalajara, 21–46.

Street, Susan. (2001b). "When Politics Becomes Pedagogy: Oppositional Discourse as Policy in Mexican Teachers' Struggles for Union Democracy." In Margaret Sutton and Bradley A. U. Levinson, eds. *Policy as Practice; Toward a Comparative Sociocultural Analysis of Educational Policy.* Westport, Conn.: ABLEX Publishing, 145–66.

UNESCO. (1992). *Educación y conocimiento: eje de la transformación productiva con equidad.* Santiago de Chile: Naciones Unidas.

9

While Gender Sleeps
Neoliberalism's Impact
on Educational Policies in Latin America

NELLY P. STROMQUIST

In the past twenty years the world has seen an unprecedented movement, generally known as globalization, toward greater connectivity between countries, characterized by rapid and intense communications, by denser and easier flows of goods and people across national boundaries, and by an increased imitation in the South of economic and cultural models operating in the North. While the tendency is to see globalization mostly in economic and technological terms, contemporary processes of globalization have been associated with peculiar views about the role of the market in public policy; hence globalization, although not inherently so, has emerged under conditions of strong linkage with reduced functions for the state in both general and compensatory social interventions. Among the countries that suffer the negative effects of the perceived virtues of the market, the phenomenon is known as "neoliberalism"; among the countries that have benefited from it, the paradigm is referred to simply as market-led policies.

Neoliberalism prescribes a limited function for the state in the areas of social welfare, arguing that free competition in the labor and production markets will ensure greater efficiency, creativity, and quality, which in turn will create better jobs and wealth that will reach all levels of society. Under neoliberalism, the role of the state is important yet limited to ensuring that the rule of law protects the market, specifically, the entrepreneurs, who need to operate under conditions of physical safety and profit protection. Latin America, being close to the epicenter of neoliberal thought—the United States—clearly reflects the principles and initiatives linked to the expanded role of the market. Not only are those principles well known, but the consequences of their applications have been felt and studied. Latin America, therefore, constitutes a very appropriate setting for exploring the impact of neoliberal influences on its social fiber.

Education becomes implicated in globalization because the discourse and practices of the market asserts that we are now in the process of creating a "knowledge society" and that to benefit from all of the technological developments, countries need to produce highly trained workers. This assertion has

199

become a mantra and remains unquestioned and unexamined as an empirical claim.[1] Key disseminators of the new ideas about knowledge are the international development agencies, which promote them through grants and loans to the developing countries to foster "educational reforms" through an ever-growing set of policies.

The expansion of public policies in education has received the attention of several constituencies, two in particular. Sociologists of education are increasingly concerned with educational policy today because their work has been relatively marginal to the design and implementation of these policies, as many of their research efforts—showing the intricate connections between educational practice and the encompassing social context—have been ignored (Shain and Ozga 2001, document this in the case of the UK, but their finding might well be extended to many other countries). The second group comprises activists and scholars in the women's movement. After a long initial period of discarding collaboration with the state, the women's movement, for the most part, now considers it necessary to influence public policy. From a gender perspective, public policies acquire importance because of their potential for the attribution of legitimacy to a given problem, because of the national coverage they may offer, because of their access to substantial financial and human resources, and because of the government's ability to provide incentives and, conversely, to impose sanctions for policy implementation.

This chapter seeks to examine some of the manifestations of neoliberalism in education from a gender perspective by focusing on Latin America and using political economy frameworks. The connection between economic and political objectives reveals the importance of material interests. As Caporaso and Levine (1992) observe, the economic approach to the understanding of politics enables analysts to decompose the state and consider its numerous elements and processes. Specifically, this chapter seeks to show the myriad ways, the variety of actors, and the consequences through which neoliberalism is impacting women's education and women's use of education as a liberating tool. The political economy perspective highlights the material, as opposed to discursive properties, of neoliberal dynamics and, in so doing, exposes the tensions among institutional actors as new equilibria are sought, prevented, and negotiated. While neoliberalism has succeeded in rendering discussion of politics as useless—at best a result of market failure—the interplay of desire and power continues to be as patent and real as ever.

Global attributes of neoliberalism

Under neoliberalism, not only are market forces instrumental in creating what is perceived to be a desirable society, but the economy acquires greater importance over other dimensions of human existence. The school becomes an institution that must serve the economy; this means generating knowledge to serve economic production and training students primarily in response to labor needs. Demands are then made to create a trained labor force, which touches basic education (the importance of following instructions and being disciplined) as well as higher education (the need to increase the number of trained scientists and engineers). Neoliberalism, in its search for expanded markets, looks at the educational system as a potential business arena and argues therefore for the development and expansion of private initiatives in providing schooling.

The unyielding confidence in the efficiency of the market simultaneously decreases the need for the state to provide remedial or compensatory measures to address inequalities in society. Neoliberalism sees inequalities as the product of people's deficient cognitive abilities or individual traits, such as motivation, lack of skills, or constraining beliefs. Hence, the notion of social policies to foster improvement in the disadvantaged individual is seen as unnecessary and creating unwelcome distortions. Social policies are enacted only to help people in very dire situations; this is done in cases of exceptional circumstance to produce safety nets for the poorest of the poor, with the expectation that short-term relief work or assistance will be sufficient.

Neoliberal principles result in the defense of a competitive market (and thus in less attention to policies seeking to provide compensatory measures for asymmetrical conditions linked to race, gender, or social class), a retrenched state (and thus one delinked from social welfare), and a predominance of individualism (with the concomitant reduction of solidarity values). The rapid expansion of communications, especially through the entertainment media, brings to the world's people images of realities that are promptly adopted. Specifically in the case of gender, women are confronted with incompatible images that, on the one hand, show them in responsible professional positions and, on the other, continue to present them in highly sexualized views.

The Latin American education situation

While Latin America appears to enable its people satisfactory access to primary education, with net enrollment rates close to universal, these educational statistics portray a situation that minimizes the degree of actual exclusion affecting many children in rural areas. Such rates undergo rapid decline when it is possible to calculate enrollment rates disaggregated by sex, economic level, urban/rural residence, and ethnic affiliation. There is a strong connection between education and socioeconomic status, with such final consequences that girls from poor families are negatively affected in their schooling and, inversely, girls from wealthy families enjoy high levels of education. Access to schooling by girls and boys in rural areas of Latin America continues to be very limited. It is well know that indigenous girls from poor rural families are those with the least access to schooling and the fewest years of schooling (Stromquist 1992).Further, the participation of the region's young people in secondary education is much lower than that of other regions (with a regional gross enrollment rate of 62 percent, in contrast to 108 percent in OCED countries). As has been observed by Carlson (2001), the rates of growth for secondary education are currently faster in East and Southeast Asia than in Latin America, where a less educated labor force is forecast, as compared to other regions in the world, a decade or so from now.

Since education is increasingly seen as an economic tool, some concern is expressed about the low proportion of secondary-level students in Latin America, who move into technical and vocational education. Presumably the more students who enroll in these forms of education, the greater the match between education and the labor market. Compared to the Organization for Cooperation and Economic Development (OCED) countries, Latin American countries do not promote technical or vocational education; few nations register more than 30 percent of their secondary-level enrollment in technical education (Carlson 2001, 16). But, as an indicator of the schooling/work fit, this evidence must be viewed with caution. In Japan, a highly successful productive country, the proportion of secondary enrollment in technical/vocational education is low, at 26 percent, which suggests that it is the skills acquired at higher levels of education, as opposed to specialized skills, that contribute to better economic performance.

Important institutions in the region have manifested concern regarding the absence of a generalized curriculum content. For instance, PREAL (Programs de Promoción de la Reforma Educativa en América Latina of el Caribe), an influential NGO working on education, states: "To date no country in [Latin America] has established, disseminated, and implemented comprehensive national standards in education, which leaves countries without a clear sense of where they are, where they want to go, and how far they are from getting there" (PREAL 2001, 12).

Over time, educational systems in Latin America are becoming increasingly unable to address social inequalities. Not only is access to schooling based on one's social class, but education is not able to generate similar incomes for similar years of schooling. According to a study of five countries, which included two of the largest economies (Brazil and Argentina) and one considered the most vibrant economy in the region (Chile), young people from lower income families earn 35 to 40 percent less than youths with the same level of education from higher-income families. Education itself contributes to salary differences, as there is a growing income disparity between workers with high and low levels of education (Weller, cited in Carlson 2001). Those with higher levels of education are entering into stable and relatively well-paid jobs while those with lower levels of education are more vulnerable to unemployment and find jobs with fewer social benefits. What these statistics do not show is that economies, despite today's "knowledge society," tend to provide relatively few positions in the most desirable segment of the labor market; further, educational benefits accrue primarily to advantaged social classes.

Characteristics of contemporary reforms in education

Guided by neoliberal logic, there is substantial convergence in the advice promoted by international financial institutions functioning in the area of education, such as the World Bank and the Inter-American Development Bank, and the direction of most of the contemporary educational reforms enacted by national governments in Latin America. Both international agencies and national actors seek to improve the efficiency and the effectiveness of schools—that is, making them run at lower costs and producing students who can successfully join the new economy. Many policies aim at reorganizing and decentralizing school administration, improving quality through greater investment in infrastructure (such as buildings and equipment), engaging in curriculum reform for a better alignment of school and economy, strengthening the teaching force through the professionalization of teaching, and increasing student learning by promoting nationwide testing of students (PREAL 2001, Carlson 2001, OREALC 2002).

As part of globalization and linked to the emerging Free Trade Zone of the Americas (Area of Libre Comercio de las Américas, ALCA), there have been already three hemispheric summits (Miami, 1994; Santiago, 1998; and Quebec, 2001) in which common areas of work are identified by the governments of the Americas. Education appears as one of twenty-three areas of action and has been reflected in the Plan de Acción Hemisférico sobre Educación (PAHE). This plan identifies ten objectives, among which access to schooling takes important place. PAHE intends by 2010 to reach universal access to primary educational, an enrollment of at least 75 percent at the secondary school level, and an expansion and quality improvement of higher education. PAHE also seeks to eliminate illiteracy and promote decentralization at the school level with adequate financing and the participation of parents, community leaders, and government officials.

The current education sector document by the World Bank, which presents "recommendations" that governments find difficult to refute when negotiating loans, promotes the establishment of curriculum standards and the concomitant practice of monitoring school performance. It also advocates more application of the inputs known to improve school performance, but simultaneously calls for "flexibility" in the acquisition and use of such inputs, which usually translates into having parents and communities contribute to them in kind or monetary terms. In terms of financial resources, the World Bank document calls for the sharing of educational costs by parents and communities, the charging of student fees at the higher education levels, the provision of educational loans, and the funding of schools based on student outcomes and overall quality. More autonomy is solicited for principals; but with few resources all they can do is lesser activities such as setting the school calendar and the daily schedules. On the subject of the participation of parents and communities, their economic contribution figures prominently, although mention is also made of their school choice (which augurs voucher and charter school options) and their involvement in school management (World Bank 1996).

Concrete manifestations of neoliberal educational reforms have been decentralization, privatization, parental choice, and accountability—all justified through invoking the principles of quality, efficiency, and even equality. While these principles are generally accepted as positive, they acquire particular characteristics under present educational reform efforts. From a gender perspective, quality and efficiency are positive goals in general but they are gender-indifferent; that is, by themselves they do not address gender. The concept of equality—perhaps the highest goal for women—can be implemented in gender-blind (i.e., ineffective) ways if the specificity of the group called "women" is not recognized in the proposed solutions.

The concept of quality has attained ubiquitous presence in today's educational reforms. One definition of quality education, proposed by Method (cited in USAID, 2000), considers that it would be characterized by 1) equal academic objectives for all students, 2) the provision of opportunities to learn and the acknowledgement of different learning needs, and 3) the creation of a solid infrastructure to enable the first two objectives. According to Espinola (1995), quality could include three meanings: more and better learning by students; greater responsiveness to community demands; and noticeable impact on social, economic, and cultural factors at the macro levels. The UNESCO Regional Office for Latin America and the Caribbean (OREALC) in its regional educational project defines quality as "an education that teaches how to be, how to learn, how to live together, and how to be proactive" (OREALC 2002, 4). In most official documents, however, the concept is reduced to student cognitive performance, which in turn is determined by standardized testing of reading and math, with consequent limited attention to other subject matters, such as civics, the environment, social justice, and reflexion on current social arrangements, including those pertaining to gender. It can be asserted that prevailing notions of quality seek higher learning by students, but this learning does not touch central issues such as the reordering of gender relations.

In current discourse, efficiency usually becomes translated into creating a more competitive labor force and thus into modernizing the educational system through management, better textbooks, and some teacher training in narrowly selected disciplines. Important regional agencies in the Latin American context such as the Economic Commission for Latin American and the Caribbean (ECLAC) argue for the need to produce a competitive labor force, thus clearly emphasizing economic knowledge and skills over other subjects. Decentralization is advocated as a means to efficiency, under the assumption that increased parental participation will lead to improved functioning of schools via the parents' monitoring of teachers' practices and the larger community contribution to educational resources at the school level. But since crucial issues of funding at the local level have not been resolved (a large number of decentralization efforts tend to devolve responsibility but create a limited reallocation of resources), decentralization as a policy objective has been found to be more linked to cost-reducing measures than to well-funded initiatives to democratize schooling (Carnoy 2000). Increasingly, the concept of efficiency is also used in public policy to mean that schools are better run by market-guided signals; thus privatization is advocated as a means to more efficient and effective schools.

Regarding two of the most visible manifestations of neoliberal policies in education—decentralization and privatization—there is no evidence that decentralization with increase responsiveness to gender concerns; in fact, logic tells us that conservative communities may successfully endorse gender codes long ago surpassed by global agreements. Privatization, by introducing school fees for schooling, may sharpen the parents' position that education for their daughters is an investment that has to be compared to that of sons, with the possible consequence that parents might think it is safer to expect greater returns for sons. One study based on Peruvian data found that willingess to pay for education is higher among the wealthy families and that parents are less willing to cover educational costs for girls than for boys (Glewwe and Gertler, 1991).

Equality is usually defined in public policy as providing education to all students, thereby making education a means to reduce poverty. It is usually reflected in calls for measures that seek to diminish the gap between rural and urban areas, to a lesser extent translated into policies that seek to reduce social class differences throughout the country, and much less into policies that pursue the elimination of gender distinctions.[2] In general, references to equality in official policies seem empty, for they seldom make reference to the prevalence of the one-teacher multi-grade schools in rural areas, which are often incomplete schools (i.e., do not offer complete primary education) staffed with non-credential teachers and a major source of poor and terminal education for the rural poor.

The concept of equity, which refers to fairness and thus calls for special measures beyond equality to generate actual equality of results, is also being utilized, although to a much smaller degree. One particular interpretation of equity among World Bank documents is the assertion that publicly supported higher education is inequitable because, in being tuition-free and in having a majority of students from middle- and upper-social class origins, this level of education de facto subsidizes the education of the rich and thus is inequitable to the poor (Klees forthcoming, World Bank 2001). Equity for the World Bank is reduced to making the middle-class and the rich pay for their higher education, something that indirectly promotes the privatization of higher education but does not consider to any substantial degree how education can be made less inequitable at the other levels and across social class, ethnic affiliation, and gender. OREALC offers a more expansive definition of equity, stating that it means "education for all, devoting greater efforts and resources in favor of the most vulnerable groups" (OREALC 2002, 4). Exactly who are the "most vulnerable groups" is left unidentified. By not referring specifically to gender, many of the principles in today's educational reforms are gender-blind, assuming that it is not necessary to go beyond unspecified declarations of equality.

Policies expressed in the educational sector plans of each country seek mainly to advance the efficiency dimension, thus following the discussion that decentralization should reach the school level, a concept exported by the U.S. to developing countries. Another visible influence is the trend toward nationwide standardized testing and the use of educational technologies, especially the use of computers.

Exactly what of the various priorities is being implemented is not clearly known, but some data from the five Central American countries (Salvador, Costa Rica, Guatemala, Honduras, Panama, and Nicaragua) and the Dominican Republic indicate that the most advanced nationwide implementations have taken place in the "design and distribution of texts" and in "decentralization at the regional or state levels." Significant nationwide implementation has also occurred in the establishment of "national curriculum standards" and in their concomitant use of "standardized student testing." More uneven has been the "transfer of resources to school level," which is reported as problematic by three of the six countries in the study (PREAL 2000).

Another development linked to the technological advances of the current globalization process and the growing importance attached to knowledge is the continuous effort by multilateral and bilateral organizations to move into "knowledge-based aid." This initiative, clearly led by the World Bank and followed by other institutions, calls for drawing lessons from previous experiences and from other institutions in the development field. Assessments so far indicate that the use of computerized data banks and entries about projects by the various agencies tend to confuse the concept of "information" with that of "knowledge" (see, for instance, Samoff and Stromquist 2001). These assessments also suggest that the knowledge generated tends to focus excessively on internal (organization-focused) experiences, that they tend to ignore the large body of research produced in the academic world, and that they give inordinate emphasis to contributions from the North rather than the South. Were these trends to continue, they forecast limited attention to indigenous knowledge and gender issues, since many insightful studies of women's conditions tend to be generated by activists and scholars in the South, whose reports may not reach personnel working in development agencies.

Gender and neoliberalism

With the increased exchange of information and the transnational nature of many efforts in education, the environment, health, and human rights, gender as a political issue is receiving considerable attention in globalized times. In response to highly publicized agreements, governments have set up "women's units" in ministries, passed pertinent legislation, drafted women's national plans, and allocated some resources for gender-related activities. Action has indeed taken place. Yet, the implementation of laws and the resources allotted to various gender initiatives have been quite meager relative to the goals.

Ironically, the emergence and consolidation of the women's movement in Latin America—facilitated by the spread of communications and ideas made possible through globalization—has been accompanied by times of economic austerity and state retrenchment, the first due to pressing repayment needs of international loans and the adoption of structural adjustment programs (SAPs), and the second due to neoliberal economic models and concomitant political regimes that call for reduced state interference in social welfare matters, including the redressing of inequalities (Deere and León 2001). Neoliberalism has been constant in its appeals for the democratization of governments in developing countries. Yet, recent political outcomes indicate that it is possible to have democracy today without necessarily being preoccupied with human rights and equity.

In the labor force, gender inequities in Latin America are becoming more intense. One thinks of human rights as protection from false imprisonment, protection from violence, on the ability to live one's life. But one important indicator of human rights is the ability to benefit equally from schooling. Labor data for 1999 indicates that there has been a moderate generational improvement in the disparity between women and men's earnings among workers with the same educational qualifications, but disparities among younger workers have worsened (ages 25–34 compared to the 15–64 age group). Table 1 shows that in eleven out of fifteen possible comparison points (i.e., comparing two time periods) income disparities have increased during the 1993–1999 period.

Not only are women earning less than men for equal levels of education, but they are facing greater levels of unemployment, irrespective of level of education. Table 2 shows this to be the case in thirteen of nineteen possible comparison points (comparing women to men). The growing disparities suggest that beneficial intergenerational change may have been reversed under neoliberalized times. Interestingly, Table 2 shows that women's unemployment is also higher at all levels of education in OCED countries, suggesting that women are facing challenges in both industrialized and developing countries. An earlier study of several Latin American countries found that a minimum of

Table 1. Mean Annual Earnings of Women as a Percentage of Mean Annual Earnings of Men 25–34 and 15–64 Years of Age, by Level of Educational Attainment. Selected Latin American Countries, 1993–1999

Level of educational attainment	Age group	Argentina 1994	Argentina 1999	Brazil 1993	Brazil 1999	Chile 1996	Chile 1999	Paraguay 1994	Paraguay 1999	Uruguay 1994	Uruguay 1999
Below upper	25–34	66	62	51	46	77	60	59	68	56	52
secondary	15–64		62		55		66		67		61
Upper	25–34	70	69	55	44	76	72	77	75	65	68
secondary	15–64		64		56		71		73		62
Nonuniversity	25–34	72	72	..	..	63	70	64	..	62	57
tertiary	15–64		57		..		67		..		69
University	25–34	..	66	57[a]	48[a]	70	67	68	..	..	74
tertiary	15–64		56		56[a]		57		72		58

Source: Carlson 2001, 27.
a. Includes university and nonuniversity.

twelve years of education is the threshold that provides an 80 percent chance of earning an income that will keep workers out of poverty (ECLAC 1997). If to this we add our knowledge that women need more years of education than men to earn comparable salaries, schooling in contemporary times is a resource for women that comes with a heavier cost.

Specific Developments Regarding Gender Policies in Education

Public policies addressing gender and education have existed since the early 1970s in English-speaking countries. In Latin America, they are more recent, dating from the early 1990s. To a significant extent, gender policies in educa-

Table 2. Unemployment Rates of Population Ages 25–64, by Level of Educational Attainment. Selected Latin American Countries, 1998

Country		Below upper secondary (%)	Upper secondary and non-tertiary post secondary (%)	Tertiary type B (%)	Tertiary type A (%)
Brazil	men	5.9	4.7	2.7	3.7
	women	12.5	9.0	3.4	1.5
Chile	men	4.7	4.1	5.6	2.4
	women	3.6	5.0	7.7	2.3
Mexico	men	1.7	2.0	2.1	2.4
	women	3.3	4.6	1.9	2.6
Paraguay	men	2.6	2.8	3.5	2.8
	women	5.5	4.5	2.5	2.7
Uruguay	men	5.4	5.2	—	1.4[a]
	women	12.8	8.7	—	2.7[a]
OECD	men	8.9	5.3	4.3	3.3
Country mean	women	10.0	7.6	5.2	4.6

Source: Carlson 2001, 21.
a. All tertiary.
Tertiary type B: not leading to entry into research programs.
Tertiary type A: leading to entry into research programs.

tion have been influenced by international agreements, notably the Education for All (EFA) commitments (1990), and those signed in Nairobi (1985), Beijing (1995), and Hamburg (1996, on adult education).

Public policies in education and gender typically focus on issues of young girls accessing and completing school. By implication, the obstacles that tend to be recognized in women's education are those originating either in the household (parents who do not allow daughters to attend school) or in the *provision* of schools (insufficient, distant, or unprotected schools). What access and completion strategies do not consider is that schools may be not be fostering attitudes, knowledge, or practices that transform the gender relations that create these obstacles—and in fact may be reproducing them. A persuasive body of sociological research finds that schools are fundamental for the promotion of social and political stability and thus for the reproduction of gender ideologies (Arnot 2000, Acker 1994, Connell 1996, among others). Thus, the *nature of schooling and the experience it affords to students* (as well as to teachers), far from being gender-neutral, carry with them powerful messages in the creation and maintenance of masculinity and femininity. Consequently, from a gender perspective, the social impact of schooling cannot be simply left unexamined, nor can the institution be expected to operate in ways that warrant no further discussion. The notion that political action regarding the schooling of girls must be seen in phases—namely concerns of access first followed later by concerns of content—cannot be accepted in light of the empirical evidence regarding the constant gendering effect of schools. Likewise, the emphasis on girls as opposed to considering both girls and women suggests a limited understanding of gender issues, since adult women are also affected by gender discrimination and ideologies and therefore should be considered for additional education, which might take the modality of nonformal education (NFE).

The most encompassing public policies in education in the region almost never mention gender. The content of a 1994 international seminar bringing together educators and policy makers from Bolivia, Chile, Mexico, and Peru (Edwards and Osorio 1995) is quite illustrative. The proceedings revealed that significant nationwide improvements in the quality of education had been occurring in some countries, which were assigning greater instructional, nutritional, and health resources to schools and also improving the pedagogical level of teachers, notably through such efforts as the 900 Schools Program and the Program for the Improvement of Quality and Equity in Education, both in Chile (Nuñez 1995) and the Program to Eliminate Educational Retention in Chile (Ezpeleta 1995). Yet, the proceedings revealed also an absolute silence regarding gender issues, as references to girls and women simply do not appear in the text.

Reflecting in an even stronger way the denial of gender issues is the UNESCO-sponsored International Education Conference, which takes place annually at the global level in Geneva and at the regional level on a rotational basis in a

Latin American city. In the 2001 meeting in Geneva, ministers of education representing Latin American and Caribbean nations made formal declarations on the educational policies they consider top priority. These discourses showed that the themes of educational inequalities and social exclusion are the leading priorities (mentioned in seven of thirteen national declarations), followed by a concern for the creation of full citizenship and the creation of high-quality schools. None of these declarations makes explicit reference to gender (IBE 2001), despite the fact that social inequality is conceptually close to gender discrimination.

Nonetheless, Latin America today is witnessing the enactment of a variety of educational measures to promote the advancement of women in education and reduce disparities in school access and treatment.[3] By and large, these measures represent minor efforts seeking marginal improvements for girls and women and include measures in national education plans to provide girls with more access to basic education, to remove sexual stereotypes from textbooks, and to offer literacy programs for adult women. While an increasingly large number of countries have undertaken textbook revisions, there have been no studies comparing the new texts with the previous ones in terms of their treatment of gender issues. Textbook design is usually left in the hands of teams comprising curriculum specialists but seldom persons with expertise in gender or specifically gender in education. Moreover, given the expanding allocation of textbook production to external bidding companies, often the authors and publishing houses come with a minimal understanding of gender issues. This was noted in a personal communication (2001) by a high-level authority in the Department of Education in the Dominican Republic, who observed that valuable training on gender issues given to curriculum personnel in the ministry had been made de facto useless by assigning the book production to firms outside the ministry. Besides textbooks, the other important component of the educational experience is teachers. Teacher training on gender issues is provided annually by most ministries of education in the region, yet it is limited to a small number of teachers as part of in-service training. Little is known of the degree of treatment of gender in the pre-service of teachers, although it is believed that no Latin American country has been able to integrate teacher training on gender issues in its initial teacher training programs. Mexico, the country with the largest teacher union and one of the most powerful economies in the region, does not have a gender component in its various teacher training programs (Cortina 2001). However, several pedagogical universities are beginning to offer a gender and education specialization at the graduate level (e.g., Universidad Pedagógica Nacional, Universidad Pedagógica de Ajusco, and Universidad Pedagógica de Guadalajara) (Palencia 2001).

Few countries in Latin America have comprehensive gender equity policies in education (as opposed to isolated measures). They include Paraguay (Colazo 2000), Bolivia (Lazarte and Lanza 2000), and Argentina (Bonder 1999).

Paraguay's gender policies have sought curriculum reforms, teacher training, and the review of textbooks. According to personnel in charge of the Gender Unit in the Ministry of Education, they were able to begin a change in the curriculum to reflect women's contributions to society and initiate a debate with teachers on sexuality. The unit produced modules on gender and sexuality, but as supplementary, not core materials (Colazo 2000).[4] Bolivia's policies have sought to make gender a cross-cutting theme throughout the curriculum and incorporate such issues as health, sexuality, equity, and sustainable development. So far, gender reformers have been able to provide training to resource teachers (those assisting classroom teachers) and design general orientations and curriculum content with a gender perspective for the first three years of primary school. The reformers have also provided training on school violence (by teachers to students and among students through a module—also supplementary material—entitled "Guidelines to Prevent School Violence") (Lazarte and Lanza 2000).

In Argentina, which had the first national policy on education and gender in Latin America, its National Program for Equal Opportunity of Women in Education (PIOM) functioned for four years in an active development mode. It created teacher teams in some twenty provinces, using contacts with universities and NGOs to develop its interventions. PIOM was able to promote the use of nonsexist language in education in the national education reform of 1993. Moreover, it eliminated sexual stereotypes from textbooks, and introduced a discourse about the need for greater equality of opportunity between women and men. It worked with the mass media through exhibits for one year to promote alternative messages on gender. As PIOM was about to translate its pilot efforts into a national scale, the Catholic Church intervened to stop the dissemination of new textbooks and teacher strategies, charging that the new texts were promoting homosexuality, were against the nuclear family, and opposed the "natural differences between men and women" (Bonder 1999). The work on education and gender continues in Argentina today but with much milder objectives and very subdued strategies.

In general, it would seem that the only gender policies that become implemented are those that do not attract contestation. Usually, such policies address access rather than content of schooling. These are also policies that seek to provide a neutral language, which means more reference to women and girls in the text, and more illustrations and stories focusing on them.[5] Since an in-depth analysis of these textbooks from a gender perspective does not exist for recent textbook revisions, it is unknown to what extent these changes have actually taken place. It appears unlikely that many modifications have reached the extent of being *nonsexist* (defined as removing all detrimental sexual stereotypes beyond the use of neutral language) or *antisexist* (defined as portraying a reality in which women occupy more assertive and less traditional roles).

Only two policy measures in the region can be identified as specifically targeting girls: PROGRESA in Mexico (Stromquist 2001b) and the provision of stipends for poor girls in Guatemala (Stromquist et al. 2000c). The first measure, a component of the government's poverty alleviation strategies, centers on the poorest families, and provides additional funds for girls in the first three years of high school. The second measure also focuses on the poorest of the poor and operates in rural areas. Both policies consider gender, but only as a manifestation of exclusion among the poor, not as a prevailing and widely diffused societal marker.

In sum, the prevailing gender policies in education in the region tend to be symbolic in nature in that they are frequently present in the official discourse but limited in nationwide application, and few resources are assigned to their implementation. Often, gender initiatives in education (as well as other sectors) are funded through external efforts (e.g., the gender equity policies in Paraguay and Bolivia), giving them an unstable nature. Ramachandran (1997) observes that, in the case of India, rarely are lessons from successful pilot initiatives taken into the mainstream. A similar observation may be made about Latin America, where successful interventions such as the subsidies for girl's schooling in Guatemala and the potentially transformative new textbooks and curriculum in sex education in several Latin American countries were blocked before they could move to a larger scale.[6] A notable exception to this pattern is the case of an innovation for gender-sensitive training of parents (mothers *and* fathers) and teachers of preschool children in gender-sensitive practices in Mexico D.F., which has now been assumed by the entire municipality, or about 20 million people (Valenzuela 2001).

Important actors in the policy-formation process

International influences in education have existed for a long time; they certainly predate the 1980s, the period in which globalization forces became quite discernable. Inkeles and Sirowy (1983) noted that already in the '70s there was a trend toward convergence among educational systems, denoting similarities in curriculum content in math, language, and science; administrative structures and roles; and demographic characteristics such as growth in enrollment and decreases in student/teacher ratios. But what has been substantially affected by both globalization and neoliberalism is the set of dominant actors. If before international development agencies provided some support and key ideas, today the business sector has a much greater voice than before. And international financial agencies, such as the World Bank and the regional development banks, which used to be circumscribed to the provision of loans for the infrastructure of schools, have now moved into advice and persuasion in the areas of key educational processes affecting school administration, objectives, content, and evaluation (Carnoy 2000, Stromquist forthcoming).

In Latin America today three different action circuits can be identified: 1) that promoted by international development and financial agencies and the national governments, 2) that which reflects a growing network of educators and activists and promotes democratic education in general, and 3) a circuit that comprises activists in the women's movement. The last involves NGOs led by women who are interested particularly in nonformal education; to a lesser extent it involves feminist educators working within universities.

International development agencies and states

It can be ascertained that there are closer ties than ever before between international agencies and government machineries working in education. While studies of these ties are still incipient, educational policies in developing countries (including those in Latin America) are typically established by the executive, not the legislative branch, and increasingly with the participation of international agencies, particularly the World Bank. The World Bank covers a very small proportion of any country's education budget (except perhaps those of the sub-Saharan countries), but its influence is considerable given the bank's association with the International Monetary Fund (IMF) in shaping national economies, and extending their influence to include social policies. This influence generally assures that funds will be available to pay the external debt, with the comcomitant reduction or slow growth education and health expenditures. Under the current climate of neoliberalism and economic competitiveness, most governmental efforts are aimed at addressing quality, efficiency, and equality, concepts constantly enforced by the World Bank (Pisani 1995) and endorsed by regional banks and most other development agencies. The way in which these concepts have been framed—in ways that do not enhance women's well being—has been discussed earlier in this chapter. Case studies of policy formation in education produced by Latin American scholars (Buenfil for Mexico, 2000; and Vior for Argentina, 2001) detail how the content of such policies was profoundly shaped by the World Bank.

Certainly, one of the most influential circuits in Latin America is PREAL. Since 1995, PREAL has functioned as the result of joint action between the Inter-American Dialogue (IAD) and the Corporation of Research for Development (Corporación de Investigación para el Desarrollo; CINDE), with the financial support of the Inter-American Development Bank (IDB), the International Development Research Centre (IDRC, Canada), USAID, and the General Electric Fund. PREAL operates with two offices: one in Washington, D.C., and the other in Santiago, Chile. Basically, PREAL seeks to promote themes and measures initiated in industrialized countries, particularly the United States. Thus, its publication department has edited books on preschool, effective classrooms and schools, teaching and learning, national education standards, and decentralization. PREAL has nine associated centers, among them mostly private research centers.[7] Its educational policy is coordinated by an International Commission on Education, Equity, and Competitiveness comprised of sixteen persons—seven from the academic and research spheres, and nine from business firms. According to a self-evaluation of its first two years, PREAL has been successful in its number of publications and their distribution. Its impact on the educational reforms of Latin American countries it considered as "varying," but it believes that it has had a larger impact in countries that have carried out smaller efforts to discuss and develop consensus (PREAL 1997b).

PREAL began its work by focusing on universal access to basic education; today it seeks wider objectives. According to a position paper, PREAL's main areas of action focus on quality (defined as improved performance in math and reading), decentralization of schooling, greater investment per student, and improvement of the teaching profession. Most of the measures promoted by PREAL will contribute to a bettering of public schools; however, it neglects gender issues. The only references to gender PREAL makes in its position paper note that girls outnumber boys in enrollment, that there is a need to eliminate gender stereotypes, and that there is a need to "provide girls with the same rewards as boys so that they may perform well in difficult subjects, such as math and science" (PREAL 1997a, 9). PREAL is also interested in new forms and innovative mechanisms in educational finance (PREAL 1997a, 7); this preoccupation with *alternative* ways of funding education suggests that PREAL favors privatization of schools.

The same document speaks of equity in its observation that poor families are those that send their children to public schools and notes that rural schools receive less funding and offer fewer grade levels. This section on equity makes a brief reference to gender:

> Around the early 1980s, girls represented more than 59 percent of the total enrollment of students in the region. Today's challenge is to treat girls in an equal manner once they are attending school, and for this it is necessary to eliminate gender stereotypes and to ensure that girls receive the same stimuli as boys to perform well in difficult subjects, such as math and science (PREAL 1997a, 9).

Beyond this paragraph, the document does not deal with any other gender issue that might exist in Latin American schools. Not surprisingly, the specific actions proposed by the PREAL document do not identify any activity touching gender equity.

In a later paper, entitled authoritatively *Lagging Behind: A Report Card on Education in Latin America*, PREAL discusses inequalities when stating that "living in rural areas compounds educational inequalities" and when affirming that "inequalities in student achievement mirror those in access to quality education" (PREAL 2001, 9). The same document acknowledges that groups from indigenous and African backgrounds "have at least three fewer years of education than their white counterparts" but it neither proposes nor examines anything further (PREAL 2001, 10). Concerning gender issues, the document specifically states: "With respect to gender equity, Latin America is doing relatively well. Boys and girls are each as likely to attend and complete schooling at all levels, and the gender bias in some countries actually tips away from boys in favor of girls," except in Bolivia and Guatemala (10). But the tables the document cites as evidence for this assertion (Tables A.20 to A.25) present data for twenty-three Latin American and Caribbean countries that only weakly support the PREAL enrollment claim, showing that girls do better than boys in eleven countries at the pre-primary education level, in three countries at the primary level, and in thirteen countries at the secondary school level (PREAL 2001, 40). The data regarding completion is stronger, showing that a slightly higher proportion of girls than boys complete grade five (the case in nine of sixteen countries) and that girls tend to complete secondary education more than boys (citing greater completion rates in all four Latin American countries for which data seem to be available) (PREAL 2001, 41).

Cognizant of the growing exclusion of poor children in the region, both international agencies and national governments seek to provide more schooling and schooling of better quality for poor, rural, and indigenous children (PREAL 2001, OREALC 2002). This is reflected in the few interventions that address educational equity. Four countries in the region—Mexico, Guatemala, Honduras and Brazil—are undertaking investments of substantial economic scope to help children of the poorest families in those countries. The Mexican initiative, known as PROGRESA, has existed since 1997 and represents an investment of about U.S. $2 billion, covering by 2000 about 2.6 million families (Parker and Skoufias 2000). This effort seeks to increase the participation of rural children in basic education by giving their families subsidies for attendance from the third grade of primary school to the third grade of secondary school; family subsidies for health and nutrition are also provided. Since poor girls in rural areas evince secondary-school enrollment rates lower than those of boys, PROGRESA gives those girls between $2 and $5 dollars more than boys per month.[8] As noted earlier, the Guatemalan intervention offers subsidies exclusively to girls of poor families, both rural and urban. In the case of Brazil, subsidies are granted to poor families in practically all municipalities, but these subsidies do not consider additional payments in favor of girls' participation in school. The Honduras effort centers presently covers approximately 62,000 boys and girls. In all three cases (Brazil, Guatemala, and Honduras), the monthly subsidy per child is about $4.

A summative evaluation of PROGRESA indicates that this intervention has increased the annual enrollment rate of poor boys in primary schools by between 0.74 and 1.07 percent and that the enrollment of girls has increased by between 0.96 and 1.45 percent.[9] Access to secondary schools has also increased by 3.5 and 5.8 percent for boys and 7.2 and 9.3 percent for girls (Schultz, cited in Skoufias and McClafferty 2001, 24). It is estimated that since PROGRESA is also reducing drop-out rates, as a whole the program will increase the number of years of education attained by the rural population by 10 percent (Skoufias and McClafferty 2001). It is interesting to observe that this evaluation of PRO-GRESA indicates that although the number of boys and girls who work outside the home has decreased, the boys and girls working at home continue to contribute a large number of hours, particularly in domestic (i.e., household) tasks—functions mainly performed by girls. PROGRESA's findings reflect that, while it is possible to make progress in girls' access to school, the intervention is not modifying the gender conceptions that produce differential domestic roles and notions linked to femininity and masculinity. Qualitative data for PROGRESA show one unintended benefit: by giving the stipends to mothers for further allocation to their sons and daughters, these adult women are gaining a discernable sense of self-importance, higher levels of community engagement, and thus empowerment (Parker and Skoufias 2000). The evaluations of the impact of subsidies in Guatemala indicate that the financial support for the family contributes to an increase in school attendance and performance of girls in school (Stromquist et al. 2000). Putting together the results drawn from Mexico and Guatemala, it can be asserted that school access among poor families can be increased if these families are granted economic resources that enable them to mitigate the pressures of economic survival and parallel women's domestic work.

International agencies express public concern for gender issues. However, they frame gender problems and solutions in different ways. The most influential agency, the World Bank, has adopted a very mild version of gender transformation, emphasizing access, and essentially access to basic education, not all levels. Other agencies, such as bilateral and semi-autonomous agencies from Sweden, Norway, and the Netherlands, endorse more transformative policies; yet, they refrain from exerting substantial pressure upon recipient states, with the result that many such states manage in the end to do less than promised.

Intentionally or not, some international agencies have developed policies that reframe a given situation so that the conflictual, transformative edge of a given solution is taken out, making them instances in which rich concepts are often co-opted or redefined. For instance, according to its World Development Report 2000/2001, *Attacking Poverty*, the World Bank wants to work with "civil society" and with "empowerment" (World Bank 2000), yet the document does not give due attention to nongovernmental organizations (NGOs). From a gender perspective, it would be essential to identify these organizations, since they are the ones most likely to advance the cause of women. Further, the *Attacking Poverty* report defines "empowerment" as participation in formal elections, without considering other fundamental elements of the concept, such as consciousness-raising, identity formation, and mobilization carried out by women-led NGOs. In other words, the World Bank's implicit policy fails to acknowledge key institutions constituting civil society and does not acknowledge the importance of individual and collective change outside formal politics.

A key document for the region has been the *Programa Regional de Acción para las Mujeres de América Latina y el Caribe, 1995–2001*, prepared by the Economic Commission for Latin America and the Caribbean (ECLAC 1995, also, Stromquist 1996). This document recognizes the importance for girls and women to have access to formal and informal education to prepare them for a future of citizenship, equal participation in policy making, and a fair distribution of tasks within the family or domestic unit. The *Programa Regional* calls upon governments to develop joint actions with women-led NGOs. The document also states that there should be "respect for diversity and cultural identities," but this could work as a loophole in efforts to engage in gender transformative policies. It is not known to what extent the *Programa Regional* has been implemented by the Latin American governments.[10] What is known is that women's organizations and feminist groups have seldom been invited to participate in governmental meetings on this matter.

An interesting initiative on gender and education is that proposed by USAID. Asserting that "the government cannot be the only provider of educational services," it calls upon "other sectors, such as the mass media, religious groups and the business sector . . . to participate increasingly more in education to render complementary services or to influence public opinion" (USAID 2000, 26). This initiative clearly reflects the diminishing amount of public funds available for educational renewal. What this invitation leaves untreated is why these sectors would be interested in proposing alternative views of gender and how their current practices might be changed. There is very little empirical evidence supporting the claim that private business and religious sectors may become strong advocates of transformational gender issues simply by invitation to join a new table of stakeholders.

The Catholic Church

While not a recent position, and thus not associated with either globalization or neoliberal models, the top echelon of the Catholic Church in Latin America continues to present opposition to efforts to alter the content of the curriculum to make it more gender sensitive. Perhaps indirectly linked to the inequalities generated by neoliberal practices in the world, the Jesuits—a progressive Catholic order in Latin America—decided about ten years ago to delink from private education (which they saw as serving mostly the upper classes) and to provide schools for the poor. This left a vacuum that according to many observers has been filled by conservative segments of the Catholic Church. Salient among the new Catholic actors is the Opus Dei, a religious as well as secular order that, in its secular version, comprises wealthy industrialists and businessmen. The current pope is considered to favor the Opus Dei, a position reflected in his appointment of the first Opus Dei cardinal in the Latin American region (Juan Luis Cipriani in Peru).

The Catholic Church has deployed a consistent opposition to any substantial effort to modify the treatment of gender issues in school textbooks, particularly regarding the introduction of transformative sex education. From the evidence accumulated thus far, it is clear that content regarding sex education is a highly contested terrain. The Catholic Church, an institution of substantial influence in the region, has kept its opposition out of the public eye. Yet, at those moments in which important curriculum modifications have been proposed in the area of sex education, it has intervened to forestall any change. This has been documented in the cases of Argentina (Bonder 1999), Mexico (Bayardo 1996), and the Dominican Republic (Stromquist 2001a). It is also known anecdotally that similar experiences have occurred in Colombia and Peru. The Catholic Church, which has played a substantial role as protector of the status quo, continues unchallenged by the women's movement.

Counterhegemonic actors

In the Latin American context, those who oppose neoliberal economic and political models, and their subsequent influence upon education, do not have a consensual opinion regarding the importance of addressing gender issues.

A network of academic and democratic educators

Since many government actions reflect more the influence of international agencies than an accurate diagnosis of the national context, an endogenous response to the dominant action by many governments and international development agencies is slowly emerging.

Pronunciamiento Latinoamericano

Pronunciamiento Latinoamericano is a coalition composed of more than two hundred NGOs working in both formal and nonformal education. It does not have a specific headquarters but its activities are coordinated by Fronesis, an NGO based in Ecuador; it functions mostly as a virtual organization, since most of its communications and connections occur through the Internet. Pronunciamiento Latinoamericano is undertaking strong initiatives to defend a *democratic* and *high-quality* public school in Latin America. It opposes measures that reflect mostly an administrative and technocratic approach to educational problems. While treating themes closely related to gender equality and equity, the positions and writings of this coalition so far are oblivious to the treatment of gender in education. Pronunciamiento Latinomericano collaborated toward the preparation of the first World Educational Forum (that took place in Porto Alegre, Brazil, on 24–27 October 2001). This forum, led by the municipal educational secretariat of Porto Alegre, selected as the conference theme, "Education in a globalized world." A reading of the themes that were debated indicate concern with equality and social justice, children's rights, the environment, the teachers' situation, education for citizenship, identity as a right, education as resistance, and the role of social movements and labor unions in education. While it treated themes that had much relevance for gender equity and equality, the forum treated gender issues mostly as subsets of other concerns.

Feminist networks in education
These groups are comprised of both long-lasting and emerging networks. A network with a well recognized influence upon women, though not so upon governments, is the Women's Network on Popular Education (Red de Educación Popular entre Mujeres, or REPEM), whose principal office is based in Montevideo. REPEM functions with very limited resources but considerable efficiency. It enjoys a formal membership of more than two hundred NGOs (both NGOs focusing exclusively on gender and NGOs dealing with development issues but containing work on gender issues). REPEM has been one of the few feminist institutions that have addressed the social reproductivist role of the school through the presence of sexual stereotypes, something that REPEM has sought to change through the revision of school textbooks and the provision of gender training for teachers. REPEM has also conducted several successful efforts in the creation of new gender visions that are reflected in the textbooks of several countries, even though, as observed earlier, accepted gender revisions have centered on the use of a more inclusive language and more references to the participation of women in history and contemporary society. REPEM played a crucial role in the drafting of the final agreement at the V International Conference on Adult Education (held in Hamburg in 1996) when it introduced elements for a wider recognition of women's needs and a proposal of specific strategies to transform gender relations through education for adult men and women.[11]

A second feminist network—still undecided about the importance of education as an area of priority—is one comprised of feminist academics. Many gender and women's studies still function precariously in the large majority of countries in the world (Stromquist 2001b). In the United States, where it is frequently asserted that such programs are widely "institutionalized," many of them face survival problems. Though these programs have existed in universities for almost twenty years, few such programs have succeeded in becoming independent. The majority of these programs function attached to (and dependent upon) an established discipline department, and have no capacity to grant university degrees or appoint their own professors. Generally, the gender and women's studies programs offer certificates, diplomas, or specializations. An example of the fragility of these programs is reflected in the example of the

Center of Women and Gender Studies at the University of Texas at San Antonio, which in August 2001 was closed by university administrators because the center "failed to finance itself with external funding as required by university policy."

It can be observed, in addition, that among universities with great intellectual reputation there is a tendency to delink the curricula of women and gender studies programs from their political and material component, while operating mainly in the world of the symbolic and discursive. These influences derive, in part, from postmodernist philosophical approaches, which have made undeniable contributions in the area of discourse analysis and in the recognition of the constant construction of identities. This approach has also gravitated toward an emphasis on cultural aspects and, thus, retreated a certain distance from economic and political issues. This, in turn, is promoting deepening discussions on aspects of identity and difference but also somewhat removing the discussions from issues of social justice and collective political action.

A third important feminist network is constituted by women-led NGOs in general. Because of the serious economic conditions facing Latin America and the Caribbean, many NGOs that advocate the advancement of women concentrate on the solution of immediate and crucial problems such as the elimination of violence against women, the provision of reproductive and sexual health, migration concerns, and improvements in the legal code so that fathers are held more accountable for the provision of children's living stipends in case of the dissolution of a marriage or partnership (Dominguez 2001, Stromquist 2000). The women's movement—as represented by the women-led NGOs—has also been investing in political strategies, promoting expanded notions of citizenship and human rights, and mobilizing to get more women elected to political office, at both national and community (municipality) levels. The women's and feminist movements have most certainly used education as a means to persuade others. On the other hand, they have taken a relatively mild position vis-à-vis *schooling* or formal education as a site for the creation and maintenance of gendered social relations.

Further weakening the possibility of an educational agenda from a gender perspective has been the absence of more education-focused women-led NGOs and feminist scholars at many of the negotiating tables and in the subsequent design of policies dealing with textbook modifications and teacher training. Their absence has permitted national governments to enact educational policies with weak content regarding the treatment of gender. There are, however, instances of improvements in the treatment of gender coming from women-led NGOs. One example is the vigorous participation of these groups in the shaping of the ten-year educational plan in the Dominican Republic. A second example comes from the initiatives by GEM, a Mexican NGO that developed a training program for teachers and parents (mothers and fathers) in preschool education in Mexico, D.F. that is now gradually expanding to other states in the country (Valenzuela 2000). A third positive example also comes from Mexico, where there are growing instances of collaboration by universities and NGOs for the development of training programs for in-service teachers from a gender perspective, and where emerging collaboration between academics working in teacher training institutions and universities have responded to requests by the government to provide teacher training from a gender perspective (Cortina 2001).

Attempting a balance

Looking at gender issues globally, it can be asserted that women today aspire to, and gain access to, many more jobs than in the past. Women hold more political positions, including those at higher national and international levels. Men and women have enacted legislation that protects women against domestic violence, against lack of spouse or partner support for children, and against rape. In several countries, there have been advances in sexual and reproductive health, and in women's access to credit and land holding. While many of these changes are attributed to education and women's increased understanding of their social and political world, the formal education system remains curiously unreformed.

A reason for suspecting that the educational system is failing to promote gender transformations is that although rates of access to schooling and the number of years of schooling attained have been going up in recent decades, at the same time some cultural aspects have not undergone modification. In Latin America, there is still reluctance by young women to use or demand contraceptives when engaging in sexual relations, a passive behavior that cuts across social classes (Stern et al. 2001). Women continue to bear the responsibility of most of the domestic tasks even when they work or study (Echarri and Pérez 2001). Women enter parenthood (childbearing in their case) about three years younger than men. They also experience a much shorter interval between first sexual intercourse and entry into conjugal union, which reflects the double standard sex practices and norms (Echarri and Pérez 2001).[12]

Nonetheless, the notions of democracy, competition, and individual merit that accompany the rhetoric of neoliberalism have facilitated changes in individual conceptions of control over one's life and the right to make demands upon the state. Educational systems have been brought to the fore as essential tools to move into the "knowledge society." Changes specifically connected with the transformation of gender are few. Access to schooling has been steadily increasing, but the nature of the schooling experience and the knowledge that students are gaining neither contests nor transforms the traditional conceptions of masculinity and femininity. The language in educational policies and in textbooks has become more gender-inclusive: the generic masculine has been replaced by the more inclusive double male/female form. There would seem to be a greater presence of women and girls in the content of courses and books. Missing in the measures to achieve these advances are strong and institutionalized forms of collaboration between the state and women-led NGOs, which would permit a greater incorporation of messages that can be transformative and facilitate girls' empowerment in the social relations of gender, particularly in the understanding and negotiating of one's sexuality. Also missing is the promotion of a curriculum that makes schooling an experience that raises awareness about gender inequalities, that considers the role of the mass media in the transmission of prevalent gender ideologies, and that attempts to bring the mass media into greater congruence with transformative gender messages. In general, the questioning of established gender roles in existing educational policies tends to be mild, and the potential of sex education to build an awareness of the asymmetrical relations between women and men in various areas of social life, particularly in the social relations of sex, has been placed out of bounds by both the Catholic Church and by market-led educational reforms that assume an asexual workplace or, more precisely, a workplace in which current gender relations are totally acceptable.

Under neoliberal influences, educational activities in Latin America and the Caribbean are much more propelled by issues linked to economic and technological globalization than to reasons of social justice, including those of gender. Influential NGOs working on education in the region are either calling for the modernization of the educational system (the case of PREAL) or the adoption of more egalitarian and democratic practices in the school (the case of Pronunciamiento Latinoamericano), but in the final analysis, gender issues remain ignored. While the concept of equity is not being challenged and, in fact, is recognized in official documents as a major problem in Latin America given the increasing social exclusion of some groups, it is typically defined to mean equity between rural and urban areas, and secondarily between the rich and the poor. In terms of action, equity is not a priority at this point since efforts to increase economic productivity displace humanist considerations. With an increasingly reduced state, it is difficult to design and implement actions that will not lead to immediate benefits for the market. Such measures do exist but are infrequent and consider only the poorest sectors and provide little attention to gender. With neoliberal priorities placed on the market, equity policies are limited and center on the poorest segment of the population. If women appear on the policy agenda, it is because many of them belong to the poorest sector. The fact that they center on the poorest of the poor, including the poorest women, contributes to reframing social problems as *class* rather than *gender* problems, which is a partial reframing at that, since other social classes are not brought into the analysis. The retrenchment of the state from social arenas does not help the consideration of how gender operates to create social inequalities and how gender operates as a fundamental marker that cuts across social classes, ethnicity, and "race."

But what accounts for the various attempts to promulgate educational policy addressing gender, only to have them persistently weakened in content or by the failure to provide funds or other means of implementation? Several factors are involved. As states modernize, they endorse values that coincide with democratic governance, such as the participation of all citizens (including women). This leads them to recognize the host of obstacles girls and women face. Incentives and financial resources offered by bilateral development agencies also prod governments into focusing on gender and education. But gender ideologies are deep, pervasive, and difficult to eliminate. Fears then arise—in the form of opposition from influential social and political groups—that any changes to the status quo may alter the current equilibrium and create unpredictable consequences for power and authority relations in public and private spheres. In many Latin American countries there are still widespread beliefs, encouraged by the Catholic Church, that feminism means opposition to the family and to the established masculine and feminine order of gender. The global media, more interested in marketing and material consumption than in reflexivity, presents contradictory images of women. Young women appear as beautiful, successful, and satisfied with their surrounding society. In an apolitical world, where expressions of dissent alone are increasingly seen as unacceptable opposition, new generations of women are not mobilizing for action, and the more experienced and active generations of women are running out of energy to monitor educational policies.

No situation is completely bleak or irresolvable. What this chapter has highlighted is that globalization and neoliberal models create a veneer of democratic change that has enraptured the minds of many and thus makes it quite difficult to present and defend alternatives. Traditionally, feminist educators and scholars working in universities have maintained a distance from women-led NGOs (Araya 2001, Stromquist 2001b), which has not facilitated recognition of the limitation of current public policies in gender and education. More recently, however, exchanges between women-led NGOs and feminist academics are reported to be increasing. It is anticipated that these exchanges of information and experiences will generate a greater understanding of accomplishments and failures, and that this in turn will foster greater unified action.

Notes

1. The expectation that countries will move into "knowledge societies" must be examined carefully. New technologies do require people who are highly trained; however, firms engaged in technology development or application generate a small fraction of the jobs in the labor force. Most people will occupy service jobs in the new societies, which usually are poorly paid and unstable work. In developing countries, where levels of technology seem to be long destined to be fewer than in the countries of the North, the promise of the "knowledge society" is all the more elusive.

2. The suggestions presented by the regional office of UNESCO in its regional framework of action for Latin America (Marco de Acción Regional de la Educación de Personas Jóvenes y Adultas en América Latina y El Caribe, OREALC, 2000), recognizes seven "priority action

lines." One of these lines is gender, which is to be implemented as a cross-cutting theme in all educational reform components (curriculum, teacher training, administration, innovation, learning resources, etc.). The document's section on gender also mentions the need to work on gender equity in the areas of "access, process, and outcomes" and proposes to work with "strategic actors," including women's organizations—something very progressive in the context of public policies. It remains to be seen how the various states in Latin America respond to these recommendations.

3. According to ECLAC, nine Latin American countries had by 1998 developed national plans on gender and equal opportunity (Krawczyk 1998). It is not known at present how central education figures in these plans.
4. Language has a crucial function in shaping reality, including gender identities. Modification in the language to refer explicitly to women and girls is not underestimated here. I simply note the limitations of many educational initiatives.
5. Supplementary materials face the possibility—quite strong at times—that teachers may not use them since they must first cover the required curriculum.
6. The Guatemala stipends for girls were part of an experiment sponsored by USAID that, if proven successful, was to be implemented nationally through loans from the World Bank and the Inter-American Development Bank. When these loans materialized, despite the positive impact of the intervention, neither institution continued the stipend for rural girls (Stromquist et al. 2000).
7. The nine affiliated centers are: Fundación Getulio Vargas (Brazil), Centro de Investigación y Desarrollo de la Educación (Chile), Instituto SER de Investigación (Colombia), Asociación de Investigación y Estudios Sociales (Guatemala), Universidad Centroamericana (Nicaragua), *Foro Educativo* (Peru), FLACSO/Plan Educativo (Dominican Republic), and Instituto de Estudios Superiores de Administración and Venezuela Competitiva (Venezuela). As of 2000, PREAL stated to comprise 23 "affiliated institutions" in 17 countries.
8. PROGRESA functions (as of 2001) in fifty thousand communities in thirty-one Mexican states, serving about 40 percent of all rural Mexican families. The monthly stipend amounts to the equivalent of an increase of 22 percent in the daily incomes of the rural families in the program (Parker and Skoufias 2000). Rural families in PROGRESA receive an amount that increases with the grade of the student, from 90 pesos (about $10 for a student, girl or boy, in the third grade of primary school to 335 pesos (about $37) for a girl in the third grade of secondary education, who receives $5 more than a boy would at that level of schooling (Parker and Skoufias 2000).
9. Two numbers are given to indicate the range across the three grades of primary and the three grades of secondary schooling covered by PROGRESA.
10. It is known, however, that policies in the Latin American region to expand the number of compulsory years of schooling to cover eighth and ninth grades are resulting in the construction of more secondary schools in rural areas. This is having the effect, albeit indirect, of increasing the access of rural girls to schooling (Schmelkes 2001).
11. A current concern of REPEM focuses on the design and implementation of a monitoring strategy based on the development and use of three types of indicators: of situation, of situation in relation to goals, and of "political will" (Bonino 1998). Conceptually, these indicators have much merit. To be implemented they require that the state collect these data and share it with NGOs. They also need national level researchers available to process the information. Herein reside some of the major difficulties.
12. According to Mexican data drawn from the 2000 National Youth Survey, the median time span between first sexual intercourse and entry into conjugal union is 0.66 years for rural women and 0.66 years for urban women. In contrast, it is 5.04 years for rural men and 7.08 years for urban men (Echarri and Pérez 2001, 12).

References

Acker, Sandra. (1994). *Gendered Education.* Buckingham: Open University Press.

Araya Umaña, Sandra. (2001). Los procesos de formación docente: Retos para la equidad de género. Paper presented at the Latin American conference on Gender and Education, organized by Programa Universitario de Estudios de Género, UNAM, Mexico, 22–26 October.

Arnot, Madeleine. (2000). Gender Relations and Schooling in the New Century: Conflicts and Challenges. *Compare,* vol. 30, no. 3, pp. 293–302.

Bayardo, Barbara. (1996). "Sex and the Curriculum in Mexico and the United States." In Nelly P. Stromquist, ed. *Gender Dimensions in Education in Latin America*. Washington, D.C.: Organization of American States, 157–186.

Behrman, Jere, Piyali Sengupta, and Petra Todd. (2001). Progressing through PROGRESA: An Impact Assessment of a School Subsidy Experiment. Philadelphia: University of Pennsylvania, April.

Bonder, Gloria. (1999). La equidad de género en las políticas educativas: La necesidad de una mirada reflexiva sobre premisas, experiencias y metas. Draft.

Bonino, Maria. (1998). Hacia la construcción de un índice de compromisos cumplidos en educación de mujeres en la V Conferencia Internacional de Educación de Adultos. Taller internacional de Seguimiento a Beijing y Hamburgo, organizado por REPEM y GEO. Santa Cruz de la Sierra, Bolivia, July.

Buenfil, Rosa Nidia. Globalization and Educational Policies in Mexico, 1988–1994: A Meeting of the Universal and the Particular. In Nelly P. Stromquist and Karen Monkman (eds.). *Globalization and Education. Integration and Contestation across Cultures*. Lanham: Rowman & Littlefield, pp. 275–297.

Caporaso, James and David Levine. (1992). *Theories of Political Economy*. Cambridge: Cambridge University Press.

Carlson, Barbara. (2001). *Education and the Labour Market in Latin America: Why Measurement is Important and What It Tells Us about Policies, Reforms and Performance*. Santiago: CEPAL.

Carnoy, Martin. (2000). "Globalization and Educational Reform." In Nelly P. Stromquist and Karen Monkman, eds. *Globalization and Education. Integration and Contestation across Cultures*. Boulder: Rowman and Littlefield, 43–61.

Colazo, Carmen. (2000). "Public Policies on Gender and Education in Paraguay: The Project for Equal Opportunities." In Regina Cortina and Nelly P. Stromquist, eds. *Distant Alliances: Promoting the Education for Girls and Women in Latin America*. New York: RoutledgeFalmer, 13–27.

Connell, Robert. Teaching the Boys: New Research on Masculinity, and Gender Strategies for Schools. *Teachers College Record*, vol. 98, no. 2, 1996, pp. 206–235.

Cortina, Regina. (2001). Políticas públicas y formación docente: Una mirada desde la perspectiva de género. Paper presented at the Latin American Conference on Gender and Education, UNAM, México, 22–26 October.

Deere, Carmen Diana and Magdalena León. (2001). "Institutional Reform and Agriculture under Neoliberalism." *Latin American Research Review* 36, no. 2: 31–63.

Domínguez, María Elvia. (2001). *Género, diversidad y educación formal en Colombia: Tendencias investigativas e implicaciones políticas*. Paper presented at the Latin American conference on Gender and Education, organized by Programa Universitario de Estudios de Género, UNAM, Mexico, 22–26 October.

Echarri, Carlos and Julieta Pérez. (2001). "Becoming Adults: Life Course Transitions in Mexican Young People." Paper presented at the XIV General Popular Conference, Salvador, Brazil, 18–24 August.

ECLAC. (1997). *Social Panorama of Latin America*. Santiago: ECLAC.

ECLAC. (1995). *Regional Programme of Action for the Women of Latin America and the Caribbean, 1995–2001*. Santiago: Economic Commission for Latin America and the Caribbean and the United Nations Development Fund for Women.

Edwards, Verónica and Jorge Osorio, eds. (1995). *La Construcción de las Políticas Educativas en América Latina*. Lima: CEAAL and Tarea.

Espinola, Viola. (1995). Algunas reflexiones sobre el concepto de calidad de la educación. In Verónica Edwards and Jorge Osorio, eds. *La Construcción de las Políticas Educativas en América Latina*. Lima: CEAAL and Tarea, 119–131.

Ezpeleta, Justa. (1995). *El caso del PARE: Programa para abatir el rezago educativo*. In Veronica Edwards and Jorge Osorio, eds. *La Construcción de las Políticas Educativas en América Latina*. Lima: CEAAL and Tarea, 107–118.

Glewwe, Paul and Paul Gertler. (1991). The Willingness to Pay for Education in Developing Countries: Evidence from Rural Peru. *Journal of Development Economics*, pp. 377–386.

IBE. (2001). Cuarentava Conferencia Internacional de Educación. Ginebra: International Bureau of Education, 5–8 September. Available at http://www.ibe.unesco.org/International/ICE/46 espanol/46miniss.htm.

Inkeles, Alex and Larry Sirowy. (1983). "Convergent and Divergent Trends in National Educational Systems." *Social Forces* 62, no. 2: 303–337.

Klees, Steven. (forthcoming). "World Bank Education Policy: New Rhetoric, Old Ideology." *International Journal of Educational Development*, forthcoming.

Krawczyk, Miriam. (1998). Algunos elementos para la agenda: Mujeres en América Latina y el Caribe a fines de los noventa. Santiago: ECLAC, draft.

Lazarte, Cecilia and Martha Lanza. (2000). "Gender Equity in Bolivian Educational Policies: Experiences and Challenges." In Regina Cortina and Nelly P. Stromquist, eds. *Distant Alliances: Promoting the Education for Girls and Women in Latin America.* New York: RoutledgeFalmer, 29–46.

Nuñez, Ivan. (1995). *El caso chileno.* In Verónica Edwards and Jorge Osorio, eds. *La Construcción de las Políticas Educativas en América Latina.* Lima: CEAAL and Tarea, 159–168.

OREALC. (2002). Proyecto Regional de Educacion para America Latina y el Caribe. Santiago: OREALC. Available at http://www.foro.unesco.cl/DocEs.pdf

Palencia Villa, Mercedes. (2001). *De Políticas Públicas a una Nueva Cultura Escolar.* Paper presented at the Latin American conference on Gender and Education, organized by Programa Universitario de Estudios de Género, UNAM, México, 22–26 October.

Parker, Susan and Emmanuel Skoufias. (2000). *Final Report. The Impact of PROGRESA on Work, Leisure, and Time Allocation.* Washington, D.C.: International Food Policy Research Institute, October.

Pisani, Luis. (1995). *Políticas del Banco Mundial en el campo de la educación.* In Verónica Edwards and Jorge Osorio, eds. *La Construcción de las Políticas Educativas en América Latina.* Lima: CEAAL and Tarea, 55–60.

PREAL. (2000). *Comisión Centroamericana para la Reforma Educativa.* Santiago: Inter-American Dialogue and CINDE.

PREAL. (1997a). *La Educación en las Américas: El Futuro está en Juego.* Informe de la Comisión Internacional sobre Educación, Equidad y Competitividad Económica en las Américas. Santiago: Inter-American Dialogue and CINDE.

PREAL. (2001). *Lagging Behind. A Report Card on Education in Latin America.* Washington, D.C. and Santiago: Inter-American Dialogue and CINDE.

PREAL. (1997b). *Evaluación del Proyecto PREAL.* Santiago: CINDE. draft.

Ramachandran, Vimala. (1997). *Girls and Women's Access to Basic Education. Bridging the Gap between Intent and Action. The Indian Experience.* New Delhi: Asia South Pacific Bureau of Education, February.

Samoff, Joel and Nelly P. Stromquist. (2001). "Managing Knowledge and Storing Wisdom? New Forms of Foreign Aid?" *Development and Change* 32, no. 4: 631–656.

Shain, Farzana and Jenny Ozga. (2001). "Identity Crisis? Problems and Issues in the Sociology of Education." *British Journal of Sociology of Education*, 22, no. 2: 109–120.

Skoufias, Emmanuel and Bonnie McClafferty. (2001). *Is PROGRESA Working? Summary of the Results of an Evaluation by IFPRI.* Washington, D.C.: International Food Policy Research Institute, July.

Stern, Claudio, Elizabeth Cueva, Elizabeth García, Alicia Pereda, and Yuriria Rodríguez. (2001). "Gender Stereotypes, Sexual Relations, and Adolescent Pregnancy in the Lives of Youngsters of Different Socio-cultural Groups in Mexico." Paper presented at the XIV General Popular Conference, Salvador, Brazil, 18–24 August.

Stromquist, Nelly P. (2001a). El conocimiento y el poder en la política feminista: La experiencia del CIPAF. Los Angeles: University of Southern California, 2001a, draft.

Stromquist, Nelly P. (2002). *Education in a Globalized World: The Connectivity of Economic Power, Technology, and Knowledge.* Boulder, Colo.: Rowman and Littlefield.

Stromquist, Nelly P. (1996). "Gender Delusions and Exclusions in the Democratization of Schooling in Latin America." *Comparative Education Review* 40, no. 4: 404–425.

Stromquist, Nelly P. (2001b). "Gender Studies: A Global Perspective of their Evolution and Challenges to Comparative Higher Education." *Higher Education* 41, no. 4.

Stromquist, Nelly P. (1992). "Women and Literacy in Latin America." In Nelly P. Stromquist, ed. *Women and Education in Latin America: Knowledge, Power, and Change.* Boulder, Colo.: Lynne Rienner, 19–32.

Stromquist, Nelly P. (2001c). "Caminos Recorridos y por Recorrer en la Educación y Género. Ligando la Acción al Conocimiento." Paper presented at the Latin American conference on Feminism and Education. Mexico: UNAM.

Stromquist, Nelly P. (2000). "Learning for the Construction of a Feminist Agenda within Organizations in Civil Society." In Regina Cortina and Nelly P. Stromquist, eds. *Distant*

Alliances: Promoting the Education for Girls and Women in Latin America. New York: RoutledgeFalmer, 75–101.

Stromquist, Nelly P., Steven Klees and Shirley Miske. (2000). "USAID Efforts to Expand and Improve Girls' Primary Education in Guatemala." In Regina Cortina and Nelly P. Stromquist, eds. *Distant Alliances: Promoting the Education for Girls and Women in Latin America.* New York: RoutledgeFalmer, 239–260.

UNESCO, CEAAL, CREFAL, INEA. *(2000). Marco de Acción Regional de la Educación de Personas Jóvenes y Adultas en América Latina y El Caribe.* Santiago: UNESCO.

USAID. (2000). Simposio sobre Educación de Niñas. Evidencias, Temas, Acciones. Washington, D.C.: USAID.

Valenzuela and Gomez Gallardo, Malú. (2000). "Other Ways to Be Teachers, Mothers, and Fathers." In Regina Cortina and Nelly P. Stromquist, eds. *Distant Alliances: Promoting the Education for Girls and Women in Latin America.* New York: RoutledgeFalmer, 103–118.

Vior, Susan. (2001). Neoliberalismo y formación de docentes. Argentina 1989–1999. In Rute Baquero and Cecília Brolio (eds.). *Pesquisando e gestando outra escola: desafios contemporâneos.* Sao Leopoldo, Brazil: Editora UNISINOS, pp. 65–93.

World Bank. (1996). *Priorities and Strategies for Education. Sectoral Study.* Washington, D.C.: The World Bank.

World Bank. (2000). *World Development Report 2000/2001. Attacking Poverty.* Washington, D.C.: The World Bank.

World Bank. (2001). *Engendering Development through Gender Equality in Rights, Resources, and Voice.* Washington, D.C.: The World Bank.

10

The Northern Influence and Colombian Education Reform of the 1990s

PATRICIA VANEGAS

The 1990s started with the enactment of a new constitution in Colombia. Public and political life were infused with the possibilities of modernization and reform. An educational reform of major proportions was one of several that were initiated at this time.

This chapter focuses on the international influence exerted on this educational reform,[1] specifically on how global trends of thought, in this case neoliberalism, pervaded the creation of reform. I aim to define and describe this influence as a relationship of power between the international context and Colombian educational policy making. I use the concept of "Northern influence" to explore the specificities of this relationship of power for the Colombian educational context. I argue that the Northern influence does not simply happen as a result of imposition from the North to the South, but rather through a complex relationship of power that impacts greatly on the capability of individuals to exert change (Vanegas 2001).

At the heart of this work is a preoccupation with the popular debate in social sciences of structure versus agency. For sake of space I will not analyze in depth the structural but limit myself to a brief description of the elements of the international context that I recognize as structural influences on educational reform. I propose that the international context is a hegemonic project that strongly influences national affairs and educational policy, and raises important questions about the capacity of individual people to exert change (agency). My analysis focuses on the development of a working definition of power that fits the Colombian reality and then moves on to provide a link between structure and agency that allows for a way forward for the individual.

The tensions between structure and agency, and the assumptions that I make about the relationship between the international context and the individual, follow Giddens' theory of structuration. Giddens says that a social system reproduces through the way in which individual agents act. Social systems consist of "regularised relations of interdependence between individuals or groups, that typically can be best analysed as recurrent social practices" (Giddens 1979, 66). Individuals reproduce the structuring properties of society by regularly using similar sets of rules and resources in their interaction. Thus, for Giddens there is not a structure that is independent from people and that imposes itself on them to restrict their actions. It is people who, employing the same tools and resources embedded in their practical consciousness, reproduce the way society is.I believe that the reproduction of structures in a social system may be altered by processes of reflexivity in the individual. This is what drives my work: the belief that research may provide the basis for increased awareness and criticality about the big picture, which in turn may allow for possibilities of alternative action, if desired, at the individual level. This motive underpinning my work relates to the concept of the "recursiveness of social knowledge": "the notion that social science informs actors in society who may then act to change their society, which requires new social analysis and so on. Sociology and social change are linked by internal feedback" (Bilton, Bonnett, Jones, Skinner, Stanworth, and Webster, 1996, 650).

In addition, "Only societies reflexively capable of modifying their institutions in the face of accelerated social change will be able to confront the future with any confidence" (Bilton, et al. 1996, 649).

The national and international context of Colombian reform

In this short section I intend to provide a flavor of what was happening in the Colombian arena in the 1990s, and I will briefly describe the main features of the international context that most impacted the educational process in Colombia.

Civil war, endemic violence, kidnapping, and economic recession, amongst other challenges, have been an everyday feature of ordinary life in Colombia for some time. Some commentators see this period of Colombian history as the worst crisis that the country has suffered. As Juan Manuel Santos describes it: "Colombia is going through one of the most critical moments of its history. . . . [T]he country is immersed in such a severe and huge crisis that for many national and international commentators the state is at risk of crumbling" (Santos 1999, 9). Other commentators see the current state of affairs more as an inevitable result of the way in which the country has been governed for more than a century (Caballero 1996, Caballero 1997). For whichever reason, there is national consensus that the country is in grave danger of social disintegration.

At this time, education in Colombia faced, and still faces, immense challenges. There are problems related to coverage, quality, equity, and educational administration amongst many. Educational policy makers place their hopes in education in every statement. These are hopes both for a better education that will help Colombia in its race toward development and for an education that will create better citizens imbued with positive qualities. The national development plan for education in 1990 stated:

> The programme of economic opening up requires the strengthening of the social infrastructure. Within this perspective, education plays a fundamental role: a higher educational level of the working population, or human capital accumulation, represents higher productive capacity for the whole economic system; higher education for women means smaller size families and healthier and better nourished children; and, in general terms, more education means more social mobility.
>
> In addition to the economic virtues emanating from the transmission of basic knowledge, the educational process must produce critical, free, creative and solidary spirits; committed to the search for peace and tolerance, and who are able to be aware participants in collective processes. (DNP 1991, 87, my translation).

As already mentioned, the 1990s began with the enactment of a new constitution that in turn triggered a major educational reform, amongst many others. At the same time, many other countries in the world had either undertaken or were undertaking educational reforms, many of these along very similar policy lines. A kind of global educational paradigm seemed to be high on the agenda of policy makers (Whitty et al. 1998). This global educational paradigm has followed neoliberal ideas that strongly promote the insertion of markets into education. These policies claim to improve educational provision and its outcomes by enhancing parental choice. The arguments in favor of market-oriented educational provision are that privatized and decentralized provision generates effectiveness and efficiency in school provision, with increased community and parent involvement and empowerment to teachers through the enhanced autonomy of the school. Therefore, an effective school reform is more likely in an environment where the school is more responsive to the needs of the local community and more democratic and accountable (Chubb and Moe 1990, Whitty et al. 1998). However, these claims have been subjected to immense controversy and criticisms (Torres and Puiggrós 1997b, Halsey, Lauder, Brown, and Stuart Wells 1997). One of the main weaknesses of market-oriented educational policies is that these polarize school intakes and thus increase social inequality:

> The consequence of marketization is likely to be the polarization of school intakes, since middle-class parents will have the material and cultural capital to exercise choice in a way denied to working-class parents. Market reforms in education also affect both the role of schools in a democracy and outcomes. In terms of democracy, the polarization of intakes means that students from different social-class and ethnic backgrounds are unlikely to mix. Hence, the possibility for the kinds of

mutual understanding between students from different backgrounds . . . as the basis for the democratic qualities of tolerance and respect for persons will be lost. A further consequence of polarization is that it will lead to an overall decline in standards, since unpopular schools will suffer a decline in resources and morale. (Halsey et al. 1997, 357)

Research in other countries shows that "recent education policies are doing little to alleviate existing inequalities in access and participation and, in many cases, may be exacerbating them." (Whitty et al. 1998, 127, Arnove 1997). Not only is the raising of quality for all sections of society via the use of markets in doubt but, more importantly, the values that the market carries with it may permeate the educational system and the pedagogies in unanticipated ways. As Ball concludes for the United Kingdom: "[I]nsofar as students are influenced and affected by the hidden curriculum of their institutional environment then the system of morality 'taught' by schools is increasingly well accommodated to the values complex of the enterprise culture" (Ball 1994b, 146).

Values of the market such as competition, survival of the best, and self interest appear to be in contradiction with the actual needs of the Colombian society as expressed by the government (that is, solidary spirits committed to the search for peace and tolerance, and who are able to be aware participants in collective processes). Nevertheless, Colombian educational reform was strongly influenced by the global educational paradigm.

Colombia, as all Latinamerican and developing countries, has been profoundly influenced in its history by the developed world and this influence was as potent at the end of the twentieth century as ever before. However, attention to the way in which the international context shapes national affairs is generally not included in the analysis or in the design of policy. Policies are presented as technical instruments, stripped of all the context and values in which they are imbued. It is, then, very difficult to know what these policies mean for the country in the long term or which interests they are serving and which values they are reproducing.

The international context has economic, political, and cultural dimensions, and reveals current and historical processes, which have combined with more local features in specific ways to shape the Colombian national culture. It seems obvious to state that the international context has an impact on the life of any country. In an increasingly globalized world, boundaries of nation-states seem to be weakening in some senses under the impact of advancing communication and technology. The dimensions of the international influence are multifaceted; these can be seen in so many aspects of daily life in a country like Colombia, that the influence tends to be naturalized—that is, accepted as the norm. I propose that it is important to look again at the naturalized features of the culture to increase awareness of them. I do not intend to make a judgement as to whether this influence is positive or negative, but rather define it more carefully in order to understand its specificities and un-tangle all of the various facets that are part of it. In other words, I want to ex-amine, for Colombia, how and why this international context pervades the culture.

The main features of the world in the late-twentieth century were capital-ism, globalization, and the prevalence of new right ideologies.

The capitalist economic model that has prevailed across the world in the last decades can be traced back to the late-fifteenth century (Wallerstein 1974, 1980a, 1980b), when Latin America was inserted into the evolving world capi-talist system.[2]

The late-twentieth and early-twenty-first century version of capitalism is rooted in modernist goals of development and growth, which assume contin-ued expansion of production. Production ensures access to a share of a bigger cake for all.[3] These goals of development and growth have been criticized since the 1960s (Schumacher 1963, Sachs 1992a, Rahnema and Bawtree 1997) but they are still deeply ingrained in the prevailing policies for the "development" of countries around the globe. One particular criticism relates to the assump-tion that production can expand infinitely, in spite of the unavoidable fact that the planet has finite and exhaustible natural resources—that is, the cake can-not grow endlessly (Sachs 1992b). Hence, it is not possible for all countries in the world to grow to acquire the levels of development and consumption that the developed economies have achieved. The concept of "developing country" implies a promise to its people that it can achieve developed status. But, as Gandhi said, "if it took England the exploitation of half the globe to be what it is today, how many globes will it take India?" (quoted in Oxfam 1995b, 151). Most countries in the world, including Colombia, have implemented growth-led reforms in the last decades in order to pursue development.

Bilton et al. define globalization as "the process whereby political, social, economic and cultural relations increasingly take place on a global scale, and which has profound consequences for individuals' local experiences and everyday lives" (Bilton et al, 1996, 660). The economic facets of globalization are defined within the context of the end of communism, which raises capital-ism to its status as the only alternative for development. Current capitalist eco-nomic ideas are rooted in neoliberal orthodoxy.

Radical changes have occurred since the 1950s when welfare state systems were implemented in many capitalist economies around the world. During the 1970s a strand of right-wing Conservatism, described in various literatures as the New Right, began to be increasingly influential in the world. Reaganomics in the United States and Thatcherism in the United Kingdom were particular manifestations of New Right politics. New Right theories combined radical liberal economic ideas (neoliberal) with neoconservative orthodoxies.

Neoliberal economics is based on two principles: first, that of the essential role of the free market in economic and social development; and second, the

Table 10.1 Global educational paradigm and Colombian policies compared

Global educational paradigm	Colombian educational policies
Education for economic development (investment in human capital)	Education for economic development and for better human beings
Decentralizing the management of public education	Decentralizing and modernizing the educational sector
—School autonomy	—School autonomy
—Local management of schools	—School development plan
Providing loans and selective scholarships	Selective scholarships project (PACES)
Encouraging the expansion of private and community supported schools (Psacharopoulos et al. 1986, 2)	Encouraging expansion of private schools
Markets into education; increasing competition amongst schools	Promoting competition amongst private and state schools to offer more and "better" education
	Increasing parental "choice"
	Closer focus on results by establishing national assessments of quality
	Assessments and more information to parents to increase their "choice"
Taken from (Psacharopoulos et al. 1986)	Taken from (DNP 1991a and MEN 1994)

superiority of the private sector over the public sector, which leads to proposals for the reduction of public spending and for the reform of the public sector for development. Neoliberal policies provide the basis for concepts such as the free market, reduction of the state, individual freedom, choice, and competition, which are now so common in the world.

Capitalism, globalization and the prevalence of new right ideologies in the Colombian international context are features that influenced educational reform of the 1990s. The Colombian Development Plan for Education and the final text of the General Law of Education reproduced many policies that can be identified as elements of the global educational paradigm (Table 10.1). Hence, it can be argued that there is an important level of correspondence between the main trends in policy at the international level and the policies of the Gaviria Government (1990–1994). Of course there are differences between international and national policies; the correspondence is not absolute and direct.

I have briefly described structural features of educational analysis and established a correspondence between international educational policies and Colombian policies in order to show that the international context did influence Colombian educational policy agendas at the time of reform.

The Northern influence

Influence is defined in the *Concise Oxford Dictionary* as "the inflowing or infusion (into a person or thing) of any kind of divine, moral or other secret power or principle" or as "the capacity of producing effects by insensible or invisible means" (Fowler and Fowler 1969). These definitions imply two things at least: First, that there is a relationship between influence and power, which will be analyzed later in the chapter; second, that at least two parties are needed for the exercise of influence, the one who influences and the one who is influenced.

To achieve a clear focus I identify the international context as the "influencer" and the national context as the "influenced." I have then chosen to use the World Bank to stand in as the main "carrier" of international influence, and Colombian top civil servants who played a key role in developing the Colombian General Law of Education as the representatives of the national context. The interaction between these two sets of chosen actors in the relationship of influence, the World Bank and high level civil servants who were active in shaping the education law, will be identified herein as the Northern influence.

The concept of "Northern influence" is used as a lens through which to examine how and why the international context pervades the national educational policy making arena in Colombia—to examine the specificities of this relationship and to untangle all the various facets that are part of it. I use "Northern" to identify influences originating in U.S. and European culture. Geographically, these countries are described as being located to the north of Latin America rather than to the west. I chose "Northern" because I wanted to capture the strength and resonance of the influence, to make it easily identifiable since it is my belief that this influence sometimes gets lost in the midst of the common sense of Colombian reality.

There are two qualifiers to the concept of Northern influence and to the argument that follow. First, the fact of choosing a particular institution and group of players to explore the Northern influence by no means implies that these two are the only important sites where the Northern influence takes shape in Colombia. I have deliberately chosen to reduce the scope in order to gain depth in the analysis. Second, the concept of "influence" used through out this analysis does not imply that the side that exerts influence is active, while the influenced side is a passive recipient. Rather, this is a complex relation of power in which both sides play an active role in its construction. The Northern influence can be related to Giddens' (1979) conception of the "dialectic of control," which will be explored in further detail later in the chapter.

The World Bank: a conduit of Northern Influence

Economic globalization is promoted by developed nations and by multilateral organizations such as the International Monetary Fund (IMF), the World Bank (WB), the Organization for Economic Cooperation and Development

(OECD) and the World Trade Organization (WTO) (Open University 1998).[4] Influence in Latin America has been exerted mainly by the IMF and WB (Torres and Puiggrós 1997a) specifically through "adjustment lending" (Ilon, 1994).[5] However, irrespective of whether these international agencies have promoted positive or negative styles of development for the region, their operation and ideology cannot be isolated from the wider international trend that locates them as just a mechanism for communicating and promoting the prevailing economic theories and needs of the global capitalist game. Hence, a basic step in this analysis is to set these international organizations within a context. As Ilon suggests, "structural adjustment effects on education have largely been viewed as policies imposed by the IMF and the WB. This view overlooks the larger process of structural adjustment in a rapidly growing global economy" (Ilon 1994, 95). It is simplistic and naive to see the international agencies themselves as "guilty" of imposing socially costly and deleterious policies. This location within a wider context helps to approach the analyses in a more strategic way:

> If structural adjustment is simply a bad policy promulgated by misinformed bureaucrats or high powered experts promoting a global agenda of domination, then the appropriate education response is to identify these forces and attempt to change or neutralise them. If, however, structural adjustment is a process that grows out of a large global system of economic exchange, albeit advantaging groups differentially, then the education response must be systematic as well. (Ilon 1994, 95)

The international context does not pervade the Colombian culture through the World Bank alone, but it has been chosen as the site for analysis for specific reasons. The World Bank is one of several multilateral organizations in the world that has consistently worked in the field of education for more than three decades.[6] The bank accounts for 25 percent of all external support for education in developing countries, with 24 percent of its total lending channelled into Latin America and the Caribbean Region in 1997. The World Bank has particular relevance to Colombia since it has funded several major educational projects in the last twenty years (e.g., Plan de Universalización, see Duarte 1995b). Lastly, the World Bank was the one organization that was referred to by a number of respondents at the initial stages of the research; it appears in interviews with civil servants, who either referred to documents published by the WB or mentioned the participation of WB employees as influencing their ideas about educational policy.

The World Bank is not a development assistance agency with a charitable mission; it is a bank that does not hold a value-free stance toward development or education policies (Jones 1997). This statement may at first seem simplistic, but the bank's image, constituted by elements such as it being a United Nations (UN) agency and its publicized aim as poverty alleviation, contributes to obscure the World Bank's main bottom line (Jones 1997).[7] Even the term "development assistance" obscures the ways in which this "assistance" works. Jones describes the World Bank's agenda as centerd upon global economic standarization and integration:

> The Bank's narrow basis of human capital theory implies an education lending rationale which needs to appear scrupulous in its bearing upon its broader range of economic, financial, political and social operations—all undertaken in the name of poverty alleviation but in reality more *centred upon global economic standardisation and integration.* (Jones 1997, 368, my emphasis)

The bulk of the World Bank's capital is raised commercially and its capacity to lend is determined by its ability to borrow (Jones 1995, 1). The majority of funds allocated to projects in the Third World are not necessarily cheap loans. The voting rights of the member states of the World Bank are in direct relation to their subscribed capital, unlike other UN agencies where voting rights are equal (Jones 1993). This feature confers on big economies the power to decide over the future of small economies; it provides a space for agendas to be pushed through without any power of interference by recipient member states (Oxfam 1995a, 4). The World Bank and the IMF work in close association. The bank provides funds for long-term development programs or projects for the member states, and the IMF has a shorter term stabilizing function. As Jones (1993) points out, these two different functions overlap and require close collaboration. In short, The World Bank is not a value-free institution.

On the other hand, I use extracts from interviews with top civil servants and people who influenced the creation of the educational reform to provide the other side of the analysis into the Northern Influence. The names provided after each extract are pseudonyms.

The Colombian state: power and the Northern influence

The first part of this chapter has briefly described some features of the national and international context of the Colombian reform of the 1990s and has identified arelationship of influence over the Colombian national processes of policy making in education in the 1990s. I will now go on to explore the ways in which this influence pervades the national context. The argument tries to move away from explanations of imposition in which the national actors are conceptualized as passive recipients of an imperialistic context, which forces them into supporting specific educational agendas. Instead, it aims to show that a set of complex practices in society reproduce an international system that reflects a Gramscian hegemonic project. It also aims to show how agents reinstate practices through their actions to perpetuate the same kind of power relation. This calls then for some kind of theory of the agent that can help explain why people act in ways that perpetuate a given relationship of power.

I suggest that an analysis of the forms of power embedded in the relationship between the international context (World Bank) and Colombia provides increased reflexivity and criticality about the process and, consequently possibilities of alternative action at the Colombian policy-making level. In other words, I suggest that the reproduction of structural properties in a social system may be altered by processes of reflexivity. The analysis draws on research data and several theoretical frameworks in order to identify the workings of the Northern influence on the Colombian educational policy-making context. I recognize that there are gaps and tensions between the different theoretical frameworks used in this analysis but still I think that the analysis benefits from their use.

In the following section I use extracts from research data and look at them through the lens of power theories to develop a concept of power that fits the Colombian reality at the time of reform. I develop this conceptualization of power by examining assumptions about power that were in play within and around the formulation of the educational reform. I do not intend to portray the conceptualizations of power that institutions or players hold per se, but to analyze the way in which participants understand the relations of power in which they were enmeshed. The aim is to show the complex ways in which power operates.

My first assumption in developing a definition of power, that can usefully illuminate the workings of the Northern influence, is that power only exists when there are at least two actors. Power arises from a relation between A and B. How this relation works, or what is needed for power to be realized requires further examination. Power has been conceptualized by a number of commentators in a way that reflects the duality of structure and agency (Giddens 1979). Some authors, such as Dahl (1957), stress that power is voluntaristic by placing it at the level of the capability of individuals to succeed in imposing their agendas. On the other hand, other authors, like Marx or Parsons, albeit in different ways, see power as imposed by social structures (Giddens 1979).

The first extract taken from the teacher union's magazine in Colombia illustrates the conception of power deployed by the Federación Colombiana de Educadores, FECODE. It describes the origins of one of the main policies of Gaviria's government: the privatization of several state services. I believe that this extract reflects a structural conception of power rather than a voluntaristic one (related to the action of agents). That is, power is understood as structural imposition or domination:

The big secret, known to everyone, of privatisation lies in the *demands* posed by the IMF and WB for the payment of both the Colombian and Latin American (external) debt. *The state is forced*[8] to reduce expenses, impose new loads on the people, support austerity policies in public expenditure, increase public service fees and transfer as much of the burden of expenses as is possible from state to citizens, so that states can pay the service of the debt and be punctual with it, no matter what social cost it may create. . . . The example of the Opening up of Education in Colombia aims at saving state resources. (Ocampo 1991, 33, my emphasis and my translation)

Expressions like "demands" and "the state is forced" in the paragraph describe a particular conceptualization of the relationship of power between the Colombian state and the IMF and WB as one of force: the Colombian state does not seem to have any choice; it is forced to go for privatisation. "Force" is defined by Bachrach and Baratz as a relation in which "A achieves his objectives in the face of B's non-compliance by stripping him of the choice between compliance and non-compliance" (Bachrach and Baratz 1970 quoted in Lukes 1974, 18).

Power, as portrayed in the extract, is easily identifiable through the demands that the IMF/WB impose on the state: it is visible and not subtle. The extract highlights the agenda of the multilateral organizations and suggests that it is forced on to Latin American states. Hence, the underlying conception of power in this extract is that there is a clear domination by the multilateral organizations by unspecified means of force.

In 1957, Dahl formulated a definition, which he later reworked, that is particularly useful at this point: "A has power over B to the extent that he can get B to do something that he would not otherwise do" (Dahl 1957). Dahl's definition will be used as a starting point to help in the clarification of the issue of power in my analysis. According to Dahl's definition, the union's perspective implies that the IMF and WB have power over the Colombian state in relation to the drawing up of policy. Dahl's definition has been criticized for providing such a straightforward conception of power that focuses only on its visible aspects (Hill 1997). Also, there are limitations to the use of this concept of power in my evolving analysis.[9] Nonetheless it seems to be helpful in understanding the way in which FECODE portrays the relationship between IMF-WB and the state as one of visible power relations. The power exerted by A (IMF and WB) over B (the Colombian state) seems to be an independent force that operates entirely above and out of reach of individuals. In other words, the conception of power portrayed by the union in this quote involves three elements. First, that this is a relationship of force; second, that it is structural (that is, independent and out of the reach of individuals); and third, that it is visible.

The second extract comes from an interview with a top executive of the teachers' union (FECODE):

[O]f course the World Bank comes and *imposes* and the minister's desire for money, the civil servant's desire for money, makes any set of values, if there is any, disappear. That is the whole secret, and that is where the jobs are, they just sell themselves, they sell themselves because they see dollars coming; they sell themselves because in Colombia they just think of money; they just think of their career progress; there is huge snobbism, the desire to get a job in the World Bank, "How am I going to get a job in the World Bank? How do I get a job here or there?" That is the most important thing. We have not had profound educational projects, we have not imposed them, the World Bank has imposed them or someone has imposed them because *without any perspective or project, how can we negotiate*, how can we say what the aim is? (Juan Pedro Vargas, 127 my emphasis)

This extract describes a relation of imposition. The World Bank imposes policies on the Colombian state. However, the concept of power portrayed here is more complex than that in extract 1 in that it looks inside the Colombian state as well. Extract 1 proposes in its relationship between A (multilateral organizations) and B (Colombian state) that an action is exercised over B. The agendas of A are highlighted while B is presented as a passive subject (i.e., not having perspectives). Extract 2 draws attention to the fact that B holds agendas as well; it refers to civil servants as part of the state. The point here is not to agree or disagree with what is said about some civil servants.[10] This extract stresses a very important element of the relationship of power: not only that there are two players (at least) in this relationship as already seen in extract 1, but that both have a role in the shaping of the relationship of power. Policies are not imposed on inactive, passive states; there is the role of the state, too, in accepting these policies; there is agency in both parts. As Giddens says:

> Power relations . . . are always two-way, even if the power of one actor or party in a social relation is minimal compared to another. Power relations are relations of autonomy and dependence, but even the most autonomous agent is in some degree dependent, and the most dependent actor or party in a relationship retains some autonomy. (Giddens 1979, 91)

Extract 1 proposes that power is exercised through force and shows the state as a passive recipient. Extract 2 shows that there are agendas on both sides, the state is not as passive as portrayed in extract 1. The observations in extract 2 about the personal advantage of civil servants are definitely part of the picture of power, but still extract 2 overlooks an essential feature of power that is signalled in extract 3:

> AL: . . . which is, more or less how education in free-market worlds has been organised without it being neo-liberal, no! *It is just logical: a public service cannot be managed from the state.* . . .
>
> PV: OK, at some point you said: "without it being neo-liberal." Is there any kind of reluctance on your part to it being neo-liberal?
>
> AL: Yes, yes. Many of the criticisms of the project were about it being neo-liberal. (Alejandra Lema, 128 my emphasis)

In extract 3 there is a language of acceptance of the international influence but not because of imposition or force; this top civil servant openly expresses consent, rather than oppression, through her commitment to the market paradigm. Gramsci uses the concept of *hegemony* to describe the successful establishment of a particular political project in a society, a unity of economic, political, intellectual and moral aims; the concept of hegemony refers to the "practices of a capitalist class or its representatives, both in gaining state power, and in maintaining that power once it has been achieved" (Simon 1991, 23). The exploration of the relationship between the World Bank and the educational policy makers in Colombia throws some light on what is really a wider phenomenon of a hegemonic global project pervading all areas of life of the Colombian society. Gramsci understands power as a relationship and suggests that hegemony is achieved through the organization of consent:

> Hegemony is a relationship between classes and other social forces. A hegemonic class, or part of a class, is one which gains the consent of other classes and social forces through creating and maintaining a system of alliances by means of political and ideological struggle. (Simon 1991, 23)

Gramsci argues that power in civil society is exercised through a combination of coercion and consent—the organization of consent happens through hegemony. In an hegemonic project a number of elements collaborate in its construction, for example, its establishment in the common sense of the culture, in the intellectual and moral reforms, and in the economic realm. No one of these elements alone constructs a hegemonic project; it is their combination that does so (Gramsci 1971). *Common sense* can be defined as "the incoherent set of generally held assumptions and beliefs common to any society" (Gramsci 1971, 323, footnote). In a way, all people are philosophers who hold some conception of the world. Common sense is necessarily fragmentary, contradictory in nature and sendimentary.[11] Extract 3 shows consent for international policies and agendas through their insertion into the common sense of the policymaker.

The elements I want to stress as important for the analysis that follows are that power is a capability that takes place in a relationship: power only exists when there are at least two actors. Power arises from a relation between A and B; both A and B play a role in the shaping of that particular relationship, therefore the conceptualization of a relation of power where one of the parts is presented as a passive recipient, as in extract 1, is inadequate. The final element that I want to stress is that power is exercised through a combination of coercion and consent.

The Northern influence in Colombian education

The World Bank has exerted an important influence on educational policies in many countries around the world. The case of Colombia is no exception.

There are examples of how direct force operates—that is, the ways in which the IMF and the WB operate, as described in extract 1. In contrast, the following section briefly describes ways in which this influence pervades the national political culture and shows that, even though there are clear instances of force, there are other subtle mechanisms involved in achieving a complex relationship of power. Each of these mechanisms is just one of the building blocks that help give shape to the Northern influence. The World Bank as "the influencer" shapes policy making in Colombia in different ways, some more subtle than others. These ways of exercising power, be them coercive (economic assessments of country performance and creditworthiness, which are an important reference for the world financial community, or conditionality in lending) or more subtle (provision of advice and policy solutions, pervading the common sense of Colombian culture both through permanent flow of information into Colombia and through its permanent "presence" in national affairs (Vanegas 2001)) have an individual impact. More importantly, they combine and work together to shape a power relationship that results in effective influence at the national policy making level.

On the other hand, "the influenced" Colombian state shapes its side of the relationship of power through active consent. Gramsci wrote that the "hegemony of a dominant class is exercised in civil society by persuading the subordinate classes to accept the values and ideas which the dominant class has itself adopted, and by building a network of alliances based on these values" (Simon 1991, 18). Alliances, I propose, are built in several ways in the Colombian educational policy making context: through the education of Colombian people who study abroad, and through the inclusion of nationals in an international policy elite that moves between international agencies and influences national affairs. These factors are surrounded by the values of a Colombian society that regards those people who access these levels as having achieved a high status (Vanegas 2001). I have argued that consent works alongside coercion. Coercion is also present in this relationship of power. Both sides are clearly contributing to its reproduction. Power can be usefully conceptualized as a capability that takes place in social interaction: "power is instantiated in action as a regular and routine phenomenon" (Giddens 1979, 91), which involves reproduced relations of autonomy and dependence.

The link between structure and agency

I have argued that the international context pervades Colombian culture via a relation of power, which is exercised both through coercion and consent, and that the organization of this consent results in it being a hegemonic project. I have presented some examples of coercion and other more subtle examples of the exercise of power as the very elements that provide for the organization of consent, and hence for the perpetuation of the international context as a hegemonic project. This matter raises for me important questions about the capacity of individuals to exert change. These questions relate to issues of structure and agency. Gidden's structuration theory provides for an understanding that individuals are at the heart of social reproduction. This section explores how, at the individual level, the hegemonic project is constantly "at work" to perpetuate its influence, independently of whether it is completely beneficial for the country.

Giddens says that a social system is reproduced through the way in which individual agents act.[12] Social systems consist of "regularised relations of interdependence between individuals or groups, that typically can be best analysed as recurrent social practices" (Giddens 1979, 66). Individuals reproduce the structuring properties of society by regularly using similar sets of rules and resources in their interaction. Thus, for Giddens there is not a structure independent from people that imposes on them, restricting their actions. It is people who, through employing the same rules and resources embedded in their practical consciousness, reproduce the way society is. Practical consciousness is the "knowledge embodied in what actors "know how to do" (Giddens 1979, 73). Giddens believes that people within a society are highly knowledgeable about the way in which that society works. They carry with them information about how to interact in it and they use this information to act in one way or another: practical consciousness is "the tacit knowledge that is skillfully applied in the enactment of courses of conduct, but which the actor is not able to formulate discursively" (Giddens 1979, 57).

The concept of practical consciousness seems to me similar to Gramsci's concept of common sense, as defined previously. Common sense is the "uncritical and largely unconscious way in which a person perceives the world" (Simon, 1991: 64). This similarity provides a gentle move into Giddens' theory of structuration.[13]

Giddens' theory of structuration relates structure and agency in a way in which they are no longer conceptualized as antinomies. Structuration recognizes a mutual dependence of structure and agency. Structure does not exist independently from the individual to constrain her actions.[14] What exists are structuring properties such as tools and resources that actors draw upon in their interactions and then, through those actors' actions, social systems are reinstated: "To study the structuration of a social system is to study the ways in which that system, via the application of generative rules and resources, and in the context of unintended outcomes, is produced and reproduced in interaction" (Giddens 1979: 66). Hence, if individuals are the ones reproducing the social system, then this reproduction can be disrupted by processes of reflexivity.[15] As already mentioned, this is important in providing a basis for possibilities of change in societies like Colombia. Levels of reflexivity and awareness in individuals about the way the social system works and about the structuring properties operating in that social system may vary. I propose that lower levels of reflexivity provide for a higher degree of reproduction of social systems.

That is, there is still agency in individuals, but it is all used to reproduce the same kind of social system: "[E]very process of action is the production of something new, a fresh act; but at the same time all action exists in continuity with the past, which supplies the means for its initiation. Structure thus is not to be conceptualised as a barrier to action, but as essentially involved in its production" (Giddens 1979, 70).

On the other hand, higher levels of awareness may provide for reflexive agency and for changing the social system. This may be the path for change. My argument is that, in respect of the structuring properties of the international system, there was not a high level of criticality and awareness at the time of the production of the Colombian educational reform. In none of the documents that I looked at were there studies of alternatives to the market policies promoted by policy makers. These policies were not the result of a deliberate choice from many alternatives, but of following what internationally was acclaimed and promoted as "the right way." This means that the international influence in the educational reform and the consequent action of actors involved provided for the reproduction of the hegemonic social system. I do not suggest that there was a lack of criticality because people promoted ideas that I do not agree with. I welcome opposing views and ideas. My point is that there was an absence of debate and a failure to consider alternatives.

This does not mean that people supporting the free market paradigm are uncritical or simply selling themselves to the prevailing trends. My speculation is that the profile of the individual at the policy-making level may be of a person who needs to work to provide for him/her or himself; who has ambition to climb to top roles; who deals daily with many pressures that do not provide for focused or deep thinking to analyze all of the issues in play in his/her decision-making processes; and one who for that reason looks for solutions and chooses, with the best intention, those which that s/he thinks are the best. (I also allow for the existence of civil servants who are aware of these issues and unequivocally believe that free-market policies are the best path for the country.) Although contradictions between personal advantage and national advantage may interplay in this chain of decision making, this may not be clearly recognized in the midst of pressures at the level of policy making. As C. Wright Mills wrote:

> Great and rational organisations—in brief, bureaucracies—have indeed increased, but the substantive reason of the individual at large has not. Caught in the limited milieux of everyday lives, ordinary men often cannot reason about the great structures—rational and irrational—of which their milieux are subordinate parts. Accordingly they often carry out series of apparently rational actions without any ideas of the ends they serve, and there is increasing suspicion that those at the top as

well—like Tolstoy's generals—only pretend they know. (Mills 1963, 237–238)

Furthermore, the analysis of the stances of top civil servants highlights features of a relationship of power, but it cannot be used to argue that this policy community is more guilty than the rest of society for how things happen. The less awareness there is about how the international context influences the national system and the individual, the fewer possibilities there are to alter the status quo with its ingrained relations of power. A further question related directly to the Colombian context is how all of these influences work in the agent's mind. The task of the next section is to explore this question.

Theorizing the subject at the individual level

This section considers individuals in two ways: first, it looks at the way in which disourses construct their actions. I use the concept of "coincidence of agendas" to analyse the way in which discourses "speak the individual." However, I believe that discourses are not everything there is to an individual's actions. In other words, if discourses disappeared there would still be an individual with the capacity to act (unlike Foucault's theory). Hence, the second way in which I explore the individual is an adventure into what, I believe, exists beyond discourses within the individual.

Coincidence of agendas

An argument found several times in the testimonies of interviewees relates to a denial of World Bank influence in the educational process, explaining the relationship as a "coincidence of agendas" between the WB and the Colombian state, rather than imposition. It was not that the WB had imposed the agenda, but that the Colombian state had developed a similar one from independent work as can be seen in the following text:

> [I]t is important for you not to perceive that the World Bank is either a very solid institution intellectually; or that it was very influential, because it wasn't. The person in charge [at the WB] was extremely frustrated with the project for primary education [a previous World Bank project in Colombia] and he did not believe in our proposal [voucher scheme for Education]. Hence, this was a neo liberal proposal that out flanked the WB. The WB did not propose it, we created it. (Federico Gómez, 148, my translation)

Foucault uses the concept of discourse to explain the existence of master narratives that "construct certain possibilities for thought. . . . [D]iscourses are, therefore, about what can be said and thought" (Ball 1990c, 18). Foucault puts it in these words: "What I have said is not 'what I think' but often what I wonder whether it couldn't be thought" (Foucault 1979a, 58).

Discourse "appears across a range of texts, forms of conduct and at a number of different sites at any one time" (Ball 1998a, 126). Therefore, the way in which we perceive is shaped by discursive constraints. The "coincidence of agendas" can be seen as the product of a discourse, the neoliberal market solution, which pervades educational policy through several conduits, the World Bank being just one of them. Hence, the Northern influence can be traced to other institutions or other literature, which articulate the global discourse or global paradigm of market-oriented policies. Even though tracing these other conduits of articulation of discourse is not within the reach of this analysis, it is important to bear in mind that these exist and that even if all of the direct influence did not come from the World Bank, the same discourse was pervading the context of policy making by other means.

The way in which discourse constructs perceptions and actions of people is powerful and subtle. An example of how a top civil servant is thinking within the "free market" discourse, as she denies the influence of the World Bank's ideas, is shown in the following passage:

> But I would say that it is much more about a *coincidence of agendas* and what many of the international publications say; and our leaders study in the U.S. hmm but I would say that many of these things are *common sense*; and that they were discovered by business managers a long time ago, people from big companies: how to make services *efficient*. Banks who provide services or any other service industry know that very *flexible schemes* are needed.
>
> Therefore I wouldn't say that one was absolutely copying the World Bank. There were even terrible arguments between the Colombian state and the bank; all the people who came from the World Bank in that period said that it was a challenge for them to work in Colombia because Colombians did not accept things without *criticality*. (Alejandra Lema, 149, my emphasis)

This passage in part relates to the argument of coincidence of agendas. It shows how the World Bank is not the only site of articulation of free-market discourse. It also illustrates how free-market discourse can impinge on the civil servant's mind in a way in which it becomes "common sense" and therefore the only possible framework for thought. Terms like "flexible schemes" or "efficiency" become the desired goals. The discourse is constructed and conveyed in part through a new language of signification, in which remakes key elements of practice. Even though human life can continue without these goals, it seems here the obvious and only alternative way to go forward. That is the power of discourse. My last observation about the quote relates to the "criticality" that the civil servant refers to. The question that arises is how much criticality can there be in a negotiation in which the two sides are thinking within the same paradigm. Criticality may still be there, but any issue in a negotiation of this kind may be just minor tinkering; the overall framework is in place and both sides are striving for the same goals even if they do not agree in small detail, as shown in the following quote:

> [W]hen missions arrive [to the DNP], the [World] Bank brings its agenda and the country has its agenda as well; many times these agendas are similar because *obviously* the Bank has influenced a lot but still there are nuances or items where there isn't agreement, so DNP negotiates a little those differences. (Diana Losada, 151, my emphasis)

Also, Levels of reflexivity or criticality may not be high or easy to achieve by some of those in top policy making levels:

> One must not overestimate the degree of conviction with which even those in dominant classes, or other positions of authority, accept ideological symbol systems. . . . Those who in a largely unquestioning way accept certain dominant perspectives may be more imprisoned within them than others are, even though these perspectives help the former to sustain their position of dominance. (Giddens 1979, 72)

As I have tried to establish throughout the analysis, the Northern influence is not a simple relationship of oppression from "the North" to "the South." Many of the international influences are appropriated by Colombian people, accepted, admired, reproduced, and sometimes invisible to their (our) eyes. As Foucault said: "If power was never anything but repressive, if it never did anything but to say no, do you really believe that we should manage to obey it?" (Foucault 1979b, 36).

The individual beyond discourse

I propose that there is a way to disrupt the reproduction of social systems through reflexive agency. Work at the personal level aimed at increasing awareness of the workings of the social system may be the most powerful tool to achieve change in society.

If there is an increase in the levels of awareness at the individual level, the practical consciousness and therefore the tools and resources that individuals may choose to utilize in their interactions may be different. The structuring properties of the social system may change as a result. An example of increased awareness in the data can be seen in the following passage:

> When one is working in Colombia, I think that this happens everywhere, one thinks that what is being proposed and pursued in education policy for example, . . . is all an original idea, and that that is what is needed; afterwards one discovers two things: first, that those policies are not only part of a Colombian agenda, but that they are part of an international

agenda, which is shared by all the international organisations for development. Second, that Colombia is not the only country pursuing these policies, but that they are happening in many countries, especially developing countries. But it is not like one realises how these things happen when working there. (Diana Losada, 7)

Processes of developing awareness at the individual level are important for both sides in the relationship of power analysed in this chapter. What this chapter provides is an example of agents who are dependent on other cultures to design the future of their country. For Colombia, research into the far-reaching impact of neocolonialism (Fanon 1968, Rahnema and Bawtree 1997, Sachs 1992) on the agent's mind may be an important way to develop understanding and increase awareness about this dependence. The literature on neocolonialism makes visible the subtle ways in which dependent minds work, therefore increasing awareness about dependence and serving as a step towards liberation.

I should provide some clarification at this point. I am not intending to argue simply that the 'educational policy makers' are solely responsible for reproducing a system characterized by its deference to the international context, mainly to the "developed world." This group just happens to be the one under scrutiny here. Research into other policy communities or into specific social groups could be valuable in exploring what I see as a much more generalized phenomenon. I would even take the risk of saying that this deference exists within most Colombian people and it is the aggregate of these individual actions that shapes society as a whole.

An individual who grows up in a dependent culture (historically, economically, and politically) may grow to accept his or her inferiority within the developed world. The desire to feel equal and accepted may lead someone down the path of copying rather than creating. This, combined with the valuing of personal advantage learned through the culture, provides for an environment for the reproduction of power relations at the international level in which alliances and consent are how Colombians shape and reproduce the Northern influence. The problem at this point is crucial. If a significant number of top Colombian educational policy makers are geared for consent, and strive to copy policies developed internationally, then the educational system that they impact may inherit the same values. Two questions to be raised are: Are the children in Colombia the only ones in need of a more critical education? What about the adults who are constructing society and reproducing the same values?

Conclusion

The aim of this chapter has been to provide an interpretation of how the world that we are in shapes the educational system in Colombia. I have defined and described this influence as a relationship of power between the international context and the Colombian educational policymakers. I use the concept of Northern influence to explore the specificities of this relationship of power for the Colombian educational context. I propose that the international context is a hegemonic project which strongly influences national affairs and educational policy, and raises important questions about the capacity of individual people to exert change (agency). I have argued that the international influence is reproduced uncritically by agents within the state. A final thought by Gandhi explains my own view about how the international influence should be considered as an alternative but not followed at any cost: "I do not want my house to be walled in on all sides and my windows to be stuffed. I want the cultures of all lands to be blown about my house as freely as possible. But I refuse to be blown off my feet" (quoted in Nanda 1995, vi).

The analysis of international context has identified the international scene as an essential element that shaped Colombian educational reform of the nineties. The chapter provides context to a reform that is usually analized as an isolated instrument of educational policy; and highlights values and agendas behind the written texts of reform.

Notes

1. The Colombian Education Reform of the 1990s is formally shaped by a framework of legislation: The National Constitution enacted in 1991, The Gaviria Development Plan for 1990–1994, The Decentralisation Law (Law 60, 1993), The General Law of Education (Law 115, 1994). The Higher Education Law (Law 30, 1993), regulations to develop Law 60 in respect to education, regulations to the General Law of Education, Ten year Plan. Other laws and decrees that are part of the reform are: Decree 2127/December 29th, 1992 (Restructuring of the Ministry of Education), Decree 1953/1994 (Revision and restructuring of the Ministry of Education demanded by the General Law of Education in its Art.220). This article is based on a PhD research thesis which narrows its focus to the General Law of Education and considers other legislation only in so far as this impinges on or throws light on the General Law of Education's processes and influences (Vanegas 2001).

2. Wallerstein argues that the current "modern world-system" in which we are living stretches back to the year 1500 and that its main characteristic is the "capitalist" mode of production. There is an interesting debate related to world-systems and how far they stretch back. Wallerstein argues that five hundred years is the time that covers the existence of the current world-system. Frank and Gills (1993) argue for a five thousand year existence, providing a very good overview and in-depth analysis of the debate. The main point of interest for this analysis is that all countries of the world are part of a one world system and so it is essential to look at the international context in order to understand national affairs.

3. Bilton et al. define "modernity" as "a term designed to encapsulate the distinctiveness, complexity and dynamism of social processes unleashed during the eighteenth and nineteenth centuries, which mark a distinct break from traditional ways of living" (Bilton, et al. 1996, 664).

4. A very interesting study of the influence of the OECD on Australian education can be found in Taylor et al. 1997.

5. For a brief introductory explanation and critique of structural adjustment programs, see Oxfam 1995a, 6–25.

6. The WB started to consider education as a bankable sector in 1962 (Jones 1997). Other agencies with major educational commitments are UNESCO, the United Nations Development Program (UNDP), the OECD, the Commonwealth Secretariat, and regional development banks (Jones 1993).

7. "[N]o task should command a higher priority for the world's policy makers than that of reducing global poverty" (World Bank, 1990b, 1). "In 1992, the WB's president, Lewis Preston, declared: 'Sustainable poverty reduction is the overarching objective of the World

Bank. It is the benchmark by which our performance as a development institution will be measured" (in Oxfam 1995a, 1).

8. "The state is *forced*" is translated from "*se obliga* al estado."

9. Dahl's definition of power is part of a research project where the intention was to analyze how power operated in New Haven, Connecticut, U.S. The definition includes ways in which power can be measured for the research. The research chose three key issues (public education, urban redevelopment, and political nominations) where there seemed to be more than two different perspectives about how they should be tackled by policy. He analyzes the different perspectives through focusing on the conflict created and then by looking at the final decision; the successful perspective finally adopted corresponded to the representative or group that had more power in this society. His conclusion was that no one group succeeded in achieving its policy preferences in all the three areas of policy under analysis; that all groups in society had the possibility of representation through their elected candidates; and that there was no concentration of power (Dahl 1961). This definition of power has been related to the pluralist concept of power. My interest in using Dahl is limited to what his conception of power implies for furthering understanding about power. For a deeper analysis of Dahl see a critique by Lukes (1974), Giddens' (1979) analysis of power, and Bachrach and Baratz (1970).

10. The statement in extract 2 about civil servants or ministers provides, I believe, only one of the pieces that are part of the whole relationship of power. There is an unresolved tension between personal advantage and national advantage. It is not necessarily true that decisions made by top civil servants to further their career prospects are always positive for the nation. This is an issue that outflanks the limits of this analysis. Still, it may be considered as part of the bigger picture, which will appear clearer as my argument evolves.

11. Hall refers to the sedimentary nature of common sense: "The subject is necessarily divided—an ensemble: one half Stone Age, the other containing principles of advanced science, prejudices from all past phases of history, intuitions of a future philosophy" (Hall 1988, 169).

12. For Giddens, "the notion of human action logically implies that of power, understood as transformative capacity: 'action' only exists when an agent has the capability of intervening, or refraining from intervening, in a series of events so as to be able to influence their course" (Giddens 1979, 256).

13. Key sources here are: *Central Problems in Social Theory* (Giddens 1979), *The Constitution of Society* (Giddens 1984), which constitutes the most comprehensive work on structuration, and *Conversations with Anthony Giddens* (Giddens and Pierson 1998), which provides an updated view, through an interview with Giddens, of his thinking about structuration. Shilling provides a very good description of structuration and he relates it to research in the sociology of education (Shilling 1992).

14. The "duality of structure" is central to Giddens' structuration. Duality of structure means that "the structural properties of social systems are both the medium and the outcome of the practices that constitute those systems. . . . The same structural characteristics participate in the subject (the actor) as in the object (society). Structure forms personality and society simultaneously—but in neither case exhaustively." (Giddens 1979, 69)

15. I am aware that there are three types of circumstances that are relevant and that combine in individuals' actions in the reproduction of social systems: unconscious elements in action, practical consciousness, and the unintended consequences of action (Giddens 1979). This combination means that the agent is not fully able to understand all motives or the impact of his or her action. However, reflexivity about action can still be a powerful means of increasing this understanding and altering aspects of action as a result.

References

Arnove, R. F. (1997). "Neoliberal Education Policies in Latin America: Arguments in Favor and Against." In C. A. Torres and A. Puiggrós, eds. *Latin American Education: Comparative Perspectives*. Oxford: Westview Press, 79–100.

Bachrach, P. and Baratz, M. S. (1970). *Power and Poverty. Theory and Practice*. New York: Oxford University Press.

Ball, S. J. (1990). *Politics and Policy Making in Education*. London: Routledge.

Ball, S. J. (1994). *Education Reform: A Critical and Post-structural Approach*. Buckingham: Open University Press.

Ball, S. J. (1998). "Big Policies/Small World: An Introduction to International Perspectives in Education Policy." *Comparative Education,* 34, no. 2, 119–130.

Bilton, T., K. Bonnett, P. Jones, D. Skinner, M. Stanworth, and A. Webster. (1996). *Introductory Sociology* 3d. ed. London: MacMillan Press Limited.

Caballero, A. (1996). *Quince años de mal agüero.* Medellín: La Hoja Mes S.A.

Caballero, A. (1997). El hombre que inventó un pueblo. In G. González Uribe, ed. *El Saqueo de una Ilusión—el 9 de Abril: 50 años después.* Santafé de Bogotá: Número Ediciones, 71–80.

Chubb, J. and T. Moe. (1990). *Politics, Markets and American Schools.* Washington D.C.: Brookings Institution.

Dahl, R. A. (1957). "The Concept of Power." *Behavioural Science,* 2, no. 1: 32–45.

Dahl, R. A. (1961). *Who Governs? Democracy and Power in an American City.* New Haven and London: Yale University Press.

DNP. (1991). *La Revolución Pacífica: Plan de Desarrollo Económico y Social 1990–1994.* Santafé de Bogotá: Departamento Nacional de Planeación y Presidencia de la República de Colombia.

Duarte, J. (1995) "State Education and Clientelism in Colombia. (The politics of state education administration and of implementation of educational investment projects in two Colombian regions)." Ph.D. diss, St. Anthony's College, University of Oxford.

Fanon, F. (1968). *Black Skin, White Masks.* London: MacGibbon & Gee.

Foucault, M. (1979a). "Powers and Strategies: Interview Between Michel Foucault and Revoltes Logiques Collective." In Meaghan Morris and P. Patton, eds. *Michel Foucault: Power/Truth/Strategy.* Sydney: Feral Publications, 48–58.

Foucault, M. (1979b). "Truth and Power: An interview with Alessandro Fontano and Pasquale Pasquino." In Meaghan Morris and P. Patton, eds. *Michel Foucault: Power/Truth/Strategy.* Sydney: Feral Publications, 29–48.

Foucault, M. (1982). "Afterword: The Subject and Power." In H. L. Dreyfus and P. Rabinow, eds. *Michel Foucault: Beyond Structuralism and Hermeneutics* Brighton: Harvester.

Fowler, H. W., and F. G. Fowler, eds. (1969). *Shorter Oxford English Dictionary.* London: Oxford University Press.

Giddens, A. (1979). *Central Problems in Social Theory—Action, Structure and Contradiction in Social Analysis.* London: The MacMillan Press Ltd.

Giddens, A. (1984). *The Constitution of Society.* Cambridge, UK: Polity Press.

Giddens, A. (1991). *The Consequences of Modernity.* Cambridge: Polity Press.

Giddens, A. (1998). *The Third Way.* Cambridge: Polity Press.

Giddens, A. and C. Pierson. (1998). *Conversations with Anthony Giddens—Making sense of modernity.* Cambridge: Polity Press.

Gómez, Federico (pseudonym). (1997). Extract of interview transcription. In Patricia Vanegas. (2001). *Colombian Educational Reform of the 1990s: A Critical Study of the Policy Process.* Ph.D. diss., King's College London, University of London.

Gramsci, A. (1971). *Selections from the Prison Notebooks.* London: Lawrence & Wishart Ltd.

Hall, S. (1988). *The hard road to renewal: Thatcherism and the crisis of the left.* London: Verso 1988.

Halsey, A. H., H. Lauder, P. Brown, and A. Stuart Wells, eds. (1997). *Education—Culture, Economy, Society.* Oxford: Oxford University Press.

Hill, M. (1997). *The Policy Process in the Modern State,* (3d ed.). Hertfordshire: Prentice Hall/Harvester Wheatsheaf.

Ilon, L. (1994). "Structural Adjustment and Education: Adapting to a Growing Global Market." *International Journal of Educational Development,* 14, no. 2: 95–108.

Jones, P. W. (1993). "United Nations Agencies." In *Encyclopedia of Educational Research.* New York: MacMillan, 1450–1459.

Jones, P. W. (1995). "On World Bank Education Financing: Review Article." *Comparative Education* (May 1997) 120–128.

Jones, P. W. (1997). "The World Bank and the Literacy Question: Orthodoxy, Heresy, and Ideology. *International Review of Education,* 43, no. 4: 367–375.

Lema, Alejandra (pseudonym) (1997). Extract of interview transcription. In Patricia Vanegas. (2001). *Colombian Educational Reform of the 1990s: A Critical Study of the Policy Process.* Ph.D. diss., King's College London, University of London.

Losada, Diana (pseudonym) (1997). Extract of interview transcription. In Patricia Vanegas. (2001). *Colombian Educational Reform of the 1990s: A Critical Study of the Policy Process.* Ph.D. diss., King's College London, University of London.

Lukes, S. (1974). *Power: A Radical View.* London: The MacMillan Press Ltd.

MEN. (1994). *Ley General de Educación* No. 115 of 1994. Bogotá: Ministerio de Educación Nacional.

Mills, C. W. (1963). "Culture and Politics." In C. W. Mills, ed. *Power, Politics, and People.* New York: Oxford University Press.

Nanda, B. R., ed. (1995). *Mahatma Gandhi—125 years.* New Delhi: Wiley Eastern Limited.

Ocampo, J. F. (1991). La apertura económica y la apertura educativa: Dos planes y un objetivo. *Revista Educación y Cultura* (June): 25–33.

Open University. (1998). *Education, Training, and the Future of Work OU—E837.* Unpublished.

Oxfam. (1995a). *A Case for Reform: Fifty Years of the IMF and World Bank.* Policy Department. Oxford: Oxfam Publication.

Oxfam. (1995b). *The Oxfam Poverty Report.* Policy Department. Oxford: Oxfam Publication.

Psacharopoulos, G., J. P. Tan, J. Emmanuel, and World Bank's Education and Training Department. (1986). *Financing Education in Developing Countries.* Washington, D.C.: International Bank for Reconstruction and Development/The World Bank.

Rahnema, M. and V. Bawtree, eds. (1997). *The Post-Development Reader.* London: Zed Books Ltd.

Sachs, W. (Ed.). (1992). *The Development Dictionary.* London: Zed Books Ltd.

Santos, J. M. (1999). *La Tercera Vía: Una Alternativa Para Colombia.* Santafé de Bogotá: Distribuidora y Editora Aguilar, Altea, Taurus, Alfaguara, S.A.

Schumacher, E. F. (1963). *Small Is Beautiful—A Study of Economics as if People Mattered.* London: Abacus.

Shilling, C. (1992). Reconceptualising Structure and Agency in the Sociology of Education: structuration theory and schooling. *British Journal of Sociology in Education* 13, no. 1: 69–87.

Simon, R. (1991). *Gramsci's Political Thought: An Introduction.* London: Lawrence & Wishart Limited.

Torres, C.A., and A. Puiggrós, eds. (1997). *Latin American Education: Comparative Perspectives.* Oxford: Westview Press.

Vanegas, P. (2001). "Colombian Educational Reform of the 1990s: A Critical Study of the Policy Process." Ph.D. diss, King's College London, University of London.

Vargas, Juan Pedro (pseudonym) (1997). Extract of interview transcription. In Patricia Vanegas. (2001). *Colombian Educational Reform of the 1990s: A Critical Study of the Policy Process.* Ph.D. diss., King's College London, University of London.

Wallerstein, I. (1974). *The Modern World System.* New York: Academic Books.

Wallerstein, I. (1980a). *The Modern World System.* Vol. 2. New York: Academic Books.

Wallerstein, I. (1980b). *The Modern World System.* Vol. 3. New York: Academic Books.

Whitty, G. (1992). "Education, Economy and National Culture." In R. Bocock and K. Thompson, eds. *Social and Cultural Forms of Modernity.* Buckingham: Open University Press.

Whitty, G., S. Power, and D. Halpin. (1998). *Devolution and Choice in Education: The School, the State and the Market.* Bristol: Open University Press.

Index

Index note: page references in *italics* indicate a figure or table.

For Product Safety Concerns and Information please contact our EU
representative GPSR@taylorandfrancis.com Taylor & Francis Verlag GmbH,
Kaufingerstraße 24, 80331 München, Germany

Batch number: 08153776

Printed by Printforce, the Netherlands